CHALLENGING AND CONTROVERSIAL PICTUREBOOKS

It is often assumed that picturebooks are for very young readers because of their emphasis on the illustrations and their scarcity of text; however, there are increasing numbers of picturebooks where the age of the implied reader is questionable. These are picturebooks whose controversial subject matter and unconventional, often unsettling style of illustration challenge the reader, pushing them to question and probe deeper to understand what the book is about. In addition to the book challenging the reader, the reader often challenges the book in an attempt to understand what is being said.

These increasingly popular picturebooks work on many different levels; they are truly polysemic and worthy of in-depth analysis. They push the reader to ask questions and in many instances are intrinsically philosophical, often dealing with fundamental life issues.

Challenging and Controversial Picturebooks examines these unconventional, non-conformist picturebooks, considering what they are, their audience and their purpose. It also considers:

- Children's and adults' thoughts on these kinds of picturebooks.
- How challenging and unsettling wordless picturebooks can play with the mind and promote philosophical thought.
- What creates non-conformity and strangeness ... is it the illustrations and their style, the subject matter or a combination of both?
- Why certain countries create, promote and accept these picturebooks more than others.
- Why certain picturebooks are censored and what factors are in play when these decisions are made.
- The role of publishers in translating and publishing these picturebooks.
- Children's creative and critical responses to strange, unsettling and often disturbing visual texts.

This inspiring and thought-provoking volume explores the work of a number of highly respected, international picturebook experts and includes an exclusive interview with the legendary Klaus Flugge, Managing Director of Andersen Press, one of the few remaining independent children's book publishers in England.

It is an indispensable reference for all interested in or working with picturebooks, including researchers, students in higher and teacher education, English advisors/ inspectors, literacy consultants and classroom teachers.

Janet Evans is an Independent Scholar, freelance Literacy and Educational Consultant and former Senior Lecturer in Education at Liverpool Hope University, UK.

CHALLENGING AND CONTROVERSIAL PICTUREBOOKS

Creative and critical responses to visual texts

Edited by Janet Evans

Routledge
Taylor & Francis Group

LONDON AND NEW YORK

First published 2015
by Routledge
2 Park Square, Milton Park, Abingdon, Oxon OX14 4RN

and by Routledge
711 Third Avenue, New York, NY 10017

Routledge is an imprint of the Taylor & Francis Group, an informa business

British Library Cataloguing in Publication Data
A catalogue record for this book is available from the British Library

Library of Congress Cataloging in Publication Data
Challenging and controversial picturebooks: creative and critical responses to
visual texts / edited by Janet Evans.
pages cm
1. Picture books for children—Educational aspects. 2. Visual learning. I. Evans,
Janet, 1952–
LB1044.9.P49C43 2015
372.133—dc23
2014044961

ISBN: 978-1-138-79774-1 (hbk)
ISBN: 978-1-138-79777-2 (pbk)
ISBN: 978-1-315-75691-2 (ebk)

Typeset in Bembo
by Book Now Ltd, London

To Les, my husband

This academic book would not have been written if it had not been for Les. He has given unconditional support both emotionally and literally at all times. Whenever I felt downhearted he cheered me up, whenever I needed advice he offered suitable, soothing words; then, more time consuming than anything else, whenever the computer decided 'not to play', or when I needed help with images, charts and 'difficult things', Les was there for me, always willing to give help and sort me out.

My heartfelt thanks Les. Your patience and forebearing is legend; I couldn't have done this book without you.

CONTENTS

ACKNOWLEDGEMENTS

Writing this book has been hard, indeed quite challenging at times, but it has always been totally absorbing and personally satisfying. I have been fortunate to have expert writers, each of them specialists in their field, who have contributed to this volume. Their time, effort and professional expertise are truly appreciated and I thank them wholeheartedly.

Since I began researching the subject of challenging and controversial picturebooks many individual picturebooks and picturebook creators have influenced me. Two books in particular stand out as having planting the seed of this book idea in my mind. The first was Wolf Erlbruch's exquisite picturebook, *Duck, Death and the Tulip*. I was immediately intrigued and instantly obsessed by this book. How could a 'mere picturebook for children' focus on such a dark and potentially foreboding subject in such a passionate and aesthetic way? At the same time I was introduced to the work of Danish picturebook creators, Oscar K and Dorte Karrebæk, in particular, Karrebæk's audaciously disturbing and uncompromising picturebook, *The Black Book: On the Seven Deadly Sins*. My fascination with unconventional, non-conformist picturebooks had begun and I was hooked!

There are many other people to whom I am grateful.

I must initially mention the crucial role that my research scholarship at the International Youth Library in Munich had to play. There, with help from experts such as Jochen Weber, and the whole team of knowledgeable specialists, I was exposed to strange, ambiguous and unconventional picturebooks from around the world.

A particular mention goes to Evelyn Arizpe who very kindly agreed to write the foreword for this book. She has done so in an informed manner that clearly links some of the thought-provoking themes in the book with the disturbing and distinctly unsettling events currently happening in the world around us.

Finally I would like to thank the children at Gilded Hollins County Primary School, Leigh, Lancashire, who have willingly shared their thoughts and ideas and who have had no problems discussing and responding to certain picturebooks that many adults would consider unsuitable for children. A special thank you goes to 11-year-old Molly Hatton whose accomplished illustration from Erlbruch's *Duck, Death and the Tulip* graces the front cover of the book. Then, of course, Wolf Erlbruch must once again be thanked, as without him there would be no duck, death or tulip.

Janet Evans
January 2015

PERMISSIONS

Acknowledgements are gratefully expressed for permission to use the following artwork:

Children's thoughts on challenging and controversial picturebooks

Cover and two double-page spreads from *Smoke* by Anton Fortes and Joanna Concejo (2009). Permission given by OQO Publishers, Spain

Chapter 1

One double-page spread from *Hello Baby* by Jenni Overend and Julie Vivas (1999). Permission given by Frances Lincoln Children's Books, London

One image from *Snowhite* by Ana Juan (2001). Permission given by Ana Juan

One image from *Die Menschenfresserin* by Valérie Dayre and Wolf Erlbruch (1996). Permission given by Wolf Elbruch

One double-page spread from 14–18: *Une minute de silence à nos arrière-grands-pères courageux* by Thierry Dedieu (2014). Permission given by Editions du Seuil, France

One image from *Hansel and Gretel* by Jacob Grimm, Wilhelm Grimm and Anthony Browne (1995). Walker Books, London. Permission given by Anthony Browne

One double-page spread from *Hansel and Gretel* by Jacob Grimm, Wilhelm Grimm and Susanne Janssen (2007). Rostock, Germany. Permission given by Susanne Janssen

One image from *La Barbe-bleue* (2005) by Thierry Dedieu. Permission given by Editions du Seuil, France

One image from *Capitan Omicidio* by Charles Dickens and Fabian Negrin (2006). Permission given by Orecchio Acerbo, Italy

One double-page spread from *The Story of the Little Mole who Knew It Was None of His Business* by Werner Holzwarth and Wolf Erlbruch (1989). Koch, Neff and Oetinger & Co, Germany. Permission given by Wolf Erlbruch

Cover from *Nu (Nude)* (2009) by Sara. Permission given by Editions du Seuil

One single page from *Duck, Death and the Tulip* by Wolf Erlbruch (2008). Gecko Press, New Zealand. Permission given by Wolf Erlbruch

Cover from *Ratten (Rats)* by Wolf Erlbruch (2009). Jacoby and Stuart, Germany. Permission given by Wolf Erlbruch

Cover from *Bornenes Bedemand (The Children's Undertaker)* by Oscar K and Dorte Karrebæk (2008). Gyldendal Norsk Forlag, Copenhagen, Denmark. Permission given by Oscar K and Dorte Karrebæk

Cover from *Idiot* by Oscar K and Dorte Karrebæk (2009). Høst og Søn, Copenhagen, Denmark. Permission given by Oscar K and Dorte Karrebæk

Double-page from *Hamlet* by Oscar K and Dorte Karrebæk (2009). Dansklærerforeningens Forlag, Copenhagen, Denmark. Permission given by Oscar K and Dorte Karrebæk

One image from *Lejren (Camp)* by Oscar K and Dorte Karrebæk (2011). Høst og Søn, Copenhagen, Denmark. Permission given by Oscar K and Dorte Karrebæk

Cover from *Knokkelmanden's Cirkus (Death's Circus)* by Oscar K and Dorte Karrebæk (2014). Høst og Søn, Copenhagen, Denmark. Permission given by Oscar K and Dorte Karrebæk

Chapter 3

One image from La Barbe Bleue by Charles Perrault and Jean Claverie (1991). Editions Albin Michel, France. Permission given by Jean Claverie

One image from *Ma Peau d'Âne* (2002) by Anne Ikhlef and Alan Gauthier. Editions du Seuil, France. Permission given by Alain Gauthier

One image from *Little Red Riding Hood* by Charles Perrault and Sarah Moon (1983). Permission given by The Creative Company, Mankato, Canada

Preliminary work on *The Girl in Red* image by Roberto Innocenti (1988). Reprinted by permission of The Creative Company, Mankato, MN © 2012 Roberto Innocenti

One image from *Snowhite* by Ana Juan (2001). Permission given by Ana Juan

One image from *Rotkäppchen* by Jacob Grimm, Wilhelm Grimm and Susanne Janssen (2001). Carl Hanser Verlag, Germany. Permission given by Susanne Janssen

One image from *John Chatterton détective* by Yvan Pommaux (1993). L'Ecole des loisirs, France. Permission given by Yvan Pommaux

One image from *Rødhatten og Ulven* by Fam Ekman (1985). Cappelen Damm, Norway. Permission given by Fam Ekman

Rood Rood Roodkapje by Edward van de Vendel and Isabelle Vandenabeele (2003). Uitg. De Eenhoorn, Belgium. Permission given by De Eenhoorn Publishers, Belgium

One image from *Mon Chaperon Rouge* (1998) by Anne Ikhlef and Alain Gauthier. Editions du Seuil, France. Permission given by Alain Gauthier

One double-page spread from *Les Cubes* by Béatrice Poncelet (2003). Editions du Seuil, France. Permission given by Béatrice Poncelet

One image from *L'Ogresse en pleurs* by Valérie Dayre and Wolf Erlbruch (2004). Editions Milan, France. Permission given by Wolf Elbruch

One image from *Vous oubliez votre cheval* by Christian Bruel and Pierre Wachs (1986). Le Sourire qui mord, France. Permission given by Christian Bruel

Chapter 4

Cover, three images and two double-page spreads from *De skæve smil* by Oscar K and Lilian Brøgger (2008). Klematis, Denmark. Permission given by Oscar K

Cover and five double-page spreads from *Krigen* by Gro Dahle and Kaia Dahle Nyhus (2013). Cappelen Damm, Norway. Permission given by Gro Dahle

Chapter 5

Cover, one double-page spread and one image from *The Wolves in the Wall* by Neil Gaiman and Dave McKean (2003). Bloomsbury Publishing, London. Permission given by Dave McKean

Cover and four images from *The Tragical Comedy or Comical Tragedy of Mr. Punch* by Neil Gaiman and Dave McKean (2006). Bloomsbury Publishing, London. Permission given by Dave McKean

One double-page spread from *Pictures That Tick* by Dave McKean (2009). Darkhorse, London. Permission given by Dave McKean

One image from *The Day I Swapped My Dad for Two Goldfish* by Neil Gaiman and Dave McKean (2005). Bloomsbury Publishing, London. Permission given by Dave McKean

One double-page spread from *Crazy Hair* by Neil Gaiman and Dave McKean (2015). Bloomsbury Publishing, London. Permission given by Dave McKean

Chapter 6

One image from *Hänsel e Gretel* by Wilhelm Grimm, Jacob Grimm and Lorenzo Mattotti (2009). Permission given by Orecchio Acerbo, Italy

Cover, six double-page spreads and one images from *Capitan Omicidio* by Charles Dickens and Fabian Negrin (2006). Permission given by Orecchio Acerbo, Italy

Chapter 7

Cover, one double-page spread one single page from *Fox* by Margaret Wild and Ron Brooks (2000). Permission given by Allen and Unwin, Australia

Chapter 8

Cover and three images from *The Girl in Red* by Aaron Frisch and Roberto Innocenti (2012). Reprinted by permission of The Creative Company, Mankato, MN © 2012 Roberto Innocenti

Chapter 9

Cover and five double-page spreads from *Loup Noir* by Antoine Guilloppé (2004). Permission given by Albums Casterman, France

Chapter 10

Cover and three double-page spreads from *Wolves* by Emily Gravett (2005). Permission given by Macmillan Children's Books, London

Cover, one double-page spread and two single pages from *Guess Who's Coming for Dinner?* by Cathy Tincknell and John Kelly (2004). Templar Publishing, Surrey. Permission given by Bonnier Publishing, London

Chapter 11

Cover and three double-page spreads from *The Red Tree* by Shaun Tan (2001). Lothian Books, Melbourne. Permission given by Shaun Tan

Chapter 12

Cover from *Home and Away* by John Marsden and Matt Ottley (2008). Lothian Books, Melbourne. Permission given by Hachette Books, Sydney

Chapter 13

Cover and one double-page spread from *Angry Arthur* by Hiawyn Oram and Satoshi Kitamura (1982). Permission given by Andersen Press, London

Cover and one double-page spread from *Not Now Bernard* by David McKee (1980). Permission given by Andersen Press, London

Cover and one double-page spread from *Chicken Clicking* by Jeanne Willis and Tony Ross (2014). Permission given by Andersen Press, London

Cover from *Tadpole's Promise* by Jeanne Willis and Tony Ross (2005). Permission given by Andersen Press, London

One double-page spread from *Frog and the Birdsong* by Max Velthuijs (1991). Permission given by Andersen Press, London

One double-page spread from *Lovely Old Lion* by Julia Jarman and Susan Varley (2014). Permission given by Andersen Press, London

One single and one double-page spread from *Denver* by David McKee (2010). Permission given by Andersen Press, London

One double-page spread from *I Hate My Teddy Bear* by David McKee (1982). Permission given by Andersen Press, London

Cover and one double-page spread from *Tusk Tusk* by David McKee (1978). Permission given by Andersen Press, London

Cover and three single pages from *Letters to Klaus* by Klaus Flugge (2013). Permission given by Andersen Press, London

FOREWORD

At the time of writing this foreword the world is reeling from, and trying to make sense of, the massacre in Paris of the cartoonists, writers and editors from the satirical magazine *Charlie Hebdo*. While the 'Je suis Charlie' signs dominate, there are also many who disagree with the satirical magazine's interpretation of freedom of speech. Heated discussions about respect, tolerance, culture and the right to express oneself will no doubt continue for some time in the media, as we reflect on where we place ourselves within the range of opinions. This is as it should be because the debate prevents the issues from becoming 'black or white' and reveals the many shades of grey in-between. Whatever interpretation of freedom of speech one agrees with, one thing comes across clearly from these tragic events: despite the ubiquity of images of every imaginable (and unimaginable) sort in the media, the impact of the visual text has not lessened. It reminds us that for every person who laughs at a picture, there will be another who will be saddened, offended or find it distasteful in some way. Regarding the massacre in Paris, Gary Younge, one of *The Guardian* columnists, argued that 'freedom of speech is always contingent'.[1] This implies that the meaning of an image will always be contingent on a given context and moment in time and hence has the potential to be regarded as controversial.

This collection of essays on controversial and challenging picturebooks is therefore timely and important as it exemplifies the kind of discussion – informed, revealing and enquiring – that can be held around images and their companion words. Works of art or literature have never been distanced from controversy but there is something about the way both word and image are brought together in these highly crafted picturebooks that doubles the impact – on our minds, our emotions and even our bodies. In addition, by their very nature picturebooks are controversial because they challenge expectations about intermediality, format, directionality and textual boundaries, among others. Finally, and perhaps most significantly, because they are ostensibly for a particular yet undefined audience, picturebooks challenge notions of childhood.

As in her previous collections of essays on picturebooks, Janet Evans has done an excellent job of pulling together voices from different perspectives and different parts of the world and introducing the reader to a rich and exciting list of picturebooks unknown in the English-speaking world. Not having translations in English is a loss highlighted by many of the authors of these essays. What is it that publishers are afraid of? Why not treat these picturebooks as one would any other form of literature or art book? A bookshop I recently visited in Spain simply had a section called 'picturebooks for adults' on a high shelf, not only an acknowledgement that picturebooks can be for adults but also that not all picturebooks are for children.

Janet starts the discussion by asking questions which will occur to people who look at the books mentioned in the chapters that follow. However, it is in the first essay that Perry Nodelman, with his customary incisive tone, shoots down any assumptions we may hold about what is 'acceptable' and what is 'controversial'. He does this by making us look again at what we take for granted, which is what the best literary criticism does no matter if it is for adult or children's books. The rest of the essays continue in this vein, questioning widely held notions of childhood and suitability through a discussion of a variety of international picturebooks, also providing a variety of lenses through which we can see that challenge, controversy and censorship are indeed contingent and contextual.

The power of image perhaps also has to do with the feeling that the impact of words can be immediately soothed over by other, comforting words but that the impact of images, as educators such as John Locke and François Fenelon maintained more than three centuries ago, could be even deeper and therefore less easily mitigated or erased. Yet the evidence from children's responses to difficult and haunting images suggests that even very young children find ways of coping with them. The accounts of readers discussing some of the 'challenging and controversial' picturebooks mentioned in the book support the main finding from a study from 2003 involving response to picturebooks, which is that children can be sophisticated readers of complex texts (Arizpe & Styles, 2003).[2] Since then, more than ten years later, children have been exposed to increasingly multimodal texts and can employ strategies from these experiences in their reading. Furthermore, the empirical work that appears in the chapters in this book shows that the children involved not only enjoyed these encounters but were motivated to search for their own answers and reflect on their interpretations, acting with sensitivity and independence. It seems that the problems about suitability arise when adults condemn a book before taking the time to read it carefully, to think about it or to discuss it with children. After all, it is adults, not children who have come up with the labels 'controversial' and 'challenging'.

The argument about protecting children from particular realities is a hard one to resolve, given that definitions of 'child' and 'reality' are continually modified as the historical boundaries between childhood, adolescence and adulthood are constantly being redrawn. Often this urge to protect seems to be an unconscious way of dealing with the guilt we adults feel about having made the world such a dangerous and endangered place for children. Therefore, before we share picturebooks that are in some way problematic or disturbing, whether it be with younger children or older students, we have to start by first being honest with ourselves about our own reactions to the picturebooks and our motives for wanting others to read them. This involves rethinking our conceptions about childhood and the idea of innocence, questioning any nostalgic or sentimental notions we may have but also reflecting on our own participation in the political, social, moral or environmental issues that created controversy or the need for 'protection' in the first place. Reading is a social practice, so once we have acknowledged our position, we then need to listen to points of view that differ from our own and consider these as we look closely at text and image so that we become aware of as many multiple layers of meaning as we can. Reading essays such as the ones in this book should help us in this self-reflexive and critical endeavour.

Finally, we need to consider why we want readers to engage with challenging picturebooks, whether it be as parents, educationalists or researchers (and, I would suggest, also as booksellers and publishers). Picturebooks about certain topics such as violence, depression or death can act as a trigger or support for broaching and reflecting on the way they touch the lives of young readers. However, there is a danger of encouraging a merely 'functional' reading that ignores both the aesthetic and pleasurable experience of reading and the status of the picturebook as an aesthetic object. There is also a danger, unless we are trained in some form of therapy, of causing upset by inviting discussion of sensitive issues. Depending on the readers, we need to create strategies to make sure that they are supported in approaching challenging themes and, if they so require it, provide a safety net to restore a sense of balance after plunging into some of these dark areas. More so than with other books, some of the picturebooks mentioned in this collection require many re-readings and a space for readers to talk, when they are ready and willing to do so, about what they found disturbing (or not). Providing readers with some analytical tools, a critical vocabulary and an invitation to respond creatively can enable them to view the text more objectively and perhaps deconstruct some of their anxieties and fears.

In a recent project in Mexico on adolescent reading, one of the books we looked at and discussed was *The Girl in Red* by Roberto Innocenti and Aaron Frisch[3] with two groups of 14-year-old students (one of the contributors to this edited collection, Elizabeth Marshall, presents an insightful analysis of how girls and women appear as objects of violation in this picturebook and also how student teachers respond to the idea of reading it in the classroom). While all eighteen participants in my project (Adolescents, Young Adult Literature and Literacy Practices in Mexico, http://readingchanges.blogspot.mx/) were familiar with the original tale of 'Little Red Riding Hood', only a few of them were familiar with picturebooks and they were amazed and fascinated by the design, colour, style, peritext and storyline in this particular picturebook. They were also intrigued by the choice of endings – happy or sad – that the authors of *The Girl in Red* offer the reader. Given that the climate of violence in Mexico became more extreme around the time of the project with the unexplained, forced disappearance of 43 student teachers, it is not surprising that the adolescent readers referred to the implicit and explicit threat of violence running through the picturebook and that most of them considered the unhappy ending to be the most 'realistic'. They linked the threat to their own lives, to the fears they faced either because of their gender, because of the area where they lived, because of the people they could come across or because of all of three. Armed with a disposable camera, they set out to create their own 'picturebook' version of the fairy tale which would be set in their communities. While many of the photographs reflected a sinister atmosphere and the beginning of the narratives tended to be alarming or bleak, most of the endings had either a twist which allowed the characters to arrive safely at their destination or a brief reflection on how we must not let our fears overcome us. It was my turn to be surprised: given our conversations, I had expected darker endings. I cannot prove it but it seemed that through the group discussions and the creative responses they came to the realization that they had the power to change their stories and so this challenging and controversial book contributed to some extent to their resilience.

As it becomes evident throughout the essays in this volume, serious artists, from Erlbruch and Sendak to Innocenti and Oscar K not only deeply respect the intelligence and independence of their readers but are also clearly aware of their responsibility to their young audiences. The images and words stir up fantasies deep inside our unconscious and push at the boundaries of what is difficult and demanding, yet at the same time they help us tolerate the anxieties they awaken. The different layers of meaning suggest that the creators are happy for their readers to decide what they can cope with. Wise publishers like Klaus Flugge, with deep knowledge of their craft, are also very much aware of the issues involved and Flugge's views are a breath of fresh air within a market where profit determines production on the one hand and arrogant and blinkered politicians come up with misguided government policies that result in library closures and narrow education on the other.

Making sense of how others think and feel is a complex cognitive activity, so awareness, self-reflection and discussion are essential if an understanding of what is challenging and controversial in a picturebook both for ourselves and for others, is to be reached. The authors of the essays in *Challenging and Controversial Picturebooks* show how much we have to learn from the insights of those closest to the creative process – authors, illustrators and readers – all involved in making meaning from image and text.

Evelyn Arizpe
25 January 2015

Notes

1 Younge, Gary (2015) Charlie Hebdo: The Danger of Polarised Debate, *The Guardian*, 11 January. Last accessed 18 January 2015 at www.theguardian.com/commentisfree/2015/jan/11/charie-hebdo-danger-polarised-debate-paris-attacks
2 Arizpe, E. & Styles, M. (2003) *Children Reading Pictures: Interpreting Visual Texts*. London: Routledge.
3 Innocenti, R. (2012) Story and illus Innocenti, R., text Frisch, A. *The Girl in Red*. Mankato, MN: Creative Editions.

CONTRIBUTORS

Sandra L. Beckett is Professor Emeritus of French at Brock University (Canada). She is a former president of the International Research Society for Children's Literature. She has authored numerous books, including *Revisioning Red Riding Hood Around the World: An Anthology of International Retellings* (2014), *Crossover Picturebooks: A Genre for All Ages* (2011), *Crossover Fiction: Global and Historical Perspectives* (2009), *Red Riding Hood for All Ages: A Fairy-Tale Icon in Cross-Cultural Contexts* (2008), *Recycling Red Riding Hood* (2002), and *De grands romanciers écrivent pour les enfants* (1997). She serves on the boards of several international journals.

Marnie Campagnaro has a PhD in Pedagogical and Educational Sciences and teaches Theory and History of Children's Literature in Educational and Training Sciences at the University of Padua. Her research interests include children's literature, reading promotion, visual literacy, and narrative and imaginative thinking in children. In 2013 she successfully hosted the *Ninth Annual International Conference 'The Child and the Book 2013'* at the University of Padua. Two of her most recent publications are in collaboration with Marco Dallari, *Incanto e racconto nel labirinto delle figure. Albi illustrati e relazione educative* (*Enchantment and Stories in the Maze of Pictures. Picturebooks and Education*) (2013), and *Le terre della fantasia. Leggere la letteratura per l'infanzia e l'adolescenza* (*Fantasy Lands. Reading Children's Literature*) (2014).

Janet Evans is an Independent Scholar, freelance Literacy and Educational Consultant, and former Senior Lecturer in Education at Liverpool Hope University. She has written numerous articles and book chapters and nine books on language, literacy and maths education. Her last academic book, *Talking Beyond the Page: Reading and Responding to Picturebooks*, focused on a reader response approach to responding orally to picturebooks and was published in March 2009 by Routledge. Her current research interests include an exploration of children's responses to strange, ambiguous and unconventional picturebooks. Janet has taught in India, Nigeria, Australia, America, Canada, Chile and Spain. She has given professional development courses at international schools and has presented keynotes speeches and papers at many international conferences. In 2010 she was awarded a research scholarship to study at the International Youth Library in Munich.

Klaus Flugge launched his own publishing company, Andersen Press (named after Hans Christian Andersen) in 1976. Since the early days there have been more than 2,000 titles for children by the likes of Michael Foreman, Satoshi Kitamura, David McKee and Tony Ross. The fiction list includes prize-winning work by Melvin Burgess and Sharon Creech. Andersen Press is responsible for modern classics such as *I Want My Potty!* by Tony Ross and *Badger's Parting Gifts* by Susan Varley. Probably the best-known character of all is Elmer the Patchwork Elephant created by David McKee. Klaus has received many prestigious awards and in 2013 was awarded the honorary citizenship of Bologna for his commitment in the field of children's books and to the Bologna Book Fair.

Kerenza Ghosh is a Senior Lecturer in English Education at the University of Roehampton. Formally a primary school teacher and English Coordinator, she convenes two English Specialism modules on the Primary Initial Teacher Education Degree. She has presented research papers at conferences within the United Kingdom, and has a chapter published, entitled 'Walking with Wolves: Children's Responses to the Wolf Tradition in Stories', in *Beyond the Book: Transforming Children's Literature* (Cambridge Scholars Publishing, 2014). Her ongoing research interests include polysemy within picturebooks and reader response with children.

Bettina Kümmerling-Meibauer is Professor in the German Department at the University of Tübingen. She is an active international editor of research volumes on picturebook theory, including *New Directions in Picturebook Research* (2010), *Emergent Literacy. Children's books from 0 to 3* (2011), *Manga's Cultural Crossroads* (2013), and *Picturebooks. Representation and Narration* (2014), and co-editor of the international book series 'Children's Literature, Culture and Cognition' (John Benjamins). She was speaker at the international research project 'Children's Literature and European Avant-garde', funded by the European Science Foundation. Her joint work with Jörg Meibauer focuses on picturebook theory as well as on lying in children's literature.

Elizabeth Marshall is an associate professor at Simon Fraser University, Canada, where she teaches children's and young adult literature. Her scholarship critically examines representations of childhood and adolescence within texts produced for, marketed to, and/or consumed by youth. She is the co-editor (with Özlem Sensoy) of *Rethinking Popular Culture and Media*. She has published articles on Little Red Riding Hood, Nancy Drew, American Girl, *Shrek*, and coming-of-age memoirs, including *Girl, Interrupted*, *The Kiss*, and *Stitches*. Her work has been published in the *Harvard Educational Review, Feminist Studies, Prose Studies, Gender and Education, Reading Research Quarterly, Journal of Adolescent and Adult Literacy, College English* and *Children's Literature Quarterly*.

Jörg Meibauer holds the chair of German language and linguistics at the Johannes Gutenberg University in Mainz, Germany, and is Affiliated Professor at the University of Stockholm, Sweden. His research focuses on the semantics–pragmatics interface, the grammar of German, word formation, lexical acquisition, and the linguistics of children's literature, especially picturebook theory (in cooperation with Bettina Kümmerling-Meibauer). His monographs include *Rhetorische Fragen* (1986), *Modaler Kontrast und konzeptuelle Verschiebung* (1994), *Pragmatik* (1999) and *Lying at the Semantics-Pragmatics Interface* (2014). Among his many co-edited books is the handbook *Satztypen des Deutschen* (2013). Currently, he is editing *The Oxford Handbook of Lying*.

Sandie Mourao is an independent scholar based in Portugal where she works as a teacher educator, author and consultant in the field of English language education, specialising in early years. She has an MA in TESOL from the University of Manchester and a PhD in Didactics and Teacher Education from the University of Aveiro in Portugal. Sandie's interest in picturebooks involves her in a number of activities that include preparing materials for and with teachers to use picturebooks in English language classrooms, as well as classroom-based, reader response research with children from pre-primary through to upper secondary education. Sandie writes an award-winning blog, Picturebooks in ELT: http://picturebooksinelt.blogspot.com/

Perry Nodelman, Professor Emeritus at the University of Winnipeg in Canada, is the author of *Words About Pictures: The Narrative Art of Children's Picture Books, The Pleasures of Children's Literature* (third edition in collaboration with Mavis Reimer), and *The Hidden Adult: Defining Children's Literature*, as well as publishing over 150 articles on various aspects of children's literature in academic journals and essay collections. He has also written a number of books for young readers, both on his own and in collaboration with Carol Matas.

Åse Marie Ommundsen is an Associate Professor in the Faculty of Education at Oslo and Akershus University College of Applied Sciences, Norway. She has her PhD from the University of Oslo on Children's Literature, with a thesis on *Literary Boundary Crossings. Erasing the Borders between Literature for Children and Adults* (2010). Her earlier publications include a book on religious magazines for children from 1875 to 1910 (1998), and *Looking Out and Looking In: National Identity in Picturebooks of the New Millennium* (ed., 2013). Her current interest is in contemporary Scandinavian children's literature, crossover picturebooks and picturebooks for adults, on which she has published several articles in Norwegian, English, French and Dutch and lectured as a guest lecturer and keynote speaker. Her ongoing research project is 'Norwegian children's literature in the aftermath of 22/7'. Most recent publication: 'Picturebooks for Adults', in: Bettina Kümmerling-Meibauer (ed.) *Picturebooks: Representation and Narration* (2014). In 2013 Ommundsen was awarded *The Kari Skjønsberg award* for her research on children's literature.

Sylvia Pantaleo is a Professor in the Department of Curriculum and Instruction in the Faculty of Education at the University of Victoria, Canada. She teaches courses in language and literacy, and children's and young adult literature at both the under-graduate and graduate level. Grants from the International Reading Association, the Social Sciences and Humanities Research Council of Canada, and the University of Victoria have assisted in funding her programme of research. Her multiple classroom-based studies have explored how 6 to 13-year-old school children respond to, understand, interpret and analyse literary elements and elements of visual art and design in picturebooks and graphic novels, and other multimodal texts.

CHILDREN'S THOUGHTS ON CHALLENGING AND CONTROVERSIAL PICTUREBOOKS

Over the years ... we have built up expectations of how hard and challenging picturebooks can be and our expectations have risen so that we now expect the picturebooks we read to be very challenging and demanding in terms of their content.

Edward, 11 years old

Over a period of seven years I worked with a class of 30 children, from their start at school at the age of 4/5 years to their final year at primary school at the age of 11 years. The class was made up of 14 boys and 16 girls. Over this period of time the children read, shared, thought about and responded to a variety of different books, mostly picturebooks. We considered the picturebook as something to read for pleasure; to think about, talk about and discuss (Evans, 2009; Styles & Noble, 2009); to respond to in the form of writing (Horner & Wing Jan, 2001), drawing (Anning & Ring, 2004; Styles & Noble, 2009), role play and drama (Heathcote, 1991); and as a catalyst for artistic expression (Craft, 2001; Brice Heath & Wolf, 2004). We also considered the picturebook as an art form and as a vehicle for discussing controversial and philosophical issues such as death and dying, war and conflict, drugs, immigration, loneliness and old age.

Many of the picturebooks were challenging, visual texts that prompted much thought and discussion. On occasion there were texts that made the children feel uneasy in relation to the subject matter; invariably, however, they invited the children to respond to texts by asking more questions and by sharing their personal thoughts and points of view.

The children were in their last year at primary school and I worked with the whole class prior to focusing on a small group of 6 children. We revisited some of the books we had previously read and worked with and examined what we thought challenging and controversial picturebooks actually were.

The children addressed a series of questions including:

What does challenging mean?

What does controversial mean?

What is a challenging picturebook?

Who are challenging picturebooks for?

What makes a picturebook challenging?

Would you choose to read a challenging picturebook and which one would you choose to read?

Initially the children were asked to write their individual ideas prior to discussion with the other group members. Then they shared them with their peers. Their responses were thoughtful and often quite profound.

What does challenging mean?

I think challenging means something that is a bit out of your comfort zone and something you are not used to doing. For example the first time you go to work it may be challenging but once you get used to it, it is not a challenge any more. There is more than one kind of challenge ... there are mental challenges where you find something hard because you are in troubling times, and physical challenges that might make your body ache.

Molly

Challenging means something that isn't easy; something that takes you a while to work out.

Edward

I think challenging means hard and difficult. I also think it means a task, like something you have been asked to do. Challenging is something that one person may find difficult or confusing that other people may find easy. I also think to challenge somebody is to ask them to do something they may not like.

Charlotte

Other words that mean challenging

The children thought of other words that could be used to describe challenging. They used the dictionary then the thesaurus to find synonyms for challenging (Figure 0.1).

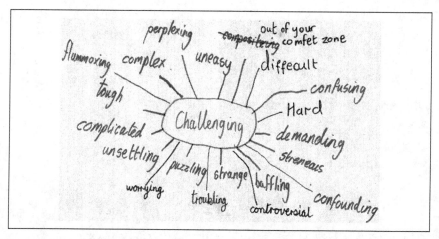

FIGURE 0.1 'Other words that mean challenging'.

What does controversial mean?

Charlotte and Megan both considered what the word controversial might mean although not all the children found this easy to define.

> I am not sure what controversial means but after our discussion I think it means causing a problem by saying something that someone disagrees with. So, if someone says something completely different to everyone else to cause an argument they are being controversial.
>
> *Charlotte*

> If something is controversial it means you can disagree with someone else and have an argument.
>
> *Megan*

> I've just looked it up in the dictionary and a controversial book is a book dealing with shocking issues such as the death penalty that not everyone has the same opinion of.
>
> *Edward*

What is a challenging picturebook?

> A challenging picturebook is a book that you have to think about 'out-of-the-box' as well as 'in-the-box'.
>
> *Molly*

> A challenging picturebook is a book that invites discussion and scrutiny so you can understand it.
>
> *Emily*

A challenging picturebook may be challenging for one person but not for someone else. I mean it might be really hard for one person but not hard for another person.

Patrick

Who are challenging picturebooks for?

I think that challenging picturebooks are for children aged 9–14. Too young and they wouldn't understand but too old and they wouldn't be challenging enough.

Edward

I would aim a challenging picturebook for an 11 year old or for people at high school or over because they are something that younger children won't understand because they're beyond their knowledge and experiences.

Molly

Sorting and classifying challenging picturebooks

After the 11 year olds had shared their thoughts and suggestions they looked at a selection of 35 picturebooks. From looking at just the title and book cover image they were asked to classify them according to if they thought they would be 'challenging', 'not challenging' or 'not sure'. Some of the books were classed as challenging by all of the children, and they began to talk about what makes a picturebook challenging.

What makes a picturebook challenging?

They were then asked to consider what might make a reader think a picturebook will be challenging. Emily's thoughts were quite comprehensive and she noted that book titles and subtitles, style of illustrations, text type and font and use of colour were all factors that can make a book look challenging or not:

I think illustrations can make a picturebook challenging. If they are childish pictures, it ticks in my brain saying easy, but if they are formal drawings and it looks more grown-up, I say challenging. For example, *Duck! Rabbit!* [Rosenthal & Lichtenheld, 2009] has cartoon type pictures, whereas *The Sweetest Fig* [Van Allsburg, 1993] has painted pictures, which are fully fledged.

The title can make a book challenging. If the title is long and in very formal writing it makes you feel like it's an adult book.

The font also makes a difference because if it looks posh, you automatically think it is more challenging.

Colour can affect my decision because lighter and warmer colours can make me think a picturebook is not as challenging but picturebooks with darker colours can make me think they are more challenging. For example with *Lola and the Rent a Cat* [Josephus Jitta, 2007] and *Woolvs in the Sitee* [Wild & Spudvilas, 2007]. *Woolvs in the Sitee* has dark and more complex colours but *Lola and the Rent a Cat*'s colours are brighter and simpler so it is less challenging.

Cartoon images and computer-generated images make a book look simpler but painted images can make it look more mature.

The subtitle of the book affects your opinion of the book, because even though *Underground* [Evans, 2011] is hand drawn and cartoon like, the subtitle writing at the bottom saying *Finding The Light To Freedom* make it sound much more mature and interesting.

Emily

Would you choose to read a challenging picturebook ... which one would you choose?

After looking at, classifying and discussing the reasons for their choice the children were extremely motivated to read the books and they each chose one to focus on. They predicted what they thought the challenge in their book would be before reading it. They then illustrated the book cover, wrote a caption for their illustration and concluded by summarising the book.

After reading the book they revisited their original challenge to see if their prediction had been 'correct'.

Once again the children showed great maturity of thought. They remarked that the reason they felt so at ease in responding was because they had been used to reading and talking about picturebooks like this for many years and they knew there was no right or wrong answer (Evans, 2009).

Children's choices and responses to six challenging books

The Island by Armin Greder

The Enemy by David Cali, illus. Sergei Bloch

Norton's Hut by John Marsden, illus. Peter Gouldthorpe

The Sweetest Fig by Chris Van Allsburg

The Wolves in the Wall by Neil Gaiman, illus. Dave McKean

Smoke by Anton Fortes, illus. Joanna Concejo

Emily's choice
The Island by Armin Greder

Before the read:

I think the challenge will be understanding and empathising with the person in the book.

After the read:

> I now know *The Island* is very challenging and the challenge is understanding why the other islanders didn't accept the man because he was apparently different when he wasn't. Just because the man seems different doesn't mean the islanders should treat him cruelly.
>
> The illustrations are sad, disturbing and horrifying. The look on the islanders' faces is angry and worrying and the book is very upsetting with a storyline that is related to things that are going on in the world now.

FIGURE 0.2 Emily's cover drawing and caption for *The Island*.

The illustration shows a man being attacked by the islanders simply because they perceive him as being different to them.

Megan's choice

The Enemy by David Cali, illus. Sergei Bloch

Before the read:

> I think the challenge will be for the soldier who is at war but wants to make peace.

After the read:

> I like this book a lot now I have read it. At first it didn't make much sense and I wondered what would happen if it continued but then you start to understand what the man is trying to do and it made a lot of sense.

FIGURE 0.3 Megan's cover drawing and caption for *The Enemy*.

The soldier is going to war to kill the enemy. However, he doesn't look like a fighting soldier, he looks like someone who wants to make peace because he has a flower in his mouth and a smile on his face.

Patrick's choice

Norton's Hut by John Marsden, illus. Peter Gouldthorpe

Before the read:

> I think the challenge for this book will be understanding it because the title doesn't give much away.

After the read:

> *Norton's Hut* is challenging because it was difficult to understand and to figure out what happened at the end.

FIGURE 0.4 Patrick's cover drawing and caption for *Norton's Hut*.

This image represents the ghostly part of the story with the man trembling next to the fire in fear that the hut will burn down and he will become a ghost.

Charlotte's choice

The Sweetest Fig by Chris Van Allsburg

Before the read:

> I think the challenge will be trying to understand why they called it *The Sweetest Fig.*

After the read:

> I don't think it is challenging because I understood what was going on and now I know why it is called *The Sweetest Fig.* It is called *The Sweetest Fig* because the fig tasted sweet and it is sweet to have a fig that could make your wishes come true.

FIGURE 0.5 Charlotte's cover drawing and caption for *The Sweetest Fig.*

The figs in this image represent the greed of the man who thought he could have everything in the world, however, in the end he ended up worse off than at the beginning.

Edward's choice

The Wolves in the Wall by Neil Gaiman, illus. Dave McKean

Before the read:

> I think the challenge will be finding out why there is a wolf in the wall.

After the read:

> I found my book was challenging because it was random and although I understood the book, it took me a while to accept what was happening.

FIGURE 0.6   Edward's cover drawing and caption for *The Wolves in the Wall*.

This picture of a wolf sliding down the banister represents the mischief, chaos, mayhem and destruction that the wolves were causing in the walls of the house.

Molly's choice

Smoke by Anton Fortes, illus. Joanna Concejo

Before the read:

> I think the challenge is going to be trying to understand the characters and why it is called *Smoke* and why it has got that particular illustration on the front.

After the read:

> Now I have read the book I think *Smoke* is a **very** challenging book. It is challenging because it doesn't tell you anything, it just gives you clues. The children don't know what's happening, but their families suffer a great deal of loss.

FIGURE 0.7 Molly's cover drawing and caption for *Smoke*.

The suit in the image represents the people who have lost their lives because they got gassed in the concentration camps and the tree represents new life and new hope because it is growing new shoots and leaves.

The children focused on *Smoke* by Anton Fortes and Joanna Concejo

Some books evidently looked much more challenging than others and although it was Molly who initially chose *Smoke* by Anton Fortes and illustrated by Joanna Concejo to focus on in detail, the other group members were also intrigued by the title and cover of this White Raven selected picturebook (2009) and they all chose it as their second book to read and discuss (Figure 0.8).

A harrowing yet poignant picturebook, *Smoke* describes the holocaust using a powerful blend of words and pictures. The reader sees how the little boy protagonist survives in the concentration camp, initially with his mother (his father having gone in a different line) and other prisoners, then alone with his only friend, Pali. Fortes' descriptive and haunting words are partnered by Concejo's equally graphic and emotive images drawn in pale, muted colours to evoke the transience of a previously short but sweet life. The reader is never sure if the boy knows where he is or what will happen to him but his innocence is never in question and, although many readers know what will finally happen, the end is still shocking.

The children's discussion about *Smoke* showed just how willing they were to predict, speculate and tolerate uncertainty in relation to challenging picturebooks; they even commented on how their own willingness and ability to do this had improved over the years. They knew there were no right and wrong answers and even though the book was very challenging and controversial, they took risks and shared their personal, sometimes audacious viewpoints as they knew these would be accepted by the other group members.

In thinking about this kind of qualitative reader response research in relation to picturebooks, Perry Nodelman questioned if it could be classed as 'real' research

FIGURE 0.8 *Smoke* by Anton Fortes, illus. Joanna Concejo (2009).

and asked, 'what might legitimately be learned … from work with a specific child or group of children?' (2010: 10). Nodelman felt that this kind of research could be classed as too subjective and idiosyncratic and he alluded to David Lewis's articulation of two routes to picturebook research, one involving, 'careful and patient listening to what children say as they read' and the other, 'an equally patient, careful description of individual books' (1996: 113). After consideration of both routes Nodelman admitted that there was great value in the former, whereby researchers work with children as they read and respond to picturebooks. He then proceeded to comment on the effectiveness of the researchers in this kind of response work and noted that in their attempt to praise the children for being so capable of precocious responses, 'researchers are often so determined to make their point about how clever children can be that they seriously underplay how clever they are themselves' (Nodelman, 2010: 11).

Children's thoughts and responses

The children with whom I worked were certainly capable of precocious responses and in relation to challenging and controversial picturebooks they showed: a willingness to be open minded; an awareness of deep, profound issues; and a level of maturity beyond their years, which at times was quite disconcerting. They were enthusiastic and willing to offer points of view and to learn from each other in this 'community of learners' environment.

Patrick:	I bet *Smoke* is about war and lots of people die. I also think the cover symbolises something strange.
Janet:	One thing is for sure, the book cover *is* very symbolic.
Molly:	What does symbolic mean?
Patrick:	I think symbolic means to represent something.
Edward:	Symbolic means it's a symbol of something, for example, if a bamboo farmer wrote this book maybe the cover is the bamboo farmer's symbol or logo for his farm.
Patrick:	We could draw a picture to symbolise the meaning of the book. We haven't actually written down or talked about what the front cover of *Smoke* could symbolise.
Megan:	I think *Smoke* will be very challenging.
Molly:	I think it is about some kind of religion; it's trying to say that people regenerate when they die.
Edward:	A bit like reincarnation?
Megan:	So how does the title, *Smoke*, come into it?
Molly:	Well, when people die some of them are cremated and that makes smoke.
Emily:	I think *Smoke* is about some people who have lost their family in a fire and then there are some trees left and because there is only one person left he is lonely so he puts the burnt people's clothes on a tree to show respect for them.
Edward:	I've just thought of what *Smoke* could be about. The person who survives the fire dresses up the bamboo plants so that he has someone to talk to like in the film *I Am Legend* where Will Smith talks to mannequins in shops. Also in the film *Cast Away* where Tom Hanks draws a face on a football to have someone to talk to.
Janet:	If your predictions are right would you expect a picturebook to be dealing with this kind of subject?
Emily:	No, because I would expect it to be in an autobiography about someone who has been through this kind of trauma but escaped, as opposed to someone who hasn't experienced this kind of thing.
Molly:	Most people expect picturebooks to be for babies.
Patrick:	People would expect subjects like this, to do with war, and concentration camps and stuff, to be in hard books.
Janet:	So what do you mean 'hard books'?
Patrick:	Books without pictures.
Edward:	Thicker books that are harder.
Janet:	Are picturebooks not hard?
Edward:	Yes they are hard but I know that some thick books without pictures can be harder.
Molly:	*The Boy in the Striped Pyjamas* [Boyne, 2006] is a hard subject but from a different point of view. This one, *Smoke*, is deeper in thoughts than *The Boy in the Striped Pyjamas*.
Edward:	If you hadn't been in this group for a while you would not expect picturebooks to be hard, you would expect them to be for babies.

Janet: Do you think picturebooks are challenging because of your personal expectations?

Edward: Yes but over the years, working with you, we have built up expectations of how hard and challenging picturebooks can be and our expectations have risen so that we now expect the picturebooks we read to be very challenging and demanding in terms of their content.

Patrick: Yes, we have built up a knowledge of picturebooks and what to expect. If we hadn't previously read picturebooks like these we would expect simple subjects and even after seeing the covers we would still expect them to be easy … but then after reading the pictures, we would think like, wow!

Edward: I've just thought of something, do you think authors just randomly choose to draw a book cover image in any way? Do they choose images that are not relevant to the story at all?

Janet: What do you think? You said the cover of *Smoke* was very symbolic so why do you think that image was chosen?

Emily: Maybe they made a tree and put clothes on the tree to pretend it's a dad.

Molly had previously read *Smoke* as it was her book of choice. At this point in the discussion she shared some of the story with the other group members.

Molly: I think the suit in the image represents the people who have lost their lives because they got gassed in the concentration camps and the tree represents new life and new hope because it is growing new shoots and leaves.

Patrick: They put this on the cover to sway us in one way and then when we read the book it has a totally different impact on us. The cover makes us think one thing but the book itself is completely different.

Edward: You would think the authors would put something on the cover that actually shows that it is going to be about, for example, a concentration camp. If you were one of those people who were actually in a concentration camp and then escaped, you might want to read the book, but you wouldn't know that it's about a concentration camp from the cover image.

Emily: Maybe people are attracted to it because it is so unusual.

Edward: I think it should have a label saying World War II, so people would know if they would want to read it.

Emily: They are gassing people's memories. It shows on the page about the green dragon.

Patrick: The green bit represents the grass and the house represents the smoke house where they go to get gassed and the dragon represents the people trying to get them into the smoke house to gas them. I think the person who is dreaming about the dragon dreams that the dragon is inside the chimney breathing gas to kill the people [Figure 0.9] (Plate 1).

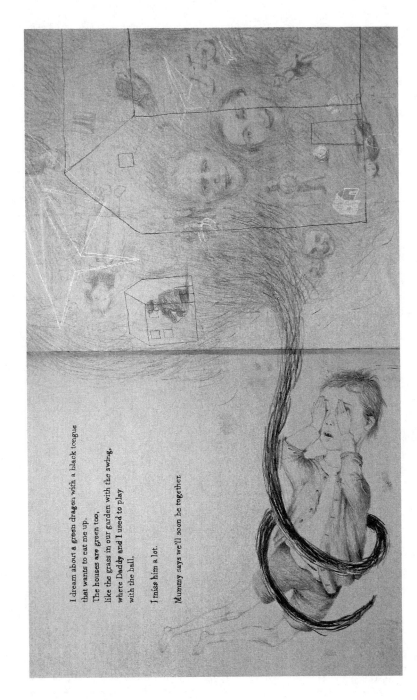

I dream about a green dragon with a black tongue that wants to eat me up.

The houses are green too,
like the grass in our garden with the swing,
where Daddy and I used to play
with the ball.

I miss him a lot.

Mummy says we'll soon be together.

FIGURE 0.9 (Plate 1) *Smoke:* The green dragon with a black tongue.

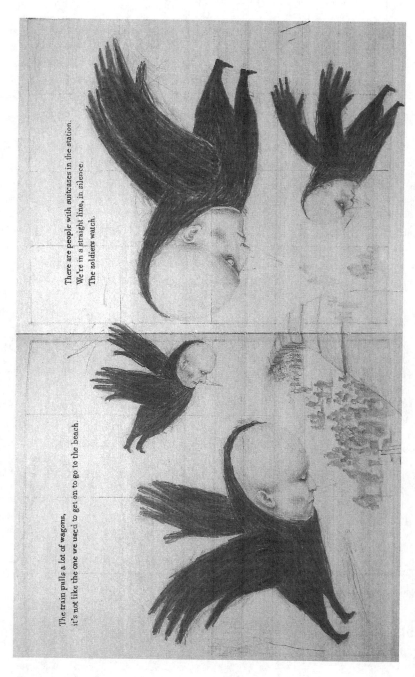

The train pulls a lot of wagons,
it's not like the one we used to get on to go to the beach.

There are people with suitcases in the station.
We're in a straight line, in silence.
The soldiers watch.

FIGURE 0.10 *Smoke*: The soldiers (as ravens) watch.

Molly's understanding of *Smoke* sums up for many readers just how challenging and controversial this kind of picturebook can be:

> Now I have read the book again I have a lump in my throat. On the first page of the story I now understand why the soldiers look like ravens because the symbol of death is a raven [Figure 0.10]. The mums and the children are in different queues to the men because the men have to go for war and the mums and the children go to the concentration camp. When I read books about concentration camps they always make me disturbed. I think it is cruel that the people that manage the concentration camps tell lies about the shower, and then 'gas-shower' the people. I cannot empathise with the characters but I do feel really sorry for them. The challenge for me is that they don't tell you much about the story and the cover doesn't link in.
>
> *Molly*

Quite evidently, even taking this very small snippet of conversation into consideration, responding to challenging and controversial picturebooks is not something that children are afraid of. It is more likely to be adults – parents, teachers and carers – who are unwilling, indeed incapable of making relevant, mature responses.

Academic references

Anning, A. & Ring, K. (2004) *Making Sense of Children's Drawings*, Maidenhead: Open University Press.

Brice Heath, S. & Wolf, S. (2004) *Art Is All About Looking: Drawing and Detail*, London: Creative Partnerships.

Craft, A. (2001) *Creativity in Education*, London: QCA.

Evans, J. (ed.) (2009) *Talking Beyond the Page: Reading and Responding to Picturebooks*, London: Routledge.

Heathcote, D. (1991) *Collected Writings on Education and Drama*, Evanston, IL: Northwestern University Press.

Horner, D. & Wing Jan, L. (2001) Writing as a Response to Literature, in Evans, J. (ed.) *The Writing Classroom: Aspects of Writing and the Primary Child 3–11*, London: Routledge.

Lewis, D. (1996) Going Along with Mr Gumpy: Polysystemy and Play in the Modern Picture Book, *Signal*, (80): 105–129.

Nodelman, P. (2010) On the Border between Implication and Actuality: Children Inside and Outside of Picture Books, *Journal of Children's Literature Studies*, 2(June): 1–21.

Styles, M. & Noble, K. (2009) Thinking in Action: Analysing Children's Multimodal Responses to Multimodal Picturebooks, in Evans, J. (ed.) *Talking Beyond the Page: Reading and Responding to Picturebooks*, London: Routledge.

Children's literature

Boyne, J. (2006) *The Boy in the Striped Pyjamas*. Oxford: David Fickling Books.

Cali, D. & Bloch, S. (2009) *The Enemy: A Book about Peace*. New York: Schwartz & Wade Books.

Evans, S. W. (2011) *Underground: Finding the Light to Freedom*. New York: Roaring Brook Press.

Fortes, A. & Concejo, J. (2009) *Smoke*. Pontevedra: OQO Books.

Gaiman, N. & McKean, D. (2003) *The Wolves in the Wall*. New York: HarperCollins.

Greder, A. (2007) *The Island*. Crows Nest, NSW: Allen and Unwin.

Josephus Jitta, C. (2007) *Lola and the Rent a Cat*. Mechelen: Bacckens Books.

Marsden, J. & Gouldthorpe, P. (1998) *Norton's Hut*. Melbourne: Lothian Books.

Rosenthal, A.K. & Lichtenheld, T. (2009) *Duck! Rabbit!* San Francisco: Chronicle Books.

Van Allsburg, C. (1993) *The Sweetest Fig*. Boston, MA: Houghton Mifflin.

Wild, M. & Spudvilas, A. (2007*) Woolvs in the Sitee*. Asheville, NC: Front Street.

ADULTS' THOUGHTS ON CHALLENGING AND CONTROVERSIAL PICTUREBOOKS

A small group of adults were asked what they thought challenging and controversial picturebooks were.

> *Challenging and controversial picturebooks are demanding, dangerous and difficult. Unexpected twists and treats emerge as each page is turned. They are fascinating, frightening, frustrating. They are a risk.*
>
> *Carmel*

It seems to me that as teachers, our energies are increasingly channelled into finding answers which are irrefutable, undeniable and measurable in order to satisfy the requirements of external accountabilities. Consequently, the texts we choose are an agreeable enough if slightly boring companion on our journey towards the literate, demonstrating tried and tested formulae in comprehension, grammar and punctuation. Limited by their primary purpose, such books are predictable, prim and proper. They are safe.

Challenging and controversial picturebooks offer neither safe passage nor guaranteed results for teacher or pupil. They call into question our beliefs; they stimulate our ideas in directions we may never even have dreamed of and lay claim to our emotions. They invoke a passionate response which can sometimes be so overwhelming that they leave the reader exhausted from the effort expended in trying to make sense of the puzzle in the visual feast before them. Such books cannot be fully appreciated in splendid isolation but instead need discussion with others, consideration and conjecture, careful observation. They are demanding, dangerous and difficult. Unexpected twists and treats emerge as each page is turned. They are fascinating, frightening, frustrating. They are a risk.

But the freedom of expression, creativity and collaboration they facilitate provides riches for the soul and lessons in life which reach far beyond the confines of the classroom.

And therein lies their immeasurable reward.

Carmel (parent and teacher)

A controversial picturebook is, I believe, a book that some people will find affecting and intriguing, whilst others will be uncomfortable with the content for any number of reasons; it could be the style of the imagery, the audience it's aimed at or the issues being tackled. A controversial picturebook is never a 'safe' book. It does not make us feel warm, content or happy; it's all about the challenge – the challenge of interpreting the imagery and text, the challenge of facing the not-so-nice aspects of reality, the challenge of reflecting and questioning your own experiences and opinions, the challenge of discussing all these things with others who have read the book. Sounds like hard work – maybe, but with that challenge comes revelations, excitement, curiousness, engagement and personal development.

The actual imagery used in such books can vary enormously. Sometimes illustrations are vivid, shocking and detailed. In other examples the surprising thing is the simplicity of the illustrations. It is the clever thought behind the imagery that provides opportunity for so many interpretations and reflections to be made about the storyline.

When reading such books we are entwining our thoughts, feelings and experiences with the imagery and text presented to us. In essence, these books are as challenging and controversial as the reader makes them.

Lizzie (parent and teacher)

Challenging for who? What is challenging for one person isn't necessarily challenging for someone else. It's a value judgement. Challenging picturebooks often raise more questions than answers.

Sue (parent and teacher)

Mmm … challenging picturebooks? Well they promote discussion. The ones I like have themes that are not too obvious or didactic and therefore the children don't realise the message at first and begin to question/challenge the thoughts of others as they all compare completely different imagined scenarios. Also, the same book brings up different things with different children as they digest the content at their own pace/understanding and have different interpretations so controversy about themes being 'too old' for younger readers isn't always relevant because unless something is pointed out, it often goes over their heads! A lot of the challenging picturebooks I've read seem to have open endings too which can be quite powerful and thought provoking even when the book is finished and placed back on the shelf and I like that.

Lisa (parent and teacher)

Picturebooks have become an art form in their own right and a powerful medium for exploring ideas. Many authors and illustrators are now employing a range of sophisticated techniques to engage the reader in the creative process by encouraging them to construct their own meaning from the narrative and visual clues. Imaginative illustrations, humour, wordplay and provocative subject matter are some of the ways the reader is challenged to think, interact and respond to powerful picturebooks. The potential for their creative use in the classroom makes picturebooks, in my opinion, the best resource available for teachers in the primary age range.

Ann (parent and teacher)

The term 'challenging' implies that the level of skill needed to 'read' a picturebook will be high. As the term refers to picturebooks this goes beyond a person's ability to read the written word and in order to fully engage with the book they would need a set of skills in addition to the ability to read text. For example, the reader must be able to focus on the pictorial element, interpreting the meaning in the pictures through inference and deduction, looking beyond the printed word. A truly challenging picturebook will ask the reader to respond to the pictures emotionally, using their wider experience of the world and the human condition in order to fully understand and experience the narrative.

The interpretation of the term 'controversial' in relation to picturebooks depends on one's exposure to the wider genre. Many may expect picturebooks to be limited to stories aimed at children aged seven years and under and picturebooks for older children would therefore be deemed to be controversial. However, I am fortunate to have had the joy of being exposed to picturebooks for older readers and for adults and for me, 'controversial' picturebooks are those with themes and content that ask us to question more deeply our preconceived ideas on any given topic.

Challenging and controversial picturebooks therefore, are the books which ask us to immerse ourselves in the written and pictorial narrative, drawing on our knowledge of all that makes us human and inviting us to perceive new realities.

Margaret (parent and teacher)

PART I

Challenging and controversial picturebooks

What are they and who are they for?

1

PICTUREBOOKS AS STRANGE, CHALLENGING AND CONTROVERSIAL TEXTS

Janet Evans

This opening chapter endeavours to consider what is meant by challenging and controversial picturebooks and some of the issues surrounding them. Issues such as: who they are for; how do we respond to them; will they be 'liked' by all readers; does 'challenging' mean the same for all readers; what are the origins of these contemporary visual texts; are they equally available in all countries; can wordless picturebooks be challenging; is it the words, the pictures or a combination of both that create the unconventionality – the sometimes very disturbing, troubling 'look' that these picturebooks can portray?

Oskar K has clear thoughts about these kinds of books:

> Every so often, books appear that are hard to categorise, because they are not aimed at a particular age group but at readers in general; they do not have monochord themes and plot sequences but are complex; they allow the dizzyingly incomprehensible to become the object of a reader's wonder – books that do not invite rapid and comfortable reading but require effort and contemplation.
>
> With great love, subtlety and humour, they depict offbeat characters, lonely children and adults, death and hope and love, they (the creators of these books) talk about incest, lies, violence, God, sexuality, alcoholism and drug abuse, abortion and euthanasia . . . everything that belongs to a more accurate description of the world shared by children and adults. A world many adults feel we should spare our children – at least, in books. A pleasant thought. And somewhat mendacious, when one considers the things that children encounter every day – on television, films and on the Internet.
>
> Journalists wallow incoherently through terror, war and destruction, sex scandals, raw violence and bestial murder. There is not much gentle grace there – at most, quickly pronounced judgements and titillating warnings about clips with bloody scenes.

But a book can be something else. A nuanced, artistic presentation of characters and worlds – without condemnation – can provide a completely different and complex experience from that of the disjointed assaults of the news. It is not about what you say but how and why you say it. It is not about provoking or offending someone but telling a story that means something. Books should not necessarily be understood but elicit a desire to understand.

Oscar K (2008: 46–48)

Is it usual to find picturebooks where a children's undertaker sings barbershop songs while he is laying out children's bodies in the mortuary; where aborted foetuses reflect on some of the reasons why they were never given a life, a name and an identity; where grotesque insects are bred to represent the seven deadly sins and where a mentally retarded boy is shown growing up in his own simple world to be eventually taken in death by, and alongside, his mother?

Well, yes it is, especially in certain countries. However we need to ask who these picturebooks, often dealing with controversial issues that evoke fearful responses about the psychological safety of the reader, are for. Who exactly is the audience? Are they for children or should we be asking if picturebooks such as *Idiot* by Oscar K and Dorte Karrebæk, *Smoke* by Anton Fortes and Joanna Concejo, and *Duck, Death and the Tulip* by Wolf Erlbruch are actually 'poetic and philosophical works of art for young adults' (Rhedin, 2009).

In the past couple of decades there has been an upsurge of interest in unusual, thought-provoking picturebooks – visual texts where the text and image work together to create the whole. Many people have previously assumed that picturebooks are for very young readers because of their emphasis on the illustrations and scarcity of text; however, there are increasing numbers of picturebooks where the age of the implied reader is questionable. These are picturebooks whose controversial subject matter and unconventional, often unsettling style of illustration challenge the readers, pushing them to question and probe deeper to understand what the book is about. In addition to the book challenging the reader, the reader often challenges the book, delving into the gaps in an attempt to understand what is being said. Very often these books are exquisitely beautiful to look at, touch and hold; they are art books and are frequently created by author/illustrators who are also artists in their own right.

Many of these picturebooks work on many different levels, they are truly polysemic and worthy of in-depth analysis. They compel the reader to respond to them and ask questions and in many instances are intrinsically philosophical, dealing with fundamental issues and asking 'big questions' which often form the basis of life.

Challenging and controversial picturebooks

Considering the terms

There is no existing term that is commonly used in the academic field of children's literature to describe/classify the picturebooks that this book focuses on, words such as: *strange, unusual, controversial, disturbing, challenging, shocking, troubling, curious, demanding* and *philosophical* are all suitable for describing *some* of these books but not *all* of them. Increasingly it seems there is no one single word that is suitable to identify and label these books. In an attempt to find such a word I have encountered more questions than answers; questions which have led me to better understand and classify these books. In considering this same issue, Perry Nodelman questioned what qualities and characteristics a book has to possess in order to be classed as controversial. He discovered that some mainstream, bestselling picturebooks were often more strange than the ones classed as strange (Chapter 2, this volume).

Children's personal challenges

Many adults feel that challenging and controversial picturebooks are not suitable for children to read, however, it is they, as adults, who have problems coping with these challenging texts and not the children. In reality, many young children have to deal with troubling, personal problems on a day-to-day basis in their own lives: real-life problems needing real-life solutions that are not just found on the pages of books. Some of the 11-year-old children with whom I was working shared their personal challenges:

> A big challenge for me was when my sister was in hospital because she had leukaemia.
> Another challenge for me is about my mum and dad's divorce. My dad has sent us to court asking for more contact when I don't want it. It has only just happened so it's a bit out of my comfort zone but I'm getting used to it.
>
> *Olly*

> A challenge for me a few years ago was when my mum was diagnosed with bowel cancer. It was especially hard for me and my dad because she was in hospital for three months. All the family was affected because she did a lot for us and it became a very hard time. Visiting mum was the hardest because seeing her like this made us feel sad because we had to do lots for her as if she was a baby whereas she used to do lots for us before. My challenge is mental and physical.
>
> *Emy*

> My first personal challenge was when I went to Manchester velodrome because I was the only girl there and I'd never done it before, plus everyone else could ride and I couldn't. What I found hard was that you can't take your feet out of the pedals and you can easily fall over and really hurt yourself.
> My second challenge was when my granddad had cancer and was always in hospital. I was challenged because I had to be brave and that was really hard because my great nan had cancer and died so I was scared I was going to

lose granddad. Unfortunately I did. It was also really hard and a challenge for my nan, uncle and mum because they were there when granddad died. My last challenge was going to my granddad's funeral because I started to cry as soon as I saw his coffin. I had a challenge trying to keep the tears back.

Meg

Personal challenges and picturebook themes

These were just some of the challenges facing these children at the age of 11 years; however, many of them had already experienced serious worries when they were younger. Of course, children have to cope with the challenges that life brings, we cannot and should not 'wrap them up in cotton wool', that is not the reality of life and this is where challenging picturebooks can be seen as being helpful, often therapeutic texts. As Oscar K (2008) noted so very emotively at the beginning of this chapter, fiction is a narrative and picturebook narratives very often reflect the reality of life, sometimes directly, other times making allusions to real-life situations as part of the story. Picturebooks can help children relate to, and come to terms with, troubling, disturbing and sometimes controversial issues in life.

Olly, Emy and Meg's personal challenges are issues often covered by picturebooks: *Jenny Angel* (Wild & Spudvilas, 1999) deals with child illness and eventual death; *Krigen* (*The War*) (Dahle & Nyhus, 2013) (discussed by Ommundson, Chapter 4, this volume) depicts the nightmarish reality of parental divorce as 'a dramatic war scene'; *The Scar* (Moundlic & Tallec, 2009) tells how a little boy deals with his mother's death and the associated emotions ranging from upset and anger to eventual acceptance of his loss; *La Visite de Petite Mort* (*Little Death's Visit*) (Crowther, 2004) shows in a poignant, and yet gently humorous way, how dying can be made more palatable and less frightening by a little girl who, in accepting her own death, endeavours to help others accept theirs; *Lola and the Rent a Cat* (Josephus Jitta, 2007) tells how Lola deals with the loss of John, her husband after 56 married years; and then, Wolf Erlbruch's award-winning picturebook, *Duck, Death and the Tulip* (2008) allows a child reader to see death in a different, unexpected light – as a character with a personality and emotions just like a living person. Finally, *Don't Let Go!* (Willis & Ross, 2002) is an incredibly emotional picturebook telling of a little girl's very close relationship with her father and the way he helps with her challenging physical struggle to ride a bicycle for the first time and in so doing to take her first move in becoming independent. These picturebooks, each challenging in different ways, evoke the children's personal worries and concerns and help them to come to terms with them by finding solutions.

Many children who are not allowed access to these kinds of challenging picturebooks, on the grounds that they are too young or immature, are being patronised. Their everyday lives are often filled with far greater personal worries and challenges than those they may find in books. Whatever challenge a picturebook presents is by definition 'at one remove', it is not one's own personal problem and can be thought about and reflected on, 'at a distance'. Carole Scott (2005) considered whether some of these challenging picturebooks were 'a challenge to innocence'. She concluded that they weren't and in some earlier research she stated that rather than deny children access to these thought-provoking texts adults should share them with children and talk about them, thereby mediating any potentially upsetting content of a controversial book (Scott, 1999). Challenging and controversial picturebooks often dealing with shocking material should be for all ages; 'It isn't enough to just read a book, one must talk about it as well' (Evans, 2009: 3).

Readers' responses: age, maturity and previous experience

The maturity shown by children as they read, think about and respond to challenging texts is often quite amazing; they can cope with and respond to both real-life and picturebook problems in a manner that adults frequently have found almost unbelievable (Evans, 1998, 2009, 2013, 2014). Most children who read these books find no problems with them and accept them at face value; their previous experiences and level of maturity allow them to respond in appropriate ways for their age. Hence, potentially distressing picturebooks about the holocaust such as *Smoke* (Fortes & Concejo, 2008), *Let the Celebrations Begin* (Wild & Vivas, 1991) and *Lejren (Camp)* (K & Karrebæk, 2011), are unlikely to be as upsetting or troubling to a 9-year-old child, who isn't fully aware of the atrocities perpetrated in the concentration camps, and in the World War 2 fighting leading up to these atrocities, as they would be to an 89-year-old war veteran.

Even beautifully tender books such as *Happy Birth Day!* (Harris & Emberley, 1996), depicting the still attached new born baby and mum breast feeding, and *Hello Baby* by Jenni Overend and Julie Vivas (1999) (Figure 1.1) (Plate 2), which depicts a mum giving birth standing up with members of her family around her to give support and to honour the new baby, are more acceptable to young children, who see the baby as a potential brother or sister and are more interested in how it arrives, than to adults, many of whom see birth as an explicit, shocking image, rather than the natural and celebratory event that it genuinely is.

Attempting to protect? Adult censorship of challenging picturebooks

Many writers, academics and picturebook creators have voiced opinions about the way adults control children's readership of challenging texts.

In relation to sharing such books with children Maurice Sendak wrote:

> I don't think I'm stretching the point when I suggest that this 'let's-make-the-world-a-happy-easy-frustration-less-place-for-the-kids' attitude is often propounded in children's literature today. . . . I believe there exists a quiet but highly effective adult censorship of subjects that are supposedly too frightening, or morbid, or not optimistic enough for boys and girls.
>
> *Sendak (1988: 158)*

FIGURE 1.1 (Plate 2) *Hello Baby* (Overend & Vivas, 1999): Mum gives birth.

In concurring with Sendak, Wolf Erlbruch, who also feels that children are underestimated by adults, stated:

> No child is ignorant. That's only what adults like to think, they like to have the edge on them. But it is the other way round. Grown ups live with so many restrictions, they just can't fathom the intellectual depth of children.
>
> *Erlbruch (2006: 2)*

Erlbruch felt that over 90 per cent of children's books are 'entirely dispensable'. Maria Nikolajeva agreed, stating, 'to be very provocative, I distinguish between children's books and children's literature. 95% of the market is (*made up of*) books that are flat, simplistic predictable, etc. and I'm not interested in them' (2009, personal email).

In addressing this same issue, Perry Nodelman wrote, 'We will be further ahead if we treat children not as different sorts of beings incapable of mature thought but as beginners at mature thought who need and are able to acquire experience of it' (1988: 282). Nodelman and Reimer later wrote:

> To deprive children of the opportunity to read about confusing or painful matters like those they might actually be experiencing will either make literature irrelevant to them or else leave them feeling they are alone in their thoughts or experience.
>
> *Nodelman & Reimer (2003:102–103)*

Challenging for who? Controversial for who?

Crossover picturebooks and picturebooks for adults: an implied audience?

What is challenging and controversial to one reader may not be to another; however, there are increasing numbers of picturebooks that are ever more strange, ambiguous and unconventional in their subject matter, form and illustrative style. So who are these picturebooks for? They are not simply for very young children as some people think. They can be so powerful and moving that even adults find them extremely emotional and thought-provoking. The majority of people do not realise how complex picturebooks actually are. In reviewing the *Picture This* exhibition at the British Library in 2013, Jenny Colgan noted that many illustrators did not pander to the perceived needs of children, not caring about frightening them or needing to keep them safe. She noted that in creating different worlds for children they are given space and freedom to let their imaginations run wild. She said, 'Children will always risk a nightmare as long as there is somebody to soothe them when they wake' (Colgan, 2013).

The question of who is the audience for children's literature is not new. In 2008 Rachel Falconer and Sandra Beckett both wrote about crossover literature, books that address both children and adults. A decade earlier, Beckett (1999) wrote about this same issue in her book on dual audience in children's literature. Even earlier than this, Kimmel asked if there could be children's literature without children? He saw that adults as well as children were reading children's picturebooks and he noticed 'the appearance of a growing number of exotically illustrated, high-priced picture books that appear to be far too unusual or sophisticated to attract many children' (Kimmel, 1982: 41).

In 2012 Beckett used the term *Crossover Picturebooks: A Genre for all Ages*, to describe picturebooks that can be read by people of any age, not just children. Her extensively researched book describes and analyses differing categories of picture-books, many of which deal with difficult subjects as her chapter focusing on cross-generational themes shows. Beckett also considers the connections between early children's stories, to include traditional tales, fairy tales and cautionary tales, with some of the dark, disturbing contemporary crossover picturebooks (Chapter 3, this volume).

Åse Marie Ommundsen takes this question of audience one stage further and focuses on picturebooks for adults, whereby the intended audience are adults and not children (Chapter 4, this volume). Ommundson defines this kind of picturebook as 'a narrative text addressed to adults with a picture on each spread' (2014: 17); she notes that they are a new trend in Scandinavian literature and although there are various types they all 'borrow their visual expression from advanced picturebooks for children' (2014: 32). The idea of picturebooks for adults is an unusual concept to accept for many people who grew up read-ing picturebooks in their own childhood and now think of them as being for young children.

Taboo subjects, translation, and censorship of picturebooks

In looking at the differing ways in which picturebook creators have approached the depiction of taboo subjects, Salisbury and Styles noted that 'there are many cultures where discussing the less cosy aspects of life (and death) in picturebooks is more commonplace that it is elsewhere . . .' (2012: 113). Countries such as France, Germany, Italy, Spain, the Far East and the Scandinavian countries of Norway, Denmark and Sweden all have picturebook creators and publishers who seem unafraid to publish challenging and controversial picturebooks. However, not all countries show this openness and many British and American publishers are quite conservative in relation to the type of picturebooks they publish. Challenging or even slightly controversial books are often considered only if they are created by well-known and extensively published authors/illustrators. David McKee is such an example, although, he cannot be used as a typical example as his work is published by Andersen Press, with owner and Managing Director Klaus Flugge at the helm. Klaus is known for being liberal in relation to books that are slightly different, challenging and unusual; he shares some of his views in this volume (Chapter 13).

This lack of openness to taboo subjects means that many challenging picturebooks don't get published at all or are published only in their first language and not translated into English. This covert censorship of books is more common than is often thought. It appears that many challenging books are censored by the publishers even before the reader gets the chance to read them; they are not published in translation meaning that many of the large, powerful publishing houses are changing the way in which children read (Hade, Paul & Mason, 2003). Givens (2009) writes of hidden forms of censorship and their impact on the reader, whilst Noll (1994), in talking about banned books in America, considers how censorship can seriously affect the kind of books teachers use in the classroom situation and how they are used. Patrick Shannon considered overt and covert forms of censorship and noted, 'censorship appears to be a form of silencing, in which groups are denied certain information, and therefore, are unable to speak about the topic in any way' (1992: 6). Elizabeth Marshall touches on the issue of censorship in her work with student teachers, in addition to considering how a particular picturebook offers a challenge for thinking about the way in which graphic knowledge about gender and sexuality operates (Chapter 8, this volume).

Nina Christensen from the Centre for Children's Literature in Copenhagen, Denmark wondered why more picturebooks were not translated into English. She felt that one explanation could be differing views of childhood and of the role of the adult in relation to children's books. She noted:

> You might find it a provocative statement but when I enter a children's bookshop in England – or Sweden for that matter – I find that the majority of books are written in a way so that neither child nor parent/adult is challenged too much. Generally speaking, picturebooks seem to confirm existing

norms and conventions. A lot of Danish picturebooks are also like this but I think there is also a tendency in picturebooks from Denmark and Norway to expand the borders of how you can address small children and which kind of stories you can tell them. Very simply put – in some Danish and Norwegian picture books children are exposed to issues such as cruelty towards children, naked children, sex and less than ideal behaviour presented in an ironic manner etc. In relation to these examples the child reader is supposed to be 'competent', not an individual who should always be protected from strong or strange impressions. I think this is one of the reasons why so few of them are translated. I might be wrong.

(2011, personal email)

What makes a picturebook challenging?

Words, pictures and subject matter

In considering crossover picturebooks, and picturebooks for adults, it is evident that although both will have things in common with more 'traditional' picturebooks, there will also be many differences, especially in relation to the subject matter of these books and the way they are presented. The way in which the words and pictures, the iconotext (Hallberg, 1982), mesh is important but the subject matter is critical in determining if a picturebook is regarded as being challenging and/or controversial. Some books, as noted by Lehr (1995) in her work on controversial issues in children's literature, deal with disturbing and often intensely thought-provoking subjects such as: death and dying; love, sex and violence; depression, sadness and loneliness; intolerance; murder; suicide; drugs; bullying; racism; the holocaust; domestic abuse; abortion and even child burial!

Many people would argue these are unsuitable subjects for picturebooks; however, we need only look at the origins of some of these stories and themes. They are not new! In the early nineteenth century the Grimm Brothers were recounting stories such as these; traditional folktales that reflected life as it existed at that time. Subjects such as murder, cannibalism, incest, child cruelty, sex and violence were all significant elements in the original Grimms' folktales and were accepted in their stories. The Grimm Brothers' stories and those, half a century later, of Hans Christian Andersen, who also wrote stories with disturbing themes, have always been viewed as suitable for children. Many adults allow, even encourage, children to read these traditional stories dealing with dark, psychological, sometimes harrowing themes and yet, those same children are often denied access to contemporary picturebooks covering similar themes.

Whether a text has illustrations or not affects how a story is viewed. The style of the illustrations and the way they 'work' with the words is central to how the book as a whole is judged and responded to. If a very explicit style is used to illustrate a narrative then there will undoubtedly be adults who see these picturebooks as being unsuitable for children. The original folktales recounted by the Grimm

Brothers were not originally written down, let alone illustrated, and it is now the explicit nature of some illustrations that creates the controversy and which is most certainly one of the reasons why certain contemporary picturebooks are sometimes seen as being unsuitable for children. Paula Rego's very dark, distressing and intensely troubling illustrations of nursery rhymes and traditional folktales bear testament to this (Rego, 2010).

Sex, violence and other taboo subjects

In relation to the existence of violence in fairy stories, Bengtsson (2009) considered whether these elements of horror and violence should be omitted from fairy tales. In looking back at some of the original stories he noted that the Grimm Brothers actually self-censored their own work, especially when they realised they were being viewed as children's stories. Their folktales, not originally for children, contained stories of sex and violence that included incest and the abuse of children. Tatar (1987) noted that in editing them the Grimms judged sex as being unsuitable but violence as being suitable. Bengtsson added, 'some of the abuse of children – such as starving them to death and the cruel punishments they endured – were not censored'. He went on to say that, 'without evil there cannot be a clear sense of good either' (2009: 16).

In stating that the use of violence in picturebooks is nothing new, Tomlinson noted how children in ancient Greece were exposed to tales such as that of Cronus, one of the Greek gods, swallowing his newborn children and keeping them imprisoned in his stomach. Tomlinson went on to say that, 'Abandonment, decapitations, disembowellings, serial murders, and poisonings were everyday fare in the folktales of the Middle Ages' (1995: 39). His view is that violence runs through every inch of the fabric of children's literature.

Despite the fact that the use of taboo subjects, to include violence is nothing new, some picturebooks are *so* complex, with subject matter that is *so* intense and difficult to grasp, that it is sometimes hard to accept that they may be considered suitable for children. Many of these books are troubling and frequently shocking. *Sinna mann (Angry Man)* by Gro Dahle and Svein Nyhus (2003) is a book about domestic violence and a little boy's way of coping. Bjorvand (2010) called this book 'a revolution in children's literature', not just because of the subject matter but because of the way in which physical abuse and domestic violence is portrayed in a picturebook. *Snowhite*, Ana Juan's hypnotic adaptation of the Grimm Brothers' traditional fairy tale, is a story of jealousy, hatred, cruelty, murder and cannibalism where, instead of a poisoned apple, Snowhite is given drugs and instead of the prince giving her a kiss, he rapes her (Figure 1.2). This book mesmerises the adult reader for its sensational coverage of universal themes in the guise of a traditional folktale.

In studying extremely controversial picturebooks Kunnemann (2005) focused on *Die Menschenfresserin (The Female Cannibal)* by Valérie Dayre, illustrated by Wolf Erlbruch (1996). Lissa Paul (2003) also studied this picturebook, becoming quite

FIGURE 1.2 *Snowhite* (Juan, 2001): Snowhite is raped.

obsessed with it in the process. The book, now almost 20 years old, is about a female ogress who eats her own son. It is about cannibalism! One of the most disturbing illustrations in this book is when the female cannibal has just devoured her own child. Erlbruch depicts this scene in the most compelling and powerfully shocking manner: the wind-up toy monkey previously depicted quietly regarding the little boy playing his bandonium, is shown screaming hysterically, his mouth wide open and his eyes wildly protruding in shock at what he is seeing (Figure 1.3) (Plate 3).

In listening to adults' responses when this picturebook was read aloud, Paul noted, 'The initial reaction was the same everywhere: a dismayed intake of breath, a shiver of horror, instinctive recoil. I felt it every time. The message was clear:

FIGURE 1.3 (Plate 3) *Die Menschenfresserin* (illus. by Erlbruch, 1996): The boy is devoured.

keep this book away from children' (2003: 173). Despite this message Paul did use this book with a class of 10 and 11-year-old children and found, 'Unlike the adults, the children did not respond with revulsion. Not even a hint. There was no shock, horror or fear. They engaged in the story with calm, intense interest and curiosity . . .' (2003: 177).

Bully by David Hughes (1993) is a strangely illustrated, upsetting and unsettling picturebook dealing overtly with aggression, hatred and gratuitous violence, triggered by one character who seems innately vicious and who passes his viciousness onto the other characters. The setting is a children's playground and the characters, depicted as both real children and wild animals are seen taking obvious pleasure in barbaric terrorism against their peers. Although *Bully* is over 20 years old it is a book for our time, covering issues of pointless violence and making people think about their senseless actions.

Then, drawing on our knowledge of history and the challenge of violent conflict is Thierry Dedieu's beautifully executed, powerfully affecting, almost wordless picturebook depicting World War 1 from a very human viewpoint, *14–18: Une minute de silence à nos arrière-grands-pères courageux* (2014) (*14–18: A Minute of Silence for Our Courageous Great Grandfathers*) (my translation) (Figure 1.4) (Plate 4).

Other books dealing with taboos, sometimes less violent but equally strange and unconventional, include: Armin Greder's darkly allegorical book, *The Island* (2007), Libby Gleeson's perplexing picturebook, *I am Thomas* (2011), which Greder illustrated, and Kitty Crowther's strangely philosophical and somewhat heart-warming

FIGURE 1.4 (Plate 4) *14–18: Une minute de silence à nos arrière-grands-pères courageux* (Dedieu, 2014).

texts such as *Le Petit homme et Dieu* (*The Little Man and God*) (2010), *Dans Moi* (*In Me*) (2007) and *La Visite de Petite Mort* (2004).

The troubling and very distressing book *Caja de Carton* (*Cardboard Box*) (2010) by Txabi Arnal and Hassan Amckan tells of loss of home and life and migration to another place. The subject of migration, refugees and the plight of asylum seekers is considered by Janet Evans (Chapter 12, this volume).

The House that Crack Built by Clark Taylor and Jan Thompson Dicks (1992) focuses the reader's attention on the effects that growing, selling and taking crack cocaine has on human beings; an important issue which Koehnecke (2001) felt was treated with sensitivity and honesty in the book. The picturebooks of Shaun Tan are all strange, visual texts but his profoundly complex book *The Red Tree* (2001) (Figures 11.1 to 11.4 in Chapter 11) is about despondency and depression as experienced by a little girl. Sylvia Pantaleo explored the gaps exposed by this book then elicited the responses of young children as they responded to it (Chapter 11, this volume). Bettina Kümmerling Meibauer and Jorg Meibauer (Chapter 7, this volume) worked with the thought-provoking, philosophical book *Fox* (2000) by Margaret Wild and Ron Brooks. In studying this picturebook they looked at the emotional issues of friendship, love, loyalty and deception and the way in which the text–picture relationships often play with the viewer's mind as they try to interpret the book.

It is increasingly evident that these and many other such picturebooks are crossover picturebooks aimed at both children and adults (Beckett, 2012; Ommundson, 2014).

Differently challenging: illustrations make a difference

How the words and illustrations work together in any kind of picturebook is crucial, as of course is the subject matter; however, as previously mentioned, the illustrations can change the way in which a contemporary picturebook is viewed and responded to. Different picturebooks may use exactly the same story (often a traditional fairy tale) but may be illustrated and presented in totally different ways, making one version easy to read and understand whilst the other can be more difficult to read and understand. *Hansel and Gretel* is one such example. Originally by the Grimm Brothers, the subject matter of this story is dark and threatening, dealing with themes of murderous intent and cannibalism. One might presume that all readers would respond to this folktale with horror and revulsion and yet different illustrations affect how the reader sees and responds to the story. Picturebook creators Anthony Browne and Susanne Janssen both did versions of *Hansel and Gretel*. While both versions are strangely disturbing, the Browne version (Figure 1.5) suggests an implied child audience, whilst Janssen's much darker, psychological version (Figure 1.6) (Plate 5) suggests an implied adult audience. The illustrations create these differences. Although both written versions may be the same, the illustrative style, colour, technique and links with the words all make a considerable difference to how a reader perceives and responds to the book.

FIGURE 1.5 *Hansel and Gretel* (illus. by Browne, 1995): Father and stepmother.

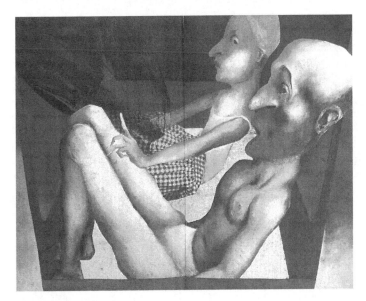

FIGURE 1.6 (Plate 5) *Hansel and Gretel* (illus. by Janssen, 2007): Father and stepmother.

Bluebeard by Charles Perrault, once again dealing with murder and cannibalism, is another example where the illustrations used make an impression on how the book is viewed. Many versions and interpretations of this story have been done but two very different adaptations, clearly showing how important the illustrations are in affecting how readers respond to a book, are *La Barbe Bleue* by Dedieu (2005) and *Capitan Omicidio* (*Captain Murderer*), a version of Bluebeard using Charles

Dickens' variation interpreted and illustrated by Fabian Negrin (2006). Dedieu's version uses bold blocks of colour and a paper tearing/layering style to create disturbingly explicit, graphic images (Figure 1.7) (Plate 6), whilst Negrin uses enigmatic somewhat ethereal pastel coloured images to represent Bluebeard, the ogre, in a metaphorical and symbolic manner (Figure 1.8). Marnie Campagnaro looked at

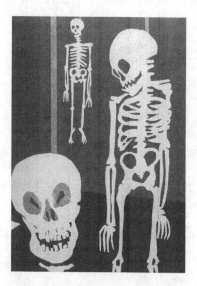

FIGURE 1.7   (Plate 6) *La Barbe Bleue* (illus. by Dedieu, 2005): The dead wives.

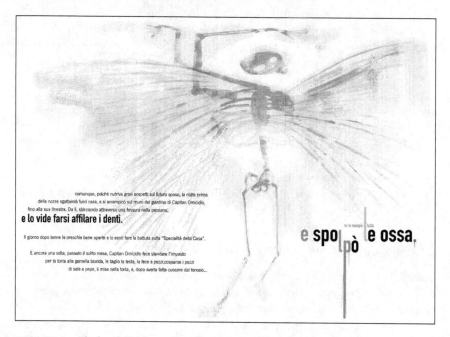

FIGURE 1.8   *Bluebeard* (Dickens, illus. by Negrin, 2006): The dead wife.

some children's responses to Negrin's illustrations. She considered how the children preferred the more connotative style of illustration where they had to think and delve beyond the text to fully understand the narrative (Chapter 6, this volume). In Chapter 5, Janet Evans considers how this kind of blending and merging of challenging subject matter with multiple, differing illustrative styles often creates a fusion-like appearance and requires that the reader thinks deeply about the narrative in order to fully appreciate and understand it.

Differently challenging: humour makes a difference

Although controversial picturebooks can be read by both children and adults alike, there are occasions when what is challenging and controversial for adults may be quite the opposite for children. Humour is often the cause, scatological humour in particular. In *Die Schopfung* (*The Creation*) by F.K. Watcher (2002) the male character who creates the world engages in some essential bodily functions in order to do so: he wees to create the seas, lakes and rivers; he passes wind to create air, breezes and the wind; and he poos to create the planet's land masses. Finally, he falls in love with one of his own kind, made by him, in his own likeness, and so the world as we know it begins. The children reading this book thought it was hilarious, they laughed at it and although it was evident they felt it was rather risqué and slightly shocking they loved it and returned to it again and again.

Another controversial picturebook which children are delighted by even after 20 years is *The Story of the Little Mole who Knew It Was None of His Business* (Holzwarth & Erlbruch, 1989). The book tells of mole, who, on emerging from his hole, is poo-ed on. His quest to find the culprit leads him to see and identify different animal poos (Figure 1.9) (Plate 7). Eventually, through a process of elimination, he finds the guilty animal. Erlbruch's wonderful, true to life illustrations almost make it a non-fiction science book instead of a narrative picturebook.

These humorous, mildly controversial books aren't necessarily appreciated by adults but children love them, finding them hilarious. McKenzie (2005) noted that adults have problems with the increasing number of picturebooks dealing with scatological humour despite children's evident enjoyment of such books.

In looking at how children's literature frequently offers stereotyped caricatures of wolves, Kerenza Ghosh (Chapter 10, this volume) analysed the way in which two picturebook creators used satire, irony and spoof humour to present 'the big, bad, wicked wolf' in a different light; as a somewhat comical character, not to be taken too seriously as he doesn't always get things right.

Challenging but not controversial

Some books are challenging to understand and yet not controversial. Once again it is the illustrations that form the challenge, as with the picturebooks created by illustrators such as Czech-born Kveta Pacovska and French-born Sara, to name but two of very many such picturebook creators. Pacovska has won many awards,

"Me? No, how could I? I do it like this!" she replied. And plippety plop — a pile of toffee-coloured little balls tumbled on the grass. The little mole found them almost appealing.

FIGURE 1.9   (Plate 7) *The Story of the Little Mole who Knew It Was None of His Business* (illus. by Erlbruch, 1989): 'I do it like this' said the goat.

including the prestigious Hans Christian Andersen Award in 1992. Her semi-abstract style, very much influenced by avant-garde art is first and foremost outrageously, gloriously bright! Her use of vibrant colours, a paper collage technique layering glittery, silver and gold paper with blocks of colour interspersed with line sketches and text, make her picturebooks challenging to 'interpret' in a non-threatening way. Her illustrative style, initially influenced by avant-garde art, is now applied to diverse subject matters, although her love for creating adaptations of traditional stories and fairly tales is clear as her books *Hansel and Gretel* (Grimm, J. & W., & Pacovska, 2008), *Cinderella* (Perrault & Pacovska, 2010) and *The Little Match Girl* (Andersen & Pacovska, 2006) show.

Like Pacovska, Sara's mainly wordless picturebooks have won many awards. *Nu (Nude)* (2009), a White Raven nomination, is an unusual book telling a simple but enigmatic story based on one of the caryatids from a Greek temple swapping places with a human being. Sara uses torn paper blocks of brown, black and white colour to depict the heat of the day, the white of the marble and the shadowiness of the temple (Figure 1.10).

Sara's style of illustration and the manner in which she communicates with the viewer is slightly unsettling at times; it links seamlessly with her subjects of loneliness, loss, sadness and sometimes cruelty – normally depicted through the eyes of an animal.

Wordless books can be strange, ambiguous and unconventional in their subject matter, form and illustrative style. They can also be quite disturbing, *A Day, a Dog* by Gabrielle Vincent (2000) is such a book and tells of an unwanted dog who is

FIGURE 1.10 *Nu* (*Nude*) (Sara, 2009).

thrown out of a moving car. This action triggers off a set of events that results in the death of many in a motorway pile-up. The dog wanders on in search of a home and some love.

The cover blurb states:

> *A Day, a Dog* is a book that defies pigeonholing. It can neither be called a work for children nor one for adults. It is, instead, a powerful documentary in picturebook form for caring human beings of all ages anywhere on Planet Earth. It speaks with understated eloquence to our best instincts, without the benefit of – or need for – words.

Due to their lack of words, visual texts require that the reader make sense of the text through pictures alone. Multiple interpretations are possible and as complex illustrations play with the viewer's mind they are obliged to respond to the challenge in different ways. Using the wordless book *Loup Noir*, by Guilloppé (2004), Sandie Mourao worked with a group of Portuguese children as they tried to determine what was real and what wasn't in relation to the story (Chapter 9, this volume).

Challenging picturebooks as an art form

Many complex, challenging picturebooks are artistic multimodal, fusion texts, all of which exhibit high levels of creativity in their illustrative style and presentation.

The rationale of some publishers, such as the Italian publisher Orrechio, is to publish 'beautiful' picturebooks . . . 'Children's books that do not harm adults/adult books that do not harm children'. Similar to this, the catalogue of the French publishers Sourire qui mord states, 'One is never too young to like texts and images or too old to no longer need them'.

Some books, in addition to their complex, thought-provoking, often troubling subject matter and content, are very often exquisitely beautiful to look at and feel and lead one to consider the picturebook as art and the art of the picturebook. The picturebook is an art form that combines visual and verbal narratives in a book format (Evans, 2009, 2012; Schwarcz, 1982; Sipe 2006; Stanton, 1998; Wolfenbarger & Sipe, 2007). In commenting on the link between picturebooks and art and the implications for using such books with children, Nodelman, states:

> A consciousness of what stories are, of what art is, offers us an even greater freedom – the freedom that comes at the end of innocence, when one knows that what one takes for granted is not all there but is merely a set of expectations that can, indeed, be delightfully or sometimes even horribly thwarted.

He goes on to say:

> Good picture books . . . offer us what all good art offers us: greater con-sciousness – the opportunity, in other words, to be more human. That means to be less innocent, more wise.
>
> *Nodelman (1988: 285)*

Wolf Erlbruch creates such picturebooks, with *Duck, Death and the Tulip* being perhaps his greatest masterpiece. It is aesthetically beautiful to smell, touch, feel, look at and read and is innately challenging in its very substance (Figure 1.11) (Plate 8).

Some picturebooks, not necessarily challenging, or controversial, are about particular artists and their art and are beautiful in their own right: books such as, *Why is Blue Dog Blue?* (George Rodrigue, 2001) and *Pish, Posh, said Hieronymus Bosch* (Nancy Willard, 1991). Others feature works of art as part of the narrative, for example: *Willy's Pictures* (2000) and *The Shape Game* (2003) by Anthony Browne; *Picturescape* by Eliza Gutierrez (2005) and *Katie's Picture Show* by James Mayhew (2004). Each of these has a protagonist who 'discovers' works of art and in so doing becomes involved in their own personal set of adventures.

However, even when wearing the potentially conservative 'robe' of a work of art some of these art books are both extremely controversial AND unconventional. Wolf Erlbruch created *Ratten* (*Rats*) (2009) a book based on Gottfried Benn's expressionist poem *Schöne Jugend* (*The Splendour of Youth* or *A Fine Childhood*). It has been described as 'a masterly composition of drawings and collage' and a 'rather unusual artist's book'. A philosophical and political text such as this is of course a crossover picturebook and a picturebook for adults (Figure 1.12). Erlbruch's expressionist illustrations perfectly partner the words of Benn's poem:

FIGURE 1.11 (Plate 8) *Duck, Death and the Tulip* (Erlbruch, 2008).

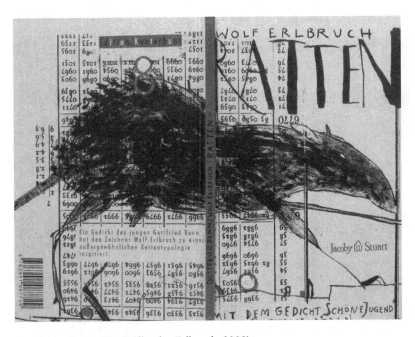

FIGURE 1.12 *Ratten* (*Rats*) (illus. by Erlbruch, 2009).

The mouth of a girl who had long lain in the reeds looked so chewed up.

When we finally broke the torso, the oesophagus was so full of holes.

Finally in a bower under the diaphragm,

We found a nest of young rats.

One little sister rat lay dead.

The others were living off liver and kidney,

Drinking the cold blood and enjoying a fine childhood.

And fine and fast was their death too:

We threw the whole bunch into water.

Oh, how those little snouts squeaked!

The epitome of challenging and controversial picturebooks: the work of Dorte Karrebæk and Oscar K

Dorte Karrebæk and Oscar K are a husband and wife team from Denmark who have a clear vision of the audience for their picturebooks. They see children's picturebooks as art; they themselves are creative artists and thus feel free to explore everything and anything! Because of this the subject matter they consider is portrayed in many unexpected, creative and often quite unsettling ways. Dorte Karrebæk, whose art sometimes reminds one of the strange, very disturbing work of Michael Kvium, is famous for transgressing normal boundaries and conventions in relation to picturebooks. Throughout her career she has continuously challenged established conceptions of picturebooks, and in so doing has expanded readers' ideas of the roles of text and image, between children and adults, and between reality and fantasy.

In talking about their work, which has won many awards, Ulla Rhedin, respected Swedish children's literature critic states, 'In a series of remarkable books, old taboos fall like bowling pins, where one ball after another, comes streaking' (2009). Their books are disturbingly challenging and almost always contentious, dealing as they do with subjects not normally seen as appropriate for picturebooks. For the most part they remain untranslated into English and because of this are not widely discussed and disseminated in English-speaking countries. This is most certainly a great loss for many readers in those countries.

They have co-created many picturebooks and are prolific in their output. Some of their more recent ones, virtually all of which have won awards, have really pushed the limits of what some would see as being acceptable in the picturebook genre. In 2007 Dorte Karrebæk created *Den sorte bog: om de syv dodssynder* (*The Black Book of the Seven Deadly Sins*). It tells of a boy who finds a book in which seven species of grotesque insects are presented, one for each of the seven deadly sins: Pride, Greed, Lust, Envy, Anger, Gluttony and Sloth. The specially bred insects

FIGURE 1.13   (Plate 9) *Bornenes Bedemand* (*The Children's Undertaker*) (K & Karrebæk, 2008).

are often depicted undertaking sexually explicit acts and this really requires one to question the audience for such a visual text. Despite this question the book is a perfect work of art with multiple interpretation possibilities about an eternal subject. It is evil, nasty, and bloody but with Karrebæk's inimitable style of humour weaving through.

Oscar K teamed up with illustrator, Lillian Brøgger to create *De skæve Smil* (*The Crooked Smiles*) (2008) (Figures 4.1 to 4.6, Chapter 4). It tells of a group of aborted foetuses who wonder why they were not given a chance to live and who question the people who conceived them and then killed them before they were born. Ase Marie Ommundson writes about this quite extraordinary picturebook (Chapter 4, this volume).

For Oscar K and Dorte Karrebæk 2008 and 2009 were a busy years, as three of their books were published. *Bornenes Bedemand* (*The Children's Undertaker*) (2008) tells of Mr Jorgenson, a children's undertaker who sings barbershop songs while he is laying out children's bodies in the mortuary (Figure 1.13) (Plate 9). This is a beautiful, emotional book which, although it deals with subject matter that seems utterly inconceivable in a picturebook, is a poignant, sensitively created book, produced with a clear tenderness of heart.

This evidence of sensitivity, warmth and tenderness, when teamed up with passion and signs of true caring and awareness of individual and group suffering in the world, are traits that move through all of K and Karrebæk's books. There is also frequently an underlying religious trait. *Idiot* (2009) shows many of these traits (Figure 1.14) (Plate 10). The book is about August, a mentally retarded boy shown

FIGURE 1.14   (Plate 10) *Idiot* (K & Karrebæk, 2009).

wearing a flying helmet and a jumpsuit, pulling his best friend, a little monster bag on a drawstring. August grows up in his own simple world but his mother is finally so exhausted with worry about what will become of him when she dies that she chooses the seemingly incomprehensible, that is, to kill herself and take her idiot child with her. *Idiot* raises serious questions about bullying, murder, suicide and of course mental disabilities. It is poetic and reminiscent of Danish poetry and one reviewer simply stated, 'when I finished this book, I cried!' Of course we shouldn't be shocked! Why should we be? This happens much more than we think in real life. In England there was the case of a mother who was driven by the action of local bullies to kill herself and her mentally disabled daughter in a burning car. She had contacted the police over 20 times in a 7-year period and nothing had been done; hence, as a frighteningly real last result, she had committed murder and suicide. Real life is frequently mirrored in literature and this is the case with *Idiot*.

A further book published in 2009 was *Hamlet*. In creating this picturebook K and Karrebæk produced a provocatively illustrated new-take on Shakespeare's play. This book holds nothing back; it is as sexually explicit and violent as Shakespeare's play dictates (Figure 1.15) (Plate 11).

In 2011 *Lejren* (*Camp*) was published. In this harrowing picturebook, the words tell one story, the illustrations another. It is a deeply shocking and yet at the same time powerfully moving picturebook portraying children's frightening and sinister experiences of brutal conflict from the recent past and present time (Figure 1.16)

FIGURE 1.15   (Plate 11) *Hamlet* (K & Karrebæk, 2009).

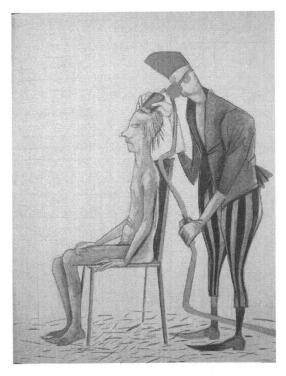

FIGURE 1.16   (Plate 12) *Lejren* (*Camp*) (K & Karrebæk, 2011).

(Plate 12). Not for the faint hearted, *Camp* is the perfect example of a pictorial work for adults and young adults dealing with the holocaust and concentration camps. It won first prize in the National Arts Council's competition for the illustrated book in 2010.

K and Karrebæk's latest book is the very original and strange, *Knokkelmanden's Cirkus (Death's Circus)* (2014) (Figure 1.17) (Plate 13). This zigzag book is a version of an original song by Septimus Winner (1868) entitled *Ten Little Injuns*. Frank Green changed the title to *Ten Little Niggers* in 1869 and it was performed for 'minstrel shows – a form of American entertainment consisting of comic skits, variety acts, dancing, and music' (Jennings, 2012). This adapted book shows and tells how performers in an eerily sinister circus 'disappear' one by one until none are left, just like the original song.

All of these picturebooks by Oscar K and Dorte Karrebæk and of course many others not considered here, are thought-provoking and worthy of detailed consideration. They are aesthetically beautiful, philosophical texts dealing with powerful issues. They frequently provoke extreme responses from adult readers,

FIGURE 1.17   (Plate 13) *Knokkelmanden's Cirkus (Death's Circus)* (K & Karrebæk, 2014).

many of whom steer away from them as they feel uncomfortable discussing such disturbing, potentially upsetting psychological themes. Conversely, however, there are many adults who are powerfully moved by these books as the many awards they have been given holds testament to.

More questions than answers

Many of the questions I started with remain. Questions such as:

- Who they are for?
- How should we respond to them?
- Will they be 'liked' by all readers?
- Does 'challenging' mean the same for all readers?
- What are the origins of these contemporary visual texts?
- Are they equally available and translated in all countries?
- What is the role of the publisher and how much power do publishers have?
- Are these books often censored before they are published?
- Can wordless picturebooks and art books be challenging?
- Is it the words, the pictures or a combination of both that create the disturbing, troubling 'look' that these picturebooks often portray?
- Might texts such as these shape our thoughts and our future?

I have tried to address these questions but many are still left unresolved. Maybe this is how it should be; these kinds of challenging and controversial picturebooks demand that they are simply read, debated and discussed by children and adults alike in order to be understood.

Final thoughts: Which kind of book would you want to read?

These books are by author/illustrators who are 'pushing the boundaries' of what is and what isn't deemed acceptable. They are crossover picturebooks for older children, adolescents and adults as well as for younger children and they offer many opportunities to talk about important philosophical and existential issues in life. All readers respond to these picturebooks in their own ways because nothing is explicit, the issues are often implied, nudging our thoughts and frequently making us feel uncomfortable about what we see and read.

What kind of reader are you and which kind of book would you read? There are choices to be made:

> I was only given children's books that were chosen with care. They acknowledged the same truths and values as those of my parents and teachers; the good were rewarded, the bad were punished; misfortune only befell ridiculous and stupid people.
>
> *Simone de Beauvoir*

One should only read books that prick and bite. If the book that one is reading doesn't wake one up with a blow to the head, then why read it? A book should be the hatchet that breaks the frozen sea within.

Franz Kafka

There is no art for children, there is Art. There are no graphics for children, there are graphics . . . There is no literature for children, there is literature.

Francois Ruy-Vidal

Think carefully!

Academic references

Beckett, S. (ed.) (1999) *Transcending Boundaries: Writing for a Dual Audience of Children and Adults.* London: Taylor and Francis.

Beckett, S. (2008) *Crossover Fiction: Global and Historical Perspectives.* London: Routledge.

Beckett, S. (2012) *Crossover Picturebooks: A Genre for all Ages.* London: Routledge.

Bengtsson, N. (2009) Sex and Violence in Fairy Tales for Children, *Bookbird*, 47(3): 15–21.

Bjorvand, A.M. (2010) Do Sons Inherit The Sins Of Their Fathers? An Analysis of the Picturebook *Angry Man*, in Colomer, T., Kummerling-Meibauer, B. & Silva-Diaz, C. (eds) *New Directions in Picturebook Research.* London: Routledge.

Christensen, N. (2011) Personal email.

Colgan, J. (2013) Children's book illustrations depict a glorious, dangerous world, *The Guardian*, 6 October 2013. www.theguardian.com/profile/jennycolgan

Erlbruch, W. (2006) Nomination for the Hans Christian Andersen Award 2006. Illustrator's Award German Section, International Board on Books for Young People, p. 2.

Evans, J. (ed.) (1998) *What's in the Picture: Responding to Illustrations in Picture Books.* London: Paul Chapman.

Evans, J. (ed.) (2009) *Talking Beyond the Page: Reading and Responding to Picturebooks.* London: Routledge Education.

Evans, J. (2012) The Picturebook as Art: Responding to Picturebooks, Responding to Art in English, Drama, Media, *NATE (National Association for the Teaching of English)*, (22): 23–30.

Evans, J. (2013) Do You Live a Life of Riley? Thinking and Talking about the Purpose of Life in Picturebook Responses, in Arizpe, E., Farrell, M. & McAdam, J. (eds) *Beyond the Borders of Art, Narrative and Culture.* London: Routledge.

Evans, J. (2014) Audience, Theme and Symbolism in Wolf Erlbruch's *Duck, Death and the Tulip*, in Kummerling-Meibauer, B. (ed.) *Picturebooks: Representation and Narration.* London: Routledge.

Falconer, R. (2008) *The Crossover Novel: Contemporary Children's Fiction and its Adult Readership.* London: Routledge.

Givens, C.L. (2009) Hidden Forms of Censorship and Their Impact, *Bookbird*, 47(3): 22–28.

Hade, D., Paul, L. & Mason, J. (2003) Are Children's Book Publishers Changing the Way Children Read? A Panel Discussion, *Children's Literature Association Quarterly*, 28(3): 137–143.

Hallberg, K. (1982) Litteraturvetenskapen och bilderboksforskningen, *Tidsskrift for literaturvetenskap (Journal of Literary Studies)*, 3–4/82: 163–168.

Jennings, J. (2012) *The History of Ten Little Indians.* http://indiancountrytodaymedianetwork.com/2012/10/11/history-ten-little-indians (accessed 7 October 2014).

K, O. (2008) It's Not the Fact That It Is Said, In Fact It's Just the Way You Say It, *Danish Literary Magazine*, (Autumn): 46–48.

Kimmel, E. (1982) Children's Literature without Children, *Children's Literature in Education*, 13(1): 38–43.

Koehnecke, D. (2001) Smoky Night and Crack: Controversial Subjects in Children's Stories, *Children's Literature in Education*, 32(1): 17–30.

Kunnemann, H. (2005) How Much Cruelty Can a Children's Picturebook Stand? The Case of Wolf Erlbruch's Die Menschenfresserin, *Bookbird*, 43(1): 14–19.

Lehr, S. (ed.) (1995) *Battling Dragons: Issues and Controversy in Children's Literature*. Portsmouth, NH: Heinemann.

McKenzie, J. (2005) Bums, Poos and Wees: Carnavalesque Spaces in the Picturebooks of Early Childhood. Or, Has Literature Gone to the Dogs? *English Teaching: Practice and Critique*, 4(1): 81–94.

Nikolajeva, M. (2009) Personal email.

Nodelman, P. (1988) *Words about Pictures: The Narrative Art of Children's Picture Books*. London: The University of Georgia.

Nodelman, P. & Reimer, M. (2003) *Pleasures of Children's Literature*, 3rd edn. Boston, MA: Allyn and Bacon.

Noll, E. (1994) The Ripple Effect of Censorship: Silencing in the Classroom, *The English Journal*, 83(8): 59–64.

Ommundson, A.M. (2014) Picturebooks for Adults, in Kummerling-Meibauer, B. (ed.) *Picturebooks: Representation and Narration*. London: Routledge.

Paul, L. (2003) Consuming Passions: Or Why I'm Obsessed with L'Ogress en Pleurs, *Signal*, 34(September): 173–190.

Rhedin, U. (2009) Interview in *Svenska Dagbladet*, 13 May 2009.

Salisbury, M. & Styles, M. (2012) *Children's Picturebooks: The Art of Visual Storytelling*. London: Lawrence King.

Schwarcz, J. (1982) *Ways of the Illustrator: Visual Communication in Children's Literature*. Chicago: American Library Association.

Scott, C. (1999) Dual Audience in Picturebooks, in Beckett, S. (ed.) *Transcending Boundaries: Writing for a Dual Audience of Children and Adults*. London: Taylor and Francis.

Scott, C. (2005) A Challenge to Innocence: 'Inappropriate' Picturebooks for Young Readers, *Bookbird*, 43(1): 5–13.

Sendak, M. (1988) *Caldecott and Co*. New York: Farrar, Strauss and Giroux.

Shannon, P. (1992) Overt and Covert Censorship of Children's Books, in Shannon, P. (ed.) *Becoming Political: Readings and Writings in the Politics of Literacy Education*. Portsmouth, NH: Heinemann.

Sipe, L. (2006) Learning from Illustrations in Picturebooks, in Fisher, D. & Frey, N. (eds) *Picture This! The Role Visual Information Plays in Literacy Learning*. Thousand Oaks, CA: Corwin Press.

Stanton, J. (1998) The Important Books: Appreciating the Children's Picturebook as a Form of Art, *American Art*, 12(2): 2–5.

Tatar, M. (1987) *The Hard Facts of the Grimms' Fairy Tales*. Princeton, NJ: Princeton University Press.

Tomlinson, C. (1995) Justifying Violence in Children's Literature, in Lehr, S. (ed.) *Battling Dragons: Issues and Controversy in Children's Literature*. Portsmouth, NH: Heinemann.

Wolfenbarger, C.D. & Sipe, L. (2007) A Unique Visual and Literary Art Form: Recent Research on Picturebooks, *Language Arts*, 84(3): 273–280.

Children's literature

Andersen, H.C., illus. Pacovska, K. trans. Bell A. (2006) *The Little Match Girl*. New York: Minedition.

Arnal, T. & Amckan, H. (2010) *Caja de Carton*. Pontevedra: OQO Books.

Benn, G. & Erlbruch, W. (2009) *Ratten*. Berlin: Jacoby &Stuart.

Browne, A. (2000) *Willy's Pictures*. London: Walker Books.

Browne, A. (2003) *The Shape Game*. London: Doubleday.

Crowther, K. (2004) *La Visite de Petite Mort*. Paris: L'ecole de Loisirs.

Crowther, K. (2007) *Dans Moi*. Paris: L'ecole de Loisirs.

Crowther, K. (2010) *Le Petit homme et Dieu*. Paris: L'ecole de Loisirs.

Dahle, G. & Nyhus, K.D. (2013) *Krigen*. Oslo: Cappelen Damm.

Dahle, G. & Nyhus, S. (2003) *Sinna Mann*. Oslo: Cappelen.

Dayre, V. & Erlbruch, W. (1996) *Die Menschenfresserin*. Wuppertal: Peter Hammer Verlag.

Dedieu, T., after Perrault, C. (2005) *La Barbe Bleue*. Paris: Editions du Seuil.

Dedieu, T. (2014) *14–18: Une minute de silence à nos arrière-grands-pères courageux*. Paris: Editions du Seuil.

Dickens, C. & Negrin, F. (2006) *Capitan Omicidio*. Rome: Orecchio Acerbo.

Erlbruch, W. (2008) *Duck, Death and the Tulip*. Auckland: Gecko Press.

Fortes, A. & Concejo, J. (2008) *Smoke*. Pontevedra: OQO Books.

Gleeson, L. & Greder, A. (2011) *I am Thomas*. Crows Nest, NSW: Allen & Unwin.

Greder, A. (2007) *The Island*. Crows Nest, NSW: Allen & Unwin.

Grimm, J. & W. & Browne, A. (1995) *Hansel and Gretel*. London: Walker Books.

Grimm J. & W. & Janssen, S. (2007) *Hansel und Gretel*. Rostock: Hinstorff Verlag.

Grimm, J. & W., illus. Pacovska, K. (2008) *Hansel and Gretel*. New York: Minedition.

Guilloppé, A. (2004) *Loup Noir*. Paris: Casterman.

Gutierrez, E. (2005) *Picturescape*. Vancouver: Simply Read Books.

Harris, R.H. & Emberley, M. (1996) *Happy Birth Day!* London: Walker Books.

Holzwarth, W., illus. Erlbruch, W. (1989) *The Story of the Little Mole who Knew It Was None of His Business*. Wuppertal: Peter Hammer Verlag.

Hughes, D. (1993) *Bully*. London: Walker Books.

Josephus Jitta, C. (2007) *Lola and the Rent a Cat*. Mechelen: Bacckens Books.

Juan, A. (2001) *Snowhite*. Onil: Edicions de Ponent.

K, O. & Brøgger, L. (2008) *De skæve Smil*. Risskov: Clematis.

K, O. & Karrebæk, D. (2008) *Bornenes Bedemand*. Copenhagen: Gyldendal.

K, O. & Karrebæk, D. (2009) *Hamlet*. Copenhagen: Dansk Laerer Publishers.

K, O. & Karrebæk, D. (2009) *Idiot*. Copenhagen: Rosinante & Co.

K, O. & Karrebæk, D. (2011) *Lejren*. Copenhagen: Rosinante & Co.

K, O. & Karrebæk, D. (2014) *Knokkelmandens Cirkus*. Copenhagen: Rosinante & Co.

Karrebæk, D. (2007) *Den sorte bog: om de syv dodssynder*. Hillerød: Alma.

Mayhew, J. (2004) *Katie's Picture Show*. London: Orchard Books.

Moundlic, C. & Tallec, O. (2009) *The Scar*. Somerville, MA: Candlewick Press.

Overend, J. & Vivas, J. (1999) *Hello Baby*. London: Francis Lincoln.

Perrault, C. & Pacovska K. (2010) *Cinderella*. Hong Kong: Neugebauer Publishing.

Rego, P. (2010) *Nursery Rhymes*. London: Thames & Hudson.

Rodrigue, G. (2001) *Why is Blue Dog Blue?* New York: Abrams.

Sara (2009) *Nu*. Paris: Seuil Jeunesse.

Tan, S. (2001) *The Red Tree*. Melbourne: Lothian Books.

Taylor, C. & Thompson Dicks, J. (1992) *The House that Crack Built*. San Francisco: Chronicle Books.

Vincent, G. (2000) *A Day, a Dog*. Asheville, NC: Front Street Publishers.

Watcher, F.K. (2002) *Die Schopfung*. Zurich: Diogenes Publishers.

Wild, M. & Brooks, R. (2000) *Fox*. Crows Nest, NSW: Allen & Unwin.

Wild, M. & Spudvilas, A. (1999) *Jenny Angel*. Ringwood, Victoria: Viking Press.

Wild, M. & Vivas, J. (1991) *Let the Celebrations Begin*. New York: Orchard Books.

Willard, N., illus. The Dillons (1991) *Pish, Posh, said Hieronymus Bosch*. New York: Harcourt Brace.

Willis, J. & Ross, T. (2002) *Don't Let Go!* London: Andersen Press.

2

THE SCANDAL OF THE COMMONPLACE

The strangeness of best-selling picturebooks

Perry Nodelman

Asked to discuss controversial picturebooks, I felt stymied by my lack of a sense of what qualities a book has to possess in order to be assigned to that category. Isn't what a reader finds controversial a matter of individual taste, so that any and all books might strike somebody as distressing or disturbing? On the other hand, though, I had a strong sense of which books have aroused the least controversy: the ones that appear most often on best-seller lists and that large numbers of people like and recommend to each other. Assuming that controversy arises when a book diverges from the characteristics of such books, I decided to identify a list of current picturebook best-sellers and take a closer look at what happens in them, what they might seem to have in common, and how controversy might emerge from divergences from their shared features. Rather than defining a norm, however, my exploration reveals the surprising oddity of the books we most take for granted—why they might become controversial if they were not so widely assumed to be harmless.

What is controversial about children's picturebooks? Just about everything. Children's literature as a whole is a category built on restrictions; special books for children would not exist if adults did not believe that children want or need to know less about their world than there actually is, and so children's literature as a whole is, almost by definition, a literature defined by what it leaves out. Inevitably, however, different adults have different ideas about what needs to be left out, and as a result, just about any book is likely to seem challenging or unsettling and be deemed unsuitable for young readers by somebody somewhere. What is controversial is in the eye of the beholder, and different eyes manage to be upset by different aspects of different books.

Nevertheless, I suspect that most adults would agree that, even though the books being discussed in this volume are quite different from each other, they are indeed ones that are likely to be widely contested—ones that deserve the label "controversial." Indeed, it is their difference from each other—and from the many other children's picturebooks that seem less likely to be so generally perceived as unsettling—that identifies the books under discussion here as deserving of that label. The books being written about here are not merely controversial to some people who love wolves because they have bad wolves in them, or controversial to some people who enjoy childhood exuberance because they take it for granted that children should be seen and not heard, or controversial to some people who believe children are in a certain developmental stage because they use difficult language. They are distinct enough to convey a more general aura of what I want to call "controversiality" to a much larger group of adult readers.

But then the distinctive difference that underpins that controversiality, gives rise to another important question: just what it is that they are different from? They are most different, clearly, from picturebooks that are not so obviously controversial—the ones that strike most people as quite conventional and acceptable even though the occasional adult might be distressed by some aspects of them. While there are those who might have reasons for finding Dr. Seuss's *Green Eggs and Ham*, or Julia Donaldson and Axel Scheffler's *The Gruffalo*, or Dorothy Kunhardt's *Pat the Bunny*, unsuitable for sharing with children, the wide popularity and massive sales of books like these make it clear that most people interested in children's books take them to be harmless. The continuing popularity of these books suggests that they represent widely held expectations about what is appropriate for children—the expectations that more obviously controversial books defy.

It occurred to me, then, that I might develop some further understanding of controversial books as a group by taking a closer look at the kinds of conventional books that more obviously controversial books excite controversy by varying from. What specific mainstream conventions do the controversial books under discussion in this volume not represent or confirm?

A group of uncontroversial books

In order to try to figure that out, I developed a list of clearly conventional and therefore, presumably, generally acceptable and therefore generally non-controversial picturebooks to take a closer look at—ideally, ones that represent current main-stream views of what is acceptable in children's picturebooks. I did so through the highly unscientific process of Googling lists of best-selling picturebooks on one specific day. The day I chose was 13 October 2013. I decided to focus my attention on English-language books produced in countries with sizeable populations and mainstream children's publishing industries—the United Kingdom and the USA. I looked at a variety of best-seller lists: the daily lists of best-selling children's books at Amazon.com and the Barnes and Noble website in the United States, as well as Amazon's more specific list of best-selling picturebooks for specific ages from 0 to 12 and Barnes and Noble's list of best-sellers for various ages 0 to 12; the best-sellers at the Amazon.co.uk and Waterstones websites in the United Kingdom; the lists of Children's Picturebooks Best Sellers provided by the *New York Times* and by *Publishers Weekly*; and *The Bookseller*'s best-sellers for pre-school for Saturday,

2 October—the closest I could find to a picturebook list. Together, these sources listed a large number of different books; but many titles appeared on more than one list—many of them, in fact transcending national tastes by being identified as best-sellers in both the United States and the United Kingdom.

In the end, I felt fairly comfortable in choosing twelve books that were unquestionably popular, unquestionably sold in large numbers, and likely therefore to be representative of what most adult book buyers feel most comfortable with when they choose picturebooks for children. These are the books:

Mark Baker and Neville Astley's *The Story of Peppa Pig*

Drew Daywalt's *The Day the Crayons Quit*

Kimberly and James Dean's *Pete the Cat and the Magic Sunglasses*

Anna Dewdney's *Llama Llama and the Bully Goat*

Sherri Duskey Rinker's *Goodnight, Goodnight, Construction Site*

Julia Donaldson and Axel Scheffler's *Room on the Broom*

Julia Donaldson and Axel Scheffler's *Tabby McTat*

Julia Donaldson and Axel Scheffler's *The Snail and the Whale*

Julia Donaldson and Axel Scheffler's *Superworm*

Timothy Knapman and Sarah Warburton's *Dinosaurs in the Supermarket*

Axel Scheffler's *Pip and Posy: The Super Scooter*

Mo Willems's *I'm a Frog*.

Presences and absences

After developing this list, my first response was to notice the overwhelming presence of Julia Donaldson and illustrator Axel Scheffler, who together account for almost half the books. Not only that, but also one of Donaldson and Scheffler's books, *Room on the Broom*, occupied both the first and second position on the *Publishers Weekly* list, in different editions. Donaldson and Scheffler clearly have their fingers on the pulse of children's book buyers, and a closer look at why that might be is in order.

But before I take that look, I need to say a little more about the list. I have to admit that in arriving at it, I did cheat a little. There were some titles prominently listed that I decided to ignore:

- First, I chose not to include the picturebook that topped the Amazon lists: a Kindle edition of Aaron Shepherd's *The Legend of Lightning Larry*. I did so because it seemed likely that the price for the Kindle edition that day—$0.01—was the incentive for the sales; that suspicion was confirmed when I

returned to the lists some months later and saw that *Lightning Larry* was missing, while the twelve titles I had chosen were still prominently featured. While
I found *Lightning Larry,* a story of a gunman who shoots love into the hearts
of his enemies, mildly amusing, I suspect I did so because of my knowledge of
the conventions of the old western movies and TV shows that it takes for
granted and builds on—a body of knowledge today's young picturebook readers are unlikely to possess. In other words: it was just odd enough in its implied
repertoire of readerly knowledge to seem unlike the twelve books I settled on,
which rarely reference matters so currently esoteric.

- Second, because I did my survey in October, the lists included many books
specifically related to Halloween. These seemed unlikely to remain best-sellers
after the holiday passed, so I left them out; I note, however, that this timing
might also be a factor in the sales of Donaldson and Scheffler's *Room on the
Broom,* whose protagonist is a witch.
- Third, there were also a few oddities that did not seem to relate to what I
wanted to learn, so I omitted them: the *One Direction Ultimate Gift Set,* consisting of a teddy bear and a paperback called *One Direction: The Ultimate Fan
Book,* and *Despicable Me 2: Make a Minion Sticker Book.* Indeed, I ignored a
number of sticker books that seemed more like toys than reading experiences.
- Finally, a number of the books on the lists were familiar titles that have been
around for some time: Eric Carle's *Very Hungry Caterpillar,* Margaret Wise
Brown's *Goodnight Moon,* Dorothy Kunhardt's *Pat the Bunny,* Bill Martin Jr.'s
Brown Bear, Brown Bear, What Do You See? I chose not to include them because
I thought it might be more revealing to concentrate on newer books with
shorter histories—books that might best represent the contemporary situation
and that were not old enough to be purchased mainly because an adult had
fond memories of them from childhood.

Popular *and* controversial?

Nevertheless, the presence of these books on the lists made me aware of another
issue: among the older books were Robert Munsch's *Love You Forever* and
Margaret Wise Brown's *Runaway Bunny,* perennial best-sellers that have also been
perennially controversial. The presence of these books on the lists seemed to be
a serious challenge to my assumptions here. If popular books can also be controversial, then the two are not in fact separate and opposite categories. I had to
acknowledge a suspicion that I would not have to dig very deep to find people
upset by *Goodnight Moon* (ageist? promotes animistic thought?) or *The Hungry
Caterpillar* (misleading nutritional information? promotes the mutilation of
books?). Controversy is in the eye of the beholder. I could not actually use these
popular books to determine what controversial books varied from because all
books are at least potentially controversial.

And yet: if reader's comments on online bookstores are anything to go by, the
twelve books I ended up with do not in fact seem to excite all that much

controversy. Indeed, in light of the well-known fractiousness of anonymous online commentators, they are surprisingly *un*controversial. Most of the readers who commented on the twelve books on Amazon and Barnes and Noble websites are very praising of them and have awarded them five stars. Indeed, a number of the books have been awarded almost nothing but four or five stars. For instance, 231 Amazon.com readers gave Donaldson's *Room on the Broom* five stars, ten others four stars, and three others three stars; of the three who gave it one star, one did not like the price and two did so as an objection to some passages in the edition they received being different from what they were used to, for, as well as changes from British idiom to American equivalents (hair plaits become braids, and chips become fries), some editions eliminate the dragon's wish to eat the witch with fries and replaces it with a bland suggestion that she "looks like a good supper." Meanwhile, on Amazon.co.uk, 427 readers gave the book five stars, twenty gave four stars, nine gave two or three stars, and just one gave one star. The two stars were from readers who disliked the American words in a specific edition they received, and the one star from a reader who expected a CD and received a book. In other words, none of these readers had any objections to the events or characters or thematic implications of this book.

By and large, those who ranked the other eleven books have the same sort of response: nothing but enthusiasm. The one minor exception relates to *The Day the Crayons Quit*; while the response to this book is generally praising, with 447 Amazon.com five-star reviews and 47 four-star ones, there are as many as thirty, one-star ones, most of them accusing the book of being either whiny or boring. The only Amazon.co.uk one-star review also calls the book boring, while thirty reviewers give it five stars and five four stars. But for most people, at any rate, there seems to be something about all twelve of my selections that separates them from the kinds of books that are more usually identified as challenging or controversial.

Shared characteristics of popular picturebook stories

So then why do these popular picturebooks not excite controversy? One possible explanation is the extent to which they conform to widespread mainstream ideas about what a children's picturebook usually is or ought to be.

- As in so many other books, all the characters in these books are humanized animals or objects. Many of them wear human clothing, live in recognizably human houses, and play in human playgrounds or attend schools. Some of the ones who do not occupy human homes nevertheless interact with and have English-language conversations with humans.
- Many of these characters seem to stand in for children, and occupy settings or have experiences of the sort readers tend to associate with childhood.
- The pictures in all of them represent the characters as simplified cartoons, often with clearly marked outlines, in bright cheerful colours, against fairly empty backgrounds, and with a scarcity of shadows.

- The texts tend to be short and often feature patterned language, with many repetitions or rhymes.
- The stories often imply the kinds of lessons that adults like to share with children: the wisdom of adults (*Peppa* and *Llama Llama*); avoiding sadness and looking for the good in every day (*Pete the Cat*); the ability of small creatures to band together to defeat a more powerful enemy (*Superworm*, *Room on the Broom*, and perhaps *The Snail on the Whale*) or the wisdom of getting an adult to deal with one (*Llama Llama*); celebrating the pleasures of pretending and creativity (*I'm a Frog*, *Crayons*, and, perhaps *Dinosaurs*); the ability of unlike creatures to become friends and the virtues of friendship (*Snail and the Whale* and *Tabby McTat*); the virtue of kindness and the wrongness of being aggressive and self-seeking (*Pip and Posy* and *Llama Llama*); accepting the inevitability of bedtime and gracefully giving in to it (*Goodnight, Goodnight*).

As these aspects suggest, these books are not unlike thousands upon thousands of undistinguished picturebooks and other stories produced for children across the decades; I suspect that most adults who work with picturebooks could offer many examples of other books with similar traits.

Popularity as a shield against controversy

But there is one way in which these twelve do stand out. They are, indeed, widely popular. They are best-sellers. Is it possible that as well as being best-sellers because they are acceptable, they are acceptable because they are best-sellers?

Or in other words: might the very fact of their popularity be what encourages new purchasers to believe these books are good choices for children? The very concept of best-seller lists engages (or encourages) a widespread assumption that certain books must be worth reading simply because so many people like them. Nor is it incidental that five of my twelve books are by a pair of creators with a history of being best-sellers, and that five more of them are representatives of series that have existed for some time: *Pete the Cat*, *Peppa Pig*, *Llama Llama*, and the elephant and pig from *I'm a Frog* have appeared in a number of other books, while fairly new characters, Pip and Posy reveal the value of multiple appearances as an incentive to new buyers by starring in seven other recently published books. Logic might suggest that if so many adults feel these books are safe and so many children have experienced them and apparently, liked them and not been harmed by them—and if so few Amazon readers have negative things to say about them—then they must be safely non-toxic. Their very popularity might then be an invitation not to pay close attention to them—not to be too worried about their potential deleterious effects on child readers, as, in my experience, most adults often do when confronted with a new children's picturebook.

If popularity does work that way, then perhaps closer attention might reveal aspects of these books that are just as unsettling and as potentially controversial as books more likely to arouse that sort of scrutiny. Consider, for instance, the books by Donaldson and Scheffler. My copies of two of these came with a gold sticker announcing that they are "by the creators of *The Gruffalo*," and the back cover of the third says that the authors are "the award-winning creators of *The Gruffalo*." Furthermore, a sticker on the cover of *Pip and Posy* identifies it as being "by the illustrator of *The Gruffalo*." The publishers clearly believe that these connections to that earlier book are an incentive to encourage purchases. It is, presumably, a familiar book, and again, therefore, a safe one. Indeed, Wikipedia informs me that *The Gruffalo* is familiar enough to have sold over three and a half million copies in various editions worldwide in the 15 short years since it appeared in 1999. While 251 of 271 Amazon.com readers and 502 of 561 Amazon.co.uk readers have awarded it five stars, fewer than thirty readers on both sites gave it anything below four stars. Indeed, one of the few negative reviewers identifies *The Gruffalo* as exactly the kind of best-seller I am discussing here: "*The Gruffalo* is a perfect example of the tipping point of hype—a spirited but basically average book whose fame happened to reach critical mass and has bathed us in a self-perpetuating supernova of books fuelling plush toys fuelling bookends fuelling jigsaws fuelling more books, for the decade and more since" (Holmeister "Hol").

A few of the other negative reviews focus on a particularly telling aspect of *The Gruffalo* and its similarities to Maurice Sendak's 1963 classic *Where the Wild Things Are*. As one reviewer says, "I can't help the feeling of 'Miss she's copying my work' I get when I read this" (humptydumpty). *The Gruffalo* does indeed share key elements with *Wild Things*, including a title character who looks very much like one of the Wild Things, a repeated use of the same adjective to describe the beast's "terrible tusks" and "terrible claws" and "terrible teeth in his terrible jaws," and some uncertainty about whether or not the monster depicted is a figment of the child protagonist's imagination; for it is certainly possible to suppose that the actual beast who emerges after a mouse invents him continues to be a projection of his own uncertainty.

I find the similarity of the two books interesting in the light of my concerns here because of the history of the reception of *Where the Wild Things Are*. Upon first publication, it was both highly praised and a cause of wide controversy, much of it centring on the extent to which the depictions of the Wild Things might frighten children. In my early years as an instructor in university-level children's literature courses, many of my students had that response to it. But as the decades passed, the intensity of that negative response diluted. The book became less controversial—in part, I suspect, because ongoing fame and sales made it seem less likely to be dangerous, in part because its success led to the publication of many other books about monsters by other authors, the existence of which made its basic premise seem much less unusual and therefore much less obviously distressing. Of the relatively few negative reviews of *Wild Things* by Amazon readers, very few worry about the book scaring children, and focus their concern instead on the obnoxiousness of the book's hero and the inappropriateness of its values. By the time *The Gruffalo* appeared, what was surprising about it was certainly not the mere presence of a monster; and what offended its few unhappy readers was not its oddity and potential to scare but rather its similarity to what was so familiar.

At any rate, the success of *The Gruffalo* might well inhibit negative responses to the other books by Donaldson and Scheffler—for how likely is it that the authors of such a successful and therefore, surely, harmless book would go on to produce harmful ones? It is no coincidence that the much-lauded *Room on the Broom* not only features a protagonist who is a stereotypically scary witch with a wart on her nose, but also, a scary fire-breathing dragon. Then for all his powers, Superworm remains a conventionally repulsive worm, and both he and the witch on the broom are frighteningly threatened with being eaten. Tabby McTat frighteningly loses his best friend long enough to marry and have a family, the whale in *Whale and the Snail* frighteningly nearly dies, and Scheffler's Posy frighteningly falls off the scooter and bloodies her knee. Yet adult readers do not seem concerned about the possibility of these elements distressing child readers. Donaldson and Scheffler are popular enough to be safe.

What lies beneath

If the safety of Donaldson and Scheffler deflects attention from elements like the ones I have just mentioned, elements that would be quite likely to elect negative responses from at least some adults if present in less widely known books, then what else might the best-selling status of these best-selling picturebooks be hiding? What other secrets does the popularity of my twelve best-sellers deflect attention from? They clearly need a closer and more consciously critical reading.

That responses to these texts depend on what they seem to be inviting readers to take for granted might be made clear by my own first response to *The Story of Peppa Pig*. For a best-selling book, it struck me as being a surprisingly absurdist text. The plot seemed to move randomly amongst a number of unconnected elements—a new house, a gardening lesson, a lost toy, a wish to jump in muddy puddles—without ever settling on or developing any of them. The apparently absurdist disconnection of these elements was confirmed for me by the decidedly cubistic depictions of the characters, each of whom always appears with two eyes facing forward and a snout protruding from one side of his or her head. But then I discovered what, innocent that I am, I had not been aware of: the book I was reading related to a pre-existing series of widely popular TV cartoons. Not only would the cubistic characters be merely expectable to the many young readers already familiar with the cartoons (the series has TV audiences in many countries, and some Peppa Peg episodes on YouTube have well over three million viewers) but what seemed so bizarrely complex and disjointed to me is in fact just a series of references to the individual plots of many separate episodes of the TV series, reminders for viewers of stories they already know and would not therefore think odd at all.

More often, however, what hides the strangeness of these texts is not a lack of knowledge of a text's specific history. It is a familiarity with the conventions of children's literature more generally. As I tried to see these books with fresh eyes, I realized that everything and anything that most adults see as conventional and expectable in these and other children's books might well be unsettling if it were not so familiar.

Characters: animals as humans

Consider, to begin with, the kinds of characters the twelve books share: animals or objects who behave like human beings. Stories for children that feature animals in human situations go back as far as Aesop. They are so central to unconsidered mainstream assumptions about children's literature that, asked to make up their own story for children, most of the university students I taught over many decades made up ones about talking animals. But if we forget that history for a moment, we might become aware of just how very odd such stories are. We tend to believe that young children are egocentric readers, interpreting stories as being significantly about themselves. Why, then, not depict them *as* themselves, rather than tell stories about animals who act like them? Do we imagine that children already think of themselves as something like humanized animals, not quite yet the fully human beings that adults are—more like puppies or kittens than adults are? If so, should not that idea be at least a little controversial? Or alternately, do we wish to delude young readers by giving them messages about their own behaviour disguised as stories about creatures apparently unlike themselves? Might we be offering them a story about a llama who has to deal with a goat who bullies as a way of hiding the fact that we want to tell them how to deal with a human bully in their own lives? If so, ought not that attempt to deceive and mislead be at least a little controversial?

Human clothing and human tools

The general strangeness of the part-human part-animal beings in so many picturebooks is compounded by specific absurdities that result from the depiction of such characters. As I read *Llama Llama* and *Peppa Pig*, I found myself wondering about how creatures with hooves such as llamas and pigs managed to get their human clothing on and off: how would they or their equally ungulate parents handle buttons? Or how does Pete the Cat manage to get onto and push his skateboard? And what holds up the earpieces of the sunglasses he wears, perched below his ears? And why, if he is wearing shoes in the earlier book, *I Love My White Shoes* (Litwin & James, 1999), is he not wearing anything else? Alternately, in *Pip and Posy*, if the characters wear ordinarily human children clothes, why do they not wear shoes? And why, if both Elephant and Piggie are unclothed in *I'm a Frog*, does Elephant nevertheless wear human spectacles (again, perched below his ears)? While my own experience of humanized animal characters led me to miss these strange and unsettling details until I considered the pictures more closely, I have to wonder if they might not confuse (or intrigue) young members of the inexperienced intended audience.

Human speech, human lifestyles

In books where the animals do not wear clothes or manipulate human objects, there are other oddities. In *Dinosaurs in the Supermarket*, *Superworm*, and *Room on the Broom*, the animals communicate with each other in what is presented as English, and in *The Snail and the Whale*, the snail communicates with humans in written English words. Where did it learn to write? The letter-writing crayons in *The Day the Crayons Quit* raise a similar question and there are also questions about the crayons' lifestyle, as there are about the construction machines in *Goodnight, Goodnight*. If these creatures are human enough to have human emotions, then what are we to make of their almost complete absence of a life outside their jobs? The crayons and trucks appear to have no families, no homes outside their workplace, no hobbies, no possessions. They appear to be living out their lives as something like slaves. Is it not just a tad imperialistic and tyrannical—and controversial—that these books ask us to take their characters' lonely servitude more or less for granted?

Human registers of difference: class, gender, race

But then, of course, I am forgetting the extent to which these characters represent aspects of human existence—that they are not merely animals and objects afflicted with human consciousness, but also, allegorical representations of actual human beings. Even then, however, they tend to depict human existence in potentially controversial ways.

In the books which depict animals in human clothing, the animals tend to live exclusively normative middle-class suburban lives. They live in pleasant semi-rural communities with lots of green space. They wear contemporary children's clothing—although, since half the characters in *Pip and Posy* wear trousers and half skirts, it seems safe to assume that the pants-wearers are all male. It becomes clear, in fact, that the lives of these characters are so normative as to represent the norm as an ideal. While there is a playground in *Pip and Posy*, it sits on a huge expanse of green lawn interspersed here and there with abundantly blooming garden plots, and the paths through the lawn lead right up to the doors of the houses. There appear to be no cars or roads, so that the entire neighbourhood sits inside a sort of park. In a similarly park-like world in *Peppa Pig*, the houses are completely surrounded by lawns and each sits atop its own small yet elevating hill, and the family car drives over the lush green lawns on an invisible road with no other traffic in view. In both these books, furthermore, the houses are few and far between, the world primarily a bucolic park.

In environments like these, the apparent gender division comes to seem ideally normative also. The apparently always-skirted girls of *Pip and Posy* are readily identifiable as female, as, it seems, they should be. In *Peppa Pig*, similarly, Peppa and her mother's outfits have the outlines of skirts, while those of her father and brother do not. Furthermore, the one other human child beside the male human protagonist wearing a sweater and jeans in *Dinosaurs* has bare legs, suggesting there is a dress under her raincoat.

Tabby McTat, the other book that prominently features humans is a somewhat different matter. It takes place in a distinctly urban version of London, and the settings include not just an elegant square with a gated park and the Thames Bankside with the dome of St. Paul's in the distance, but also, a bridge under which live what appears to be a group of homeless people. They are, however, almost the only ones of the many people the book depicts who are not smiling; for despite homelessness, this London is a decidedly happy place.

Throughout the book, furthermore, the smiling crowds who listen to buskers and shop in outdoor markets contain people with significantly darker complexions than most of the others. Some wear burqas and other traditional Arabic garb, and the family that adopts Tabby McTat are two women who might well be a lesbian couple. Nevertheless, the couple live in a comfortable middle-class house, and they and most of the human beings depicted throughout the book have white faces—as do most of the conventionally dressed supermarket customers in *Dinosaurs*, including the protagonist, and most of the humans in *Snail and the Whale*. The impression created is that people of colour form part of the background of the lives of mainstream white people—like, presumably, most young readers? The focus on mainstream white middle-class lives as the ones that implied readers are being invited to recognize and, presumably, identify with, becomes controversial only in relation to the many young readers too poor or of other racial or ethnic backgrounds to actually see something like their own lives in the books. For them, the books are a representation of what their authors take for granted as not only normal but also desirable—the presumed utopia of a white middle-class lifestyle that implied readers are invited to identify with and that real readers can then see their own lives as acceptably like or perhaps unfortunately unlike.

The presence of characters of various races in *Tabby McTat* raises the issue of the ways in which the animal characters in books like *Pip and Posy*, *Llama Llama*, *I'm a Frog*, and *Pete the Cat* might be read as representing various races and ethnicities. In a real world fraught with questions of racial and ethnic tolerance and identity, the mixed groups of animals of other species that make up the cast in these books and many others are easily and often understood as representations of an ideally multicultural world. In the playground of *Pip and Posy*, a frog, a cat, a mouse, and a rabbit all play happily together. In the playground of *Llama Llama*, a llama, a kitten, a sheep, a rhinoceros, and a giraffe all play together, all happily except for the bully goat, who must then be made to reform and join the happy community. An elephant and a pig are friends in *I'm a Frog*, and Pete the Cat's friends include a frog, a squirrel, a turtle, and an owl. And while only members of Peppa's family appear in *The Story of Peppa Pig*, other books about Peppa reveals her friendships with rabbits and other animals.

If the intention of these books is to illustrate racial harmony, most of them do so in a peculiar way: by representing only one (or two, if they are siblings) of each of the species depicted. The exception is *Pig and Posy*, which includes a number of rabbits and a couple of cats amongst its children. But the other books all ignore the real reasons why multicultural societies are difficult for most of their members: the fact that some are members of minority groups, outnumbered by a more powerful larger group, while a lot of others are not.

In books like *Peppa Pig*, and *Llama Llama*, which depict the young animals' parents, the parents are of the same species. There is, in other words, none of what used to be called miscegenation: the marriage and interbreeding of people of what are identified as different races. If Peppa's parents are both pigs and Llama's mother and, as revealed in other books in the series, father, are also llamas, then another oddity becomes apparent: the mere fact that each of the animals is identifiably of one specific species. There are no creatures in these books who are half-llama, half-goat (although I note that the main character of Donaldson and Scheffler's *Gruffalo* books is indeed such a creature—and identified therefore as being monstrous). If these books do mean to represent a multicultural society, they do so in terms of very restrictive ideas about how the cultures might relate to each other—ideas that surely ought to be controversial?

While not depicting parents, the books which describe animals without human clothing tend to follow the same one-of-each-kind pattern. Pete the Cat meets one toad, one squirrel, one turtle, and one owl. The companions the witch finds room for on her broom are one cat, one dog, one generic bird, and one frog; meanwhile, one squirrel, one owl, and one ant appear in the background. Here Donaldson and Scheffler are following a pattern established in *The Gruffalo*, which features one mouse, one fox called Fox, one owl called Owl, and one snake called Snake, the names confirming their uniqueness: a snake is not likely to be called Snake unless he is, somehow, the only snake there is. While other snails do appear in the background, *The Snail and the Whale* features one snail and one whale. *Superworm* is something of an exception, since the plot centrally involves little beings joining together to defeat a big enemy, there are a number of toads and bees and snails and centipedes; but the central characters are one worm, one crow, and one lizard. Nevertheless, there is also a sense here that smaller creatures are generally not as likely to be unique as larger ones are; and just as there are many insects here, there are also a lot of small snails in *The Snail and the Whale*. If we read these creatures as being depictions of racially marked human beings, might there be a hint of a suggestion that less visible groups of humans are less fully human than representatives of larger groups? Perhaps.

Individuality

It is possible of course, that the predominant pattern of one-animal-of-each-kind in these books might not relate to race or ethnicity at all, but be instead a matter of depicting the individuality of individual beings. It is true that the animals of *Llama Llama* share their species with the parents who come to pick them up from school, and that Peppa's parents are also pigs, but that might be mainly a matter of family resemblance, not racial purity. But while the books might be read as celebrating the uniqueness of individual personalities, I suspect most adult readers, aware of an ongoing need to educate young readers about tolerance, would find it hard not to identify the characters' species with ideas of race and ethnicity (and in any case, if their animal characteristics represent their individuality, why are they recognizable as certain specific kinds of animals—as characteristic types?). At any rate, the fact that the same set of characters might represent either racial difference or individual uniqueness suggests how strongly their assumptions about race relate to ideas about essential difference: races are somehow as unlike as we like to believe individual people are. I find that controversial.

In the books about inanimate objects, the insistence on the uniqueness of each character might suggest a clearer relationship to questions of unique personality. Each construction truck described in *Goodnight, Goodnight* is the only one of its kind in the book, and each crayon in *The Day the Crayons Quit* is also a unique representation of its kind—although the books also make it clear that the kinds are important by insisting that these unique examples do each belong to a specific type; and their appearance together in the same crayon box or construction site does almost automatically suggest a vision of racial harmony. Furthermore, in a book in which each crayon has a different problem to complain about, there do seem to be racial overtones being slyly suggested when it turns out that the problem of the peach-coloured crayon is that it has been stripped of its wrapping and is now, it says, "naked," thus evoking its connection to fleshiness: a subtle reminder, perhaps, that before 1962, what are now "Peach" Crayolas were called "Flesh"? If so, this text intriguingly raises the controversial issue of what colour flesh might be, and in the mere fact of implying a connection between a naked crayon and the colour peach evokes an assumption that naked flesh is most typically peach-like—what we most often identify as white.

Animals as humans: the descent in cuteness

The possibility that the crayon has a race suggests another potentially controversial aspect in relation to all of the humanized non-human characters in these books—that in making animals act like humans, we invite young readers to think of animals in unrealistically human ways—ways that might well have a negative effect on the members of their species in the real world. The constant and predominant depiction of animals acting like humans in these books might be helping to create attitudes that cause thoughtless humans to put themselves in danger in relation to real animals in the wild, in situations that inevitably end up in creating trouble for those animals that respond by acting naturally.

The depiction of animals as human has two other effects that apply equally to the depiction of humans as animals. First, the resulting creatures are strange enough to be funny. Second, they are funny enough—and apparently, therefore, harmless enough—to be what we usually call cute.

As bright, simplified, colourful cartoons, most of these books invite a response that focuses on their humour. Despite, or because of, the familiarity of such pictures, the depiction of a cat in sunglasses or a llama in a pair of overalls is incongruous enough that, even if it is conventional and familiar, it is more likely to elicit giggles than terror. In all these books, I think, the characters are figures of fun, absurd enough and silly enough in their combinations of human and other traits to have been rendered relatively harmless. A construction machine that gets sleepy and shuts its eyes is far less intimidating than a huge, powerful, real construction machine exuding gas fumes while looming above one's head. Dinosaurs are incongruous enough in a supermarket to create a slapstick situation that ignores their prehistoric savagery and the potential danger they once caused each other. Even a supposedly malevolent lizard has his malevolence undermined by the absurdity of his having a human-type hat on.

As a result, I think, the lizard in a hat or the sleepy-eyed construction truck invite the kind of response that identifies them as cute. Sianne Ngai (2005) identifies "the formal properties associated with cuteness" as "smallness, compactness, softness, simplicity, and pliancy"—properties displayed by many of the characters in these twelve books, sometimes in terms of the soft, simple depictions of otherwise complex organisms and objects, sometimes metaphorically, as in the implied pliancy of creatures who appear to be blind to the oddity of their looking like animals and acting like humans. Ngai suggests that, "in its exaggerated passivity and vulnerability, the cute object is as often intended to excite a consumer's sadistic desires for mastery and control as much as his or her desire to cuddle" (2005: 816). Daniel Harris (2000) agrees: "The process of conveying cuteness to the viewer disempowers its objects, forcing them into ridiculous situations and making them appear more ignorant and vulnerable than they really are" (2000: 6). Both animals who act like humans and humans who look like animals are inherently cute enough to be diminished and disempowered versions of both the humans and the animals they depict.

The desirability of powerlessness

Some of the themes of these twelve books echo either the desirability or the inevitability of vulnerability, cuteness, and disempowerment. In celebrating the ability of relatively helpless enemies to band together to defeat a more powerful enemy, as happens in *Superworm* and *Room on the Broom* and also to some extent in *Llama Llama* and *The Snail and the Whale*, these books confirm the inevitability of the smaller creature's relative individual powerlessness. The frequent reiteration of this theme implies some adult anxiety both about the fragility of their smaller young and the ability of those frail creatures to protect themselves either individually or as a group—as if repeating that small beings can triumph by working together might somehow end up making it true. The anxious undertone of wish-fulfilment is echoed in the owl's insistence in *Pete the Cat* that one does not need magic sunglasses to get past bad moods, one only has to "remember to look for the good in every day." Inviting young readers to ignore what actually might upset them seems rather convenient for adults who then do not have to deal with the actual experiences that make for upset and despair. In these books generally, as the adult teacher suggests in *Llama Llama*, "being mean is not allowed"—nor are other negative actions and emotions.

I am tempted to suggest an equally negative resonance in what presents itself as a celebration of creativity in *The Day the Crayons Quit*, *Dinosaurs in the Supermarket*, *Room on a Broom*, *Superworm*, and *I'm a Frog*. What saves the day in *Broom* and *Superworm* is unrealistically successful—it is not clear why a silly-looking imaginary beast scares the dragon in *Broom*, or how a spider's web can be tough enough to fly a fairly large lizard in *Superworm*—and so there is again a whiff of anxiety; and the celebration of pretending in *I'm a Frog* is somewhat undercut by how cute and silly it makes the pretenders seem. The adults' discovery in *Dinosaurs* that the creatures they have assumed to be imaginary are real seems to me to be a particularly anxious moment of wish-fulfilment, for it flies in the face of good sense altogether. How can there be dinosaurs in the supermarket if dinosaurs are extinct? And if these creatures are actual living dinosaurs, why are they so small and so much more harmless in their antics than their real forebears once were? Implying that something so clearly imaginary is not, is an attempt to celebrate a supposedly childlike exuberance that reveals its untenability in a way that diminishes it.

The scandal of the commonplace

Having tried to look past my sense that the books I have considered are merely conventional, I have discovered a range of ways in which they seem to be very odd indeed—ways in which they ought to be more controversial. But the fact remains: they are not in fact, seen as controversial. I have to ask why. The best answer to that question that I can think of is that they represent what we do in fact usually take for granted, both about what children's literature is and ought to be and what child readers are and ought to be. They do not unsettle because they show us what we already take to be true—what we view as merely ordinary, merely conventional. They express mainstream ideologies so widespread that most people agree to them without even being aware of having made the choice of doing so. They seem incontrovertible—anything but alarming.

Indeed, that lack of alarm might be the most significant response that the books and the discourse about popularity surrounding them engender. Like much of what ideological mechanisms hide from our conscious awareness, what we most take for granted about these books might actually be unsettling enough for us to have good reasons for preferring to be unaware of it. As I have shown, it might well be scandalous. Its insistence on middle-class utopias and childlike animals might represent a response to, and a deliberate refusal to engage honestly with, the less savoury aspects both of children and of the world they live in. As Jacqueline Rose (1984) suggested some decades ago in *The Case of Peter Pan*, and as I explore in some detail in my book *The Hidden Adult* (Nodelman, 2008), the cheery world of texts like these might represent ways in which we are unwilling to be honest with children about the true complexity and difficulty of the world we are asking them to share with us. It might represent our need for them to believe that the world we have invited them into is a better place and they themselves more able to bear it than we might fear is actually the case.

In any case, the scandal hidden in the conventional might open a doorway to understanding how very much our perceptions of the surprising or inappropriate in less conventional books relate to our unconsidered ideas about what is ordinary and acceptable—ideas that are based in convention and therefore might well be changed. Working toward making more adults—and more children—aware of the strangeness of the books we tend to take for granted might well allow us all to be more accepting of the less conventional books we more easily find so strange.

Academic references

Harris, D. (2000) *Cute, Quaint, Hungry, and Romantic: The Aesthetics of Consumerism*. New York: Basic Books.

Ngai, S. (2005) The Cuteness of the Avant-Garde, *Critical Inquiry*, 31: 811–847.

Nodelman, P. (2008) *The Hidden Adult: Defining Children's Literature*. Baltimore, MD: Johns Hopkins University Press.

Rose, J. (1984) *The Case of Peter Pan, or The Impossibility of Children's Fiction*. London: Macmillan.

Children's literature

Baker, M. & Neville A. (2011) *The Story of Peppa Pig*. London: Ladybird, Penguin.

Daywalt, D. illus. Oliver Jeffers (2013) *The Day the Crayons Quit*. New York: Philomel, Penguin.

Dean, K. & J. illus. James Dean (2013) *Pete the Cat and the Magic Sunglasses*. New York: Harper.

Dewdney, A. (2013) *Llama Llama and the Bully Goat*. New York: Viking, Penguin.

Donaldson, J. illus. Alex Scheffler (1999) *The Gruffalo*. London: Macmillan.

Donaldson, J. illus. Axel Scheffler (2001) *Room on the Broom*. New York: Puffin, Penguin.

Donaldson, J. illus. Axel Scheffler (2003) *The Snail and the Whale*. London: Penguin.

Donaldson, J. illus. Axel Scheffler (2009) *Tabby McTat*. London: Alison Green, Scholastic.

Donaldson, J. illus. Axel Scheffler (2012) *Superworm*. London: Alison Green, Scholastic.

Knapman, T. illus. Sarah Warburton (2013) *Dinosaurs in the Supermarket*. London: Scholastic.

Litwin, E. & James D. illus. James Dean (1999) *Pete the Cat: I Love My White Shoes*. New York: Harper.

Rinker, S.D. illus. Tom Lichtenheld (2011) *Goodnight, Goodnight, Construction Site*. San Francisco: Chronicle.

Scheffler, A. (2011) *Pip and Posy: The Super Scooter*. London: Nosy Crow.

Sendak, M. (1963) *Where the Wild Things Are*. New York: Harper.

Willems, M. (2013) *I'm a Frog*. New York: Hyperion.

3

FROM TRADITIONAL TALES, FAIRY STORIES, AND CAUTIONARY TALES TO CONTROVERSIAL VISUAL TEXTS

Do we need to be fearful?

Sandra L. Beckett

This chapter focuses on controversial picturebooks inspired directly or indirectly by the tradition of fairy tales and nursery rhymes. Such picturebooks may be considered more unsuitable for children than their sources, despite the fact that traditional tales often contain violent and gruesome details. The author examines a wide range of picturebooks to show how authors and illustrators are using the heritage of traditional tales to explore disturbing, often dark subjects that are part of the life experience of young readers as well as adults. The chapter contends that these picturebook artists respect children's ability to deal with the controversial subjects that often alarm adult mediators.

Controversial picturebooks are generally innovative and provocative works that defy current codes and conventions of the genre. Paradoxically, however, many unconventional and controversial picturebooks have their roots in the time-honoured tradition of folk and fairy tales, cautionary tales, and nursery rhymes. These may be present only in a very subtle manner, sometimes in reminiscences and allusions which go unnoticed by many readers. A large number of controversial picturebooks, however, draw heavily on traditional sources, often retelling or revisualizing the well-known stories. Although many adults consider the picturebooks to be unsuitable or threatening, they do not necessarily see the original works in the same light. These vigilant and perhaps overly protective adults may withhold picturebooks from a young audience while freely giving the same children access to the stories that inspire them, many of which contain grim, grisly, and gruesome details and events.

The traditional stories do not flinch from the hard, even sordid facts of life: child abandonment, infanticide, incest, rape, abuse, cannibalism, murder, necrophilia, and madness, among others. Yet most, if not all, of these subjects are considered taboo in children's literature. Is it the fact that fairy tales and cautionary tales purportedly contain moral lessons that make them more acceptable to the mediators of children's literature? The Grimms' *Kinder- und Hausmärchen* (*Children's and Household Tales*) claimed to be "a manual of manners" (quoted in Tatar, 2003: 19). The title of Charles Perrault's *Histoires ou contes du temps passé, avec moralités* (*Stories or Tales of Times Past, with Morals*) stresses the lessons expressed in rhyming *moralités* at the end of each tale. However, the events and lessons contained in fairy tales often seem to be anything but moral: children are imprisoned, seduced, and devoured; adults are guilty of violence, abuse, and murder. Even the most popular fairy tales contain shocking and terrifying events. Snow White is a victim of attempted murder, Hansel and Gretel of attempted cannibalism, and Little Thumbling and his brothers of child abandonment. A poor little match girl freezes to death in the street, Cinderella's cruel stepsisters have their eyes pecked out, and Snow White's step-mother dances in red-hot iron shoes until she drops dead. All these stories, despite their grim and horrific themes, have been deemed appropriate fare for children. Although they are associated with an even younger child audience, nursery rhymes also present a range of unsavoury, downright macabre subjects. In her paintings for *Nursery Rhymes*, an anthology of twenty traditional tales, the Portuguese artist Paula Rego (2010) demonstrates clearly that these beloved works are actually colourful stories about madness, cruelty, and sex. "Ring around the Rosy" ("Ring a Ring o' Roses") is claimed to be about the deadly bubonic plague and "Mary, Mary, Quite Contrary" is purported to be about Bloody Mary and instruments of torture. Even without looking beyond the literal meaning of the words, "Hush-a-Bye, Baby" describes a baby and its cradle falling out of a tree. Yet these are the tales that are told to infants and toddlers.

Challenging fairy tales

Traditional folk and fairy tales were not originally intended for children, but were told to general audiences at a time when the concept of childhood as we under-stand it did not exist and very little distinction was made between children and adults. The collection and publication of these tales coincided with the 'invention' of children's literature and they gradually passed into the children's library and the nursery. Today many authors, illustrators and publishers are trying to restore them to a crossover audience of children and adults, as I demonstrate in *Red Riding Hood for All Ages: A Fairy-Tale Icon in Cross-Cultural Contexts* (Beckett, 2008; see also Beckett, 2014). In its innovative series Libros para niños—children's books which are "¡NO SOLO para niños!" (NOT ONLY for children!)—the groundbreaking Spanish publisher Media Vaca published an illustrated collection of the Grimms' tales, titled *El señor Korbes y otros cuentos de Grimm* (*Mr. Korbes and Other Tales by the Brothers Grimm*, 2001). Winner of the Bologna Ragazzi Award in the fiction category in 2002, the unusual book was intended, according to the publisher's catalogue, "to frighten and delight both young and old." The suitability of fairy tales for children has nonetheless been questioned over the centuries, particularly in the Anglo-American world. There was much criticism of the early editions of the Grimms' tales as being totally inappropriate for children. In response, the brothers strove to alter the tales to make them more edifying for youngsters. However, the preface to the second edition warned that some parents might still find certain parts unsuitable for children (1980: 17). In their efforts to appease readers, the Grimm brothers removed sexual innuendo and heightened the violence, in order to more firmly punish the evil characters.

The Grimm brothers' approach to making the material more acceptable for children might have been questioned in the anglophone world. The eighteenth-century author and educationalist Sarah Trimmer was opposed to fairy tales because "the terrific image" that tales such as *Cinderella* "present to the imagination, usually make deep impressions, and injure the tender minds of children, by exciting unreasonable and groundless fears" (quoted in Carpenter, 1985: 3). Similar anti-fairy-tale sentiment arose in America. As Jack Zipes points out, many Americans, suspicious of anything European, "considered fairy tales . . . subversive . . . and potentially dangerous for the health and sanity of children" (2001: 84). *The Wonderful Wizard of Oz* was the result of Frank L. Baum's desire to create a "modernized fairy tale" in which the "nightmares are left out", and claimed to have eliminated "all the horrible and blood-curdling incidents devised . . . to point a fearsome moral to each tale" (Baum, 1900: unpaginated). Even today, opposition to fairy tales persists. For Banned Books Week in the year of the 200th anniversary of the first publication of the Grimms' tales, Sherry Liberman of the New York Public Library reminds readers that *The Complete Grimms' Fairy Tales* was challenged by a committee of parents, teachers, and administrators twenty years earlier due to its "excessive violence." Half of the "10 controversial kids' books" listed in an April 2013 *MSN Living* article on books that have been challenged or banned in the United States are fairy tales. Using the statistics collected in Robert P. Doyle's *Banned Books: Challenging Our Freedom to Read* (2010), the article cites Andersen's "The Little Mermaid" (for "pornographic" pictures of bare-breasted mermaids), the Grimms' "Little Red Riding Hood" (for violence and the presence of alcohol), and "Snow White" (for graphic violence). According to the *MSN Living* article, "sexually explicit content" tops the list of reasons why children's books are banned, followed by "offensive language" and "violence" (Pfeuffer, 2013). To a certain extent, fairy tales and controversial picturebooks, both of which constitute a form of crossover literature, share a similar fate in the world of children's books, at least in some countries.

Some fairy tales tend to be excluded from the children's canon and provoke controversy when they are reintroduced. The dark tale "The Juniper Tree," in which a mother kills her son and cooks him for supper, provided the title of the fairy-tale anthology *My Mother She Killed Me, My Father He Ate Me: Forty New Fairy Tales*, edited by Kate Bernheimer. When the anthology came out, "there was a controversial discussion online in which a bookstore browser—who admitted to not reading the book—accused [the editor] of seeking, through fairy tales, to 'glamorize cannibalism' for an unsuspecting generation of very young readers" (Bernheimer, n.d.). Maurice Sendak, one of the world's best-known children's illustrators, chose Grimms' "The Juniper Tree" as the title story of his 1973 collection, which includes some of the lesser-known and grimmer of the Grimms' tales. Fairy tales that are accepted fare for children in one country may not be in another. Perrault's version of "Little Red Riding Hood," which ends with the little girl being devoured, is not normally the subject of children's editions in English-speaking countries. This is explained not only by the tragic ending, but by what Bruno Bettelheim calls the "direct and obvious seduction" (1975: 169). In Perrault's tale (1697), which warns girls to beware of charming, two-legged wolves, the little girl undresses and climbs into bed with the wolf, who tells her that his strong arms are for embracing her better. It is not surprising that Britain and America, among other Western countries, favoured the German "Rotkäppchen," in which the Grimms had eliminated Perrault's sexual innuendo and added a happy ending that mitigated the violence, or at least its consequences. "Bluebeard" and "Donkeyskin" are seldom illustrated for children in the Anglo-American world, but Perrault's versions of these tales are bedtime stories for French children from an early age. One of France's most popular author-illustrators, Jean Claverie, published *La Barbe Bleue* (1991) for very young readers, which contains a very gruesome illustration of the dead wives in various states of decomposition (Figure 3.1).

The book's success is indicated by the fact that it appeared subsequently in Gallimard Jeunesse's popular Folio Cadet series for children eight to ten years of age. A few years later, another French illustrator, Sibylle Delacroix (2000), offered an only slightly less grisly depiction of the bodies in Bluebeard's chamber of horrors. The tale has also been illustrated in Italy in a striking picturebook by Chiara Carrer (2007), whose illustration of the same scene is perhaps less disturbing

FIGURE 3.1 *La Barbe Bleue* by Charles Perrault and Jean Claverie (1991).

FIGURE 3.2 *Ma Peau d'Âne* by Anne Ikhlef and Alain Gauthier (2002).

because only the women's legs are visible. Adult mediators did not seem to be particularly concerned about the graphic violence in these books for young children, but it is difficult to imagine them being published for the same audience in North America. Even in France, some illustrated editions of the more violent Perrault tales have raised eyebrows and provoked discussion of appropriate target audience. In *Ma Peau d'Âne* (*My Donkeyskin*, 2002), the author Anne Ikhlef and the illustrator Alain Gauthier offer an intimate, sensual retelling of Perrault's tale about incest (Figure 3.2).

Although the sexual innuendo in the illustrations is more subtle than in their earlier picturebook retelling of "Little Red Riding Hood," this book was published by Seuil Jeunesse for readers from nine years of age, rather than six. For the most part, critics agree that it is more appropriate for older children and adults. In the eyes of some French reviewers, it is the esoteric nature of the text and images rather than the sexual content that makes this picturebook unsuitable for young children.

Broaching dark and difficult subjects in fairy-tale picturebooks

Fairy tales and nursery rhymes do provide a filter that allows authors and illustrators to broach more difficult subjects in picturebooks for young children. Many adults seem to find so-called "adult" subjects, particularly sexuality and violence, more acceptable in recastings of classic fairy tales. This is the case for Claude Clément and Isabelle Forestier's *Un petit chaperon rouge* (*A Little Red Riding Hood*, 2000), which uses the tale—"a story about pedophilia" according to the illustrator (letter, 5 October 2003)—to tackle the subject of sexual abuse in a picturebook published by Grasset & Fasquelle for readers four years of age and older. When illustrating canonical fairy tales, illustrators may get away with more unconventional artwork, although this is not always the case. Even a rather traditional visual rendition of a classic tale can encounter opposition. The illustrated edition of the Grimms' *Little Red Riding Hood* (1983) by Caldecott medallist Trina Schart Hyman was pulled from a first-grade recommended reading list by a California school district for its depiction of the fairy-tale heroine taking a bottle of wine to her grandmother.

Some picturebook editions of popular fairy tales have raised a great deal more controversy than Hyman's. One such picturebook is Sarah Moon's interpretation of Perrault's *Little Red Riding Hood*, published, in 1983, by the Creative Company, one of the most innovative American children's publishers. The French-born fashion photographer casts a child model, Morgan, in the role of an urban Little Red Riding Hood. The sober black-and-white photographs used to document the sinister events involving a young, flesh-and-blood girl explain the book's powerful, shocking effect on viewers (see Beckett, 2002: 49–53). In a dark, deserted street, a young schoolgirl is illuminated by the glaring headlights of the large car of a predatory, unseen driver. The wolf remains an invisible, menacing presence as the little girl begins to undress (Figure 3.3).

Moon's final, disturbing image depicting only white, rumpled bedclothes confronts the reader with the sexuality and violence inherent in Perrault's tale. Awarded the Premio Grafico at the Bologna Children's Book Fair in 1984, Moon's daring portrayal of child abuse in a children's book met not only with critical praise, but also with scandalized condemnation. An Italian reader felt the jury "mistook a very refined book for adult voyeurs for a children's book" and an American reviewer and social worker thought that the Bologna Book Fair prize sticker should be accompanied by a red "HANDLE WITH CARE" stamp since the book can frighten even adults (Garrett, 1993: 9). Moon's book did not meet with the same controversy in France, where it was published by Grasset Jeunesse for five years of age and up (1983). From an early age, young French readers are exposed to what Zipes calls the "seduction scene" (1993: 355) in Gustave Doré's famous and influential nineteenth-century engraving of the encounter scene (1861). Doré's even more troubling engraving of the bed scene presents an intimate

FIGURE 3.3 *Little Red Riding Hood* by Charles Perrault and Sarah Moon (1983).

tête-à-tête of the bonneted wolf and a little girl whose long, curly hair falls seductively over her shoulders and whose chubby bare arm pulls the sheet to her bosom. The Italian illustrator Beni Montresor reworks both of these Doré engravings in a rendition of Perrault's version of *Little Red Riding Hood* published in New York in 1991. The provocative bed scene, which is featured on the cover, is followed by a second disturbing illustration, in which the little girl's head has almost completely disappeared inside the wolf's jaws. The picturebook by the 1965 Caldecott medallist was not without controversy. One reviewer suggests that Montresor's darkly disturbing and violent interpretation of the classic tale is probably "more suited to adults searching into the deeper psychological meaning of fairy tales" (Robinson, 1991: 92).

In 1988, just five years after Moon's controversial, award-winning book, Roberto Innocenti depicted a similar, troubling encounter of a young schoolgirl and a dark, dangerous, urban wolf driving, not a car, but a motorcycle.

The preliminary work, which the illustrator kindly allowed me to reproduce in *Red Riding Hood for All Ages* (Figure 3.4), was unfortunately lost before he began work on *The Girl in Red* (Innocenti, 2012), released in 2012 by the Creative Company, who had published both Moon's *Little Red Riding Hood* (1983) and Innocenti's *Rose Blanche* (1985) in the 1980s. Innocenti admitted to me at the Bologna Book Fair in 2013 that he preferred the original image, which had a decidedly darker tone than those in the book. Perhaps *The Girl in Red* would have caused more controversy had its illustrator retained the darker atmosphere of the earlier work, which is more reminiscent of his *Rose Blanche*. His first portrait of the girl in red running along a stone wall covered with graffiti bears more than a striking resemblance to Moon's Little Red Riding Hood running along a brick wall. The presence of bystanders in Innocenti's image does little to mitigate the sense of menace and dread, as they remain indifferent to the little girl's plight in a hostile cityscape.

FIGURE 3.4 Preliminary work on "Little Red Riding Hood" by Roberto Innocenti (1988).

FIGURE 3.5 *Snowhite* by Ana Juan (2001).

It would be interesting to know how the adults who restricted the Grimms' "Snow White" to students with parental permission at some public school libraries in the United States because of its graphic violence—a hunter kills a wild boar and a wicked witch orders Snow White's heart torn out—would react to Ana Juan's *Snowhite*, published in Spain in 2001. Like Moon, Juan interprets the fairy tale entirely in black and white in order to create the "mysterious and troubling" ambiance she sought (email, 30 April 2014). In a hostile, dark world, the familiar characters either "lose their 'goodness' and become abusers," as in the case of the prince and the seven dwarfs (Figure 3.5), or become silent witnesses who look the other way.

As in Wim Hofman's disturbing psychological retelling of the same tale, *Zwart als inkt is het verhaal van Sneeuwwitje en de zeven dwergen* (*Black as Ink is the Tale of Snow White and the Seven Dwarfs*, 1998), in which Snow White contemplates suicide, Juan's tragic ending brings us full circle at the end. Neither Hofman's nor Juan's young protagonist is able to escape the inexorable cycle of evil that dictates her fate. Marketed for young adults and adults, Juan's cruel, sordid tale of narcissism, prostitution, drugs, and abuse is a far cry from the sweet tone of the Disney movie that she had loved as a child (email, 28 April 2014), and that, according to Jack Zipes (2001), changed the negative attitude toward fairy tales in the United States.

The images of Susanne Janssen's *Rotkäppchen*, published by Carl Hanser in 2001, restore some of the sexuality to the Grimms' version of "Little Red Riding Hood." It is not so much the grotesqueness of the figures or the distorted perspective that disturbs adult readers, but rather the sexual innuendo that re-enters the familiar tale. Janssen focuses on faces and they tell a rather different story from the text. Setting out under her mother's somewhat disapproving stare, the little girl with the saucy red hat and seductive pink lips seems to cast a flirtatious gaze at the wolf who lolls lasciviously on its back (Figure 3.6).

FIGURE 3.6 *Rotkäppchen* by Jacob and Wilhelm Grimm and Susanne Janssen (2001).

After her encounter with the wolf, the young girl herself is sprawled across the doublespread and on her face is a look, not of fear, but of ecstasy. In the bedroom, the intimate close-up of her face that fills the picture frame portrays a dreamy gaze, shaped eyebrows that arch speculatively, and a sensual, lipstick-smeared mouth. The German critic Mattenklott Gundel finds it "hard to imagine the book in the hands of small children" pointing to "a precarious eroticisation of the pictorial narrative." In his view, Janssen's picturebook belongs "to the category of those books whose blurb points out from the outset that they are not suitable for children, but rather more so 'for adults interested in art'" (Gundel, 2002: 38). Janssen has drawn a very different tale from the Brothers Grimm's "fairy tale for little children," according to the reviewer, who feels it might be different if she had included humour or irony to distance readers, as did Yvan Pommaux in *John Chatterton détective* (1993), winner of the Deutscher Jugendliteraturpreis (German Youth Literature Award) in 1995.

Pommaux's popular picturebook retelling of "Little Red Riding Hood" none-theless has a sinister undercurrent, as it depicts a psychopathic wolf art-collector who abducts the heroine and holds her for ransom to obtain a coveted wolf paint-ing for his art collection (Figure 3.7) (Plate 14).

The eponymous black cat detective follows a trail of red items of clothing—ominous signs perhaps of the young victim's struggle with her abductor—through dark and deserted parks, streets, and alleys to the wolf's powerful, black car. However, the comic book style, humour, and happy ending of Pommaux's whodunnit mitigate the seriousness of the subject matter in this award-winning picturebook appreciated by adults and children alike. Even fairy-tale retellings in a playful, light-hearted mode can, however, be controversial. Fam Ekman (1985) adopted a humorous approach to the Grimms' version of "Little Red Riding Hood" in *Rødhatten og Ulven* (*Red Hat and the Wolf*), in which a sexy she-wolf in high heels and a low-cut red dress attempts to seduce a naïve country boy. The Norwegian public is quite accustomed to Ekman's sophisticated, challenging picturebooks, which are avidly collected by adults, so the picturebook did not meet with any controversy until it was adapted as a television film. According to the

FIGURE 3.7 (Plate 14) *John Chatterton détective* by Yvan Pommaux (1993).

author, the film was never aired due to the provocative scene in which Red Hat stares into the décolleté of the seductive saleswoman wolf in the café, a scene deemed inappropriate for children (Figure 3.8).

It is important to remember, however, that this occurred in the 1980s. The Scandinavian countries are much more tolerant toward sexual content in children's works than most other countries.

An increasing number of contemporary retellings of fairy tales in picturebook format adopt a darker, more ambiguous atmosphere and restore some of the sexuality and violence of the earlier sources. The majority of these books, however, have been published in non-English-speaking markets. Both the text and the images of *Rood Rood Roodkapje* (*Red Red Little Red Hood*), by the Dutch author Edward van de Vendel and the Belgian illustrator Isabelle Vandenabeele, received awards when

FIGURE 3.8 *Rødhatten og Ulven* by Fam Ekman (1985).

the picturebook was published in 2003 by the innovative Belgian publisher De Eenhoorn. The strikingly dramatic woodcuts create a dark, unsettling atmosphere, which becomes decidedly more troubling toward the end of the story. Vandenabeele portrays a composed little girl wielding a large, blood-drenched axe, as blood fills her grandmother's doorway and flows out into a pool on the ground beside her (Figure 3.9).

The final, ambiguous spread depicts the little girl standing in a blood-red room staring at the black wolf skin on the floor as she dreams of doing red things. More than a decade earlier, one of France's most successful children's publishing houses, L'École des loisirs, published *Mina je t'aime* (*Mina, I love you*), a picturebook by the French author Patricia Joiret and the Belgian illustrator Xavier Bruyère (1991). While there is nothing in *Mina je t'aime* that blatantly transgresses taboos, there is an underlying current of sensuality and a disturbing sense of menace. Joiret and Bruyère portray Little Red Riding Hood as a predatory seductress (she lures three young boys to her she-wolf grandmother) in a picturebook targeted at very young children. One particularly sensual portrait, inspired by Titian's *Venus of Urbino*, shows Carmina lounging on a divan in a sexy red mini-dress and red tights, her long, loose, red hair flowing erotically over her shoulder and a seductive smile on her red lips. Although it shocked my class of Canadian university students, there is no trace of any controversy in France over this picturebook, which seems to be widely used by teachers with children aged nine to eleven. Despite its apparent success in France and the fact that it was released by a major publishing house, *Mina je t'aime* has not been translated (except for an adult audience in a scholarly anthology of retellings I published in 2014, titled *Revisioning Red Riding Hood Around the World: An Anthology of International Retellings*).

One retelling of "Little Red Riding Hood" that did spark discussion of its appropriateness for young readers in France was *Mon Chaperon Rouge* (*My Red*

FIGURE 3.9 *Rood Rood Roodkapje* by Edward van de Vendel and Isabelle Vandenabeele (2003).

FIGURE 3.10 (Plate 15) *Mon Chaperon Rouge* by Anne Ikhlef and Alain Gauthier (1998).

Riding Hood, 1998) by Anne Ikhlef and Alain Gauthier (Figure 3.10) (Plate 15). Seuil Jeunesse released it for ages six years of age and up, but some critics consider it to be a sophisticated picturebook primarily for adolescents and adults. This is not due only to the sensuality and eroticism of both the text and illustrations, however, but also to the textual layering and sophisticated images. Adult readers may have difficulty with this picturebook because it is inspired by Ikhlef's earlier, rather provocative film, *La vraie histoire du Chaperon rouge* (*The real story of Red Riding Hood*), which was presented at the Cannes Film Festival in 1985. The five-year-old actress Justine Bayard is nude in the intimate bed scene, as she lovingly caresses the wolf, in the guise of the French actor Didier Sandre. In fact, the picturebook is less disturbing than the film, since the prepubescent heroine portrayed by Gauthier appears much older than the young actress who plays Little Red Riding Hood. *Mon Chaperon Rouge* nonetheless remains a daring picturebook which, like the film, presents an erotic, nocturnal version of the tale inspired largely from oral versions, notably the gruesome tale "The Story of Grandmother," with its cannibalistic scene and ritualistic striptease. Ikhlef uses what Angela Carter calls "the latent content of those traditional tales," a content that is "violently sexual," but, unlike the British author, she does so in a children's picturebook (Goldsworthy, 1985: 10). The sexual content is perhaps made more palatable in this picturebook targeted at children by the fact that Ikhlef embeds in the poetic text other popular forms from children's culture, such as nursery rhymes, counting rhymes, riddles, and songs, although some of these also have grisly overtones. The author reworks a counting rhyme to retell the story of the cannibal repast (see Beckett, 2008: 89). Ikhlef's picturebook (1998) retains the lengthy, ritualistic striptease of "The Story of Grandmother," in which the little girl asks in turn what to do with her apron, bodice, stockings, and skirt, and the wolf tells her each time to throw the article in the fire, as she won't be needing it anymore. Gauthier's illustrations turn the scene into an erotic spectacle in which readers become complicit spectators, peering voyeuristically over the man-wolf's shoulder. A red curtain is pulled back to reveal the little girl, smiling enigmatically at the wolf (and readers) as she shrugs one shoulder out of her red dress. The more risqué version of the dramatic dialogue from the popular tradition receives a strikingly provocative treatment by Gauthier. The intimate picture of a naked Little Red Riding Hood lying on top of the wolf is once again framed by red bed curtains, as if readers/viewers were watching a love scene being enacted at the theatre.

The figure of the ogre in picturebooks

The ogre is a common figure in folk and fairy tales, from where it made its way into children's literature. For many children today, the word 'ogre' is likely to evoke the grotesque, harmless figure of Shrek. In the francophone world, however, the terrifying images that Doré created for Perrault's *Le Petit Poucet* (*Little Thumbling*) are still engraved on the collective unconscious of young and old alike (Figure 3.11).

The Swiss picturebook artist Béatrice Poncelet (2003) incorporates Doré's frightening images into *Les Cubes* (*The Blocks*), a challenging picturebook about dementia. The dominant image on the book's cover is a fragment of the fearsome face of Doré's ogre in the process of cutting his own daughters' throats. Superposed over his face is a children's block that depicts the fragment of his hand on the hilt of the knife. Poncelet adds colour to Doré's images, which makes them even more nightmarish, as it highlights the blood. Fragments of this gruesome scene reappear on blocks throughout the book with more frequency than other, less disturbing childhood images. Three blocks with fragments of Doré's engraving are positioned in the centre of one doublespread so as to reconstruct the most horrific part of the image (Figure 3.12).

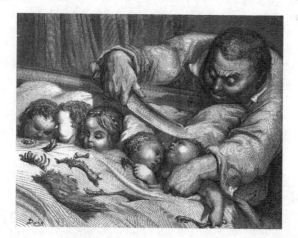

FIGURE 3.11 *Les Contes de Perrault* (*The Fairy Tales of Perrault*) by Charles Perrault and Gustave Doré (1861).

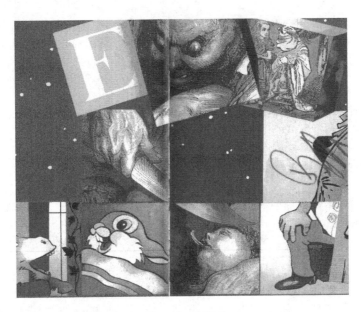

FIGURE 3.12 *Les Cubes* by Béatrice Poncelet (2003).

Midway through the story, the block bearing the ogre's face is isolated and enlarged to fill an entire page. Poncelet defends her inclusion of these images—essential images of our cultural heritage—in her picturebooks. A child reader unfamiliar with Doré's work still "sees clearly that it is an ogre, and an ogre is scary, so why not show it (wink, also small homage) since it's part of our culture" (Poncelet, 2005: 60). Doré's ogre also finds his way into her picturebook *Chez elle ou chez elle* (*At Her Place or at Her Place*) (1997). A unique ogre is the eponymous protagonist of *L'Ogresse en pleurs* (*The Ogress in Tears*) by the French author Valérie Dayre and the Hans Christian Andersen Award winner Wolf Erlbruch (1996). They use the filter of fairy tale to present the ultimate form of parental violence against a child, that of cannibalism. In Dayre's tale of "a woman so evil that she dreamed of eating a child," the sinister, grotesque ogress prowls an eerie, surreal landscape looking for a child to eat until finally she returns home and devours her own child (Figure 3.13) (Plate 16).

Erlbruch's decision not to represent the horrific cannibalistic scene was not intended to protect young readers, but rather to highlight the horror and violence, which is witnessed by a circus monkey. The animal's yellow eyes almost pop out of his head, his mouth is open wide in a terrified scream, and he beats his drum frenetically (see Figure 1.3 in Chapter 1). The truncated German title *Die Menschenfresserin* (*The Ogress*) eliminates the sentimentality of the French title, which refers to the ogress's fate as she roams the countryside at the end of the story, now seeking a child to love, not to eat. The picturebook shocks many non-French-speaking readers, perhaps in part because the wordplay in French reduces some of the anguish (the expression "à croquer" or "to eat" has the figurative meaning of

FIGURE 3.13 (Plate 16) *L'Ogresse en pleurs* by Valérie Dayre and Wolf Erlbruch (1996).

"to look good enough to eat"). In an article titled "How Much Cruelty Can a Children's Picturebook Stand?" Horst Künnemann (2005) points out that admiring critics who added the picturebook to their collection "would not read it to their own children." While Erlbruch's phenomenally successful illustrations for *Vom kleinen Maulwurf, der wissen wollte, wer ihm auf den Kopf gemacht hat* (*The Story of the Little Mole Who Knew It Was None of his Business*), by Werner Holzwarth (1989), sold well over a million copies, the German edition of *L'ogresse en pleurs*, with its darker title, was printed in only 15,000 copies. Needless to say, the picturebook has not been translated into English.

The heritage of traditional tales

It is not surprising that controversial picturebooks are often inspired by traditional tales, cautionary tales, and nursery rhymes. Many contemporary picturebook artists turn to fairy tales as models of what children's literature should be. These genres have been popular with both children and adults for centuries. The French publisher Christian Bruel acknowledged in 1981 that there is a connection between the traditional tale and the controversial picturebooks of his experimental publishing house Le Sourire qui mord (The smile that bites) (Bruel, 1985). Concerned by the fact that many children's books ignore complete chunks of the reality experienced by children, the publishing house was founded with the intention of eliminating the stereotypes and taboos in children's literature. Its complex, crossover picturebooks deal with difficult themes, notably sensuality and violence, in a manner that is particularly disturbing for adults. The wordless picturebook *Vous oubliez votre cheval* (*You are forgetting your horse*), conceived by Bruel and illustrated by Pierre Wachs (1986), is one of several enigmatic picturebooks in the groundbreaking series Grands petits livres (Large little books) that contain important allusions to fairy tales. The doublespreads that refer to "Goldilocks" and "The Frog Prince" are perplexing and unsettling, but the one devoted to "Little Red Riding Hood" is entirely unnerving. Opposite the black-and-white illustration depicting the inside of the grandmother's empty living room, where a bear trap has been set, is a colour illustration showing the bedroom, where a large, realistic wolf stands in the doorway, holding in its jaws a red slipper that evokes the absent, devoured grandmother (Figure 3.14) (Plate 17).

It is not the violence done to the old lady that disturbs adult readers, however, but rather the implied sensuality. Obligingly bringing the grandmother's slippers, the wolf fixes his yellow gaze on Little Red Riding Hood, but viewers see only two vulnerable-looking bare legs and feet that bleed suggestively off the page, conjuring up images of a naked heroine. The ambiguous illustrations, which leave readers to determine if Little Red Riding Hood is the victim or the complicit partner of the wolf, are far more disturbing for adults than children. While adults will immediately interpret these multilayered, enigmatic pictures in the light of "Little Red Riding Hood," children may simply be fascinated by their strange and sometimes playful details.

Like fairy tales, nursery rhymes have inspired some rather controversial picturebooks. Maurice Sendak chose two nursery rhymes as the text of his picturebook *We Are All in the Dumps with Jack and Guy* (1993), an origin clearly indicated in the subtitle "Two Nursery Rhymes with Pictures." It is the pictures and the added text,

FIGURE 3.14 (Plate 17) *Vous oubliez votre cheval* by Christian Bruel and Pierre Wachs (1986).

not the original nursery rhymes that are a source of alarm for adults. Cleverly combining two little known and unrelated nursery rhymes, Sendak interprets them, with a great deal of social commentary, in the context of serious contemporary problems and issues that are introduced in newspaper headlines and articles. Although the illustrations are not necessarily frightening, they remind readers of horrific things in the real world: poverty, war, crime, pollution, famine, inflation, AIDS, unemployment, and so forth. A number of critics feel *We Are All in the Dumps* is not a picturebook for children. In a review for *School Library Journal*, Kay E. Vandergrift says that "adults may question presenting serious topics to children in this imaginative form," but she points out that its subject matter is part of children's experience: "Lucky children have seen homelessness, and worse, only on TV; the unlucky have lived it." Categorizing *We Are All in the Dumps* as a picturebook for four years of age and up, the reviewer concludes: "In this beautiful, passionately concerned book, Sendak creates visual poetry, rich in symbolism, that goes to the heart of such matters better than any earnest description" (Vandergrift, 1993: 119). Jane Doonan rightly points out that "*Dumps* shares with certain other modern picture books a quality that was formerly the preserve of folk and fairy tales: an open address" (1994: 166). For decades, Sendak's books have challenged established ideas about what children's literature is and should be, in an attempt to revolutionize the picturebook genre by introducing dark, contentious themes.

From classic cautionary tales to challenging picturebooks

In addition to cautionary tales from the fairy-tale tradition, contemporary picturebook artists borrow from classic cautionary stories, in which cruel fates are purportedly offered for children's edification. The most influential of these works is Heinrich Hoffman's popular collection of moral tales, *Der Struwwelpeter*, a German classic that has often been criticized for its violence. The cruelty is, of course, mitigated by humour, as indicated by the original title, *Lustige Geschichten und drollige Bilder mit 15 schön kolorierten Tafeln für Kinder von 3-6 Jahren (Funny stories and whimsical pictures with 15 beautifully coloured panels for children aged 3 to 6*, [1845]). In these nightmarish stories with their implausible and absurd morals, a thumb-sucking boy has his thumbs cut off with giant scissors, a girl is burned to death playing with matches, and a child who refuses to eat his soup wastes away and dies. Another German classic in the same vein, published in 1865, is Wilhelm Busch's *Max und Moritz* (English trans. *Mac and Murray*), in which the boys' pranks end with them being ground to bits and devoured by a miller's ducks, to no one's regret. The Anglo-French author Hillaire Belloc parodies nineteenth-century cautionary tales in his humorous work *Cautionary Tales for Children: Designed for the Admonition of Children between the Ages of Eight and Fourteen Years* (1907), illustrated by Basil Temple Blackwood (B.T.B.) and later by Edward Gorey. The tongue-in-cheek poems recount the stories of "Jim, who ran away from his nurse, and was eaten by a lion," "Matilda, who told lies and was burnt to death," and "Henry King: Who chewed bits of string, and was early cut off in dreadful agonies."

Images from both of the German works find their way into *Chez elle ou chez elle* and Poncelet attributes this influence to the German side of her Swiss culture. Poncelet is often accused of elitism and creating picturebooks for adults, but she insists that they are intended for children as much as adults. She feels that many children's books continue to address children in the same manner they did at the beginning of the twentieth century, that is, "avoiding truly confronting them with existence" (2005: 60). The French publisher François Ruy-Vidal, who collaborated with the controversial American publisher Harlin Quist, had made the same accusation in the 1960s. Quist and Ruy-Vidal both wanted to abolish the taboos in children's literature and break down the boundaries that separated it from adult literature. In 1972, they published an adaptation of Hoffman's work, *Pierre l'ébouriffé: Histoires pas très drôles, d'un passé toujours présent* (*Dishevelled Peter: Not Very Funny Stories of a Past Still Present*), adapted by Ruy-Vidal and illustrated by Claude Lapointe. Unlike the majority of the Quist and Ruy-Vidal collaborations, *Pierre l'ébouriffé* did not appear in the United States. Although Quist's daring books gleaned critical acclaim, their European look and controversial content prevented their commercial success in the United States and to this day they remain unique in American children's publishing.

From fear to pleasure: picturebooks as an introduction to life

Assumptions about children's limited ability to deal with certain topics have often restricted their literary experiences and deprived them of fictional opportunities to explore dark, disturbing, and painful subjects that nonetheless touch them personally and constitute part of their life experience. This is particularly true in the case of the picturebook genre (see Beckett, 2012). The Danish author Oscar K laments the attempt to keep "an often harsh reality out of children's books" and wonders "for whose sake—children or adults?" (2008: 46). He and his wife Dorte Karrebæk, whose unconventional and provocative illustrations brought a new look to Danish children's literature, contend that to take children seriously is to present them with raw and undiluted reality. As we have seen, there is a particular reluctance to portray those harsh realities in the picturebooks of the Anglo-American world. In his article "Creation of a Picture Book," the English children's author and illustrator Edward Ardizzone acknowledges that we tend to "shelter [the child] too much from the harder facts of life," and expresses his belief that subjects like poverty and death, "if handled poetically, can surely all be introduced without hurt." Books for children are, in his view, "an introduction to the life that lies ahead of them," so he feels that picturebook artists are not "playing fair" if "no hint of the hard world comes into these books." In support of his argument, Ardizzone points to fairy tales, like those of Andersen, and to nursery rhymes, which consist of "the very stuff of life itself" (1980: 293). Sendak attributes the appeal of the Grimms' tales with young and old alike to the fact that they are about "the pure essence of life—incest, murder, insane mothers, love, sex" . . . (quoted in Lanes, 1980: 206). Many contemporary picturebook artists agree that it is their duty to tell young children some terrible truths even if this causes horror and distress.

Dark subjects can also cause immense pleasure, as a number of critics remind us. Maria Tatar states: "Children love fairy tales precisely because they speak the language of pain, suffering, loss, and torture with a candor they often do not encounter in real life." She admits being "hooked by the terror" as a child, explaining: "And I read voraciously, in the same way that I was also mesmerized by the images of people suffering from terrible diseases in the pages of *JAMA*, the professional medical journal that piled up over the years in my parents' bedroom" (quoted in Liberman, 2013). In *No Go the Bogeyman* (2000), Marina Warner has shown the pleasure both adults and children derive from the fantastic terrors used in tales, nursery rhymes, and cradle songs to allay real ones. A reviewer for *V&A Magazine* reported his ten-year-old child's reaction to Rego's collection of *Nursery Rhymes*: "'Really, really scary Daddy . . . But in a good way.'" In her work, Rego focuses on the fears and obsessions of childhood, conscious that those fears remain with us as adults. Should these fears not be faced while we are still children? Rego describes the cathartic nature of frightening images in the following manner: "If you put frightening things into a picture, then they can't harm you. In fact, you end becoming quite fond of them" (email from Sue Hopper on behalf of Paula Rego, 5 June 2014).

Some of the most celebrated picturebook artists, including Maurice Sendak, Tomi Ungerer, and Wolf Erlbruch, continue in the tradition of folk and fairy tales. Sendak was largely responsible for reintroducing subjects from the dark, disturbing side of childhood into picturebooks with *Where the Wild Things Are*, published in 1963. Since the 1960s, picturebooks have made great strides in freeing themselves from the rigid moral codes and taboos that long governed children's literature. They now deal with a wide range of topics that are often quite contentious and very far from the standard fare of children's books. However, the fact remains that we are still discussing "controversial" picturebooks. "The gulf between childhood and adulthood" that was demonstrated by the very different response of adult and child readers to *Where the Wild Things Are*, according to its author, still seems to exist more than fifty years later. Sendak describes the dual response to the picturebook in the following words: "Adults find the book fearful; however, they misinterpret childhood. Children find the book silly, fun to read, and fun to look at" (1995: 142–143). Of course, not all the picturebooks examined here will be "silly" and "fun" for young readers. And they will probably all be more frightening or alarming for adults than *Where the Wild Things Are*. In his essay "On Fairy-Stories," J.R.R. Tolkien, contends that fairy stories provide moral or emotional consolation through their happy ending, which he terms a "*eucatastrophe*" (1964: 68). Perhaps it is the absence of this "eucatastrophe" in many contemporary picturebooks inspired by traditional tales that accounts, at least in part, for their controversial status. Künnemann describes the horrifying events in *L'Ogresse en pleurs* as "an existential catastrophe" and "a drama of cosmic proportions" (2005: 17, 16). However, does that mean that children cannot comprehend and appreciate the appalling and tragic events? As Sendak maintains, picturebook artists understand that "children know a lot more than people give them credit for" and "are willing to deal with many dubious subjects that grownups think they shouldn't know about" (Sendak, 1988: 192). In an article devoted to "inappropriate picturebooks for young readers," Carole Scott points out quite rightly that "their authors must view their texts as appropriate, providing an introduction to our world rather than constructing a cocoon for children to shelter from it . . . as artists, they shy away from presenting 'inappropriate' works that are not truthful to the reality they perceive" (2005: 12).

Like Oscar K, Sendak insists that the "anxiety" over such books comes not from children, but "from adults who feel that the book has to conform to some set ritual of ideas about childhood" (1988: 193) Adult mediators who try to keep controversial picturebooks out of the hands of young readers feel that they are protecting children. Sendak, on the other hand, sees children's authors and illustrators as the only ones who attempt to "protect [children] from life." "All we're trying to do in a serious work is to tell them about life," he claims (Sendak, 1988: 193). Acknowledging that *We Are All in the Dumps* is a "potent, evocative book," Vandergrift contends that Sendak "respects children's ability to deal with powerful and potentially controversial issues and ideas." Such controversial picturebooks engender "discussion, speculation, and a variety of interpretations" (Vandergrift, 1993: 119), and therefore offer adults an opportunity to broach very difficult subjects with children. Scott insists on the role of the adult mediator and "the filter of adult interpretation" in children's reception of works that "may seem shocking or inappropriate for young children" (2005: 12). Picturebook artists who understand the importance of exploring the nightmare side of child experience also recognize the importance of presenting potentially disturbing images and ideas in a manner that is appropriate for their young readers.

Maybe we don't need to be fearful after all!

Academic references

Ardizzone, E. (1980) Creation of a Picture Book, in Egoff, S, Stubbs, G.T. & Ashley, L.F. (eds) *Only Connect: Readings on Children's Literature*, 2nd edn. New York: Oxford University Press, pp. 289–298.

Beckett, S. (2002) *Recycling Red Riding Hood*. London: Routledge.

Beckett, S. (2008) *Red Riding Hood for All Ages: A Fairy-Tale Icon in Cross-Cultural Contexts*. Detroit, MI: Wayne State University Press.

Beckett, S. (2012) *Crossover Picturebooks: A Genre for All Ages*. London: Routledge.

Beckett, S. (2014) *Revisioning Red Riding Hood around the World: An Anthology of International Retellings*. Detroit, MI: Wayne State University Press.

Bernheimer, K. (n.d.) The Strange, Beautiful, Subterranean Power of Fairy Tales, *The Center for Fiction*. http://centerforfiction.org/why-fairy-tales-matter#sthash.JoHpMKkY.dpuf (accessed 27 April 2014).

Bettelheim, B. (1975) *The Uses of Enchantment: The Meaning and Importance of Fairy Tales*. New York: Random House.

Bruel, C. (1985). Christian Bruel: conforter l'intime des enfants, interview, in Épin, B. *Les livres de vos enfants, parlons-en !* Paris: Éditions Messidor/La Farandole, pp. 150–151.

Carpenter, H. (1985) *Secret Gardens: The Golden Age of Children's Literature*. London: George Allen & Unwin.

Doonan, J. (1994) Into the Dangerous World: *We Are All in the Dumps with Jack and Guy* by Maurice Sendak, *Signal*, 75: 155–171.

Doyle, R. P. (2010) *Banned Books: Challenging Our Freedom to Read*. Chicago, IL: American Library Association.

Garrett, J. (1993) "With Murderous Ending, Shocking, Menacing . . .": Sarah Moon's *Little Red Riding Hood* 10 Years After, *Bookbird*, 31(3): 8–9.

Goldsworthy, K. (1985) Angela Carter, *Meanjin*, 44(1): 10.

Gundel, M. (2002) Leg dich zu mir, Rotkäppchen, *Frankfurter Allgemeine*, 5 January, 24, 38.

K, O. [O. Dalgaard] (2008) It's Not the Fact That It Is Said—In Fact It's Just the Way You Say It, *Danish Literary Magazine*, (Autumn): 46–48.

Künnemann, H. (2005) How Much Cruelty Can a Children's Picturebook Stand? The Case of Wolf Erlbruch's *Die Menschenfresserin*, *Bookbird*, 43(1): 14–19.

Lanes, S. (1980) *The Art of Maurice Sendak*. New York: Harry N. Abrams, Inc.

Liberman, S. (2013) Banned Books Week: The Complete Grimms' Fairy Tales, *New York Public Library*, 27 September. www.nypl.org/blog/2013/09/27/banned-books-week-grimms-fairy-tales (accessed 24 April 2014).

Pfeuffer, C. (2013) 10 Controversial Kids' Books, *MSN Living*, 2 April. http://living.msn.com/family-parenting/the-family-room-blog-post?post=65efcc07-75a5-468b-9532-47806b8be4b1 (accessed 5 April 2014).

Poncelet, B. (2005) À bâtons très très rompus . . ., *La lettre de l'enfance et de l'adolescence*, 3(61): 57–62.

Rego, P. *Famousquotes.com*. www.famousquotes.com/search/fact/141 (accessed 30 April 2014).

Robinson, L. (1991) Review of *Little Red Riding Hood*, by Charles Perrault, illus. by Beni Montresor, *The Horn Book Guide*, (July–December): 92.

Scott, C. (2005) A Challenge to Innocence: "Inappropriate Picturebooks for Young Readers", *Bookbird*, 43(1): 5–13.

Sendak, M. (1988) *Caldecott and Co.: Notes on Books and Pictures*, New York: Farrar, Straus and Giroux.

Sendak, M. (1995) Maurice Sendak, in Hopkins, L.B. (ed.) *Pauses: Autobiographical Reflections of 101 Creators of Children's Books*. New York: HarperCollins, pp. 142–143.

Tatar, M. (2003) *The Hard Facts of the Grimms' Fairy Tales*, 2nd edn. Princeton, NJ: Princeton University Press.

Tolkien, J.R.R. (1964) On Fairy-Stories, in *Tree and Leaf*. London: George Allen & Unwin, pp. 3–83.

Vandergrift, K.E. (1993) Review of Maurice Sendak's *We Are All in the Dumps with Jack and Guy*, *School Library Journal*, 39(10): 119.

Warner, M. (2000) *No Go the Bogeyman: Scaring, Lulling and Making Mock*. London: Vintage.

Zipes, J. (1993) *The Trials and Tribulations of Little Red Riding Hood: Versions of the Tale in Sociocultural Context*, 2nd edn. New York: Routledge.

Zipes, J. (2001) *Sticks and Stones: The Troublesome Success of Children's Literature from Slovenly Peter to Harry Potter*. New York: Routledge.

Children's literature

Baum, L.F., illus. Denslow, W.W. (1900) Introduction, *The Wonderful Wizard of Oz*. Chicago, IL: George M. Hill.

Belloc, H., illus. Temple Blackwood, B. (1907) *Cautionary Tales for Children: Designed for the Admonition of Children between the Ages of Eight and Fourteen years*. London: Eveleigh Nash.

Bruel, C., illus. Wachs, P. (1986) *Vous oubliez votre cheval*. Paris: Le Sourire qui mord.

Busch, W. (1990) *Max und Moritz: eine Bubengeschichte in sieben streichen*. Bindlach: Loewe Verlag.

Carrer, C. (2007) *Barbablù*. Rome: Editore Donzelli.

Clément, C., illus. Forestier, I. (2000) *Un petit chaperon rouge*. Paris: Grasset & Fasquelle.

Dayre, V., illus. Erlbruch, W. (1996) *L'ogresse en pleurs*. Toulouse: Milan.

Ekman, F. (1985) *Rødhatten og Ulven*. Oslo: Cappelen.

Grimm, W. & J., Segal, L. & Sendak, M. (1973) *The Juniper Tree and Other Tales from Grimm*, 2 vols. New York: Farrar Straus and Giroux.

Grimm, W. & J. (1980) *Kinder- und Hausmärchen Band 1, Märchen no 1-86*. Stuttgart: Philipp Reclam.

Grimm, W. & J., illus. Hyman T.S. (1983) *Little Red Riding Hood*. New York: Holiday House.

Grimm, W. & J., illus. Dumas, O. (2001) *El señor Korbes y otros cuentos de Grimm*. Valencia: Media Vaca.

Grimm, W. & J., illus. Janssen, S. (2001) *Rotkäppchen*. Munich: Carl Hanser Verlag.

Hoffman, H. (1845) *Lustige Geschichten und drollige Bilder*. Frankfurt am Main: Literarische Anstalt (J. Rütten).

Hoffman, H., adap. Ruy-Vidal, F., illus. Lapointe, C. (1972) *Pierre l'ébouriffé: Histoires pas très drôles, d'un passé toujours présent*. Boissy-St-Léger: F. Ruy-Vidal and Harlin Quist.

Hofman, W. (1998) *Zwart als inkt is het verhaal van Sneeuwwitje en de zeven dwergen*. Amsterdam: Querido.

Holzwarth, W., illus. Erlbruch, W. (1989) *Vom kleinen Maulwurf, der wissen wollte, wer ihm auf den Kopf gemacht hat*. Wuppertal: Peter Hammer Verlag.

Ikhlef, A., illus. Gauthier, A. (1998) *Mon Chaperon Rouge*. Paris: Seuil Jeunesse.

Ikhlef, A., illus. Gauthier, A. (2002) *Ma Peau d'Âne*. Paris: Seuil Jeunesse.

Innocenti, R. (1985) *Rose Blanche*. Story and illus. Innocenti, R., text Innocenti, R. & Gallaz, C., trans. Creative Education. Mankato, MN: Creative Education.

Innocenti, R. (2012) *The Girl in Red*. Story and illus. Innocenti, R., text Frisch, A. Mankato, MN: Creative Editions.

Joiret, P., illus. Bruyère, X. (1991) *Mina je t'aime*. Paris: L'École des loisirs.

Juan, A. (2001) *Snowhite*. Onil: Edicions de Ponent.

Perrault, C. (1697) *Histoires ou contes du temps passé avec moralités*. Paris: Claude Barbin.

Perrault, C., illus. Doré, G. (1861) *Les Contes de Perrault*. Paris: Pierre-Jules Hetzel.

Perrault, C. illus. Moon, S. (1983) *Little Red Riding Hood*. Mankato, MN: Creative Education.

Perrault, C., illus. Claverie, J. (1991) *La Barbe Bleue*. Paris: Albin Michel.

Perrault, C., illus. Montresor, B. (1991) *Little Red Riding Hood*. New York: Doubleday.

Perrault, C., illus. Delacroix, S. (2000) *La Barbe Bleue*. Tournai: Casterman.

Pommaux, Y. (1993) *John Chatterton détective*. Paris: L'École des loisirs.

Poncelet, B. (1997) *Chez elle ou chez elle*. Paris: Seuil Jeunesse.

Poncelet, B. (2003) *Les Cubes*. Paris: Seuil Jeunesse.

Rego, P. (2010) *Nursery Rhymes*. London: Thames & Hudson.

Sendak, M. (1963) *Where the Wild Things Are*. New York: Harper & Row.

Sendak, M. (1993) *We Are All in the Dumps with Jack and Guy*. New York: HarperCollins.

Van de Vendel, E., illus. Vandenabeele, I. (2003) *Rood Rood Roodkapje*. Wielsbeke: Uitgeverij De Eenhoorn.

4

WHO ARE THESE PICTUREBOOKS FOR?

Controversial picturebooks and the question of audience

Åse Marie Ommundsen

When reading contemporary Scandinavian picturebooks, one may wonder who they are aimed at. The two picturebooks to be discussed in this chapter are the Danish book De skæve smil *(The Crooked Smiles) (2008) by Oskar K and Lilian Brøgger, and the Norwegian book* Krigen *(The War) (2013) by Gro Dahle and Kaia Dahle Nyhus.* De skæve smil *is a challenging picturebook about aborted foetuses, 'those who never were born'.* Krigen *uses war metaphors to tell about a different kind of war, the war between two divorcing parents. Both books are existential picturebooks, illustrated in a naïve drawing style with complex multilayered narrative devices. They are challenging both thematically and in terms of their verbal and visual narrative devices. But unlike many other challenging Scandinavian picturebooks, they are also controversial and likely to offend their adult reader. What makes these picturebooks not only challenging but also highly controversial? This, in turn, leads to the question of audience: Who are these picturebooks for?*

Reading contemporary picturebooks, one may often wonder who they are aimed at. The question about audience is relevant when reading children's literature as well as contemporary adult literature that challenges traditional borders between literature for children and adults. One recent development in contemporary Norwegian literature is that the boundaries between children's and adult literature are constantly being challenged or even entirely erased. In previous research (Ommundsen, 2010a), I explored literary boundary crossing in a series of publications from 1994 to 2008. I found that traditional boundaries between literature for children and adults are frequently blurred or eliminated. This tendency occurs typically in prize-winning literature for children, young adults and adults, and can be said mainly to represent 'sophisticated' children's literature. What does this erasing of boundaries consist of, and which forms does it take? One way boundaries are being stretched is in crossover fiction, books written for children and adult readers alike. Crossover fiction has been an important subgenre in Norwegian literature since Jostein Gaarder published *Sophie's World* in 1991. My definition of crossover literature is that it is literature that addresses both an implied child reader and an implied adult reader at the same time, and not the one at the expense of the other (Ommundsen, 2006). In short, crossover literature must have a 'dual address', to use Barbara Wall's term (Wall, 1991).

Of course, crossover fiction is not only a Scandinavian phenomenon, as is pointed out in the research of Sandra Beckett (Beckett, 1999, 2009, 2011) and Rachel Falconer (2009). Beckett calls *Sophie's World* (Gaarder, 1991) 'a pre-Potter crossover hit', and refers to the Scandinavian term '*allalderlitteratur*' (literature for all ages), which was used in Scandinavia years before the English term 'crossover' appeared. Also, when discussing 'crossover picturebooks', Beckett points to Scandinavia, for good reason: crossover picturebooks are well established and accepted in Scandinavian children's literature (Ommundsen, 2006, 2010a). Further, the advances in picturebooks and numerous signs of children's literature coming of age (Nikolajeva, 1996) have led to another interesting picturebook phenomenon in Scandinavia: picturebooks for adults, a phenomenon rarely found beyond the Nordic countries (Ommundsen, 2010a, 2013).

Scandinavian crossover picturebooks

Why are so many crossover picturebooks published in the Nordic countries? Is it a question of cultural identity and the prevailing view of children and childhood in these nations? We could suggest economical, historical, political and ideological reasons for these challenging Norwegian picturebooks. Norway has the world's best economical structure for maintaining a national literature for children, the Norwegian purchasing system (*Innkjøpsordningen*) and picturebook funding. As only around five million people speak and read the Norwegian language, there is a strong need and political will to keep the language and national literature alive. Historically, Norway developed its own children's literature in the nation-building phase when the country liberated itself politically and culturally from Sweden and Demark. Culturally, Norwegians have a tradition of questioning authority. New pedagogic ideas made child-rearing in Norway less authoritarian and more dialogue oriented. From the time that the first Norwegian children's literature appeared in the second half of the nineteenth century, children's literature portrayed children as valuable and important contributors to society (Ommundsen, 1998). Ideologically, the view of children as competent, but in need of special care, is prevalent in the population. Norway was the first nation in the world to initiate a public child welfare service to secure child protection for all children (1896), and the second nation after Sweden to prohibit physical punishment of children (1972). The Norwegian school system may be criticised for lack of discipline, but it scores high on democratic citizenship (nrk.no, 2010). An important aim in the school curriculum is to teach children to discuss so that they can learn practical democracy and to be active citizens in a democratic nation based on an inclusive welfare system and values such as equality, free education, tolerance, freedom of religion and freedom of speech (NOU, 2011).

The relationship between children and adults in the family is firmly based – like the relationship between men and women – on the ideal of equality. Children are considered to be thinking human beings facing the same challenges as adults. This may explain the tendency to publish picturebooks on existential and philosophical matters common to all ages. In my first study of crossover literature (Ommundsen, 2006), I divided the crossover books into three main groups: Naïve, Complex and Existential, underlining that they often belong to more than one group at the same time.

Naïve

From the 1990s, a naïve writing and drawing style became popular in Norwegian adult fiction, with Erlend Loe's novel *Naiv.Super.* (1996) as a key example. What is often referred to as a naïve style means that the author or illustrator writes or draws in a childlike fashion, as a child would do. The naïve can be understood as a way to create art according to children's premises, or a way to implant child perspectives into art (Goga, 2011). Loe's children's books are marked by the same simple and naïve writing and drawing style as his adult novels, which makes it difficult to determine which audience the various books are aimed at.

Complex

In the same time period, the complex children's book developed into another dominant literary trend, as pointed out by Maria Nikolajeva (1996). Children's fiction became more and more complex, with polyphonic multilayered narrative structures and advanced literary devices traditionally thought of as adult. While the complexity demands cognitive skills of the reader, it also develops those skills (Kampp, 2002). Many of the complex books can be read at different levels, depending on the reader's frame of reference.

Existential

Existential picturebooks may be challenging for both children and adults alike, as they tackle crucial questions in human life: life and death, love, friendship and loneliness, identity and belonging. They might also treat subjects traditionally thought of as taboo in children's literature: war, domestic violence, child abuse, broken relationships and divorce. What might be considered taboo in some cultures may be normal in others. One example is Stian Hole's picturebook trilogy about Garmann (Hole, 2006, 2008, 2010). Garmann is a boy aged 6 to 8 years old who is depicted experiencing transitional stages in his life. In the first book he is about to start school, in the second book he lights a fire, and in the third book he develops a relationship with Johanne. The books have been awarded several prizes, and have been translated into several languages. *Garmanns sommer* (*Garmann's Summer*) is an example of how new techniques open the way for new expressions in picturebooks. When Stian Hole won the Bologna Ragazzi Award in 2006 with *Garmanns sommer*, it was the first Nordic picturebook in 45 years to win the award, and was also the first digitally created picturebook in the award's history (Rhedin, Eriksson & K, 2013). In Denmark the Garmann series evoked a debate as to whether the serious existential questions in the books were suitable for children (Christensen, 2013). In the translation for the American market, Hole had to censor two of the pictures in the third book: a picture where Garmann is urinating in the forest and a picture where Garmann and Johanne swim naked in a lake were considered unsuitable for American kids. In Norway, children playing in the nude is considered normal, and unlikely to offend anyone. What could be provocative in the Garmann books for a secular Norwegian audience are the existential questions about God and about life after death. Thus, it might be possible to reach a limit even for Norwegian openness and tolerance, but the limit is more likely to be linked to religion and spirituality. Picturebooks that make fun of God or religious beliefs are hardly considered provocative by a Norwegian audience. Two examples are *Frosken* (*The Frog*) (Sande & Moursund, 2003) and *Kurtby* (*Kurtville*) (Loe & Hiorthøy, 2008) (Ommundsen, 2010b, 2011b).

Aside from belonging to one of these categories, crossover picturebooks often simultaneously include traits from all three (the existential, naïve and complex). The two Scandinavian picturebooks to be discussed in this chapter are the Danish book *De skæve smil* (*The Crooked Smiles*) (2008) by Oskar K and Lilian Brøgger, and the Norwegian book *Krigen* (*The War*) (2013) by Gro Dahle and Kaia Dahle Nyhus. They are existential picturebooks illustrated in a naïve drawing style and with complex multilayered narrative devices. Thus they are challenging both thematically and in terms of verbal and visual narrative devices. But unlike many other challenging Scandinavian picturebooks, they are also controversial and likely to offend their adult reader. Critics have pointed to the fact that Danish and Norwegian picturebooks are more challenging than Swedish picturebooks (Rhedin, 2004; Nikolajeva, 2003). Catherine Renaud (2010) asks whether Denmark is a nation of picturebooks without taboos. She draws a historical line from the Danish authors Ole Lund Kierkegaard and Ib Spang Olsen to the contemporary picturebooks of Oskar K: 'the grotesque, particularly in the illustration and the representation of the body, but also in non-conformism and the rejection of authority, is the preferred instrument to break (down) the boundaries of decorum (politeness) and to overthrow taboos' (Renaud, 2010: 6, my translation).[1] Renaud refers to the subversive, anti-authoritarian tendency in Danish picturebooks, and her question as to whether Denmark is a nation without taboos is highly relevant when discussing the Danish book *De skæve smil* and the Norwegian book *Krigen*. The issue for discussion is: What makes these picturebooks not only challenging but also highly controversial? This, in turn, leads to the question of audience: Who are these picturebooks for?

De skæve smil (The Crooked Smiles)

The Danish author Oskar K (alias Ole Dalgaard) usually works with his wife, illustrator Dorte Karrebæk, and has published several challenging picturebooks in which the question of audience is highly relevant. As an author he explores the limits for picturebooks and for children's literature (Renaud, 2010: 14). The picturebook *De skæve smil* (Figure 4.1) (Plate 18) is the first he wrote in collaboration with illustrator Lilian Brøgger. It is a challenging picturebook about aborted foetuses, 'those who never were born' (all quotes are my translations). The word '*skæve*' or 'crooked' in the title, may refer to something bent or out of shape, the opposite of straight, or to deformed, crippled persons. Thus the title *De skæve smil* (*The Crooked Smiles*) refers to the aborted foetuses that play the leading roles in this book. To write a picturebook with aborted foetuses as main characters is original and controversial, and may be the reason why this book is hardly referred to by researchers. In a Scandinavian setting the book is controversial for the message it conveys, which is an exceptionally clear anti-abortion message. Still, more than providing answers, the book asks difficult questions about life, death and eternity, the same questions Oskar K and Dorte Karrebæk raised in another challenging picturebook published the same year, *Børnenes bedemand* (*The Children's Undertaker*) (K & Karrebæk, 2008). The book is

FIGURE 4.1 (Plate 18) *De skæve smil* by Oscar K and Lilian Brøgger (2008).

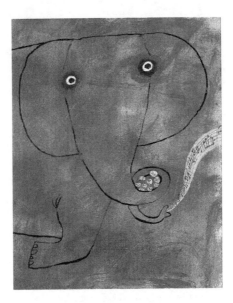

FIGURE 4.2 *De skæve smil:* The elephant's lullaby.

about Mr Jørgensen, who makes children's coffins and prepares the bodies of dead children for their funerals. Another literary device the two books have in common is the intertextual references to popular songs. In *Børnenes bedemand* the undertaker makes the dead children smile by singing for them. In *De skæve smil* the foetuses can hear women singing in the distance for their children, singing the words from the traditional Danish lullaby 'The Elephant's Lullaby' (Figure 4.2).

How to draw an aborted foetus

Most of the text in *De skæve smil* consists of dialogues between the main characters, the aborted foetuses, discussing why they were aborted and what their lives would have been like if they had been allowed to be born. Even though the text claims that they never became anyone, they did actually become someone, as the book gives them voices. By presenting the aborted foetuses the book gives the non-existent an existence – in eternity – and gives those who cannot speak a voice. They are given life through the book. The project must have been a challenge for the illustrator. How do you draw an aborted foetus? The experienced illustrator Lilian Brøgger paints them as small, crooked, but human-like characters wearing colourful clothes. They all have their unique characteristics that define them as individuals. Brøgger uses what is often referred to as a naïve drawing style, meaning she draws in a childlike way. As mentioned earlier, the naïve can be understood as a way to introduce child perspectives into art (Goga, 2011). This picturebook introduces child perspectives into the difficult adult debate on abortion, and transforms this controversial political debate into art.

The colours vary according to whether they illustrate the reality of the foetuses or their dreams. When bright colours are found in the background, they may express the children's 'pink' dreams and 'blue' longing for (happy) lives. Even if they are small and never had a life, they live in a state of eternity, and are – considering their age – highly verbal, with advanced thoughts and reflections. The text is both sad and humorous at the same time, as in the following passage where the foetuses discuss the various reasons why they were not wanted by their parents:

'I was a blunder, a fortuitous accident,' said a squinty joker.

'My mother was fourteen when she tumbled down a summer hill in summer with a boy she had hardly known for an hour.'

'My father was a clown, and my mother liked to laugh. She laughed for three evenings and nights. On free tickets. Then the circus was gone.'

. . .

'I was scanned and found too heavy,' said a little scraping

[*skrabud*] who was number eight in a family with seven siblings.

. . .

'We are leftovers from a test tube,' two Hottentots said.

'I stood in the way of my mother's career.'

'And I was removed because of a hare lip.'

'My father got cold feet.'

K & Brøgger (2008: 1–2, unpaginated)

In the original text, the word '*skrabud*' is a wordplay on two words: the original meaning of the word is a gesture of bowing the head and scraping the foot backwards, which may be translated as 'obeisance'. But in this context, the author plays with the similarity to the Danish word '*udskrab*' or '*udskrabning*', which means 'curettage' (medical scraping), part of the process performed in an abortion.

The nameless foetuses sit in the dark (literally) together with the blind old dog Sam, the world's ugliest dog (Figure 4.3). He is the only one amongst them with a name, and the only one who has ever lived. Still, as mentioned earlier, they all come to life in this book, and they all seem to live in the same state of eternity. They share their thoughts with one another on eternity and life:

They dreamed about real lives with real parents and wished for others to have a better fate than theirs. The only thing they had was thoughts, so they dreamed about a pair of twins, a boy and a girl, who would never be unhappy. They would have names and would be named Mads and Mette, and would come from a nice home with clever parents and be gifted, so that they would quickly learn to read and write and calculate.

FIGURE 4.3 *De skæve smil*: Sam and the foetuses.

But what will happen to our twins? they asked Sam, who had lived fourteen years. Sam pretended he was deaf. And they looked at him and knew that Mette and Mads would become like bad baboons that hogged down and did not wish others well but were envious and discontented with everything and everyone.

K & Brøgger (2008: 13–14) (Figure 4.4)

The children's greatest wish is to have a name, so that they can become someone: 'I would like so much to have a name . . . '. The others agreed. 'Let us ask God', the joker said. 'God', the others said. 'Does he exist?' 'Yes, yes, he does!' 'OK, so let us try.' All the crooked smiles ride away in the dark on Sam's back to find God, so that he can give them a name. When the foetuses are on their way to God, they are no longer colourful, but painted in black and white (Figure 4.5).

God is described as a soft light 'shining quietly, but so slightly that it was difficult to see in the dark'. In the illustration he is drawn as a prism or as a diamond that sheds light around itself. God's face, with eyes and mouth, can be seen in the prism, and counterpoints the verbal text's question as to whether God is at home or not. Thus the picture of the diamond-like prism challenges the text, because it may be read as an illustration of the face of God. We can see the eyes and mouth of God, and the foetuses are heading for his mouth. Kari Sønsthagen (2008) reads it differently, not as the face but as the palace of God:

The palace of God is a lamp drawn as the inner side of a great diamond, in which light and colours are majestically collected and spread, which is a big contrast to the tiny little child caricatures, that optimistically stride forward.

FIGURE 4.4 *De skæve smil*: The foetuses and their dreams.

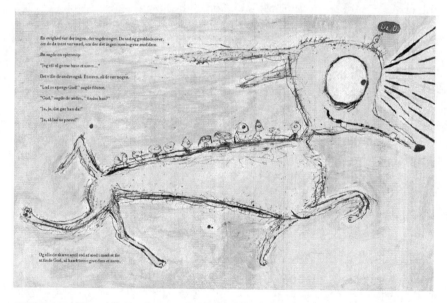

FIGURE 4.5 (Plate 19) *De skæve smil*: Sam and the foetuses on their way to God.

After Sam and the foetuses meet 'the little lamp with dusty glasses', they literally 'see the light' and everything changes. In a discussion about whether God is really there, or whether he 'only exists in dreams', Sam's final comment transforms the situation:

'Maybe we only exist in dreams', Sam said. 'Think about it, then there is someone dreaming of us', the hare lip said, astonished. And he looked so funny that the others started laughing. 'Yes, there is someone who dreams about us!' they laughed. 'And give us names', the joker said. . . . They laughed and dreamed all the names they could think of: Emma, Mathias, Mikkel and Clara, Johanne, Mohammad and Asger, Lea and Frida and Frederik and Louis, Cecilie, Julius, Alberte and Emil . . . And they all got a name. Then they returned home. Now they had names. They were someone. It happened that in the midst of the darkness someone called: 'Hey, Emma! It is Frederik. Are you there?' 'Yes, I am.'

K & Brøgger (2008: 25–28)

In the Bible, the meaning of names is of great importance, and links important qualities with the person. 'I am' is a direct reference to the Old and the New Testament, to God's name in Hebrew, 'YHWH', a form derived from the verb 'to be'. In Hebrew, the words 'I am' and 'YHWH' form a wordplay (Exodus 3:14–15; John 8: 24–58). It is not clear whether it is God who gives the foetuses names or whether they give one another names. In the Bible, God tells Adam to give names to all the animals, in order to find his own match (Genesis 2). Even more important than to receive a name from God, is the foetuses giving names to each other. By naming others, the foetuses define themselves as human beings, and thus become someone. The encounter with God and their new names alters everything, and this is underlined by the change of colours in the pictures. By receiving names, they have got an identity and become someone, so that they can answer, 'I am'. The picture on this final spread is not dark, as the text might suggest, but quite the contrary: beautiful pastel colours of blue, pink, green and yellow fill the whole doublespread. The children are smiling, they are flying. Even Sam is changed. He is also smiling, and for the first time he has normal eyes, he doesn't look blind any more. The foetuses are floating inside different elements: a plane, a hat, a car, a house, a star, a tree, a fish, symbolising things the foetuses dream and long for.

An ethical and political debate on prenatal diagnosis

The book was published in 2008, four years after early ultrasound scanning at 12 weeks of pregnancy was introduced in Danish prenatal care. This scanning, also called neck-fold-scanning, is done in order to discover and abort foetuses with Down's syndrome. Since then, 99 per cent of foetuses with Down's syndrome have been aborted in Denmark. Other, less serious diagnoses can also be discovered through this scan method; for instance 87 per cent of the foetuses with Turner's syndrome were aborted (Damgaard, 2012). In 2009 *Etisk råd*, the Ethical Council, presented a list of conditions that should be checked in the scan and those that should not. Their recommendation list is called 'Future's prenatal diagnosis'. After the new ultrasound diagnostics was implemented in pregnancy care, it was said that

Denmark was about to become a society without people with Down's syndrome. *De skæve smil* can be seen as part of the Danish debate on abortion and the future prenatal diagnosis. There was a similar debate in Norway. In the Norwegian political debate about the right to early ultrasound diagnostics, the possibility of discovering and removing foetuses with Down's syndrome at an early stage of pregnancy was discussed. Unlike in Denmark, the proposal was rejected. In 2014 strong feelings were again aroused in the Norwegian debate, as the government suggested giving doctors the right to refuse to refer women for abortion. It was not meant to be a debate on abortion, but turned out to be that as well. In 2014, at the official celebration of the 200th jubilee of the Norwegian constitution (1814–2014), one of the speakers was Marthe Wexelsen Goksøyr, who herself has Down's syndrome. 'I want to live', she concluded in her speech. Not only her speech, but also the fact that she was asked to speak, was considered provocative in the ensuing debate, as if it were a way of criticising women who abort foetuses with Down's syndrome. 'They shouldn't have let her speak, as the exclusion society is too controversial a theme', people argued in the following debate (*Vårt Land*, 2014). No one questioned the political correctness of any of the other contributors representing other, uncontroversial minorities such as immigrants and the indigenous Sami people. On 8 March 2014, a record number of participants joined the International Women's Day parades, marching under the slogan of women's right to abortion and against the new proposal to allow doctors to refuse patients referrals for abortion. If there still can be said to be any taboos left in Scandinavia, I would suggest that to be against abortion is one of the biggest. This is why *De skæve smil* is considered a controversial picturebook in Scandinavia.

Who is this picturebook for?

Who is this picturebook for? The first time I borrowed a copy of the book from a Danish library, there was a big library stamp on the book saying 'Not to be loaned to children'. In a Danish review it is called a picturebook for older children, young adults and adults (Nørholm, 2008). Even though Denmark doesn't have a category of 'picturebooks for adults' one could argue that this may be called a picturebook for adults. One could also call it a crossover picturebook, as it can be read by children and adults alike. With the author himself reading the book on his own webpage (www.oscar-k.dk/), the book is made more easily accessible for (Danish) children. It would certainly be an interesting book to study in schools, and in a Norwegian school context listening to the Danish author may also help children gain a general understanding of a neighbouring country and its language. *De skæve smil* may also be relevant for young adults, with its ethical questions and important discussions on life, death and eternity. Even though the book would probably be catalogued as a picturebook for adults under the Norwegian system, this does not mean it would not be interesting for children and young adults. The Norwegian school curriculum is full of adult literature that is presented to children. The question is, as always, how it is done. I would argue this is a picturebook for adults published as an argument against abortion. But it is also a book that can be enjoyed by children, who might read it on another level, as a fantastic story about unborn children travelling on a dog to find God. For a child, to be against abortion is not very controversial. On the contrary, most children would probably question why on earth adults would kill foetuses. But for adults, who know more about the complex reality, the standpoint might be both controversial and provocative, as one could see at the 8 March 2014 parade in Norway. *De skæve smil* addresses adults with a challenging and controversial anti-abortion message. But in doing so, the authors feel obliged to defend the mothers. When the aborted foetuses are thinking about their mothers, longing for home, they don't judge them:

> And they thought about their mothers and remembered how alone their mothers had been. Their doubt, their fear, their good intentions. And the tears. Silence befell the Crooked Smiles. Did their mothers cry over them? Were they so unhappy that they had not wanted them to live? Had their lives been so meaningless? Was life so poor? The longer they thought, the more doubtful they became. What would have become of them if they had been allowed to live?
>
> *K & Brøgger (2008: 21–22) (Figure 4.6)*

The picture of a weeping mother illustrates that the mothers themselves are victims. Depicted on a background of corrugated cardboard, painted green, a women's face is drawn as roads through a green landscape. Her face is shown in profile, yet her gaze looks directly at us. Her eye is like a lake in the landscape, with a big tear dropping out of it. A small house and some trees are drawn into her hair, representing

FIGURE 4.6 *De skæve smil*: The weeping mother.

the mother's wish for a future. She is painted in green, the colour of growth and new life. If the message is that the mothers are not to blame, but they play the victim role alongside the aborted foetuses, who are the antagonists of the narrative? Ingjerd Traavik writes about the book that, 'The aborted foetuses in the book call upon us from lonely eternity and make us feel empathy both for the foetuses and their mothers' (Traavik, 2012: 154).

Krigen (The War)

The second picturebook I would like to discuss is *Krigen* (2013) by Gro Dahle and Kaia Dahle Nyhus (Figure 4.7). Gro Dahle is a Norwegian crosswriter who is known for the challenging and controversial crossover picturebooks she makes together with her husband, the illustrator Svein Nyhus. They have published crossover picturebooks on existential issues such as invisibility, *Snill* (*Kind*) (Dahle & Nyhus, 2002); anger, *Bak Mumme bor Moni* (*Behind Mumme lives Moni*) (Dahle & Nyhus, 2000); violence, *Sinna Mann* (*Angry Man*) (Dahle & Nyhus, 2003); and mental illness, *Håret til mamma* (*Mum's Hair*) (Dahle & Nyhus, 2007). *Sinna Mann* (Dahle & Nyhus, 2003), which is about domestic violence, was adapted into a prize-winning animation film (2009). The book is challenging, as domestic violence is still a problem and has been a taboo subject. It has been used by schools in order to identify this kind of violence in the home, the message being, 'tell someone about it'. In some cases this has led the Child Welfare Service to take children away from their families and into foster care in order to protect them,

FIGURE 4.7 *Krigen* by Gro Dahle and Kaia Dahle Nyhus (2013).

and their parents have received prison sentences. Even though the book is challenging, it is not controversial in the sense that it is likely to offend anyone, as domestic violence is not considered acceptable in the Norwegian population apart from with a few immigrant groups. It would hardly be considered politically correct in any sector of Norwegian society to defend domestic violence.

Another war

In the crossover picturebook *Krigen* (Dahle & Nyhus, 2013), Gro Dahle works with her daughter Kaia Dahle Nyhus as illustrator. War ceased to be a controversial theme in Norwegian picturebooks after the publication of Gunilla Bergström's *Albert Åberg og soldatpappaen* (*Alfie Atkins and the Soldier Dad*) in 2006 (Ommundsen, 2011a). But this book is about a different kind of war, the war between two divorcing parents. As with the other Dahle/Nyhus crossover picturebooks, this one also challenges the reader both verbally and visually. It is more controversial and may be considered provocative, as it touches upon divorce as a main challenge in Norwegian society, in a non politically correct way. Divorce is so common in Norwegian society (almost 50 per cent of all couples are divorced), that it is no longer questioned. In 2013 in Norway, 23,400 couples were married and 9,700 divorced (*Statistisk sentralbyrå*, 2014). Among couples who cohabit without being married, more than 50 per cent split up. In 2012, there were 9,906 divorces, and 9,635 children under 18 experienced their parents divorcing (*Statistisk sentralbyrå*, 2014). Divorce is so common that, although research shows many children suffer from their parents' divorce, it is not a common subject for discussion. Commuting between two homes is considered normal for a Norwegian child, and is depicted in children's literature and children's television as the normal way of living, and seldom discussed as a problem. In fact, divorced parents may seem over-represented in Scandinavian children's literature. There are several books about divorce, but only a few of them deal with divorce as a problem and point to the dramatic long-term negative effects a divorce may have on the children involved. Some books do point to the negative effects the divorce may have on the abandoned parent, such as *Knute* (*Knot*) (Hagen & Düzakin, 2007). Other books on the subject are marketed as 'warm, humorous and optimistic' stories about divorce, such as *Ulla hit og dit* (*Ulla here and there*) (Tinnen & Dokken, 2010). *Krigen* is not warm, humorous or optimistic. Dahle and Dahle Nyhus use war metaphors to discuss divorce and the 50/50 existence of children who have to commute between two different homes. They write about the negative effects a divorce may have on a child, viewed from a child's perspective, and depict a divorce as a dramatic war scene, where the main character, Inga, suffers greatly.

The book starts with references to the phenomenon of war, as children would know it. Already on the title page, two guns are drawn into the title of the book *The War*, written in big fonts (called 'war typefaces' in Norwegian). A child with a peace symbol on her shirt is drawn under the title. Thus, even before the story begins, it is posed as a story about war and peace. On the first double-page spread (Figure 4.8), the verbal text is about war as we know it from the news:

> War exists.
> Inga knows, that war exists,
> because there has always been war,
> and there is war
> in many places outside in the world.
> Inga knows.
> Inga has seen pictures of war in the newspaper.
> She has seen soldiers with helmets on their head.
> She has seen guns
> and fire and smoke
> and holes in the wall after shootings
> and holes in the ground after bombs
> and tanks that can drive everywhere,
> straight over grain and grass and animals and human beings,
> straight over houses and grain fields.
>
> *Dahle & Dahle Nyhus*
> *(2013: 1–2, unpaginated) (all quotes are my translation)*

The picture shows Inga reading the newspaper. She is in the foreground and in focus in the picture. Smaller, but also in focus, we can see two small boys playing at war, one of them holding a gun in his hand. They are Inga's twin brothers, Lars and Ola. In the background, barely visible, two adults are sitting on the sofa, the man with his arm around the woman. Or perhaps not: they might have left the

FIGURE 4.8 *Krigen*: Inga and her brothers.

sofa, as we can only see a space they left behind, their shadowy contours without defining black outlines, and their eyes and other details are missing. Inga is drawn entirely in orange, and her brothers all in blue, but her parents are marked by the lack of colour, light green like the wall and the floor carpet. Using her drawing technique and the visual narratology, Dahle Nyhus warns the reader that the relationship between the parents is about to end, and they will not sit together like this on the sofa any more. Also, the look on Inga's face is troubled, while her brothers are occupied in playing. The text on the first page parallels war as Inga knows it from the news with the war Inga is about to experience in her own life: her parents' war. The poetic, repetitive language is filled with war metaphors that foreshadow Inga's feelings: gun, fire, smoke and holes after shooting and bombs will soon be felt on her own body. Later, in a very dramatic picture, the parallel is expressed directly by portraying Inga with a big hole in her body (Figure 4.9). The tanks driving over everything parallel and foreshadow Inga's feeling of being run over.

The war parallel is contrasted in the next doublespread, showing the happy family laughing together. The text tells a happy story of a happy family in a peaceful country: 'The world's best family, Inga thinks'. This is the only spread where text and picture are both positive, and the only picture in which all the family members look happy and smiling. In the next spread the mood totally changes. Words and illustration depict a fierce conflict between the parents. The parents are drawn with angry faces, and Inga looks frightened: The war has begun (Figure 4.10). The conflict and quarrelling between the parents escalates throughout the following spreads. This is underlined both in the text and in the dramatic pictures. The dramatic expression of the escalating conflict may be considered challenging for children, as was pointed out in one of the reviews: 'The combination of a painful

FIGURE 4.9 *Krigen*: Inga with a hole through her body.

FIGURE 4.10 *Krigen*: The parents at war.

theme and violent pictures makes *Krigen* almost too powerful' (Djuve, 2013). I would suggest that the book may be even more challenging for adults.

Inga's parents do not behave as responsible adults, because they are concerned with their own problems and cannot see that Inga is upset. Inga takes on responsibility for everyone: she behaves like a good girl, looks after her brothers, and later also after her father's new child. Her father is in love with a new woman, and unable to take good care of his children. Her mother is concerned with her own grief process and later also falls in love with a new partner. Inga is exhausted by moving between the two houses. She doesn't have a place where she feels at home. She has become homeless like a refugee, and also feels she has to play the role of a spy, another war metaphor. She is exhausted by having to take care of her brothers, take the bus and remember their bags. She is constantly travelling back and forth, and is exhausted by it.

> Dad sweats, smiles and laughs.
> For Dad is getting married again.
> And Mum has friends who call.
> And Lars has Ola, and Ola has Lars,
> but Inga has no one,
> for Inga travels and travels
> back and forth to school,
> back and forth to Dad,
> back and forth to Mum,
> back and forth, back and forth
> with announcements, letters, messages,
> everything she must remember,
> so that Inga gets dizzy and sick.
>
> *Dahle & Dahle Nyhus (2013: 23)*

FIGURE 4.11 *Krigen*: Inga's suffering.

Her head is full of noises from the war, and she starts to forget her belongings, her homework, everything (Figure 4.11). Inga's suffering escalates to a state where she stops eating, is unable to sleep and starts self-mutilating, cutting herself until she bleeds, as the pictures also show. Her name, Inga, means 'nobody', and this is how she feels. As her parents are concerned with themselves, they actually don't see her, and because she hides her tears they think she is alright. Her invisibility is a recurring theme in other books by Gro Dahle and Svein Nyhus, such as the picturebook *Snill* (Dahle & Nyhus, 2002), in which Lussi disappears into the wall. When Inga becomes visible for her mother again, she can finally say how tired she is and how exhausting it has been to live in a war zone. And even when the war is over, and the rest of the family have gone back to normal life, the war is still waging inside Inga – it has moved into her body. The picture expands the text, and shows that Inga is still challenged by her parents' new families.

The final spread suggests a more harmonious ending, probably to comfort the child reader (Figure 4.12) (Plate 20). But adult readers may still feel uneasy, knowing that they bear responsibility for their children's sense of security and peace. *Krigen* is certainly a challenging and controversial book, especially for adults.

So who is this book for? I would suggest it is a crossover book for both children and adults, but as in the case with *De skæve smil*, the main message is for the adult reader. As in Dahle and Nyhus' other books about psychological processes, this crossover picturebook also has one message for the implied child reader and another message for the implied adult reader (Ommundsen, 2004). Dahle and Dahle Nyhus describe the divorce from the child's perspective, taking the child's feelings seriously, trying to provide hope of relief from the trauma in the future. For the implied adult reader, the message is to be a responsible parent, to put aside one's own grief, disappointment or happiness, and instead to put the child's interests

FIGURE 4.12 (Plate 20) *Krigen*: The war is over.

first. The book can also be seen as an argument in the debate about the desirable norm after divorce, as it questions the norm in which children divide their time between their parents and live every other week with the mother or father. Is this an arrangement that only caters to what is best for the adults instead of what is best for the child? As this split child existence is generally regarded as an acceptable and common way to organise family life with children after divorce in Norway, this picturebook can be seen as controversial and provoking. Nonetheless, it has been nominated for the prestigious Nordic Council children's literature award of 2014. Another picturebook looking at the subject of divorce and nominated for the same prestigious award is the Danish picturebook *To af alting* (*Two of Everything*) (Kvist, 2013). This book is about a boy who feels his world is falling apart due to his parents' divorce. His parents tell him he will have two of everything because they are getting divorced, but the boy feels surrounded by half things, visually expressed in the pictures as a halved house, halved piano, halved TV and halved sofa. Also this picturebook maintains the child's perspective, and says divorce does not happen for the sake of the child.

Conclusion: a question of audience

According to Knud E. Løgstrup, there are two normal positions in life: to be carried by another person, or to carry another person. Life oscillates between the two positions (Løgstrup, 1956). The question is whether contemporary living conditions should be the same for children and adults alike, or whether childhood should ideally be some sort of shielded life phase in which you can be carried. If that is the case, then there must be adults who are willing to carry, who are prepared to act as adults (Ommundsen, 2010a: 52).

The two challenging picturebooks discussed here have children as protagonists, and adults who do not protect their children. In the Danish picturebook *De skæve smil*, the protagonists are the smallest, most vulnerable children of all, the aborted foetuses who were not wanted by their parents, and were therefore never born. They reflect upon how life would have been if they had been born, and understand that in the end they probably would not have got the happy life they dream of. To see life from an aborted foetus' viewpoint is probably a new experience for most readers, children and adults alike. The book will be read differently depending on whether it is read as an argument in the debate about abortion (as adults may do, and which may support the argument that it is a picturebook for adults), or simply as a fantasy narrative about some foetuses looking for God (as children might read it, and which may support the argument that it is a crossover book). The book can be read by children, young adults and adults, perhaps preferably together, as the subject would probably need explanation. As a crossover book it has the potential to stimulate interesting discussions about life, death and eternity. I have argued that it may be challenging both for children and adults, but controversial mainly for adults. The same could apply to the Norwegian picturebook *Krigen*. It is a crossover picturebook with a visually dramatic form of expression, which should preferably also be read by children and adults together. Most children will have seen their parents' angry faces at some time, even if they are not divorced, and can possibly recognise at least some of Inga's fear, and the wish to hide in the wardrobe. For some children who have been through a divorce, the book may confirm their own experiences. But for other children divorce may not have been a dramatic experience. Still, the story may be read as a true story. And each divorce is different, as the book emphasises.

The changed relations between children and adults in recent modern society provides an opportunity for crossover picturebooks that challenge traditional boundaries for children's books. To check whether a book is actually still for children, we should look for the implied reader, or model reader in the book, to see whether only an adult, or also an implied child reader is inscribed into the text (Eco, 1979; Iser, 1974).

Zohar Shavit asks the important question of whether crossover literature is really written for children, or whether the child reader is in fact ignored. Is the child reader merely a pseudo addressee, an excuse for the book (Shavit, 1999)? Barbara Wall (1991) demonstrates that analyses of how the narrator addresses the narratee in literature for children show that many authors of children's literature do not address children at all, but are more concerned with pleasing the adult reader. This is what Wall calls a 'double address'. Wall argues that more than *what* is being said, it is *how* it is said, and *to whom*, that distinguishes children's literature from literature for adults. In the challenging picturebooks discussed here, the authors are no longer concerned with pleasing the adult reader. Quite the opposite: the authors want to challenge the adult reader, and do so through a picturebook seemingly published for children. With such a strong message to the adult, one may argue whether these books have a double or dual address, according to Wall's terms. In my opinion they may be said to communicate to children and adults at different levels, which might suggest a double address. However, I would argue that in both books the narrator addresses both a child and an adult narratee at the same time, and not one at the expense of the other, and thus they both have a 'dual address', according to Wall's definition. The narrators do not exclude the child reader. Quite the contrary, the narrators are on the children's side and narrate from the children's viewpoint.

In order to answer the question, 'Who are these books for?' we can look for signs of childness, following Peter Hollindale (1997). As already mentioned, the discussed crossover picturebooks are consequently on the children's side, and see the world from their viewpoint. This may be why the questions asked are so difficult, serious and honest. Children are known for asking difficult questions, and for continuing to ask until they understand what is going on in the world. With their thought-provoking picturebooks, Dahle and K continue to ask and to challenge. As one of the reviewers wrote about Oskar K: 'Alone or together with his wife, the illustrator Dorte Karrebæk, [Oskar K] regularly shakes up the more or less firm ground of children's books' (*Information*, 2008).

The challenge of the boundaries between children's and adult literature is one of the ways in which late modern literature reflects a society where limits are constantly challenged, and where the borders between childhood and adult life are changing and partly erased. However, there still is a difference between being a child and being an adult, and I suggest that there is a boundary for what is and is not children's literature. True children's literature must also be for children, thus it must (also) address a child reader. It is not the book's content that decides whether a child reader is addressed or not, but rather the ways of writing: Who does the narrator's voice address?

Note

1 '[L]e grotesque, en particulier dans l'illustration et la representation des corps, mais aussi dans l'anticonformisme et les refus de l'autorité, est l'instrument privilégié pour sortir des frontières de la beinséance, pour renverser les tabous' (Renaud, 2010: 6).

Academic references

Beckett, S. (1999) *Transcending Boundaries: Writing for a Dual Audience of Children and Adults*. New York: Garland.

Beckett, S. (2009) *Crossover Fiction: Global and Historical Perspectives*. New York: Routledge.

Beckett, S. (2011) *Crossover Picturebooks: A Genre for All Ages*. New York: Routledge.

Christensen, N. (2013) Contemporary Picturebooks in the Nordic Countries. Concepts of Literature and Childhood, in Å. M. Ommundsen (ed.) *Looking Out and Looking In: National Identity in Picturebooks of the New Millennium*. Oslo: Novus, pp. 182–194.

Damgaard, S. (2012) Accessed at www.b.dk/nationalt/der-foedes-langt-faerre-boern-med-downs

Djuve, M.T. (2013) Accessed at www.dagbladet.no/2013/10/07/kultur/anmeldelser/litteratur/litteraturanmeldelser/bok/29452040/

Eco, U. (1979) *The Role of the Reader: Explorations in the Semiotics of Texts*. Bloomington, IN: Indiana University Press.

Falconer, R. (2009) *The Crossover Novel: Contemporary Children's Fiction and Its Adult Readership*. New York: Routledge.

Goga, N. (2011) Bildebokkritikken og det naïve, *Nordic Journal of ChildLit Aesthetics*, 2.

Hollindale, P. (1997) *Signs of Childness in Children's Books*. Stroud: The Thimble Press.

Information.dk. (2008) Drengesnd, drengestreger og skæve smil, 28 July 2008.

Iser, W. (1974) *The Implied Reader: Patterns of Communication in Prose Fiction from Bunyan to Beckett*. London: Johns Hopkins University Press.

Kampp, B. (2002) *Barnet og den voksne i det børnelitterære rum*. Copenhagen: Danmarks Pedagogiske Universitet.

Løgstrup, K.E (1956) *Den etiske fordring*. Copenhagen: Gyldendal.

Nikolajeva, M. (1996) *Children's Literature Comes of Age: Toward a New Aesthetic*. New York: Garland.

Nikolajeva, M. (2003) Danska bilderböcker gjärvere än svenska, *Opsis Kalopsis. om barn- och ungdomskultur*, No 1.

Nørholm, S. (2008) Med vid og poesi, *Kristeligt Dagblad*, 8 November 2008.

NOU (2011) Accessed at www.regjeringen.no/nb/dep/bld/dok/nouer/2011/nou-2011-20/4.html?id=668760

nrk.no (2010) Accessed at www.nrk.no/norge/norske-elever-skarer-hoyt-1.7190285

Ommundsen, Å.M. (1998) *Djevelfrø og englebarn: synet på barn i kristne barneblader i perioden 1875–1910. (Devil Seeds and Little Angels: The View upon Children in Christian Children's Magazines from 1875–1910)*, No 1. Institutt for nordistikk og litteraturvitenskap, Seksjon for nordisk språk og litteratur, Universitetet i Oslo, Oslo.

Ommundsen, Å.M. (2004) Girl Stuck in the Wall: Narrative Changes in Norwegian Children's Literature Exemplified by the Picture Book *Snill, Bookbird*, 42(1): 24–26.

Ommundsen, Å.M. (2006) All-alder-litteratur. Litteratur for alle eller ingen? (Crossover fiction. Fiction for all or for no one?), in Sverdrup, J.E.o.K. (ed.) *Kartet og terrenget: linjer og dykk i barne- og ungdomslitteraturen*. Oslo: Pax, pp. 50–70.

Ommundsen, Å.M. (2010a) *Litterære grenseoverskridelser. Når grensene mellom barne- og voksenlitteraturen viskes ut (Literary Boundary Crossings. Erasing the Borders between Literature for Children and Adults)*. Oslo: Universitetet i Oslo.

Ommundsen, Å.M. (2010b) På vei mot barnelitteraturens grense? Erlend Loes *Kurtby* (2008) (Towards the Limit of Children's Literature? Erlend Loe's *Kurtby*). *Barnboken – tidskrift för barnlitteraturforskning*, (1).

Ommundsen, Å.M. (2011a) Childhood in a multicultural society? Globalization, childhood and cultural diversity in Norwegian children's literature, *Bookbird*, 49(1): 31–40.

Ommundsen, Å.M. (2011b) A World of Permanent Change Transformed into Children's Literature: The Post-Secular Age Reflected in Late Modern Norwegian Children's Literature, in Weldy, L. (ed.) *Crossing Textual Boundaries in International Children's Literature*. Newcastle upon Tyne: Cambridge Scholars Publishing, pp. 1–19.

Ommundsen, Å.M. (2013) *Looking Out and Looking In: National Identity in Picturebooks of the New Millennium*. Oslo: Novus Press.

Renaud, C. (2010) Danemark: le pays des albums sans tabous? (Denmark: The nation of picturebooks without taboos?), *Nous voulons lire!* 186.

Rhedin, U. (2004) Med ryggen vänd mot förnyelsen, *Dagens Nyheter*, 6 September 2004.

Rhedin, U., Eriksson, L. & K, O. (2013) *En Fanfar för bilderboken!* (Vol. 122). Skärhamn, Sweden: Museet.

Shavit, Z. (1999) The Double Attribution of Texts for Children and How It Affects Writing for Children, in Beckett, S. (ed.) *Transcending Boundaries: Writing for a Dual Audience of Children and Adults*. New York: Garland.

Sønsthagen, K. (2008) Oscar K og Lilian Brøgger. De skæve smil, *Berlingske Tidende*, 21 June 2008.

Statistisk sentralbyrå (ssb). (2014) Accessed at www.ssb.no/ekteskap/ Lesedato 15 May 2014.

Traavik, I. (2012) *På liv og død: tabu i bildeboka : analyser og refleksjoner*. Oslo: Gyldendal akademisk.

Vårt Land (2014) www.vl.no/mobile/samfunn/jeg-er-ikke-syk-jeg-har-et-ekstra-kromosom-og-jeg-vil-leve-1.65389

Wall, B. (1991) *The Narrator's Voice: The Dilemma of Children's Fiction*. Basingstoke: Macmillan.

Children's literature

Bergström, G. (2006) *Albert Åberg og soldatpappaen*. Oslo: Cappelen.

Dahle, G. & Nyhus Dahle, K. (2013) *Krigen*. Oslo: Cappelen Damm.

Dahle, G. & Nyhus, S. (2000) *Bak Mumme bor Moni*. Oslo: Cappelen.

Dahle, G. & Nyhus, S. (2002) *Snill*. Oslo: Cappelen.

Dahle, G. & Nyhus, S. (2003) *Sinna Mann*. Oslo: Cappelen.

Dahle, G. & Nyhus, S. (2007) *Håret til mamma*. Oslo: Cappelen.

Gaarder, J. (1991) *Sofies verden: roman om filosofiens historie*. Oslo: Aschehoug.

Hagen, O. & Düzakin, A. (2007) *Knute*. Oslo: Samlaget.

Hole, S. (2006) *Garmanns sommer*. Oslo: Cappelen.

Hole, S. (2008) *Garmanns gate (Garmann's Street)*. Oslo: Cappelen Damm.

Hole, S. (2010) *Garmanns hemmelighet (Garmann's Secret)*. Oslo: Cappelen Damm.

K, O. & Brøgger, L. (2008) *De skæve smil*. Copenhagen: Klematis.

K, O. & Karrebæk, D. (2008) *Børnenes bedemand*. Copenhagen: Gyldendal.

Kvist, H. (2013) *To af alting*. Copenhagen: Gyldendal.

Loe, E. (1996) *Naiv. Super: roman*. Oslo: Cappelen.

Loe, E. & Hiorthøy, K. (2008) *Kurtby*. Oslo: Cappelen Damm.

Sande, H. & Moursund, G. (2003) *Frosken*. Oslo: Gyldendal.

Tinnen, K. & Dokken, S. (2010) *Ulla hit og dit*. Oslo: Gyldendal.

PART II

Controversy and ambiguity in the art of the visual

5

FUSION TEXTS – THE NEW KID ON THE BLOCK

What are they and where have they come from?

Janet Evans

This chapter will define what fusion texts are, prior to looking at their evolution with reference to comics, graphic novels and picturebooks. It will look at some of the difficulties of terminology, audience and content before focusing in particular on the work of Dave McKean, both alone and in collaboration with other authors and fusion text creators. The chapter will argue that fusion texts are challenging, often troubling texts in both their content and illustrative style but that as a genre they are here to stay.

> . . . the narratives of McKean's books are constructed through a powerful fusion of generic conventions, a combination that prompts the reader to stay constantly alert, assessing the nature of word – image interaction on each page, and switching from one mode of interpretation to another.
>
> *Panaou & Michaelides (2011: 66)*

There will be some kind of visual text – a comic, graphic novel, picturebook or illustrated text to suit most readers. Additionally, there is now a new kid on the block! A different kind of book is emerging, one that exhibits some, but not always all, of the characteristics normally thought of as belonging to comics, graphic novels and picturebooks. These books blur the boundaries, blending the characteristics of visual texts to create 'a category that is a synthesis of aspects from all of them' (Evans, 2011: 53). These are 'fusion' texts.

Fusion texts are the evolving multifaceted and multimodal close relation of comics and graphic novels and their characteristics show a merging of features from comics and graphic novels with those from picturebooks where text and image work together in harmony or discordantly. This is resulting in a form of cross-breed, hybrid text which is breaking new ground in terms of visual texts and which is providing the platform for many innovative author/illustrators to be inventive with their thoughts and ideas.

The Wolves in the Walls by Neil Gaiman and Dave McKean (2003) is one such text (Figure 5.1). It was inspired by a nightmare that Gaiman's 4-year-old daughter had that there were wolves in the walls of their house. It is an unusual, somewhat disturbing story that the reader knows is unbelievable but somehow it seems believable. In illustrating the book, McKean utilises many different techniques, including drawing, computer-generated imagery, photography and photomontage, to achieve an effect that complements but at the same time often fragments the text.

Ten-year-old Edward summarised the story:

> *The Wolves in the Walls* is about a family in a big house that has wolves in the walls. One night the wolves come out of the wall and chase the family out of the house. The wolves cause chaos and mischief and a massive mess. After a while the family retake the house and tidy the mess. But now . . . strange elephant noises are coming from . . . the walls! This book makes the reader think of whether the wolves are real or imaginary or whether the family is scared of noise!
>
> *Edward*

The Wolves in the Walls is a true fusion text, the cover implies that something really is in the walls of Lucy's house but the pencil in her hand and the childlike drawing makes the viewer question if the wolves are real or not. Yet in playing with these thoughts we note that the eyes of the wolf are disturbingly real . . . are they real? In fact they are more real than real, they are hyperreal (see Figures 5.1 and 5.4)

Jeff Garrett states, 'Hyperrealism is art that is convincingly real, but so real in our perception of it – so uber-real or hyperreal – that we are drawn to it with our eyes open. Hyperrealism is therefore not trickery, but seduction' (Garrett, 2013: 149).

Fusion texts very often include this element of seduction! The 'real' wolves' eyes are looking out at the viewer in a penetrating manner. They draw the viewer

FIGURE 5.1 *The Wolves in the Wall* by Neil Gaiman and Dave McKean (2003).

inwards making them wonder what is inside, what are the wolves doing and where does the girl come in? The eyes look real and therefore are real in our minds, even though we know they are not real and in fact, never existed. In writing about hyperrealism Umberto Eco (1986) considered the viewer's faith in fakes whereby false things are created to look more real than real . . . made to look hyperreal.

It is evident that McKean is a practitioner of hyperrealism, he uses traces of hyperrealism in his work, 'melding incredibly, credibly real and fantastic elements into a convincing new whole transcending the confused and flawed versions of truth we experience in our real-world existences' (Garrett, 2013: 148).

In looking at the artificial perfection of the real in hyperrealism, Garrett considers how surrealism as an art movement also gives us 'blatantly real, indeed impossible images made of realistically portrayed building blocks, that combined seem to correspond to a different – and even higher – form of reality' (2013: 155). McKean's art is this kind of art, a fusion of differing realities that draw the reader into thinking that what is being viewed is believable when we know it is unbelievable.

Young readers are able to pick up these hyperreal/surreal fused nuances, which in this picturebook lead them to question if the story could actually be real. Having illustrated the book cover (Figure 5.2),

FIGURE 5.2 Ten-year-old Molly's illustration for the book cover of *The Wolves in the Walls*.

10-year-old Molly wrote:

> This book is great. The pictures are not like normal pictures in picturebooks they are a combination of cartoons, photographs and drawings with words everywhere, not just going from one side of the page to the other but up and down and across the page. It's a bit like a comic with speech bubbles and little boxes everywhere. My favourite pages are where the wolves come out of the walls – that's scary –and where the wolf plays the trombone I also like it at the end where Lucy talks to pig puppet [Figure 5.3] [Plate 21].
>
> *Molly*

In a close consideration of Dave McKean's art, Panaou and Michaelides looked at how it 'breaks conventions, resists categorisation, subverts reading expectations, and yet is highly successful in communicating powerful and engaging stories' (2011: 63). They noted that *The Wolves in the Walls* is the kind of visual text whereby the viewer has to suspend belief as they interact with the book:

> One could say that the walls represent the borders between reality and fiction, which the mind can easily transgress, as Lucy does, and as the creators of the book do, showing that there are really no borders. The relations and contrasts between text and illustrations are so intense, and the combinations and alterations so vivid, that you have to go along and agree with them.
>
> *Panaou & Michaelides (2011: 66)*

The wolf's eye looking from inside the walls symbolise the borders between reality and fiction, our mind tells us the eyes are real . . . maybe there are no real borders (Figure 5.4).

FIGURE 5.3 (Plate 21) *The Wolves in the Wall*: The wolves came out of the walls.

FIGURE 5.4   *The Wolves in the Wall:* A wolf's eye looking from inside the wall.

Moving from comics, graphic novels and picturebooks to fusion texts

Comics and graphic novels are still viewed, by many, in a different light to picture-books. They have been the catalyst that has turned many children and adults, who could read, but didn't want to, into readers. Countless numbers of children and young adults love to read them and yet they are still seen by many as the poor relation of other written and illustrated texts. Although both genres show a strong unity between word and image, they do not share the same ideological frameworks. Picturebooks can serve a pedagogical function, they celebrate socially prized literacy – the teaching of reading – whilst comics are seen as being against, indeed even obstructing, this highly prized type of literacy (Hatfield & Svonkin, 2012). Joseph states that comics, in particular alternative comics, can actually disturb the reader as they resist the norms of book culture and subvert the notion of children's literature (Joseph, 2012).

Things are changing. A new breed of visual text is emerging, the fusion text. It is a 'new kid on the block', one that is presenting challenging and thought-provoking reading material in creative, artistic forms.

It was Will Eisner, the legendary cartoonist and author of *Comics and Sequential Art,* and the man who pioneered the comic-art field, who noted that since the 1980s things have changed radically and comics and graphic novels are now much more widely accepted, with the genre being extensively studied and researched academically. He was aware that 'sequential art' had been ignored for many decades for reasons linked to 'usage, subject matter and perceived audience'. In attempting to identify some of the reasons for the evident lack of status, Eisner noted, 'unless more comics addressed subjects of greater moment they could not, as a genre, hope for serious intellectual review . . ."great artwork alone is not enough"' Eisner (1985: xi).

It was whilst writing his seminal text, *Comics and Sequential Art*, that Eisner came to the conclusion that the reason this genre had taken so long to be critically accepted wasn't just the fault of the reading critic but was also the fault of the actual practitioner; the creator of sequential art. In his role as teacher of Sequential Art at the School of Visual Arts in New York in the 1980s, Eisner noted that many practitioners produced their art intuitively but that, 'Few ever had the time or the inclination to diagnose the form itself' (1985: xii). In thinking about this complex genre and the reasons for its lack of acceptance, Eisner realised that he was involved with 'an "art of communication", more than simply an application of art' (1985: xii). The whole genre needed to be analysed and taken more seriously and Eisner soon began to recognise that an increasing number of artists and writers were creating sequential art that was more worthy of scholarly discussion.

This issue of subject matter and content was picked up by Scott McCloud, who, writing ten years later, had similar concerns:

> Some of the most inspired and innovative comics of our century have never received recognition as comics, not so much in spite of their superior qualities as because of them. For much of this century the word 'comics' has had such negative connotations that many of comics' most devoted practitioners have preferred to be known as 'illustrators', 'commercial artists' or, at best, 'cartoonists'! And so, comics' low self-esteem is self-perpetuating!
>
> *McCloud (1994:18)*

Working at the same time as Eisner and McCloud, and in agreement with them, Raymond Briggs, creator of cartoon strips, graphic novels and picturebooks for readers of all ages, was aware that people often viewed the genre with contempt. He felt that it was the subject matter of many graphic novels, along with the terminology afforded to them, that posed the problem. Many of them did not deal with worthwhile subjects nor were they as widely read in England as they were in other countries where they had long been celebrated as worthwhile texts.

Comics and/or graphic novels? A question of terminology

The status of comics and graphic novels is growing and although they have always been valued amongst a certain readership they are now much more widely accepted (Arnold, 2003; Couch, 2000; Evans, 1998, 2009, 2011; Gravett, 2005; Lim, 2011; Martin, 2009; Tarhandeh, 2011). There is, however, still an issue with the terminology of the genre, with many librarians and booksellers being unsure of where to position them on their shelves; should they be placed alongside children's literature, young adult or adult literature, picturebooks, illustrated or chapter books? This question in itself poses a problem in terms of accessibility. Where do prospective readers look to find their preferred genre? The issue of terminology is not straightforward and even the great masters of the craft such as Will Eisner, Scott McCloud and Raymond Briggs have concerns about the terms being used.

In talking about the republished version of one of his earlier graphic novels, *Gentleman Jim*, Briggs shared some of his concerns with the terminology:

> It's jolly good, a book from 28 years ago being dragged out of the cellars. I read it the other day for the first time in years. I didn't think it was bad, though I don't see that it was all that revolutionary in terms of the graphic novel. Not that I like that term; they're not all novels, and 'graphic' is such a meaningless word; it just means writing. I prefer the French, bandes dessinées. If you say strip cartoons, which is what I say, it implies something a bit comic and Beano-ish. It's never been an accepted form in England, that's the trouble. I've been grumbling about this for years.
>
> *Briggs (2008)*

Shaun Tan also considered this question of terminology and in an article on graphic novels he stated:

> You'll notice that I use the terms 'comics' and 'graphic novels' interchangeably, because I don't see much difference between them; these terms both describe an arrangement of words and/or pictures as consecutive panels on a printed page (and can be extended to include picturebooks too).
>
> *Tan (2011: 2)*

Comics

Comics are an art form that features a series of static images in sequence, usually to tell a story. Eisner (1985) called comics 'sequential art'. He studied and wrote about comics until his death in 2005, demonstrating that comics have a vocabulary and grammar in both prose and illustration. He also considered what needed to be in place for a visual text to be called a comic. How were comics different from other visual texts? He realised that creators of comics use a blend of words and images to convey their message; he also noted that many comics creators were artists presenting their work in 'a series of repetitive images and recognisable symbols', hence the term 'sequential art' (Eisner, 1985).

Scott McCloud extended Eisner's work in relation to defining the art of comics. His eventual definition was more complex, stating that 'comics are juxtaposed pictorial and other images in deliberate sequence, intended to convey information and/or to produce an aesthetic response in the viewer' (McCloud, 1994: 9).

The key to comics is their format, what they look like on the page. Traditionally they have been printed on paper with boxes of drawings in sequence. Text is usually incorporated into the images, with text bubbles to represent speech and squiggly lines to indicate movement. Well-known examples showing these characteristics are comics such as *The Beano*, *Peanuts*, *The Simpsons*, and even *Rupert Bear*, which uses a sequential art format but with a less cartoony style of art and which has been continuously in print for over 90 years since its conception in 1920.

Graphic novels

It was Eisner's book *A Contract with God* which was the first published graphic novel to use the term on its cover in 1978, despite the fact that Eisner, like others, disliked the term graphic novel and preferred to use the terms, 'graphic literature' or 'graphic story'. Similar to comics and strip cartoons in form, the graphic novel, often defined as a type of comic, slightly longer than the typical comic, but produced in book form with some kind of thematic unity, is a truly multimodal form of communication. Weiner (2001) defines the graphic novel as 'a story told in comic book format with a beginning, middle and end', whilst de Vos (2005) defines them as 'bound books, fiction and non-fiction, which are created in the comic book format and are issued an ISBN'. Philip Pullman questioned whether the terminology actually matters and in speaking of the graphic novel he stated: 'Personally, I'm getting a little tired of the term. It's the form itself that is interesting, the interplay between the words and the pictures, and I'd be happy to call them comics and have done with it' (1995: 18).

Certain countries and cultures recognise this form of visual text more than others: these include France, with its celebrated bande dessinées including *The Adventures of Tintin* and *Asterix the Gaul*, and Japan with its widely read manga texts; manga being the Japanese term for comics. In Korea, Manhwa, the general term used to refer to comics and graphic novels was originally derived from Japanese manga (Lim, 2011).

Graphic novels: subject matter and audience

Graphic novels have been viewed by some as dealing with unoriginal, immature and clichéd subject matter, lacking proper storylines and sometimes being limited to violent and sexually explicit graphics. Mel Gibson stated:

> Graphic novels, comics and manga are often seen as texts specially for younger male reluctant readers, but such an assumption underestimates this enormously flexible medium as it can be used to create complex works of fiction or non-fiction for adults and young adults, male and female, as well as humorous stories for the very young.
>
> *Gibson (2008)*

Briggs was in agreement but in complaining that graphic work doesn't get the respect it deserves he sensed a change. In conversation with Nicholas Wroe, he stated:

> Partly it has itself to blame because the subject matter is often so dreadful and there is still an awful lot of sock-em-on-the-jaw stuff going on. But respectable publishers are putting out graphic novels, although I don't know if I like that term too much, and there is no reason why it shouldn't be as dignified a medium as, say, film, which they are very much like in many ways.
>
> *Wroe (2004)*

In order to be given greater consideration and respect, graphic novels need to deal with 'subjects of greater moment' (Eisner, 1985). Those published more recently cover issues ranging from eating disorders, war, and the holocaust to child abuse and drug addition:

- *Tyranny: I Keep You Thin* (2011), is Lesley Fairfield's disturbing and powerful tale of a young adult fighting a potentially life-threatening eating disorder. The graphic novel tells how the young girl, Anna, begins to accept herself after years fighting the effects of both anorexia and her personal demon, Tyranny, who constantly goads her not to eat.
- *Skim* (2008), written and illustrated in the form of a diary by Mariko Tamaki and Jillian Tamaki, depicts teen witch Skim's sexual awakening against the backdrop of the suicide of a male classmate. The story tells of her loneliness and inner grief and of her endeavour to come to terms with her own body changes when falling in love for the first time.
- In *Persepolis: The Story of a Childhood* (2003), Marjane Satrapi tells of her own life growing up in Iran in the 1970s and 80s. As the daughter of Marxist intellectuals, this beautifully illustrated graphic novel shows what it was like to grow up in Iran during the Islamic Revolution and the war with Iraq. The book, whose subject matter is now more relevant than ever, was first published in French but has since been translated into five other languages. It has won several prestigious comic-book awards along with being made into a film.
- David Reviati, an Italian comic author/illustrator, painter and screenwriter, won awards for *Morti di Sonno (The Dead Sleep)* (2009), his debut graphic novel. It describes the life of a group of children growing up on a housing estate built for workers of the local (toxic) petrochemical plant. They spend their childhood in the shadow of the pollution of the factory, exposed to heroin drug addiction, AIDS and endless games of football; the latter fuelled by the victory of Italy at the World Championships. This is an intensely powerful book, dark, harrowing and poignant all at the same time.

It isn't just recently published graphic novels that deal with challenging subject matter. As early as 1992 Art Speigelman won the Pulitzer Prize for *Maus*, a book about his father's survival in the holocaust (Spiegelman, 1973). *Maus* is often noted as being the quintessential graphic novel. Then in 1982, Raymond Briggs wrote *When the Wind Blows*. In warning of the atrocities of nuclear war in the cold-war era and the influence of political propaganda on ordinary people, this graphic novel/fusion text was considered so important and influential that copies were sent to every member of the House of Commons in England.

Picturebooks – where do they fit in?

It is apparent that there are many similarities between graphic novels and picturebooks, but although graphic novels can evidently be viewed as picturebooks, it is obvious that picturebooks cannot necessarily be viewed as graphic novels: the terms are not mutually inclusive. In the best examples of its genre a picturebook can be seen as 'an art form that combines visual and verbal narratives in a book format. A true picturebook tells the story both with words and illustrations. Sometimes they work together, sometimes separately' (Evans, 2011: 54). David Lewis indicated that:

> The words tell you something and the pictures show you something; the two things may be more or less related, but they may not. Back and forth you must go, wielding two kinds of looking that you must learn to fuse into understanding.
>
> *Lewis (2009: xii)*

Seeing a picturebook as an art object is something that Barbara Bader noted in her well-used definition from 40 years ago:

> A picturebook is text, illustrations, total design; an item of manufacture and a commercial product; a social, cultural, historical document; and foremost an experience for a child. As an art form it hinges on the interdependence of pictures and words, on the simultaneous display of two facing pages, and on the drama of the turning page.
>
> *Bader (1976: 1)*

Whilst accepting these definitions, there is increasingly a blurring of the boundaries, an overlapping and meshing of characteristics normally associated with comics and graphic novels with those associated with picturebooks. Philip Nel stated: 'The text–image relationship in a picture book is typically less complex than it is in a comic book' (2012: 447). Nodelman agreed that 'in terms of structure comics are more complicated than picture books' (2012: 437). Natalie op de Beeck (2012) noted that picturebooks have quite a few things in common with graphic novels; she stated that they are 'graphic narratives that operate in a medium called comics' (2012: 468). Despite this merging of characteristics and an awareness that although there are differences between the two genres there are also many similarities, there are still more studies of picturebooks than of comics and graphic novels. A group of scholars interested in this seeming dichotomy between the genres considered 'Why Comics Are and Are Not Picture Books'. They questioned why comics should be studied alongside picturebooks, and why it is still difficult to do so. Hatfield and Svonkin, members of this group, noted that despite sharing many similarities there are:

> different ideological frameworks: picture books are generally seen as empowering young readers to take part in a social structure that prizes official literacy, while comics, in contrast, are often seen as fugitive reading competing with or even obstructing that literacy.
>
> *Hatfield & Svonkin (2012: 431)*

Fusion texts – a new kid on the block

Things are changing!

A new breed of visual text is emerging, the fusion text.

It is a 'new kid on the block', one that is presenting challenging, thought-provoking and sometimes controversial reading material in creative, artistic forms.

At first glance fusion texts may not look very different; however, if one looks closely they are an amalgam of features from other genres – comics, graphic novels, illustrated books and picturebooks – *and* they draw on differing illustrative techniques to create the visual aspect of the text. Fusion texts are not just different because of the way they look; the subject matter too has its part to play. The visual artistry of fusion texts fuses, links and coalesces with the subject matter, which in itself is often challenging, problematic and thought-provoking. It seems that this kind of content is 'crying out' to be illustrated in a less traditional manner – in a way that merges differing genres with different illustrative techniques, such as, drawing, painting, photography, collage, photomontage, computer-generated imagery and sculpture. The art of the fusion text exhibits a unique and distinctly bold approach and the creator has been influenced by specific, often personal and emotional, experiences that have shaped their artistic vision.

Although the fusion text is a fairly new phenomenon, its precursor was starting to emerge over 30 years ago when Eisner noted: 'comic book and strip artists have been developing in their craft the interplay of words and images. They have in the process, I believe, achieved a successful cross breeding of illustration and prose' (1985: 2). It is this cross breeding of different, creative forms of illustration and prose that is one of the *key* features of fusion texts and Eisner went on to say:

> The format of comics presents a montage of both word and image, and the reader is thus required to exercise both visual and verbal interpretative skills. . . . The reading of a graphic novel is an act of both aesthetic perception and intellectual pursuit.
>
> *Eisner (1985: 2)*

It is this act of aesthetic perception and intellectual pursuit when reading a graphic novel that is also required when reading a fusion text, as this usually displays a high degree of creativity and innovation and isn't always easy to understand at first glance. Fusion texts necessitate that the reader gives both time and effort to ensure that they are fully appreciated. Indeed many fusion texts are similar to postmodern picturebooks, which often present the reader with multiple reading pathways and which are challenging to read because of their non-linear texts and their lack of a straightforward text topology; authors play with what is real and what isn't and there are numerous perspectives in terms of voice, illustrations and content (Pantaleo, 2009; Serafini, 2005; Sipe & Pantaleo, 2008).

This playing with what is and isn't real is not easy and creators of fusion texts sometime struggle with how to verbalise the creation of these texts. In talking about his search for story in his wordless graphic novel/picturebook, *The Arrival*, which is a fusion of differing styles and techniques, Shaun Tan verbalised his concerns stating:

> In particular, one question that I think about every day as an artist: how can I successfully combine written narrative and visual artwork in a way that's unique. What can an illustrated story do that other stories can't and how can it access a world that is otherwise inaccessible?
>
> *Tan (2011: 3)*

Tan further shared his thoughts:

> certain ideas demand to be expressed in certain ways, a conclusion I come to again and again as a reader, critic, writer and artist and no doubt a principle that drives so many artists and writers to constant experimentation, trying to give a tangible name and shape to ideas that might otherwise seem vague or nebulous. Something unique often emerges from that struggle.
>
> *Tan (2011: 4)*

Tan went on to note how difficult it is to find the exact way of representing what one is doing:

> When I look at the work of other creators, I always see beyond the page surface and imagine them struggling the way I do: trawling through many different fragments of drawing and writing and discovering that some compositions work – seem truthful, precise, and evocative while others appear false, inarticulate, or disjointed. After a while, every artist comes to realise that they are not just expressing an idea, they are engineering a personal language, tailored to suit that idea. For an illustrator, it's a language that involves image, text, page layout, typography, physical format, and media, all the things that work together in a complex grammar of their own, and open to constant reinvention. And this is something that almost defies the graphic novel – an experimentation, playfulness, even irreverence, when it comes to rules of form and style.
>
> *Tan (2011: 5)*

Fusion texts – complex and challenging multimodal texts

Other writers are attempting to describe this rapidly emerging cross-breed text. Panaou and Michaelides (2011) call them 'hybrid' texts, whilst Foster (2011), in comparing graphic novels with picturebooks, feels that 'graphic novel' is a slippery term to define. In his research he claims they are 'morphed' texts. This fusion, morphing or hybridising of features relates to the artistic techniques being used as well as to the use of the comic strip/graphic novel features being incorporated. In a search to find answers to *why comics are and are not picture books*, Hatfield and Svonkin, stated that by 'smashing together two similar yet culturally distinct genres, picture books and comics, we can spark a discussion that will offer new ways of thinking about the distinctions among genres, forms and modes' (2012: 432). This 'smashing together' of genres can be seen as being analogous to fusing the differing genres. Hatfield and Svonkin drew on Eisenstein's theories of dialectical montage in cinema stating meaning was created in montage 'by violently smashing image *against* image, so that images juxtaposed in opposition to each other create a new dialectical meaning each image separately could never evoke' (2012: 432). The fusion text is such a juxtaposition.

Increasing numbers of author/illustrators now create fusion texts, with Shaun Tan, Peter Sis, Matt Ottley and Dave McKean being some of the forerunners. Many of Tan's picturebooks cross the boundary into fusion texts and it is his book *The Lost Thing* (2000) that springs to mind immediately, incorporating as it does story boxes, overlapping drawn images, speech bubbles, captions and collage.

Many fusion author/illustrators have won awards for their thought-provoking, challenging texts:

- Brian Selznick won the Caldecott Award in 2008 for his fusion text *The Invention of Hugo Cabret* (2007), which combines elements of picturebooks, graphic novels and film and which has been described as a cinematic, movie-like book, evocative of early black-and-white films. This book was inspired by Georges Melies, a French filmmaker whose 1902 film *A Trip to the Moon* captivated Selznick as a child and was the inspiration for the Oscar-winning film 'Hugo', directed by Martin Scorsese (2011). Selznick states on the book's website that '*The Invention of Hugo Cabret* is not exactly a novel, and it's not quite a picture book, and it's not really a graphic novel, or a flip book, or a movie, but a combination of all these things'. Books such as these openly announce their affiliation with multiple genres – but nearly every part participates in more than any single genre.
- *The Wall* written in 2007 by Peter Sis, who was born in Czechoslovakia during the Cold War, tells of life in his Soviet-occupied country. Through remarkable drawings and diaries, blocks of print and evocative pen and ink sketches, Sis, who was awarded the Hans Christian Andersen award for illustration in 2012, shares his life story. It tells of his longing to be free of the tyranny of the Iron Curtain and to participate in the forbidden fruits he was hearing about in the news of the West; things such as, the Beatles, rock and

roll, blue jeans and Coca-Cola. This award-winning fusion text is a wonderful piece of historical fact as well as being a beautiful text.

- Matt Ottley worked with John Marsden on the fusion text *Home and Away* (2008) (see Figure 12.1 (Plate 30) in Chapter 12), an incredibly moving depiction of war, displacement and illegal immigration as seen from the point of view of a 'normal' Australian family. Matt Ottley also created *Requiem for a Beast* (2007) which was the controversial winner of the Australian Children's Book Council Award for the best picturebook of the year in 2008. The book, combining illustration, music and storylines about an Australian stockman taming a wild bull and the dark secrets of the 'stolen generation' of aboriginal children, is described by the publishers as a graphic novel aimed at young adult readers and on Matt Ottley's website as 'a multi modal work, consisting of the formats of graphic novel, picture book, novella, and musical work'.

The fusion texts of Dave McKean

All of these award-winning books show the different perspectives and characteristics of fusion texts, texts that can be challenging to read and understand and that require readers to commit energy, effort and time to read and to make sense of them. It is, however, to the work of Dave McKean that I again turn. His work is the epitome of the fusion text.

British born McKean is an artistic all-rounder (although he states that he is not an artist) and a true iconoclast. His work blends and mixes aspects of drawing, painting, photography, collage, found objects, sculpture, and computer-generated digital art for a fusion text experience unlike any other. His work was showing many of the features of the fusion text over 20 years ago but over time his style has changed, morphing into a dynamic, constantly changing style that now fuses all manner of different techniques in any one text. In his early artistic career he illustrated comics and graphic novels and was famous for his work on all the covers of Neil Gaiman's celebrated *Sandman* series. His first collaboration with Neil Gaiman was *Violent Cases* (1987), a short graphic novel portraying disturbing childhood memories. These themes of early childhood perception and the nature of memory were visited again in *The Tragical Comedy or Comical Tragedy of Mr. Punch* (2006) (Figure 5.5) (Plate 22).

This story of childhood innocence and adult pain tells of a young boy, who, whilst in his grandfather's failing seaside arcade, encounters a mysterious Punch and Judy man with a dark past, and a woman who makes her living playing a mermaid. As their lives intertwine and their stories unfold, the boy is forced to confront family secrets, strange puppets and a nightmarish world of violence and betrayal.

Gaiman's story of Mr. Punch is dark, challenging and disturbing. His text and McKean's visual images are a fusion of differing techniques which play with the passage of time and fuse to create a compelling and unsettling whole. Even the cover is unsettling and the reader knows from previous knowledge of Punch and Judy shows that violent Punch eventually kills all the other characters:

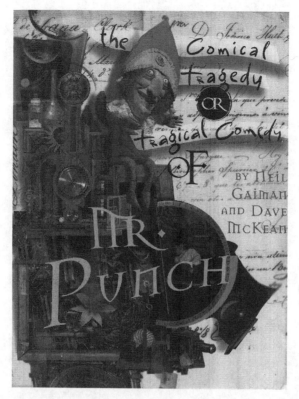

FIGURE 5.5 (Plate 22) *The Tragical Comedy or Comical Tragedy of Mr. Punch* by Neil Gaiman and Dave McKean (2006).

He threw the baby out of the window. Then he battered his wife to death. He killed a policeman who came to arrest him. He caused the hangman to be hanged in his place. He murdered a ghost. And outwitted the devil himself. He never died.

(Back cover synopsis) (Figures 5.6, 5.7, 5.8 (Plate 23) and 5.9)

In considering *Mr. Punch*, Paul Gravett (2005), comic and graphic novel researcher, noted that from a boy's perspective, adults loom as 'threatening creatures', seething with the sort of violence against the family that Mr. Punch gets away with. McKean deliberately confounds readers' expectations, by enacting some of the disturbingly 'real' everyday scenes with puppet-like figures and sets, in contrast to the 'unreal' dreaming and remembering recorded in photographs.

In *Pictures That Tick* (2009), McKean collected a variety of short comics stories from the 1990s and 2000s. As with Mr. Punch, the content of each story is dark and challenging and leaves the reader/viewer feeling uneasy as they ponder the stories' meanings. Gathered together they represent a tour-de-force achievement and the whole fusion text stretches the boundaries of comics art. Each story is

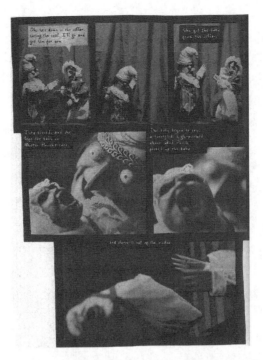

FIGURE 5.6 *The Tragical Comedy or Comical Tragedy of Mr. Punch*: He threw the baby out of the window.

FIGURE 5.7 *The Tragical Comedy or Comical Tragedy of Mr. Punch*: He battered his wife to death.

FIGURE 5.8 (Plate 23) *The Tragical Comedy or Comical Tragedy of Mr. Punch*: He caused the hangman to be hanged.

FIGURE 5.9 *The Tragical Comedy or Comical Tragedy of Mr. Punch*: He outwitted the devil.

FIGURE 5.10 *Pictures That Tick*: Yol's story.

written and illustrated in different ways many of them being made up of separate images fused together as a whole (Figure 5.10). As a 'picturebook guy' studying comics, Perry Nodelman commented that in comics 'words appear not only outside of and near pictures, but also within pictures, superimposed over images (often already busy ones), or in the speech balloons that interrupt the pictorial space depicted while implying that it continues on behind them' (2012: 437). He goes on to note that 'comics is a "mosaic art": in which lots of separate little pieces that come together through their relationships to each other form a whole, but nevertheless remain apparent as still–separate pieces' (2012: 438). Much of McKean's work exhibits this 'mosaic art' but is always much more.

Panaou and Michaelides note that McKean's work 'breaks conventions, resists categorisation, subverts reading expectations, and yet is highly successful in communicating powerful and engaging stories' (2011: 63). They also state, 'McKean's techniques take the reader on a journey between imagination and reality: drawings and paintings (fictional part), photos (the real part), collages and graphics (somewhere in between)' (2011: 65).

Fusion texts for an implied child audience

McKean is a real fusion text artist but in conjunction with inspirational authors his creations are legendary. Some of his most interesting fusion texts are aimed at a child audience and are those combining his artistic and creative talents with different authors.

Dave McKean and David Almond

Almond and McKean worked together on a set of three books all dealing with complex, disturbing issues. In the first Almond writes about bereavement and bullying. *The Savage* (2008) is a 'fusion' book which is part picturebook, part illustrated story book, and part graphic novel. The second book, *Slog's Dad* (2010) is also about the loss of a father; this time the reader hears how Slog, the young boy deals with his grief, believing as he does that his dad has come back from the dead. *Mouse, Bird, Snake, Wolf* (2013), the third of this Almond/McKean collaboration, deals with the story of the creation. It is a complex tale about the inevitability of evil (personified by a wolf), the corruptive nature of power (as portrayed by the gods), and the existence of hope and faith as portrayed through the eyes of Ben, the youngest of the three mortal characters. It is an unsettling, disturbing story that leaves lasting and troubling thoughts in one's mind.

In reviewing *Mouse, Bird, Snake, Wolf*, Jones felt there was something very special in McKean's artwork:

> There's a Dali-esque feel to some of his panels, that sort of blurring of reality and imagination, colours burning, images merging, and slightly too long limbs that don't feel grotesque but feel somehow balletic and graceful. He's very painterly in this, and it's something quite special. I loved his 'transformation' scenes where the children imagine the new things. The children 'look inside' themselves, and the images come from a dark part of their thoughts and are borne to life through the power of their imagination. The wolf panel itself is a genuinely unnerving moment and it's worthwhile, if you're sharing this or recommending it to younger readers, to take a second and look at this moment yourself.
>
> *Jones (2013)*

Dave McKean and Neil Gaiman

It is McKean's work with Neil Gaiman that exhibits fusion text characteristics most effectively. Together they create emotionally complex fusion texts that oblige the reader to tolerate ambiguity and incongruity breaking into the traditional text. They frequently disrupt previously accepted norms in terms of layout, presenting picture and text surprises from very different perspectives. In addition, the stories often hold multiple meanings that provoke, tease and cajole the reader in different ways as they read.

The Day I Swapped My Dad for Two Goldfish (1997), *The Wolves in the Wall* (2003) and award-winning *Crazy Hair* (2009) are three books created by the ingenious liaison of these two experts. They are true fusion texts in terms of their narratives and the illustrative art styles they draw on.

In the first, a little boy swaps his dad for his best friend's goldfish (Figure 5.11). When his mum finds out, he has to get dad back but that is when the trouble starts as dad has been swapped all over town and getting him back is not easy.

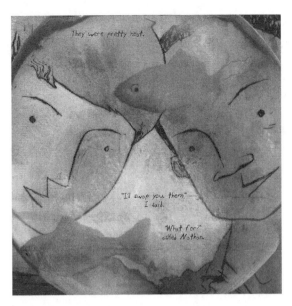

FIGURE 5.11 *The Day I Swapped My Dad for Two Goldfish*: 'They were pretty neat'.

In describing the book, Panaou and Michaelides state:

> The pages oscillate between genres. Panels and balloons are overused on one page and not used at all on the next. There is a continuous fluctuation of the text–image interaction and expressive mannerisms. The book combines forms and elements from different genres, all at the same time and sometimes on the same page. There is no specific pattern, but rather a constant change and blending. The only limitation is the story; anything that contribute to the narration of a good story is permissible, anything that enlists the different strengths of images and words and overcomes their individual inadequacies. Thus, text and illustrations break every rule forming a hybrid (fusion) picturebook, comic book, illustrated book, graphic novel.
>
> *Panaou & Michaelides (2011: 65)*

In *The Wolves in the Walls*, Gaiman's enigmatic and in places disturbing narrative is perfectly complemented by McKean's artwork; their work fuses to create an amazing whole (see Figure 5.1 and Figure 5.3 (Plate 21)).

The third book, *Crazy Hair* is a visually stunning and captivating tale of Bonnie, and the little girl's fascination with Mister's unbelievably amazing hair. The text and images fuse to create a visually stunning and captivating book, which repeatedly draws the reader back to inspect the hyperreal illustrations (Garrett, 2013), and admire the links between words and pictures (Figure 5.12) (Plate 24).

All three texts exhibit the creators' truly creative and imaginative fusion style. They are oddly humorous, rather unsettling and yet intriguing at the same time.

FIGURE 5.12   (Plate 24) *Crazy Hair*. This is Bonnie. This is me.

They invite the reader to return repeatedly to search for and discover new features in both the text and images.

In looking at McKean's artistic style, Panaou and Michaelides considered the way his books 'are constructed through a powerful fusion of generic conventions, a combination that prompts the reader to stay constantly alert, assessing the nature of word–image interaction on each page, and switching from one mode of interaction to another' (2011: 66). They go on to say:

> While these 'hybrids' certainly do imply an experienced reader – one who is familiar with the conventions of each of the enlisted genres – they also imply a reader who, being a child of the post-modern era, accepts and celebrates flexibility, fluidity, and transmutation.
>
> *Panaou & Michaelides (2011:66)*

Fusion texts – celebrating the new kid on the block

It isn't always easy to define and categorise visual texts when a totally new and different genre appears. Some readers are content that they exist whilst others want the texts to be defined and classified, maybe by their aesthetic qualities, implied audience, subject matter and/or style. Some may feel it isn't important to give these visually different books a name. However, I feel it is, and in addition I feel it is important to celebrate this new kind of text that is challenging by its visual non-conformity.

Shaun Tan felt:

> Ironically, good narrative illustration is not about 'illustration' at all, in the sense of visual clarity, definition, or empirical observation. It's all about uncertainty, open-mindedness, slipperiness, and even vagueness. There's a tacit

recognition in much graphic fiction that some things cannot be adequately expressed through words: an idea might be just so unfamiliar, an emotion so ambivalent, a concept so nameless that is best represented either wordlessly, through a visual subversion of words, or as an expansion of their meaning using careful juxtaposition.

Tan (2011:8)

... and by careful fusion!

The fusion text is here to stay and, if accomplished author/illustrators continue to produce quality visual texts like the ones considered here, then it will not be long before comics, graphic novels and picturebooks will, along with the rapidly developing and closely related, fusion texts, be seen as respectable genres, read, enjoyed and talked about by many.

Academic references

Arnold, A. (2003) The Graphic Novel Silver Anniversary. *Time Magazine*, 14 November 2003.

Bader, B. (1976) *American Picture Books: From Noah's Ark to the Beast within*. New York: Macmillan.

Briggs, R. (2008) in conversation with Rachael Cooke. Big kid, 'old git' and still in the rudest of health. *The Guardian*, 10 August 2008. www.guardian.co.uk/books/2008/aug/10/booksforchildrenandteenagers (accessed 23 February 2010).

Couch, C. (2000) The Publication and Format of Comics, Graphic Novels, and Tankobon, *Image & Narratology*, December. www.imageandnarrative.be/narratology/narratology.htm (accessed 24 February 2009).

de Vos, G. (2005) ABC's of graphic novels, *Resource Links*, 10(3): 1–8.

Eco, U. (1986) *Faith in Fakes: Travels in Hyperreality*. London: Vintage.

Eisner, W. (1985) *Comics and Sequential Art*. Tamarac, FL: Poorhouse Press.

Evans, J. (ed.) (1998) *What's in the Picture? Responding to Illustrations in Picture Books*. London: Paul Chapman.

Evans, J. (ed.) (2009) *Talking Beyond the Page: Reading and Responding to Picturebooks*. London: Routledge.

Evans, J. (2011) Raymond Briggs: Controversially Blurring Boundaries, *Bookbird*, 49(4): 49–61.

Foster, J. (2011) Picture Books as Graphic Novels and Vice Versa: The Australian Experience, *Bookbird*, 49(4): 68–75.

Garrett, J. (2013) Realism, Surrealism, and Hyperrealism in American Children's Book Illustration, in Grilli, G. (ed.) *Bologna: Fifty Years of Children's Books from around the World*. Bologna: Bologna University Press, pp. 147–158.

Gibson, M. (2008) 'So What Is This Mango, Anyway': Understanding Manga, Comics and Graphic Novels, *NATE Classroom*, 5(Summer): 8–10.

Gravett, P. (2005) *Graphic Novels: Stories to Change Your Life*. London: Aurum Press.

Hatfield, C. & Svonkin, C. (2012) Why Comics Are and Are Not Picture Books: Introduction, *Children's Literature Association Quarterly*, 37(4): 429–435.

Jones, N. (2013) *Mouse Bird Snake Wolf: David Almond & Dave McKean*, Book Review. http://didyoueverstoptothink.wordpress.com/2013/06/07/mouse-bird-snake-wolf/

Joseph, M. (2012) Seeing the Visible Book: How Graphic Novels Resist Reading, *Children's Literature Association Quarterly*, 37(4): 454–467.

Lewis, D. (2009) Foreword, in Evans, J. (ed.) *Talking Beyond the Page: Reading and Responding to Picturebooks*. London: Routledge, pp. xii–xiii.

Lim, Y. (2011) Educational Graphic Novels: Korean Children's Favorite Now, *Bookbird*, 49(4): 40–48.

McCloud, S. (1994) *Understanding Comics: The Invisible Art*. New York: HarperCollins.

Martin, M. (2009) How Comic Books Became Part of the Literary Establishment, *The Telegraph*, 2 April 2009.

Nel, P. (2012) Same Genus, Different Species? Comics and Picture Books, *Children's Literature Association Quarterly*, 37(4): 445–453.

Nodelman, P. (2012) Picture Book Guy Looks at Comics: Structural Differences in Two Kinds of Visual Narrative, *Children's Literature Association Quarterly*, 37(4): 436–444.

op de Beeck, N. (2012) On Comics-Style Picture Books and Picture-Bookish Comics, *Children's Literature Association Quarterly*, 37(4): 468–476.

Panaou, P. & Michaelides, F. (2011) Dave McKean's Art: Transcending Limitations of the Graphic Novel Genre, *Bookbird*, 49(4): 62–67.

Pantaleo, S. (2009) Exploring Children's Responses to the Postmodern Picturebook, Who's Afraid of the Big Bad Book? In Evans, J. (ed.) *Talking Beyond the Page: Reading and Responding to Picturebooks*. London: Routledge, pp. 44–61.

Pullman, P. (1995) Partners in a Dance, *Books for Keeps*, 92(May): 18–21.

Serafini, F. (2005) Voices in the Park, Voices in the Classroom: Readers responding to Postmodern Picturebooks, *Reading, Research and Instruction*, 44(3): 47–64.

Sipe, L. & Pantaleo, S. (2008) *Postmodern Picturebooks: Play, Parody and Self-Referentiality*. New York: Routledge.

Tan, S. (2011) The Accidental Graphic Novelist, *Bookbird*, 49(4): 1–9.

Tarhandeh, S. (2011) Striving to Survive: Comic Strips in Iran, *Bookbird*, 49(4): 24–31.

Weiner, S. (2001) *The 101 Best Graphic Novels*. New York: NBM Publishing.

Wroe, N. (2004) Bloomin' Christmas, *The Guardian*, 18 December 2004. www.guardian.co.uk/books/2004/dec/18/featuresreviews.guardianreview8 (accessed 24 February 2010).

Children's literature

Almond, D. & McKean, D. (2008) *The Savage*. London: Walker Books.

Almond, D. & McKean, D. (2010) *Slog's Dad*. London: Walker Books.

Almond, D. & McKean, D. (2013) *Mouse, Bird, Snake, Wolf*. London: Walker Books.

Briggs, R. (1982) *When the Wind Blows*. London: Hamish Hamilton.

Briggs, R. (2008) *Gentleman Jim*. London: Jonathan Cape.

Eisner, W. (1978) *A Contract with God*. New York: Baronet Press Books.

Fairfield, L. (2011) *Tyranny: I Keep You Thin*. London: Walker Books.

Gaiman, N. & McKean, D. (1987) *Violent Cases*. London: Escape Books.

Gaiman, N. & McKean, D. (1997) *The Day I Swapped My Dad for Two Goldfish*. New York: HarperCollins.

Gaiman, N. & McKean, D. (2003) *The Wolves in the Wall*. New York: HarperCollins.

Gaiman, N. & McKean, D. (2006) *The Tragical Comedy or Comical Tragedy of Mr. Punch*. London: Bloomsbury.

Gaiman, N. & McKean, D. (2009) *Crazy Hair*. New York: HarperCollins.

McKean, D. (2009) *Pictures That Tick*. Milwaukee, WI: Dark Horse Books.

Marsden, J., illus. Ottley, M. (2008) *Home and Away*. Melbourne: Lothian Children's Books.

Ottley, M. (2007) *Requiem for a Beast: A Work for Image, Word and Music*. Melbourne: Lothian Publishers.

Reviati, D. (2009) *Morti di Sonno*. Bologna: Coconino Press.

Satrapi, M. (2003) *Persepolis: The Story of a Childhood*. London: Pantheon.

Selznick, B. (2007) *The Invention of Hugo Cabret*. London: Scholastic.

Sis, P. (2007) *The Wall: Growing up behind the Iron Curtain*. New York: Farrar, Straus and Giroux.

Spiegelman, A. (1973) *Maus: A Survivor's Tale*. New York: Pantheon.

Tamaki, M. & Tamaki, J. (2008) *Skim*. London: Walker Books.

Tan, S. (2000) *The Lost Thing*. Melbourne: Lothian Publishers.

Tan, S. (2006) *The Arrival*. Melbourne: Lothian Publishers.

6

'THESE BOOKS MADE ME REALLY CURIOUS'

How visual explorations shape the young readers' taste

Marnie Campagnaro

There are two ways in which a text may be illustrated: an artist can use a literal, descriptive, denotative mode, or a symbolic, implied, connotative mode. In the denotative mode, an artist's illustrations are a direct and literal imitation of the 'text' reality, whilst in the connotative mode, ideas and concepts are not directly signified but are implied by the associations or meanings that are suggested or evoked. In this latter mode the artist uses metaphors and similes to illustrate a text, thus introducing additional meaning and requiring that readers must draw on previous experiences in order to interpret and draw meaning from the text. This chapter will look at young readers' responses to a selection of picturebooks using these two types of illustrative styles. It focuses in particular on Capitan Omicidio *(Captain Murderer), a version of Charles Perrault's* Blue Beard *written by Charles Dickens and illustrated by Fabian Negrin.*

There is evidence that a 'quiet revolution' (Arizpe & Styles, 2003) has been happening in children's literature over the last 20 years. Increasingly, newer editions of picturebooks have combined written aspects of older texts with contemporary and often controversial visual styles to create new picturebooks which are outstanding works of art.

Picturebooks are a valuable educational resource which encourage children's aesthetic awareness and several critical researchers have recently focused on the educational and aesthetic value of picturebooks (Colomer, Kümmerling-Meibauer & Silva-Díaz, 2010; Hamelin, 2012; Salisbury & Styles, 2012; Campagnaro & Dallari, 2013). Moreover, many qualitative researches have investigated the way children interact with picturebooks in primary and secondary school (Arizpe & Styles, 2003; Pantaleo, 2008; Sipe & Pantaleo, 2008; Evans, 2009; Arizpe, Colomer & Martínez-Roldán, 2014). These studies show that visual narration creates a shared space which affords the possibility of discussion with children and can thereby stimulate a deeper understanding of the fictional universe and the real world. In addition, they demonstrate that the visual and aesthetic literacy of a child can be developed through the reading of picturebooks.

Two visual modes of representation: the child's engagement in literal and symbolic visual narratives

Despite there being many ways in which a text can be illustrated, a visual artist can basically use two visual modes of representation: a literal, descriptive mode, or a symbolic, implied mode. In the first mode the artist illustrates the text using images which are a direct imitation of the 'text' reality, while in the second mode the artist uses metaphors and similes to illustrate the text, thereby introducing additional but implied meaning.

These two modalities recall the distinction between denotation and connotation described by Roland Barthes in his influential book, *Image, Music, Text* (1977 [1964]). According to Barthes, *denotation* is what a sign (or text) describes; at a first level of meaning, the 'literal or obvious meaning'. *Connotation* is a second level of meaning, the additional cultural meanings we can find in the image or text, including emotional associations that a sign carries.

Picturebooks can likewise be marked by these same two modes of representation: a visual denotative language (something that is signified directly or literally), or a visual connotative language (something that is not signified directly or literally but which is implied). Visual denotative picturebooks are characterized by illustrations making explicit references to the text. In these picturebooks, the pictures convey the conventional and primary meaning of the text and make it clear and explicit. The conveyed meaning is precise and unequivocal. Conversely, visual connotative picturebooks are characterized by illustrations making only implicit reference to the texts. In such picturebooks the pictures do not directly represent the text but rather fill in the textual gaps which may emerge from an interpretational reading of the text. Such picturebooks may provoke an emotional impact in the reader. The text–image relation in such picturebooks will frequently have a high degree of ambiguity. Ambiguity is an important aesthetic quality because it provides the reader with multiple opportunities to access and interpret the meaning of the story.

Pointing out the differences between visual denotative and visual connotative picturebooks is crucial because visual language affects our meaning-making process and enhances our perception of the story. For instance, visual denotative language helps children to understand the meaning of some situations or concepts, but often has little or no aesthetic potential (Schwarcz, 1982: 50). In contrast, the visual connotative language has an aesthetic potential: it engages a child's imagination and often gives 'an open invitation to the child to experience some empathy with the author' (Schwarcz, 1982: 51).

'To see is to interpret': the potential of visual texts

According to Schwarcz (1982), illustrating a text is 'a matter of interpreting and commenting on it. Coming upon a metaphor in a text he is about to illustrate, the artist has a wide range of possibilities; he chooses contents and meanings and transfers them to his pictures' (1982: 34).

This process can be analysed using the definition Gombrich gave in relation to the visual representation in his most influential book, *Art and Illusion*: 'to see is to interpret' (Gombrich, 2002: XIII [1960]). Gombrich's constructivist theory of perception reminds us that reading and commenting on an image is always a process based on the relativity of our vision. Our cultural, social and psychological history shapes our perception and representations of reality. For Gombrich, there is no such thing as an 'innocent look'; when we perceive an image and understand it, we have been influenced by our knowledge of the world.

If we look at ambiguous and controversial images in connotative texts, the feeling of disorientation and amazement that often arises can make the act of seeing even more lively and engaging. This is evident when looking at the ambiguous and challenging book *Imagine* by the English illustrator Norman Messenger (Messenger, 2005), which has illustrations of a bucolic landscape with hills, mountains, groves, pastures, glades, houses, castles and Roman ruins. On looking more carefully at these images the reader discovers a strange new world: the idyllic landscape stunningly hides behind giant faces on the hill sides!

Young readers' aesthetic explorations of ambiguous and controversial picturebooks

According to Gadamer's hermeneutics, aesthetics have a crucial role to play in life experience (Gadamer, 1986). Aesthetic investigation is vital because it disrupts and challenges a reader's customary expectations of a text; it also pushes the reader towards an aesthetic attentiveness that says something essential about the experience an individual has of the text.

For Gadamer, artwork is interrogative by nature and since the meaning transmitted can never be fully understood in the same way by all, it remains partly enigmatic and the reader's hermeneutic, interpretative involvement is required. Disclosure and hiddenness are not contraries in Gadamer's aesthetics, but mutually dependent: the disclosed reveals the presence of the undisclosed in the disclosed (Davey, 2011).

Using this hermeneutic, interpretative perspective, controversial picturebooks become valuable aesthetical tools. Ambiguities and discrepancies in a controversial picturebook have a fundamental role to play because they require the reader to become involved in interpreting a text and they help him/her to orientate his/her own meaning-making process. Understanding a plot in a picturebook is much more than the simple understanding of a sequence of sentences. It calls for far more complex abilities than just a good command of the language or good reading and writing skills; it requires children to establish a relationship between ambiguous details in a single illustration and ambiguous details in sequences of illustrations. In order to establish a relationship between characters, environments, purposes, actions and unexpected events and to grasp the content of a story, the reader has to give a meaning to ambiguities and discrepancies in a plot, to understand metaphors and to formulate hypotheses. Since the first reading of a picturebook doesn't always lead to the 'authentic' reading of the story, drawing on all of these actions is fundamental for understanding to take place.

During the reading, children have to become familiar with the existence of multiple reading levels in a story. In order to clarify this process, I will describe the picturebook reading process of a child attending primary school:

- First, the child recognizes, mentions and enumerates the characters, objects and setting of the story.
- Second, the child notices the relationships existing within a single picture in relation to other pictures and discovers some details that at first sight might have appeared 'meaningless'.
- Third, the child analyses these details and realizes that a deeper reading level is required. At this point, the child formulates a hypothesis to interpret the 'hidden' narrative plot, posing questions in relation to the ambiguous and apparently meaningless details of the story.

Due to the reader's interpretive involvement, the undisclosed meaning of a plot (that is, what has not explicitly been said or seen) may be disclosed, giving the child access to the 'authentic' pleasure and understanding of the story.

Visual explorations and young readers' taste: an observational research

The theoretical perspective I have just outlined was put into practice in an observational research project I carried out in an Italian primary school in 2010. In this qualitative study, observation was used as the investigation methodology. The aim of the study was to explore children's response to the two visual modes of representation in picturebooks (that is, visual *denotative* language and visual *connotative* language) through the reading of three popular fairy tales illustrated by different artists.

The study was inspired by some well-known critical studies carried out by scholars such as Schwarcz (1982), focusing on Cinderella, Nodelman (1988), focusing on Snow White, and Nikolajeva and Scott (2006), focusing on Thumbelina. These studies investigated the relationship between words and pictures in the three fairy tale picturebooks, but they did not discuss children's responses as this study aims to do.

Even though I was aware of the methodological difficulties in drawing demarcation lines and in applying categorization methods to fairy tale picturebooks, I planned a research project that would enable me to observe and encourage 'aesthetical development' in young readers. The children started by reading the fairy tales which used explicit denotative visual language (the favourite visual language chosen by the majority of children at the beginning of the research).

They were then asked to compare these 'unambiguous' illustrated stories with other more controversial versions which used more connotative visual language. Finally, the children were asked to state their preferences.

My aim in conducting this qualitative study was to consider:

- How children respond to fairy tale picturebooks marked by different modes of representation.
- Their mode of choice and the preference they express for either a visual denotative language, marked by a literal and descriptive referentiality to the text, or a visual connotative language, marked by a high degree of ambiguity and aesthetic potential.
- How the explicit teaching of visual exploration shapes a young reader's taste.

The structure of the observational research

The research methodology employed was developed drawing upon some valuable guidelines from a previous survey conducted on a world scale using the Delphi technique (Linstone & Turoff, 1975): a research method conducted by an expert panel of 28 experts that included scholars, publishers and illustrators from all over the world who, in this survey, had dealt with some multidimensional aspects of picturebooks (Campagnaro, 2012).

My observational study involved children aged 6, 8 and 10 and was carried out in a primary school in the Padua district of Northern Italy. It had an observation group of 62 children (52 children with Italian citizenship and 10 with foreign citizenship). The observation group was divided into three subgroups, according to their school classes: the first class consisted of 20 children aged 6 (11 girls and 9 boys); the second class consisted of a group of 17 children aged 8 (9 girls and 8 boys); and the third class consisted of a group of 25 children aged 10 (11 girls and 14 boys). I chose children aged 6, 8 and 10 from the different age groups in order to present a multifaceted children's response study based on children's cognitive and aesthetical development at different ages.

During the research I observed the modes of interaction expressed by children in relation to 21 versions of illustrated fairy tales: 7 different illustrated versions of *Little Red Riding Hood*, 7 of *Hansel and Gretel*, and 7 of *Bluebeard*.

Three factors were taken into consideration when selecting the fairy tale picturebooks.

- First, the selection needed to offer an important outlook on the richness and the variety of contemporary picturebooks: the goal was to promote a greater awareness both in children and teachers about the mentioned 'quiet revolution' (Arizpe & Styles, 2003) that has involved children's literature in recent years.
- Second, the selection needed to include fairy tale picturebooks that had been positively reviewed or whose author/illustrators had received prominent children's literary awards.
- Third, the selection needed to be equally representative of the two different visual categories.

The 21 fairy tale picturebooks were grouped into two families: 11 illustrated fairy tales marked by a denotative, explicit, visual language and 10 fairy tales marked by a connotative, less explicit, visual language.

I decided to apply the 'denotative–connotative' categorization used for picturebooks to the illustrated fairy tales because these two fields share a great number of elements. The fairy tale is an open and ductile text, which can lend itself to multiple reinterpretations: the original texts, any text innovations or rewritings of the classic fairy tale, together with the contextual genesis of a specific iconic representation and a particular graphic project, give rise to a work which is significantly close to the concept of a picturebook. Some of the works used in this study are characterized by a relationship in which text and pictures are inextricably bound to each other: the text denotes the fairy tale, but the connotation is made possible by the pictures, which give the text an *added value*.

In the fairy tales illustrated according to a denotative visual language, pictures convey the conventional and primary meaning of the text. Undoubtedly, there are notable differences between these books: in some of them, the visual narration amplifies the text and may sometimes encourage the reader to take part in the plot from an emotional point of view, but the visual language of all these books nevertheless shows a strong adherence to the text; it depicts a faithful portrait of the textual reality. Table 6.1 shows the list of the fairy tale picturebooks using denotative visual language:

TABLE 6.1 Fairy tale picturebooks using denotative visual language

Author	Illustrator	Title	Publishing house	Year	Visual language
Charles Perrault	Eric Battut	Barbablù (Bluebeard)	Bohem Press	2001	Denotative
Charles Perrault	Jean Claverie	Barbablù (Bluebeard)	Emme Edizioni	1991, 1995	Denotative
Charles Perrault	Raffaella Ligi	Barbablù (Bluebeard)	Fabbri/Rcs	2005	Denotative
Roberto Piumini	Altan	Barbablù (Bluebeard)	Edizioni EL	2008	Denotative
Jacob and Wilhelm Grimm	Lisbeth Zwerger	Cappuccetto Rosso (Little Red Riding Hood)	Nord-Sud Edizioni	1983, 2003	Denotative
Jacob and Wilhelm Grimm	Pia Valentinis	Cappuccetto Rosso (Little Red Riding Hood)	Fabbri/Rcs	2005	Denotative
Nicola Cinquetti	Stefano Morri	Cappuccetto Rosso (Little Red Riding Hood)	Edizioni Arka	2006	Denotative
Roberto Piumini	Alessandro Sanna	Cappuccetto Rosso (Little Red Riding Hood)	Edizioni EL	2005	Denotative

Jacob and Wilhelm Grimm	Giulia Orecchia	*Hansel and Gretel*	Fabbri/Rcs	2005	Denotative
Rika Lesser	Paul Zelinsky	*Hansel and Gretel*	Puffin books	1984, 1999	Denotative
Roberto Piumini	Anna Laura Cantone	*Hansel and Gretel*	Edizioni EL	2005	Denotative

Conversely, the illustrations from the fairy tale picturebooks characterized by a visual connotative language, add 'something' to the text through the use of uncommon graphic and artistic codes; for example, experimentation with unusual perspective and composition and the wise use of symbols and visual metaphors. These texts instil a sense of wonder, curiosity and emotional tension and propel the reader towards a more aesthetically aware state. For instance, they allow readers to associate different meanings/perspectives with the reading of the same narrative sequences. Table 6.2 shows the fairy tale picturebooks using connotative visual language:

TABLE 6.2 Fairy tale picturebooks using connotative visual language

Author	Illustrator	Title	Publishing house	Year	Visual language
Chiara Carrer	Chiara Carrer	*Barba-blù (Bluebeard)*	Donzelli Editore	2007	Connotative
Nicola Cinquetti	Alessandra Cimatoribus	*Barbablù (Bluebeard)*	Edizioni Arka	2009	Connotative
Charles Dickens	Fabian Negrin	*Capitan Omicidio (Captain Murderer)*	Orecchio Acerbo	2006	Connotative
Jacob and Wilhelm Grimm	Kveta Pacovská	*Cappuccetto Rosso (Little Red Riding Hood)*	Nord-Sud Edizioni	2008	Connotative
Anthony Browne	Anthony Browne	*Hansel and Gretel*	Walker books	1981, 2003	Connotative
Jacob and Wilhelm Grimm	Pablo Auladell	*La casetta di cioccolato (The Chocolate House)*	Kalandraka	2008	Connotative
Jacob and Wilhelm Grimm	Lorenzo Mattotti	*Hansel and Gretel*	Orecchio Acerbo	2009	Connotative
Jacob and Wilhelm Grimm	Susanne Janssen	*Hansel and Gretel*	Éditions Étre	2007	Connotative
Chiara Carrer	Chiara Carrer	*La bambina e il lupo (The Child and the Wolf)*	Topipittori	2005	Connotative
A. R. Almodóvar	Marc Taeger	*La vera storia di Cappuccetto Rosso (The True Story of Little Red Riding Hood)*	Kalandraka	2009	Connotative

The phases of the observational research

The observational research was divided into two phases. The first phase lasted 5 weeks (4 days a week, 5 hours a day). In the first week the main goals, the path and the children's role in the research were shared with the parents and their children. In the second week, I presented and read two picturebooks in each classroom, *Piccolo blu e piccolo giallo* (*Little Blue and Little Yellow*) by Leo Lionni and *Dentro me* (*In Me*) by Alex Cousseau and Kitty Crowther to get the children familiar with different types of visual narration (abstract and symbolic language) and with the disclosed and undisclosed elements of the picturebooks (such as details on the cover, on the endpapers, on the title page, etc.). These first two weeks were also very important in creating space and opportunity for discussion with the children.

I then started the observational research with the fairy tale picturebooks. Each week I presented a different fairy tale: initially *Little Red Riding Hood*, then *Hansel and Gretel*, and finally *Bluebeard* in the third week. I followed the same sequence each time I introduced a new fairy tale picturebook to the children: first, I presented the title, authors, illustrators and publishing house, front cover, endpapers, colophon (at the beginning or at the end of the book) and title page, then I began reading aloud (I read the first two pages of the text, then I showed children the pages I had just read so that they could see the pictures, and continued like this until the end of the picturebook).

After the shared read, the discussion phase started: the children were divided into small groups of no more than 7 or 8 children. Each group was encouraged to read, analyse and compare the seven different versions of each fairy tale, expressing their thoughts and preferences. I personally carried out both the reading phase and the analysis of the books with the children and I allowed time and space for the children's questions and doubts in relation to the previous reads. During the whole observational research period I was able to rely on the expertise of Alessandra Carraro, a sociologist specializing in ethnography from the University of Padua. She was asked to observe the children's reactions, to tape their comments with audio and video devices and to write the ethnographic notes.

During this first phase working with the different iconographic versions of the selected works, I examined the ways in which the children communicated with the text and pictures, grasping similarities and differences between the textual and the visual narration, wondering about the metaphorical and challenging illustrations of the selected fairy tales and developing a more consistent aesthetic attentiveness.

The second phase of the research focused on the children borrowing the fairy tale picturebooks to read at home. This lending-activity lasted one month (one day a week during the school timetable). The children were free to choose any of the fairy tales used during the research, take them home to read and to share with their parents. My purpose was clear: to discover which illustrated fairy tales the children were most curious about or liked the most outside the classroom context.

The results of this research were collected through a visual questionnaire completed during three subsequent surveys: the first survey was carried out before the observational research began, the second survey, one month after the first and the third at the end of the research after two months. During the research I also used some typical tools of qualitative research, that is, ethnographic notes, audio-video recordings and reading journals written at home by the children and their parents separately. The parents' journals were a valuable observational source for the reading and qualitative interpretation of the data.

The findings of the observational research

The children's responses to the books

First of all, the research highlighted that the children very much enjoyed being actively involved in hermeneutic (interpretational) reading activities. In fact, the analysis of the children's reading journals revealed that they particularly liked the discussion phase during which they were given opportunities to make comparisons, discover similarities and differences in diverse visual narrative plots, solve challenging ambiguous visual enigmas and experience different aesthetic styles. Huck's journal entry noted how the books made him curious:

> It seemed strange to see these books which didn't have a lot of differences, but instead were differences. And how!
>
> These books made me really curious because they had particular pictures which hid something strange. And then in the end in these seven books I noticed these differences in some books. So these seven books really were different one from the other.
>
> *Huck (aged 10)*

The pleasure of managing interpretive processes was stated even by those children who weren't keen on books and reading. These children were often fascinated by the dark side of a story like Bluebeard as can be seen in Billy's journal response:

> From the first day we started I liked it straightaway because you read us funny books and scary books like Bluebeard when the wife found the room where he hung his wives who found out about that room and when he was going to kill his wife because she had seen the room as well.
>
> *Billy (aged 10)*

The research points out that reading and comparing different controversial picturebooks encourages children's interpretative responses and involvement. It is a challenging activity that could be widely used and promoted at school and undertaken with other subjects or in different contexts. Luce's journal response shows this kind of involvement:

I would really like to do the project again. It would be nice to read other books about Pinocchio for instance or Puss in Boots. I'd also like to see the pictures in the books we read again.

Luce (aged 8)

In addition to the children's enjoyment of being involved, the research confirmed the existence of stereotypes in these children's choices with respect to the visual mode of representation in children's picturebooks. The existence of such stereotypes is confirmed by the choices the children made during the first observation, at the beginning of the research before they had been offered any aesthetic tools to help read visual texts. In this phase, children chose the picturebooks they preferred exclusively on the basis of a quick reading of the text and pictures, when leafing through the books for the first time.

Most of the children (83.9 per cent) chose those fairy tales in which characters, animals, objects, environment and situations were illustrated in a familiar, unambiguous and explicit way according to the unequivocal 'realism' of the visual denotative language. Only 16.1 per cent of them said they preferred a visual connotative language. Strangely, this trend was consolidated in children aged 10. These children appeared to be much more set in their artistic representational ways (90.5 per cent chose the denotative visual mode of representation) than children aged 8 (88.2 per cent) or even 6 (72.3 per cent). In effect children aged 6 were far more willing to choose fairy tale picturebooks with a visual connotative language than the older children: 27.8 per cent of children aged 6, 11.8 per cent of children aged 8 and 9.5 per cent of children aged 10.

Visual cultural conditioning does not wane as the years go by; on the contrary, it grows in older children. If not duly educated, children tend to lose their confidence in dealing with connotative (figurative and symbolic) interpretation (Gardner, 2006 [1983]). In fact the ethnographic notes reported examples in which the 10-year-old children often declared, during the first sessions of the empirical study, that characters, animals, objects, environments and situations have to be easy to identify and pictures should literally explain any narrative passage of the text. They declared that the visual narration has to tell everything and any element that could lead to ambiguity or equivocal interpretive involvement should be removed. For example, the children's desire to find a clear visual explanation for each narrative passage is evident in the following dialogue with children during the analysis of Grimms' fairy tale *Little Red Riding Hood* illustrated by Pia Valentinis (2005):

Ben:	the trees are again bare.
Viviana:	but the wolf was alive before!
Group of children:	what's that got to do with crows?
Laura:	but how could he die? Pictures don't answer these questions for a child who doesn't know the story . . . .

Ethnographic notes with 10-year-old children, 4 March 2010

At the beginning of this study, the children tended to avoid ambiguous and controversial picturebooks. They chose picturebooks characterized by explicit, denotative visual language because these books provided them with referentiality and thus reassurance. Nevertheless, as argued earlier, aesthetic investigation should be crucial in children's experience to disrupt and challenge their customary visual expectations. The data analysis, in fact, pointed out a remarkable change in the preferences expressed by children as the research progressed.

In the second survey, the percentage of children who said they preferred the fairy tales characterized by a connotative visual language rose to 45.9 per cent, while the percentage of children who said they preferred the fairy tales written with a denotative language fell to 54.1 per cent. The increase was particularly significant, as it reached + 29.8 per cent. But the highest peak was reached during the third survey, at the end of the observational research (+ 46 per cent), after the children had borrowed the books shared at school and taken them home.

The opportunity to take home, share and read again the most interesting books changed the initial situation. The children's new aesthetic attentiveness resulting from their ability to become familiar with challenging visual texts and to share interpretive processes led many of these children (62.1 per cent) to move their preferences towards picturebooks marked by a connotative visual language: John's journal reflected this change:

> I really enjoyed this experience because I found out that book illustrators have their own way of illustrating books, that there are different versions which come from the same story. For example Little Red Riding Hood, or I found out that books can be in black and white and loads of other things . . .!
>
> *John (aged 8)*

The children's preferences

At the end of the research, which fairy tale picturebooks did these children prefer?

Strong and visually challenging fairy tales, with a high aesthetic potential, emotionally pregnant, full of ambiguous and controversial details stimulated the children.

When faced with these kinds of text they asked questions, expressed their doubts, questioned ambiguous pictures. They were very curious and fascinated by dark and provocative narrations.

During the reading of Grimms' *Hansel and Gretel* illustrated by Lorenzo Mattotti (2009) (Figure 6.1) several 8-year-old children gave their thoughts:

John:	it's a mysterious book but for me also strange because I didn't expect the pictures to be like that. . . . I think they are fascinating, they were really good at illustrating it.
Piero:	you can see that they were done with a paintbrush.

FIGURE 6.1 Lorenzo Mattotti's representation of *Hänsel e Gretel* (W. & J. Grimm, & L. Mattotti, 2009).

Penelope:	for me the pictures are wonderful but they make me a bit unsure because Hansel looks big.
John:	I think they are very . . . fascinating.

Ethnographic notes with 8-year-old children, 11 March 2010

Shaping young readers' taste in picturebook choices

This research revealed that it is possible to shape a young reader's taste. The opportunity to read, share, discuss and respond to the picturebooks may support an aesthetic awareness, break some stereotyped visual habits and promote in children a more mature attitude towards reading. Additionally, the pleasure experienced in this hermeneutic involvement may lead children to choose similar picturebooks that can make them think, question and respond, and allow them to relive the same experience. Children from each of the differing age ranges were asked:

Researcher: Out of everything that we have read or looked at what struck or surprised you the most?

That we read so many books, I thought we would read only three books about three stories.

Eric (aged 6), ethnographic notes of 16 March 2010

The stories because I didn't know that so many Little Red Riding Hoods and Bluebeards existed.

Tyn (aged 8), ethnographic notes of 15 March 2010

I dream about a green dragon with a black tongue
that wants to eat me up.
The houses are green too,
like the grass in our garden with the swing,
where Daddy and I used to play
with the ball.

I miss him a lot.

Mummy says we'll soon be together.

PLATE 1

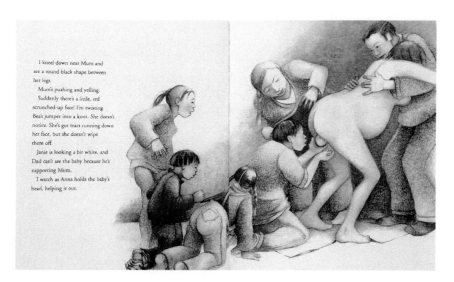

I kneel down near Mum and
see a round black shape between
her legs.
  Mum's pushing and yelling.
  Suddenly there's a little, red
scrunched-up face! I'm twisting
Bea's jumper into a knot. She doesn't
notice. She's got tears running down
her face, but she doesn't wipe
them off.
  Janie is looking a bit white, and
Dad can't see the baby because he's
supporting Mum.
  I watch as Anna holds the baby's
head, helping it out.

PLATE 2

PLATE 3

PLATE 4

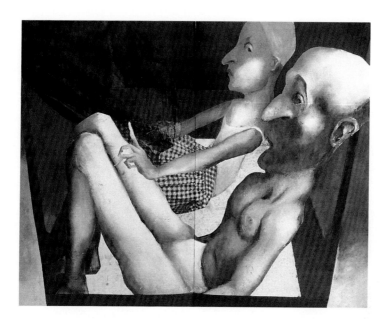

PLATE 5

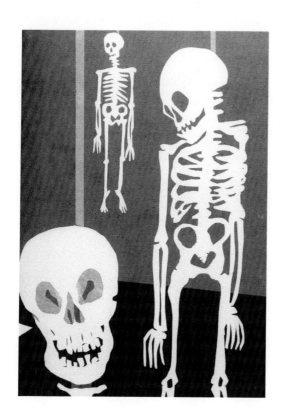

PLATE 6

PLATE 7

Death stroked a few rumpled feathers back into place,
then he carried her to the great river.

PLATE 8

PLATE 9

PLATE 10

PLATE 11

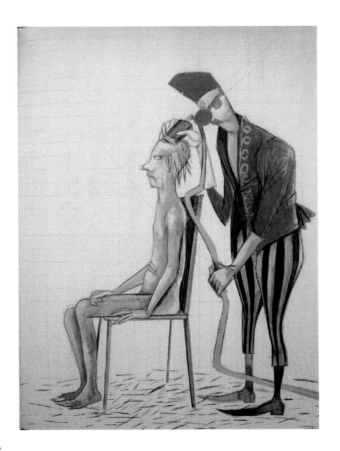

PLATE 12

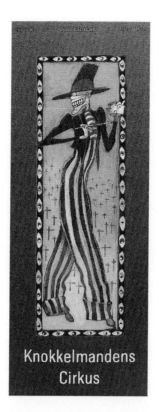

Knokkelmandens
Cirkus

PLATE 13

PLATE 14

L'enfant saute sur le lit et
dévisage la gueule noire
du loup. Elle frémit !

« Que vous avez de grands
yeux ! »

« C'est pour mieux te voir mon
enfant ! C'est pour mieux te voir ! »

Puis elle se laisse glisser sur le
corps sombre :

« Oh ma grand que vous êtes poilouse ! »

« C'est de vieillesse mon enfant !
C'est de vieillesse ! »

« Que vous avez de grands bras ! »

« C'est pour mieux t'embrasser, mon enfant !
C'est pour mieux t'embrasser ! »

« Que vous avez de grandes jambes ! »

« C'est pour mieux courir, mon enfant !
C'est pour mieux courir ! »

L'enfant se redresse tout à coup et
met sa main dans la gueule du loup :

« Que vous avez de grandes dents ! »

« C'est pour te manger ! »

PLATE 15

PLATE 16

PLATE 17

PLATE 18

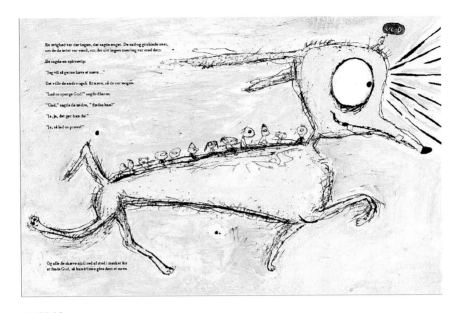

PLATE 19

PLATE 20

PLATE 21

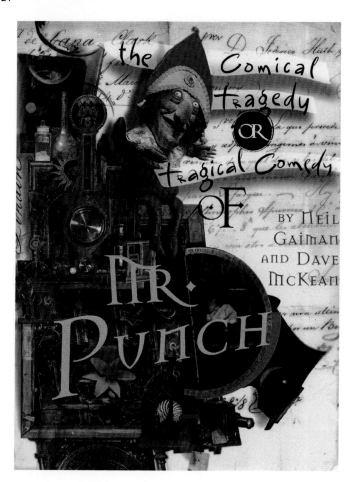

PLATE 22

PLATE 23

PLATE 24

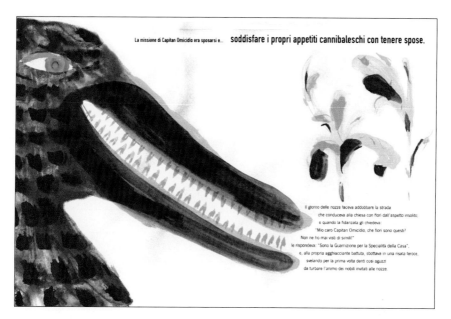

PLATE 25

PLATE 26

Suddenly, lightning splits the sky.

In the wildest parts of the forest, the law of the food chain holds sway. Small creatures give way to large ones. With a clap of thunder, the jackals are gone.

A smiling hunter. What big teeth he has. Dark and strong and perfect in his timing. Sophia tells him of her grandmother and her little home. Of the biscuits and honey.

PLATE 27

Luckily this wolf was a vegetarian, so they shared a jam sandwich, became the best of friends, and lived happily ever after.

PLATE 28

terrible fates are
inevitable

PLATE 29

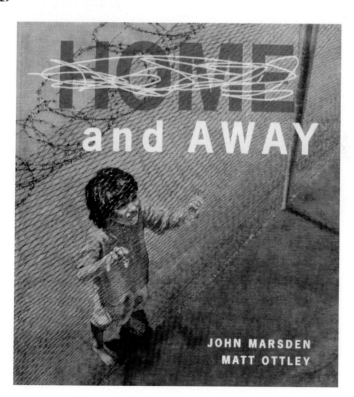

PLATE 30

Denver was rich. Very rich. Very, very rich.
He lived in a big house called Berton Manor.

PLATE 31

PLATE 32

When you read Hansel and Gretel with pictures in black and white because I had never seen it before.

Penelope (aged 8), ethnographic notes of 15 March 2010

Showing us so many books like that!

Tom (aged 10), ethnographic notes of 16 March 2010

Reading the books.

David (aged 10), ethnographic notes of 16 March 2010

So many books.

Percy (aged 10), ethnographic notes of 16 March 2010

So many books and pictures.

Goffredo (aged 10), ethnographic notes of 16 March 2010

Challenging children's curiosity: Captain Murderer, an original Bluebeard

It came as no a surprise that at the end of the research the fairy tale picturebook that best satisfied the children's curiosities and expectations was *Captain Murderer* (*Capitan Omicidio*) by Charles Dickens and Negrin, 2006. After the first read, this picturebook had a very low interest percentage (5.4 per cent), and this was only among children aged 6. Children aged 8 and 10 didn't show any interest in *Captain Murderer*. At the end of the research this situation was completely overturned: this fairy tale achieved the highest percentage of preferences among all the fairy tales (21.1 per cent expressed by children aged 6 years, 20 per cent by children aged 8 years and 29.2 per cent by children aged 10 years). It was interesting to point out that this picturebook was of interest to the majority of the children, regardless not only of the age bracket they belonged to but also of their gender.

What was so special about this picturebook? What kind of aesthetical experience does this visual narration offer to young readers?

The classical version of *Bluebeard* was first written in a literary form by Charles Perrault in 1697. This fairy tale has since been continuously rewritten, adapted and transformed over the course of the intervening centuries and many cultural variations have been produced (Tatar, 2004). *Bluebeard* is a very appealing 'tenacious cultural story' because it produces:

> the suspense of all stories in which an enigma about a killer must be solved by one of his potential victims. And by casting the killer as husband and the victim as wife, it adds the ingredients of intimacy, vulnerability, trust, and betrayal to make the story all the more captivating.
>
> *Tatar (2004: 14)*

This Bluebeardean capacity to grasp the readers' imagination affected Charles Dickens and references to this persistent folktale 'recur throughout his works from *The Pickwick Papers* (1837) to *the Mystery of Edwin Drood* (1869–70)' (Barzilai, 2004: 506).

Bluebeard is one of the most blood-curdling fairy tales of the folk tradition. Nevertheless, as Shuli Barzilai (2004) revealed, it did not seem to be blood-curdling enough for Charles Dickens, who, in effect, aimed in his *Bluebeard* retelling, called *Captain Murderer*, 'to draw on a cannibalistic variant of the taly-type [sic] and garnished it, so to speak, with further grisly flourishes' (Barzilai, 2004: 507). Charles Dickens had known of *Captain Murderer* since he was a child. A nursemaid, strangely named Mercy, told him hundreds of times in his early youth the story of an 'off-shoot of the Blue Beard family': it was this ogre who 'terrorized the young Dickens over a period of many years' (Tatar, 2004: 13).

What kind of story is Dickens' *Captain Murderer?*

Originally written by Charles Dickens as *Nurse's Stories*, in his collection of sketches and reminiscences, *The Uncommercial Traveller* (1860), *Captain Murderer* is based on a folktale that brings to mind also the plots of *The Robber Bridegroom* and *Fitcher's Bird* in Jakob and Wilhelm Grimm's *Tales for Young and Old (Kinder- und Hausmärchen)*, 1857, even if no cannibal elements are present in Grimms' tales (Barzilai, 2004). It tells the story of Bluebeard, a rich and powerful man who vented his showy cannibalistic tendencies on young women exactly one month after marrying them. These poor women become tasty morsels on his sumptuously laid table. He killed them by chopping off their heads, after which he cut them into small pieces and put them into a pie, whose dough had been prepared in advance by the very same women just before their death. He cooked the pies at the baker's and then, satisfied, he devoured them, picking even the bones. Marriages and murders followed one after the other in a seemingly unstoppable sequence until a young woman came along who, thirsting for revenge, managed to put an end to Bluebeard's terrible game.

Dickens' *Captain Murderer* is a strong mixture of genres: it belongs 'to the genre of the comic tale with socially subversive elements', but also represents 'a tale of gothic terror in which the desire touch [sic] is a *frisson*, a shudder or thrill of fear'. It is a 'comic-macabre story into the mode of carnivalization' (Barzilai, 2004: 510). Above all, *Captain Murderer* is a story 'to be shared in a public arena' (Barzilai, 2004: 511), as children revealed in their journals:

> I really liked Bluebeard because I didn't know the story and it made me curious because it has something mysterious about it, it's interesting as well as being wonderful. I really liked the two books called Captain Murderer and Bluebeard.
>
> *Suzy's journal (aged 8)*

The extraordinary narrative power of this story has been greatly increased by the visually challenging metaphors created by the illustrator Fabian Negrin. His connotative illustrations have a strong aesthetic potential, they are full of ambiguous and controversial details and contribute to an emotionally pregnant atmosphere, without shying away from the feeling of disorientation that can arise when dealing

FIGURE 6.2 Fabian Negrin's representation of *Captain Murderer* (*Capitan Omicidio*, Dickens & Negrin, 2006).

with this kind of ambiguity and controversy. Children were indeed disoriented by the representation of *Captain Murderer*. They expected him to be depicted as a 'real' cannibal ogre and not as an elegant bird; a challenging intertextual reference to the bloody fairy tale *Fitcher's Bird* mentioned above (Figure 6.2).

For these children, Fabian Negrin's illustrations became a space for visual and aesthetic experimentation. The presence of visual symbols delivered a strong emotional impact and the ingenious visual metaphors stimulated children into looking at the images with astonishment and curiosity.

Seeing and interpreting the visual metaphors

Captain Murderer demands of the reader a visual multiple level of reading. The reader is actively involved in the Gombrichean 'seeing and interpreting' process described earlier in order to grasp the meaning of the story. An example of this excellent use of visual metaphors can be seen for instance in the presence of a flower, the iris, never mentioned in the verbal text. This beautiful flower can be seen not only on the front cover (Figure 6.3), but also on the endpapers (Figure 6.4) and inside the book (Figure 6.5) (Plate 25).

The iris is a metaphor. The children liked the inclusion of the flower and although they never explicitly wrote about it, they did, on a few occasions report that this flower referred to something 'good', 'reassuring' and 'related to the butterflies'. Their intuition was surprisingly close to the undisclosed symbolic meaning of the

FIGURE 6.3 Irises on the cover: *Capitan Omicidio*, Dickens & Negrin, 2006.

FIGURE 6.4 Irises on the front endpapers: *Capitan Omicidio*, Dickens & Negrin, 2006.

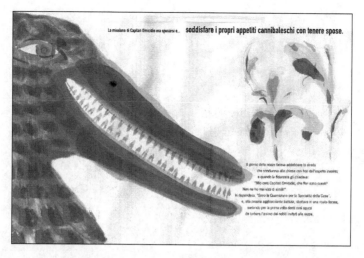

FIGURE 6.5 (Plate 25) Irises inside the book: *Capitan Omicidio*, Dickens & Negrin, 2006.

visual metaphor because in effect this flower has a double meaning: on the one hand it stands for good news; on the other it implies a symbolic reference to the Greek goddess Iris, messenger of the gods, classically depicted as a young and radiant woman, her wings the diaphanous and iridescent colours of the rainbow. According to Greek mythology this goddess, very similar to a butterfly, was chosen to take dead women's souls to the Elysian Fields (Figure 6.6).

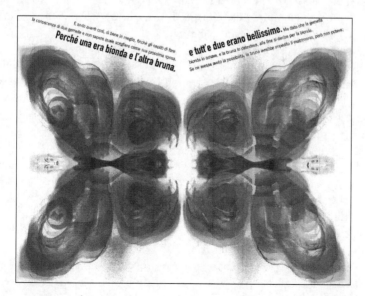

FIGURE 6.6 The two sisters became Captain Murderer's wives: *Capitan Omicidio*, Dickens & Negrin, 2006.

FIGURE 6.7   Bloodstains from Captain Murderer's wives: *Capitan Omicidio*, Dickens & Negrin, 2006.

In the picturebook Negrin depicted Captain Murderer's wives as butterflies and this visual metaphor (absolutely not present in the verbal text) had a great emotional impact on the children. It really enhanced their curiosity about the unusual but 'appropriate' aesthetic choice of the illustrator.

At the beginning of the research project, this visually ambiguous and controversial picturebook disturbed both children and adults, some of whom had conflicting (and negative) reactions towards this picturebook until the end of the observational research. The adults considered the story completely inappropriate for reading to children aged 6, 8 and even 10 years and thought that the bloodstains and the cannibalistic elements would scare children (Figure 6.7).

Despite the adults' resistance and their negative reactions to this picturebook, the children were absolutely fascinated by it. They were certainly frightened by the story but they would not have stopped it from being read to them. The sense of wonder, the thrilling plot, the visual enigmas definitely enchanted them, as is evident from the ethnographic notes made when the book was being read to the 10-year-old children (Figure 6.8).

The researcher takes the book, a lot of the children had seen it before but Gastone asks to see it:

Ben: It's gruesome.
Gildo: Even the title is scary.

The researcher begins reading and everyone moves closer to the book except Bianca and Perla.

Viviana: He eats women …
Perla comes a bit closer.
The children are silent and very attentive. …

Gastone: The bride was the ingredient! [Figure 6.9]

Ethnographic notes of 15 March 2010

FIGURE 6.8   One of Captain Murderer's wives: *Capitan Omicidio*, Dickens & Negrin, 2006.

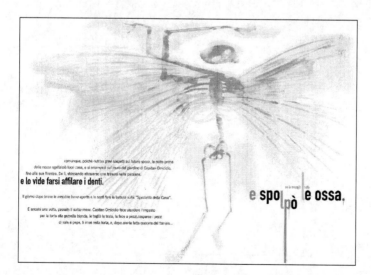

FIGURE 6.9   The death of one of Captain Murderer's wives: *Capitan Omicidio*, Dickens & Negrin, 2006.

Two months of picturebook reading and visual comparison allowed the children to refine their 'seeing and interpreting' ability and to gain an aesthetic awareness as readers. Billy's journal reflected this awareness:

> Well I liked everything we did, but the best thing was that you told us 'to see' and then 'to look' because it's a good painting technique.
>
> *Billy (aged 10)*

In *Captain Murderer* the illustrations, which acted as receptors, enriched the reading activity with riddles; after some initially unsuccessful attempts, these children formulated some interesting interpretative hypotheses. This triggered off a positive mechanism that encouraged them to look for other visually enigmatic details. It was through this process of research and interpretation that *Captain Murderer* increased its charm and fascination.

At the end, children were captured by the emotional landscape and the narrative tension emerging from *Captain Murderer*. The combination of Dickens' thrilling comic–macabre story and Negrin's fascinating, inconsistent and challenging visual metaphors made *Captain Murderer* the picturebook most chosen by these children. One of the 6-year-old children drew his preferred picturebook (Figure 6.10).

FIGURE 6.10 'The picturebook I preferred'. Drawing from the journal of a child aged 6 involved in the observational research.

Conclusion: shaping the young readers' visual and aesthetic curiosity

If during the pre-school period children like to build daring controversial and metaphorical associations even in different semantic areas, it is during the primary school years that they gradually give up the habit of using symbolic and figurative languages to read and interpret external and inner reality. It is a great loss because they thereby lose some of the antibodies that can help them to counter and fight against visual cultural conditioning.

It is crucial to ensure that children have access to books that make use of figurative language and to bring this kind of language, even in its darkest and controversial versions, into classrooms. Moreover, ambiguous and controversial picturebooks are a valuable *instrument* in cultivating this mental attitude, because they can induce in the reader astonishment and curiosity and allow him/her to undertake a process of discovery and research.

Children's desire to be presented with very realistic pictures must be satisfied. However, if teachers and educators offer young readers books that satisfy their natural need for concreteness and realism, they should also offer them books that make appropriate use of symbolic language, books whose visual validity depends above all on rich and complex aesthetic contents. This visual mode of representation gives space for things to be undisclosed and unsaid and encourages children's interpretive involvement. It is a precious tool that allows children to experiment with the relativity of points of view. In order to encourage this, it is essential to arouse children's curiosity.

Curiosity is a resource that a shrewd teacher should be able to call upon and exploit in the reading processes. As Maria Chiara Levorato (2000) points out, curiosity, as well as interest and wonder, plays a strategic role in the development of cognitive and aesthetic awareness. Curiosity activates a state of excitement that provides the child with the impetus to look for and discover new sensations, experiences and knowledge. Curiosity stimulates children's thoughts. Since children are often attracted by what is different, mysterious and forbidden, wouldn't it also be advisable to recommend to them strong controversial picturebooks?

While *Captain Murderer* was being read these children were silent and completely involved. The gruesome aspects of the book held their attention: their tension was palpable and engrossing. Each picture increased their thrilling expectations by offering a new visual enigma. With each page their worst doubts were continuously reinforced by the ambiguous and controversial details.

The Gombrichean approach 'to see is to interpret' shows that challenging visual explorations in picturebooks can effectively stimulate the reader's aesthetic response, feed his/her curiosity and shape his/her taste. Last but not least visually challenging picturebooks are a powerful tool for enjoying reading.

At the end of this research the main question is not whether a visual mode of representation is appropriate or inappropriate for a child, or whether ambiguous or unambiguous picturebooks can shape young readers' taste. The main question is whether teachers and educators are well enough 'equipped' to share with children challenging controversial picturebooks because children surely are.

Note

This paper was partially inspired by the essay Campagnaro M. (2013) Educare lo sguardo. Riflessioni pedagogiche sugli albi illustrati, *Encyclopaideia* 35, pp. 89–108 and by the essay Campagnaro M. (2014) Lo scudo di Perseo. Fiabe e metafora, in Campagnaro, M. (ed.) *Le terre della fantasia. Leggere la letteratura per l'infanzia*, Rome: Donzelli.

Academic references

Arizpe, E. & Styles, M. (2003) *Children Reading Pictures: Interpreting Visual Texts.* London: Routledge.

Arizpe, E., Colomer, T. & Martínez-Roldán, C. (eds) (2014) *Visual Journeys through Wordless Narratives: An International Inquiry with Immigrant Children and The Arrival.* London: Bloomsbury Academic.

Barthes, R. (1977 [1964]) Rhetoric of the image, in *Image, Music, Text.* New York: Hill and Wang.

Barzilai, S. (2004) The Bluebeard barometer: Charles Dickens and Captain Murderer. *Victorian Literature and Culture* 32: 505–524.

Campagnaro, M. (2012) *Narrare per immagini: uno strumento per l'indagine critica.* Lecce: Pensa Multimedia.

Campagnaro, M. & Dallari M. (2013) *Incanto e racconto nel labirinto delle figure.* Trento: Erickson.

Colomer, T., Kümmerling-Meibauer, B. & Silva-Díaz, C. (eds) (2010) *New Directions in Picturebook Research.* New York: Routledge.

Davey, N. (2011) Gadamer's aesthetics, in Edward N. Zalta (ed.) *The Stanford Encyclopedia of Philosophy.* http://plato.stanford.edu/archives/win2011/entries/gadamer-aesthetics/

Evans, J. (2009) *Talking Beyond the Page. Reading and Responding to Picturebooks.* New York: Routledge.

Gadamer, H.G. (1986) *Die Aktualität des Schönen, Kunst als Spiel, Symbol und Fest.* Stuttgart: Reclam Philipp Jun.

Gardner, H. (2009 [1983]) *Formae mentis. Saggio sulla pluralità dell'intelligenza.* Milan: Feltrinelli.

Gombrich, E.H. (2002 [1960]) *Arte e Illusione. Studio sulla psicologia della rappresentazione pittorica.* Milan: Leonardo Arte.

Hamelin (2012) *Ad occhi aperti. Leggere l'albo illustrato.* Rome: Donzelli.

Levorato, M.C. (2000) *Le emozioni della lettura.* Bologna: Il Mulino.

Linstone, H.A. & Turoff, M. (eds) (1975) *The Delphi Method: Techniques and Applications.* Reading, MA: Addison-Wesley.

Nikolajeva, M. & Scott, C. (2006) *How Picturebooks Work.* New York: Routledge.

Nodelman, P. (1988) *Words about Pictures: The Narrative Art of Children's Picture Books.* Athens: The University of Georgia Press.

Pantaleo, S. (2008) *Exploring Children's Responses to Contemporary Picturebooks.* Toronto: University of Toronto Press.

Salisbury, M. & Styles, M. (2012) *Children's Picturebooks. The Art of Visual Storytelling.* London: Laurence King.

Schwarcz, J. (1982) *Ways of Illustrator: Visual Communication in Children's Literature.* Chicago: American Library Association.

Sipe, L.R. & Pantaleo, S. (eds) (2008) *Postmodern Picturebooks. Play, Parody and Self-Referentiality.* New York: Routledge.

Tatar, M. (2004) *Secrets beyond the Door: The Story of Bluebeard and His Wives.* Princeton, NJ: Princeton University Press.

Children's literature

Almodóvar, A.R. & Taeger, M. (2009) *La vera storia di Cappuccetto Rosso*. Florence: Kalandraka.

Browne, A. (2003) *Hansel and Gretel*. London: Walker books.

Carrer, C. (2005) *La bambina e il lupo*. Milan: Topipittori.

Carrer, C. (2007) *Barba-blu*. Rome: Donzelli.

Cinquetti, N. & Cimatoribus, A. (2009) *Barbablù*. Milan: Arka.

Cinquetti, N. & Morri, S. (2006) *Cappuccetto Rosso*. Milan: Arka.

Cousseau, A. & Crowther, K. (2007) *Dentro me*. Milan: Topipittori.

Dickens, C. (1860) *The Uncommercial Traveller*. London: Chapman and Hall.

Dickens, C. & Negrin, F. (2006) *Capitan Omicidio*. Rome: Orecchio Acerbo.

Grimm, J. & W. (1992 [1857]) *Tales for Young and Old (Kinder- und Hausmärchen)*. Turin: Einaudi.

Grimm, J. & W., & Auladell, P. (2008) *La casetta di cioccolato*. Florence: Kalandraka.

Grimm, J. & W., & Janssen, S. (2007) *Hänsel et Gretel*. Paris: Éditions Être.

Grimm, J. & W., & Mattotti, L. (2009) *Hänsel e Gretel*. Rome: Orecchio Acerbo.

Grimm, J. & W., & Orecchia, G. (2005) *Hansel e Gretel*. Milan: Fabbri.

Grimm, J. & W., & Pacovská, K. (2008) *Cappuccetto Rosso*. Milan: Nord-Sud.

Grimm, J. & W., & Valentinis, P. (2005) *Cappuccetto Rosso*. Milan: Fabbri.

Grimm, J. & W., & Zwerger, L. (2003) *Cappuccetto Rosso*. Milan: Nord-Sud.

Lesser, R. & Zelinsky, P. (1999) *Hansel and Gretel*. New York: Puffin books.

Lionni, L. (1999) *Piccolo blu e piccolo giallo*. Milan: Babalibri.

Messenger, N. (2005) *Imagine*. Cambridge, MA: Candlewick Press.

Perrault, C. & Battut, E. (2001) *Barbablù*. Trieste: Bohem Press.

Perrault, C. & Claverie, J. (1995) *Barbablù*. Trieste: Emme Edizioni.

Perrault, C. & Ligi, R. (2005) *Barbablù*. Milan: Fabbri.

Piumini R. & Altan, F. (2008) *Barbablù*. Trieste: Edizioni EL.

Piumini, R. & Cantone, A.C. (2005) *Hansel e Gretel*. Trieste: Edizioni EL.

Piumini, R. & Sanna, A. (2005) *Cappuccetto Rosso*. Trieste: Edizioni EL.

7

BEWARE OF THE FOX!

Emotion and deception in *Fox* by Margaret Wild and Ron Brooks

*Bettina Kümmerling-Meibauer and
Jörg Meibauer*

From the perspective of an adult reader, Fox *by Margaret Wild and Ron Brooks certainly is a challenging picturebook. Basically, it is a love triangle between a half-blind dog, a broken-winged magpie and a fox, in which the fox seduces the magpie away from the half-blind dog by deception. The accompanying pictures give the impression of emotional arousal and despair. In order to reconstruct a possible interpretation of this particular text–picture relation from the point of view of a child reader, we analyse the fox as a specific literary character, discuss the notions of deception and seduction (with reference to the child's emerging mind-reading abilities), ask how empathy with literary characters contributes to the child's moral theme comprehension, and include emotional aspects of the pictures (especially those triggered by the colours). The comprehensive analysis shows that* Fox *can be read on multiple levels, thus qualifying for the status of a genuine crossover picturebook. On a methodological level, this chapter shows how picturebook theory can benefit from an in-depth analysis of a single picturebook when cognitive aspects related to the picturebook are taken into account.*

Introduction

This chapter analyses the challenging content of the picturebook *Fox* (2000), with text by Margaret Wild and illustrations by Ron Brooks. By 'content', we refer to both the pictorial and the textual level. Why is this picturebook 'challenging'? It is challenging, because it presents a story about love and seduction in a very condensed way; at first sight, not a topic expected to be appropriate for an audience of young children. In our analysis, we will focus not only on the content (i.e. the story and the artwork) but also on the three literary characters, Fox, Magpie and Dog, and their narrative characterisation through a network of emotions. We also look at Fox as a trickster and deceiver, embedding this character into narratives of lying and deception (Kümmerling-Meibauer & Meibauer, 2011a; Kümmerling-Meibauer & Meibauer, 2014). Analysing emotions and deception, as related to the three characters, is important for our investigation, since the perspective we take is driven by our specific approach to picturebook theory that consists in working out the cognitive underpinnings of picturebooks, both from the side of production and comprehension (Kümmerling-Meibauer & Meibauer, 2013; Kümmerling-Meibauer *et al.*, 2014). Moreover, we are interested in how assumed cognitive restrictions for children's understanding of picturebooks can be violated or transgressed, and ultimately give an answer to the question how a 'challenge' might be constituted (Kümmerling-Meibauer & Meibauer, 2011b).

Challenging story, challenging artwork

The title of the picturebook, *Fox*, refers to different entities. First of all, *fox* denotes a type of animal. It can be assumed that children have some rudimentary knowledge about foxes, be it from the zoo, from other picturebooks, or from their own experience. Second, *fox* denotes the individual literary character Fox. Thus, Fox is a fictional representative of the class of foxes. Note that there is a shift from denoting a natural class of animals to a proper name; the same holds for Magpie and Dog. Third, *fox* denotes a type of literary character. We know that animal characters have a longstanding tradition in the arts (Obermaier, 2009). Let us briefly sketch the story's plot, before we come to the artwork.

Fox focuses on the triangular relationship between a one-eyed dog, an injured magpie, and a fox. In the beginning, Dog saves Magpie whose wing has been burnt in a bush fire. Although Magpie is on the verge of abandoning hope because she would never be able to fly again, Dog finally convinces her to stay together so that they might support each other. Since Dog runs very fast, Magpie gets the impression of flying when clinging to the dog's back. After a while, their well-rehearsed teamwork is challenged by Fox who accepts Dog's offer to join their companionship. Whereas Dog confides in Fox, Magpie is mistrustful of Fox's actual intentions. She realises that Fox secretly observes her friendly conversations with Dog and stares at her broken wing. One night Fox tries to persuade Magpie to leave Dog, arguing that he can run faster than Dog. Magpie initially refuses this bargain, but also starts having doubts about her refusal. On the third occasion, she gives in to Fox's persuasiveness. Overwhelmed by new sensations caused by Fox's extraordinary speed, Magpie does not realise that Fox takes her far away to a remote desert. There Fox shakes her off his back, leaves her on her own and tells her that she will now know what it is like to be alone. At first Magpie prepares herself to die in the desert, but the thought of Dog who might worry about her disappearance prompts her to begin the arduous journey home.

Ron Brook's artwork embeds and reflects this story in a congenial way. We observe that he experimented with different artistic techniques in order to convey the multiple meanings of the story (Painter, Martin & Unsworth, 2013). He combined oil painting, acrylic painting, water colour illustration, and shellac, thus creating a sophisticated colour scheme which lights the single pages and contributes to the mysterious atmosphere. Moreover, the illustrations are cross-hatched by scratches and lines that Brooks accomplished by using kitchen tools, wires, and oil sticks (see www.allenandunwin.com/uploads/BookPdf/TeachersNotes/9781864484656.pdf). The disrupted patterns and scrapes underscore the dynamic and spontaneous character of the drawings, which often seem to be incomplete and evoke an impression of sketchiness (Figure 7.1).

All pages are fully coloured, the most prominent colours being red, different shades of brown, and black, followed by dark green, yellow, white and blue. The book cover that shows Fox gazing at the viewer reveals that red is the dominant colour, since the fox's fur, the charred forest in the background, and the book titles are all coloured in bright red, intermingled with some orange and yellow under-tones. Throughout the book, the colour red is connected with three domains: the bush fire in the beginning, the fox, and the burning sun in the desert, thus creating a tight connection between the animal, the fire, and the sun. Hence, red is marked as dangerous, since Fox threatens the harmonious relationship between Dog and Magpie, whereas the fire and the sun are depicted as life-threatening natural phenomena. Since the storyline focuses on a triangular relationship, red can also be associated with love and sexual attractiveness, all the more when Fox and Dog are interpreted as males and Magpie as female. Consequently, red arouses different associations that are closely related to strong, even controversial emotions, such as love and hatred, and to menacing situations, such as the bush fire and the hot sun in the desert.

Furthermore, the light brown fur of Dog and the black and white coat of Magpie contrast with the red fur of Fox. When Dog and Magpie enjoy their happy life together, the colour scheme of the landscape presents brownish and greenish tones, penetrated by the blue of the sky and the water. Whenever Fox emerges, the

FIGURE 7.1 *Fox* by Margaret Wild and Ron Brooks (2000).

colour red increasingly impacts the colour scheme, even causing the darkening of the landscape colours.

In addition to the unusual combination of artistic techniques and colour schemes, the typography catches the eye. Ron Brooks has handwritten the whole text in block letters, using a penholder with a thick black pen. He created spiky capitals and shaky letters by writing the text with his left hand. In this manner, Brooks gives the impression that the handcrafted lettering was made by a child or somebody who is not used to or able to write regular letters and to keep to the line. The names of the protagonists are constantly capitalised, sometimes also the word 'flying'. In addition, Brooks changes the direction and size of the font. Singular text blocks are vertically and horizontally arranged so that readers are enticed to rotate the book through 90 degrees or to twist their heads in order to read the text. This strategy slows down the reading process and thus creates a certain pace that matches with the uneven progress of the story. While most of the text is placed on the illustrations, Brooks also glued separate sheets with text onto the illustrated pages so that layers of papers are scattered on the doublespreads. Sometimes the text passages frame the characters. On other doublespreads the text blocks separate the characters from each other, thus emphasising their unbalanced relationship. For instance, the power of Fox who looks down on Magpie as she looks up to him is communicated by the vertical text block between the two (Figure 7.2) (Plate 26).

The paratexts also contribute to the sophisticated meaning of the story. As already mentioned, the book cover focuses on Fox, whose body stretches around the spine and the back cover, thus embracing the whole book. The front endpapers show a burning and partially charred forest, dominated by the colours red and yellow. The flyleaf and the front matters present the other two protagonists, Dog and Magpie. Dog is running fast, holding Magpie in his mouth. These illustrations are quite misleading, since they make the viewer suspect Dog of having caught Magpie as a prey. The fact that the injured bird is actually rescued by Dog and

FIGURE 7.2   (Plate 26) *Fox*: 'Dog beams, but Magpie shrinks away.'

brought to a safe cave is something the book does not reveal until its first doublespread (Mallan, 2013). The subsequent doublespread with the imprint on the left-hand page and the dedications on the right-hand page might be interpreted as an anticipation of the story: While Dog continues carrying Magpie in his mouth he is secretly followed by Fox. The rear endpapers show the same forest as in the front endpapers, only that the trees' foliage is thicker. Accordingly, the colours green, blue and brown dominate in this illustration. Besides the mirroring effect, the endpapers can additionally be interpreted as a sign of hope. Just as the forest has recovered from the severe bush fire, Magpie will hopefully succeed in returning to Dog.

All in all, the layout of the picturebook and the elongated form of the dog's and the fox's bodies manifest the energy of movement and the ambivalent relationship between the three animal characters. Their position and postures on the page invoke tension and highlight the complex power relations among them.

Animal characters

Considering the taxonomy of literary characters in picturebooks, like the one proposed by Nikolajeva and Scott (2001) and Nikolajeva (2002), we find a distinction between human and non-human characters. As for the non-human characters, Nikolajeva (2002) offers another distinction between animals, supernatural creatures, objects, such as toys and machines, and abstract entities, such as colours and letters.

So we can ask, what is the special narrative or aesthetic potential of these non-human characters? According to Nikolajeva (2002: 125), 'children's novels and especially picturebooks abound in clothed and humanized animals, living toys, supernatural creatures (witches, ghosts), as well as personified objects and machines, such as cars or trains'. While it is plausible that these picturebook characters are somehow related to the human reader, for instance, mirroring the reader's ecological, social, and emotional situation, it is also feasible to assume that each of these different characters has its own and very specific narrative and aesthetic potential. Each non-human character challenges certain assumptions of the child about what a 'normal' world looks like, thus introducing the concept of fictional space, where persons and things are quite different from the real world the child experiences.

The question arises, then, why picturebooks apparently show more non-human characters than children's novels. Nikolajeva's (2002: 125) basic tenet is that 'animals, toys, baby witches, and animated objects are always disguises for a child'. This approach, however, seems inadequate with respect to *Fox*. None of the characters seem to be a disguise for the child. Instead, the child is introduced into a fictional world where complex feelings reign. This world can be compared to the world of adults; it can also be compared with the child's own world but this would demand very complex processes of transfer.

With respect to characterisation in picturebooks, Nikolajeva and Scott (2001: 82) argue that:

it is clear that picturebooks allow little room for thorough characterization in the conventional sense. We may generally observe that picturebooks tend to be plot-oriented rather than character-oriented. Further, the plot is often too limited to allow much development, which means that most characters are static rather than dynamic, and flat rather than round.

Again, we think that Magpie, Dog, and Fox are flat characters in a way, yet the emotions they show and the tragic plot in which they are involved give them a more round and dynamic outlook.

What makes *Fox* so exceptional is the intricate triangular relationship between Dog, Magpie and Fox. Whereas the animals' proper names are genderless, their behaviours are certainly not: The way Dog and Fox treat Magpie makes them seem male, and Magpie's need of protection seems to represent the female sex. The ambivalence of their relationship thus switches between friendship and love attachment, additionally stressed by the colour red and the fox's pervading gaze which is perceived by Magpie only. Magpie's feeling of uneasiness is ingeniously presented in the illustration that just shows nothing but the fox's haunted eyes staring at the viewer (Figure 7.3). Fox increasingly takes over space and blocks out Dog and Magpie. Further, while Dog is often on a par with Fox concerning size and posture, Magpie is almost always forced into a corner, until right near the end when she is virtually placed in the middle of the page.

The changing relations are additionally stressed by the position of the characters on the page. In the beginning, Dog and Magpie are close to each other, they even seem to merge into one creature – as depicted in the illustration that shows Dog and Magpie staring into a water pool. In this scene, Magpie clings to the dog's back

FIGURE 7.3 *Fox*: 'Magpie can feel him watching, always watching her.'

and claims that she sees a new creature, whereas Dog explains that this creature is actually themselves reflected in the water. This picture presents a key scene, which is additionally stressed by the text blocks framing the illustrations on the left and right like a mirror.

Looking at the reflection of one's own face in the water is one of the seminal motifs in art since Antiquity, going back to the prominent myth of Narcissus. Recognising oneself in a mirror is a milestone on the path of self-knowledge that might lead to egocentrism and self-love on the one hand (as in the case of Narcissus), and to the realisation of one's own individuality and dependence on others on the other hand (as in the case of Dog and Magpie). Hence, Dog and Magpie have a deep affection for each other, which is severely menaced by Fox. He often stands between Dog and Magpie and thus contributes to their separation and gradually developing alienation. Interestingly, the animal species in this picturebook reveal another power relationship on closer consideration. While Dog is depicted as a wild dog or dingo, and Magpie evidently is an Australian magpie, Fox is also an intruder in a literal sense as this species was imported from the United Kingdom to Australia in the middle of the nineteenth century in order to introduce the traditional fox hunt in this British colony. Consequently, the fox became a rival to the dingo as predatory species.

Besides the illustrations, the relations between Dog, Magpie, and Fox become clear in the condensed dialogues, which stress the characters' emotional conditions and reveal their secret wishes. For instance, Dog is trustful and confident despite Magpie's warning of Fox's sly behaviour: 'He belongs nowhere,' she says. 'He loves no one.' But Dog says, 'He's all right. Let him be.' Dog remains optimistic although he has lost one eye and is dependent on Magpie's guidance. His attitude towards life culminates in the expression 'I am blind in one eye, but life is still good'. In comparison, Magpie is determined by conflicting feelings, fluctuating between disappointment and hope. Though Dog attempts to console her by referring to his missing eye, Magpie is not convinced since she believes that this loss cannot be compared to the inability to fly: 'An eye is nothing!' says Magpie. 'How would you feel if you couldn't run?'

Because of her unbalanced emotional condition, she is an easy prey for Fox, who is the most complex character. In the beginning, his attitude towards Dog and Magpie is dominated by jealousy, but the readers will gradually become aware that Fox is overwhelmed by a feeling of loneliness that finally leads to despair and the determination to destroy the close friendship between Dog and Magpie. In this regard, the notion of 'flying' is a leitmotif, a recurring theme that connects the three characters. By repetitious references to flying, this capacity gains in weight in the course of the picturebook story. The ability to fly is not only linked with fulminant speed, but also with a feeling of freedom which almost touches upon erotic sensations.

It is no wonder, then, that Magpie finally succumbs to Fox's seductive speech whose effect is underscored by the fox's whispering voice: 'I can run faster than Dog. Faster than the wind. Leave Dog and come with me' – and on the second night: 'Do you remember what it is like to fly? Truly fly?' Magpie litany-like answers back: 'I will never leave Dog. I am his missing eye and he is my wings.' Nevertheless, Fox succeeds in sowing seeds of doubt in Magpie, as she reproduces his thoughts when riding on the dog's back again: 'This is nothing like flying. Nothing!' Consequently, her final decision culminates in the assertion: 'I am ready.' This condensed dialogue that reoccurs on three consecutive nights convincingly shows the gradual change in Magpie's attitude towards Dog. While she refuses to abandon Dog twice, she yields after Fox's third seduction, and is now ready to betray Dog.

Fox as a trickster and deceiver

Fox, as a type of literary character, has the properties of a trickster. This term notifies a character whose main trait consists in being a cunning deceiver. In cultures around the world, the trickster is a favourite character that appears in diverse media from folktales, primordial and ancient myths, to modern literature, comic strips, picturebooks and films. The character delights in playing tricks on others, either to profit from a specific situation or just for the sport of it. Famous figures are Till Eulenspiegel in Germany, Reynard the Fox in France, Nasreddin Hodcha in Turkey, Anansi in the Caribbean, and Coyote and Rabbit in the USA. The mystery of the trickster lies in the way he acts entirely on his own, being bound neither by law nor by a moral code. The trickster might be human or an animal, male or female, acting in a way that makes it difficult to decide whether their behaviour might be classified as good or bad. This ambiguity is additionally emphasised by the fact that the trickster might also perform functions of an essential benefactor (Geider, 2012: 913).

In many European and Non-European cultures, the prototypical representative of the trickster is the fox who has played a dominant role in trickster tales since Antiquity. In these tales, be it the *Talmud*, the *Pancatantra* or the fables of Aesop, the fox is always depicted as a sly and bogus animal, characterised by asocial behaviour and the tendency to tell lies. According to the New Testament, the fox even symbolises malice and trickiness (Luke 13: 32). It is no wonder, then, that the fox mutates into a personification of the devil in medieval legends and bestiaries, thus granting the fox a demonic character (Uther, 1987: 450). Nevertheless, several trickster tales also point to the double function of the fox as deceiver and dupe, when he is outsmarted by his actual victims.

Fox is a deceiving character. He aims at leading Magpie into a false belief, the belief that he is a better partner than Dog because with him 'flying' is possible. When Magpie outbursts 'At last I am flying, really flying!', she is a victim of self-deception. And Fox, so it seems to turn out, never thought about a relationship to Magpie like the one she had with Dog. Instead, he is malicious in that he teaches a lesson to Magpie and Dog: 'Now you and Dog will know what it is like to be truly alone.' Magpie then hears 'a faraway scream' and 'she cannot tell if it is a scream of triumph or despair'.

Understanding deception is by no means an easy task for young children. Lying to others is the prototypical way of deceiving someone (Meibauer, 2014). The ability to lie and to recognise that other people lie is strongly connected with the development of metalinguistic abilities, such as irony, metaphor and joke (Leekam, 1991). While in ironical and metaphorical remarks as well as in jokes the content of the speech acts is not literally true, the speaker nevertheless wants the hearer to understand that they are true. In contrast to irony, metaphor and joke, lying is basically uncooperative. This principle of rational communication postulates that speakers should make conversational contributions that fit the 'accepted purpose or direction of the talk exchange' (Grice, 1989: 26). Since no rational conversation principally requires lying, lying is closely related to its fundamentally uncooperative character.

A milestone for the child's acquisition of lying is Theory of Mind (ToM), that is, the ability to comprehend other people's thoughts, feelings and imaginations. As several experimental studies have proved, children usually acquire this ability when they are around four years of age. Precursors of ToM are the imitation of intended actions (at 18 months), the distinction between one's own and other people's feelings and intentions, and the beginning of symbolic play. At two years of age children develop the ability to ascribe feelings and wishes to other people. In this respect, the distinction of first-order belief, that is, the understanding that one might have a false belief about an actual situation (appearance–reality distinction), and second-order belief, that is, the understanding that one might have a false belief about the belief of another person, is crucial. While first-order belief is usually acquired at age three-and-a half to four, second-order belief is acquired somewhat later, approximately at six years of age. A full understanding of different perspectives of a certain belief only begins to mature around 12 years of age and then fully develops in adolescence (Ringrose 2006; Lee, 2013; Lee & Talwar, 2014).

On reading *Fox*, children can learn about seduction and deception. And they can also learn about another important aspect of deception, namely that it is good to trust others but also to distrust others and be epistemically vigilant, that is, not to believe in false information (Mascaro & Sperber 2009; Sperber *et al.*, 2010).

Dog is certainly a trustworthy character. He is the one who shows Magpie that they could be 'one' creature: 'I will be your missing eye, and you will be my wings.' Dog is caring and he is even friendly to strangers. Yet he is not taking Magpie's concerns about Fox seriously. In the end, Dog remains a victim because his trustful and sharing relation to Magpie has been interrupted. Magpie is not vigilant enough. In fact, it is not true that Fox can fly in the literal sense of the word. Ironically, however, it is true that she knows in the end 'what it is to be truly alone'. This knowledge is so strong that Magpie 'can feel herself burning into nothingness', that is, that she is ready to die.

Recent research on the development of distrust has shown that the ability to distrust others has to be acquired. Vanderbilt, Liu and Heyman (2011), in their research on preschoolers' reasoning about the reliability of deceptive sources, showed several trials to 90 three- to five-year-olds in which an informant gave advice about the location of a hidden sticker. The informants were either 'helpers' who were happy to give correct advice, or 'trickers' who were happy to give incorrect advice. The authors found that: (a) 'three-years-olds tended to accept all advice from helpers and trickers'; (b) 'four-year-olds were more sceptical but showed no preference for advice from helpers over trickers, even though they differentiated between helpers and trickers on metacognitive measures'; and (c) 'five-year-olds systematically preferred advice from helpers'. They concluded that 'selective trust was associated with children's ability to make mental state inferences' (Vanderbilt *et al.*, 2011: 1372). These results show that it is not easy for children to be distrustful, even when they are aware of the possibility of deceptive 'trickers'.

Furthermore, there are moral themes built into the story. Moral lessons that can be learned from *Fox* are, for instance: (a) that it is better to be content with a certain state, even when it is dissatisfying, than to always strive for a better state (Dog vs Magpie); and (b) that it is better to love and be socially and emotionally bound, than to love no one and be socially isolated and lonesome (Dog/Magpie vs Fox). Research concerning moral theme comprehension conducted by Narvaez *et al.* (1999) shows that even for seven-year-olds and nine-year-olds it is by no means easy to extract moral lessons from stories. We can speculate that this holds all the more for a younger audience like the one targeted by *Fox*. (Note that the book is recommended to children from six years onwards.)

Emotion and empathy

In this section, we will relate our descriptive findings to two cognitive-narratological topics that are important for a deeper understanding of *Fox*. These topics are emotion and empathy, that is, cognitive abilities that are also related to children's development of a Theory of Mind (ToM). We will ask what kind of knowledge children might have when they read *Fox*, and what they can learn from reading *Fox*. Briefly, our point is to make clear that these considerations are in fact relevant for a deeper understanding of the 'challenging' nature of *Fox*.

We know that children have to acquire an emotional lexicon (Thompson & Lagattuta, 2006). The semantics of words denoting emotions is notoriously difficult, even for adults. In *Fox*, we find several passages in which feelings and emotions are explicitly addressed:

p. 1   How would you *feel* if you couldn't run?
       Magpie drags her body into the shadow of the rocks until *she feels herself melting into blackness.*

p. 3   Days, perhaps a week later, she wakes with *a rush of grief.*

p. 6   Magpie *feels* the wind streaming through her feathers, and she rejoices.

p. 10 Dog beams, but Magpie shrinks away. She *can feel* Fox staring at her burnt wing.

p. 11   Now and again Fox joins in the conversation, but Magpie *can feel* him watching, always watching her. And at night his smell seems to fill the cave – *a smell of rage and envy and loneliness.*

p. 12   Magpie tries to warn Dog about Fox. 'He belongs nowhere', she says. 'He *loves* no one.' But dog says, 'He's all right. Let him be.'

p. 21   She cannot tell if it is *a scream of triumph or despair.*

p. 23   She *can feel herself burning into nothingness.*

As Bretherton *et al.* (1986: 533) show, 28-month-olds have already a positive and negative emotion vocabulary, for instance *good* (moral) *love, like, have fun* or *bad* (moral), *sad, scared,* and use these and other emotion labels 'not only to comment on or explain their own or someone else's feeling state but also to guide or influence their companions' behaviour' (1986: 537). In the preschool years (from 3–5), 'children's ability to verbally reflect on emotion-related situations (antecedents, consequences, behavioural correlates) gains in accuracy, clarity and complexity' (Bretherton *et al.,* 1986: 537).

Yet it appears that:

> although preschoolers are proficient at imputing 'general purpose' emotions like happiness and sadness to story characters, social cognitive studies show that emotion terms requiring more complex understanding of interpersonal situations, for example, gratitude, guilt, or pride, are not appropriately used until later.
>
> *Bretherton et al. (1986: 538)*

Thus, it is not clear to which extent a five-year-old can understand, for instance, what *a smell of rage and envy and loneliness* means. Generally, children may have difficulties in understanding these processes and feelings, but the picturebook *Fox* is also an invitation to learn about these feelings. Interestingly, the emotions and feelings of the animal characters are tightly connected to the senses. The text emphasises several times the impact of seeing, hearing, smelling and touching on the individual characters' emotional state.

In order to understand other people's emotions, children have to acquire ToM (also called 'mindreading'). Without ToM, children are not able to feel empathy and to identify with others. However, it is still under discussion what empathy actually is and which cognitive and social requirements need to be fulfilled. The general assertion is that empathy is the capacity of an observer to get access to the emotional state of another being or fictional character. The concept of empathy plays a significant role, since it influences the multi-levelled acquisition of emotional competence, which consists of four developmental stages, culminating in the acquisition of 'empathy for another's feelings' – often equalised with ToM – and 'empathy for another's life condition', which is acquired at the age of about 11–12 (Hastings, Zahn-Waxler & McShane, 2006: 487). In comparison with 'empathy for another's feeling', 'empathy for another's life conditions' demands the ability to discern not only feelings and imaginations of individuals, but also of groups, whether it concerns the peer group, or a social, ethnic, or religious group (Frijda, 2007).

In this regard, empathy is often confused with sympathy. It is important, however, to distinguish these emotional conditions because empathy does not imply automatically that the character one empathises with should be classified as likeable. On the contrary, the interesting point is the observation that one is usually even able to empathise with emotional conditions, of people regarded as unfriendly or unappealing. Therefore, we would like to consider what children might learn about empathy when reading *Fox*.

One crucial issue in cognitive studies dealing with the impact of literary texts on readers' engagement with literature is the appreciation of other people's emotions and how this process might support children's engagement with fictional characters, thus arousing empathy. In this regard, the notion of literary character plays a seminal role: it is very important in modern narratology, not only with respect to literature for adults (Margolin, 2007; Jannidis, 2009; Eder, Jannidis & Schneider, 2010), but also with respect to children's literature (Nikolajeva, 2002; Kümmerling-Meibauer, 2012; Nikolajeva, 2014). Most interestingly, children may identify with a certain literary character. Identification itself is a complex cognitive notion, yet there appear to be textual clues that support identification; for instance: (i) 'sympathy with a character who is similar to the reader'; (ii) 'empathy for a character who is in a particular situation'; and (iii) 'attraction to a character who is a role model for the reader' (Jannidis, 2009: 24).

The degree to which a child reader's identification with a literary character is possible, depends on further conditions, such as: (iv) the ability to take over a certain perspective of the literary character (based on its characterisation); (v) the affective relation to the character that may be induced by a number of factors, some possibly of a rather idiosyncratic nature; and (vi) the evaluation of the respective character, which is in turn dependent on a set of individual attitudes and preferences, as well as on world knowledge (including historical, social and cultural knowledge) (Jannidis, 2009: 24–25). Learning 'to care about literary characters', as Vermeule (2010) puts it, is of prime relevance for literature acquisition, and it is obvious that children's literature plays a seminal role in this process.

By way of summarising our findings, we pick up these issues and relate them to the characters in *Fox*. In relation to the issue of sympathy, it could be stated that the animal characters are not similar to the reader as they are not human beings. Nevertheless, children are able to sympathise with Dog and Magpie at least, since they acknowledge that these characters are driven by emotions and feelings similar to their own. Whether children might also feel sympathy with Fox is not easy to answer. The unveiling of the reasons for Fox's behaviour, however, his feelings of loneliness and despair that increase after his encounter with Dog and Magpie, may stimulate children to reflect on Fox's inner state of mind.

This observation leads to the second issue, 'empathy for a character who is in a particular situation'. The animal characters arouse empathy because of their physical handicaps and their distressed emotional states. These are mediated by their bodily position and the dialogues, sometimes even by their facial expression with an emphasis on the eyes. In order to decipher the meanings of these depictions and the short dialogues, children should have knowledge of schemata and abstract signs. In cognitive psychology, this strategy is determined by 'emotional scripts' that refer to certain encoded emotions. Encoded emotions presuppose a general knowledge about the representations of emotions, such as joy, sadness and anger, in facial expression, gesture, posture and language. Moreover, readers must have acquired the ability to recognise visual and textual cues that refer to specific emotions. This is especially the case when characters lack relevant information that contributes to their characterisation and identification, such as proper names, age and gender. The readers of *Fox*, for example, do not get any information about the characters' individual background, let alone age, family relations and gender. Nevertheless, children are able to empathise with the animal characters, since they realise that these characters show comparable emotions and feelings to their own.

Concerning the third issue, 'attraction to a character who is a role model for the reader', we do not believe that children are attracted by the animal characters as role models in a general sense. However, children might recognise that the emotional turmoil evoked by the triangular relationship between Dog, Magpie and Fox probably mirrors their own sometimes complicated relationships with siblings, friends and peers.

The fourth issue, 'ability to take over a certain perspective of the literary character', is tightly connected to the phenomenon of empathy. In this respect, children are encouraged to develop empathy with the animal characters' feelings. Children can identify with the emotions and thoughts expressed by Dog, Magpie and Fox. While it might be easy to identify with Dog's optimism, trust and tolerance, and with Magpie's need of protection and her longing for freedom expressed in the metaphor of flying, the examination of Fox's feelings challenges the reader in multifarious ways. Fox confronts the child reader with negative emotions, such as jealousy and despair. Despite these adverse effects, children might get an insight into the causes of the Fox's behaviour and even compare it with experiences made in their own life. While Magpie is the primary victim and thus deserves the child reader's empathy, Dog is a victim, too, because he is the one who is left and betrayed. For children, it may be hard to see that Fox is also a character who deserves empathy. He loves no one, as Magpie says, and he teaches Magpie a lesson that he learned himself before: 'Now you and Dog will know what it is like to be truly alone.'

This finding is strongly connected with the fifth issue, 'affective relation to the character that may be induced by a number of factors, some possibly of a rather idiosyncratic nature'. If children accept that animals have emotions similar to those expressed by humans, they may be able to compare the animals' emotions and feelings with their own. This strategy opens up an affective relationship between child readers and the three animal characters. Children may be attuned to the various affective markers in *Fox*, which appear as strong and appealing images and dialogues.

The emotional lexicon additionally attracts readers and stimulates them to build up an affective connection with the three characters. In the beginning, children will certainly be mostly persuaded by the injured and helpless bird. Then, their affection might turn to Dog who is Magpie's lifesaver and protector. Children may obviously identify with Dog's confidence and tolerance, but may also be affected by Magpie's dream to fly again. In this regard, the final image exerts a strong impact on the viewer, since it contrasts the hostile surroundings with Magpie's determination not to lose hope and to cross the desert in order to reunite with Dog. This open ending, which refuses to show the usual 'happy ending' of picturebooks, provokes the readers' active consideration of the possible outcome of the story.

Concerning the final issue, it should be evident that the evaluation of the three characters is 'dependent on a set of individual attitudes and preferences, as well as on world knowledge' (Jannidis, 2009: 25). It is a well-known fact that children are interested in animals and that animals appear in many books targeted at children. While animals in picturebooks are often anthropomorphised, the animal characters in *Fox* are depicted in a quite realistic manner, although they can speak and show emotions comparable to those of humans. Hence, *Fox* addresses both children's attachment to animals and their interest in emotional situations of high degree. What distinguishes *Fox* from other picturebooks with animal characters, however, is the open ending and the confrontation with ambivalent, even negative feelings that challenge the reader to delve into the presentation of a complex psychological situation.

Conclusions

As our detailed description and interpretation of *Fox* has shown, this picturebook is indeed challenging on a number of counts. First of all, its artwork challenges common expectations with respect to child-appropriate aesthetics. Second, its content is challenging, since narrating a disastrous love triangle, albeit told with reference to animal characters, seems to be risky for an audience of six-year-olds. Our interpretation showed that the rewards of reading this book, for both children and adults, relate to learning about complex emotions such as jealousy and despair. These emotions appear late in the process of emotional acquisition; therefore gaining knowledge about them is by no means easy. We realised that Wild's text helps children to learn how emotions can be verbally expressed and additionally that *Fox* contains implicit moral lessons. This is undeniably challenging, because such lessons have to be inferred from all the information given in the pictures and in the text. The most demanding challenge, however, is to feel empathy for the remorseless Fox, since his malignancy is caused by his loneliness and his inability to love someone.

Academic references

Bretherton, I., Fritz, J., Ridgeway, D. & Zahn-Waxler, C. (1986) Learning to Talk about Emotions: A Functionalist Perspective, *Child Development*, 57: 529–547.

Eder, J., Jannidis, F. & Schneider, R. (eds) (2010) *Characters in Fictional Worlds. Understanding Imaginary Beings in Literature, Film, and Other Media.* Berlin: de Gruyter.

Frijda, N.H. (2007) *The Laws of Emotion.* Mahwah, NJ: Lawrence Erlbaum.

Geider, T. (2012) Trickster, in Brednich, R.W. (ed.) *Enzyklopädie des Märchens, Vol. 13.* Berlin: de Gruyter, pp. 913–923.

Grice, P. (1989) Logic and Conversation, in Grice, P. *Studies in the Way of Words.* Cambridge, MA: Harvard University Press.

Hastings, P.D., Zahn-Waxler, C. & McShane, K. (2006) We Are, by Nature, Moral Creatures: Biological Bases of Concern for Others, in Killen, L.M. & Smetana, J.G. (eds) *Handbook of Moral Development.* Mahwah, NJ: Lawrence Erlbaum, pp. 483–516.

Jannidis, F. (2009) Character, in Hühn, P., Pier, J., Schmidt, W. & Schönert, J. (eds) *Handbook of Narratology.* Berlin: de Gruyter, pp. 14–29.

Kümmerling-Meibauer, B. (2012) Emotional Connection: Representations of Emotions in Young Adult Literature, in Hilton, M. & Nikolajeva, M. (eds) *Contemporary Adolescent Literature and Culture. The Emergent Adult.* Farnham: Ashgate, pp. 127–138.

Kümmerling-Meibauer, B. & Meibauer, J. (2011a) Lügenerwerb und Geschichten vom Lügen, *LiLi. Zeitschrift für Literaturwissenschaft und Linguistik,* 162: 118–138.

Kümmerling-Meibauer, B. & Meibauer, J. (2011b) On the Strangeness of Pop Art Picturebooks: Pictures, Texts, Paratexts, *New Review of Children's Literature and Librarianship,* 17: 103–121.

Kümmerling-Meibauer, B. & Meibauer, J. (2013) Towards a Cognitive Theory of Picturebooks, *International Research in Children's Literature,* 6(2): 143–160.

Kümmerling-Meibauer, B. & Meibauer, J. (2014) Lying in Children's Literature. A Cognitive-Narratological Approach, Unpublished manuscript, Mainz–Tübingen.

Kümmerling-Meibauer, B., Meibauer, J., Nachtigäller, K. & Rohlfing, K. (eds) (2014) *Learning from Picturebooks. Perspectives from Child Development & Literacy Studies.* New York: Routledge.

Lee, K. (2013) Little Liars: Development of Verbal Deception in Children, *Child Development Perspectives,* 7(2): 91–96.

Lee, K. & Talwar, V. (2014) *Children and Lying: A Century of Scientific Research.* New York: Wiley-Blackwell.

Leekam, S. (1991) Jokes and Lies: Children's Understanding of Intentional Falsehood, in Whiten, A. (ed.) *Natural Theories of Mind.* Oxford: Blackwell, pp. 159–174.

Mallan, K. (2013) *Secrets, Lies and Children's Fictions.* Basingstoke: Palgrave Macmillan.

Margolin, U. (2007) Character, in Hermann, D. (ed.) *The Cambridge Companion to Narrative.* Cambridge: Cambridge University Press, pp. 66–79.

Mascaro, O. & Sperber, D. (2009) The Moral, Epistemic, and Mindreading Components of Children's Vigilance towards Deception, *Cognition,* 112(3): 367–380.

Meibauer, J. (2014) *Lying at the Semantics–Pragmatics Interface.* Berlin: De Gruyter Mouton (Mouton Series in Pragmatics, 14).

Narvaez, D., Gleason, T., Mitchell, C. & Bentley, J. (1999) Moral Theme Comprehension in Children, *Journal of Educational Psychology,* 91: 477–487.

Nikolajeva, M. (2002) *The Rhetoric of Character in Children's Literature.* Lanham, MD: Scarecrow.

Nikolajeva, M. (2014) *Reading for Learning. Cognitive Approaches to Children's Literature.* Amsterdam: Benjamins.

Nikolajeva, M. & Scott, C. (2001) *How Picturebooks Work.* New York: Garland.

Obermaier, S. (ed.) (2009) *Tiere und Fabelwesen im Mittelalter.* Berlin: de Gruyter.

Painter, C., Martin, J.R, & Unsworth, L. (2013) *Reading Visual Narratives. Image Analysis of Children's Picture Books.* Sheffield: Equinox.

Ringrose, C. (2006) Lying in Children's Fiction: Morality and the Imagination, *Children's Literature and Education,* 37: 229–236.

Sperber, D., Clément, F., Heintz, C., Mascarao, O., Mercier, H., Origgi, G. & Wilson, D. (2010) Epistemic Vigilance, *Mind & Language*, 25(4): 359–393.

Thompson, R.A. & Lagattuta, K. (2006) Feeling and Understanding: Early Emotional Development, in McCartney, K. & Philipps, D. (eds) *Blackwell Handbook of Early Childhood Development*. Oxford: Blackwell, pp. 317–337.

Uther, H.-J. (1987) Fuchs, in: Brednich, R.W. (ed.) *Enzyklopädie des Märchens, Vol. 5*. Berlin: de Gruyter, pp. 447–478.

Vanderbilt, K., Liu, D. & Heyman, G. (2011) The Development of Distrust, *Child Development*, 82(5): 1372–1380.

Vermeule, B. (2010) *Why Do We Care About Literary Characters?* Baltimore, MD: The Johns Hopkins University Press.www.allenandunwin.com/uploads/BookPdf/TeachersNotes/9781864484656.pdf (accessed 2 June 2014).

Children's literature

Wild, M., illus. Brooks, R. (2000) *Fox*. St Leonards, NSW: Allen & Unwin.

8

FEAR AND STRANGENESS IN PICTUREBOOKS

Fractured fairy tales, graphic knowledge, and teachers' concerns

Elizabeth Marshall

In this chapter, I provide a feminist visual analysis of the representation of girlhood in Roberto Innocenti and Aaron Frisch's picturebook The Girl in Red, *a contemporary retelling of the "Little Red Riding Hood" tale. Throughout the illustrations, Innocenti includes violent and sexualized images that challenge mainstream ideas about picturebooks as innocent texts for young children. I argue that the use of girls and women as objects of violation is part of a larger cultural pedagogy about gender, sexuality, and violence. This analysis of image and text is complemented by responses from student teachers, who discuss the book and their concerns for using it in the classroom. I conclude that* The Girl in Red *offers a forum for thinking about how graphic knowledge about gender and sexuality operates, and a challenge to confront unsettling truths about how children and adults come to know about sexuality and violence.*

Concerns about challenging picturebooks mark adult tolerances for, anxieties about, and investments in certain representations of childhood. Discussions about appropriateness, especially in the context of schooling, occur when writers and illustrators challenge what and when the child should know about sex and violence. These debates often ignore the varied material experiences of children, and usually attempt to collapse all childhoods into a coherent and idyllic vision of innocence.

However, it comes as no surprise to those familiar with children's texts that sexuality and violence are the norm rather than the exception. Literary fairy tales, for instance, are replete with implicit and explicit scenes of sexuality and violence that contemporary picturebook writers and illustrators must navigate for contemporary audiences through the lens of their own conceptions of childhood.

Not originally intended for young readers, literary fairy tales were considered children's fare by the beginning of the twentieth century. In *Off with Their Heads!: Fairy Tales and the Culture of Childhood*, Maria Tatar (1992: 30) writes: "Using intimidation, cautionary tales persuade children to obey the laws set down by parental authority, celebrating docility and conformity while discouraging curiosity and will-fulness." Parents and caregivers hoped the brutality of the tales would control children's behaviours. These cautionary tales sought to warn children of real dangers, but also sought to deter the young from deviating from norms. In the common cautionary tale, disobedient children, usually curious or stubborn ones, receive a severe physical punishment. Stories written to control children's behaviour through these graphic depictions most likely produced competing interpretations. Child listeners may have revelled in the gory details of the characters' afflictions, and as Tatar points out, the brutality of these oral fairy tales might not have necessarily frightened children.

Maurice Sendak described fairy tales as a way to tell stories through metaphor so as not to upset anyone. In a 1976 interview for *Rolling Stone* magazine (reprinted Cott, 2012) Sendak stated:

> It's something we've always known about fairy tales—they talk about incest, the Oedipus complex, about psychotic mothers, like those of Snow White and Hansel and Gretel, who throw their children out. They tell things about life which children know instinctively, and the pleasure and relief lie in finding these things expressed in language that children can live with. You can't eradicate these feelings—they exist and they're a great source of creative inspiration.
>
> *Cott (2012: unpaginated)*

As Sendak points out, fairy tales are marked by uncomfortable truths about child-hood that are often cloaked in more or less child friendly ways—depending on author and audience. Most fairy tale picturebooks published and circulated within North America are sanitized versions of earlier grittier narratives in which children were routinely the subjects of abuse, abandonment, and other harm.

Tatar (1992: 5) argues that folktales had to lose their bawdy, subversive edge to be included in the official canon of children's literature, which has "always been more interested in producing docile minds than playful bodies." These literary tales were also edited to emphasize certain ideologies about gender. For instance, as the brothers Grimm revised their collection for a wider and younger audience, inces-tuous fathers were written out of tales while abusive stepmothers took centre stage, curious girls like Bluebeard's wife or Little Red Riding Hood were punished while inquisitive or disobedient boys were rewarded for their pluck (Bottigheimer, 1987; Tatar, 1992; Zipes, 1993). Contemporary fairy tale picturebooks continue to privilege variants by Perrault and the brothers Grimm rather than other authors and in the process reaffirm normative ideas about heterosexual femininity and masculinity. Folklorist Christina Bacchilega argues that the fairy tale shares a "complicity with 'exhausted' narrative and gender ideologies" (1997: 50). As fairy tale scholars have pointed out (Bacchilega, 1997; Jones & Schacker, 2012; Warner, 1994; Zipes, 2012) there is also a long history of women fairy tale authors and illustrators into which contemporary picturebook creators such as Sarah Moon, Babette Cole, Ana Juan and others fit as they continue the work of subverting "exhausted" ideologies about gender. Regardless, the bulk of fairy tale picturebooks available to young readers, especially in schools, reify normative lessons about gender and sexuality.

Thus, contemporary picturebook creators face a number of interesting challenges when they decide to explicitly reference violent and sexual material in their texts. Charlotte Huck and Anita Lobel's controversial *Princess Furball*, a retelling of the Grimms' "All-Kinds of Fur" a version of Cinderella, in which a feisty heroine escapes her home after her father proposes marriage (and therefore incest) serves as a good example here. Charlotte Huck (1995) has written on the ways her concepts of childhood influenced how she told the tale and what knowledge she relayed to her audience. In Huck and Lobel's (1989) retelling of the tale, the father promises his daughter's hand to an ogre in exchange for fifty wagons of silver. Of her decision to replace the incestuous father with an ogre Huck (1995: 80) writes:

> The decisions I faced in retelling were challenging. First of all I had to decide whether to include the incest or not. With the rise of incest in our society, one could argue that it should not be eliminated from the story. While I do believe that somewhere in the sexual education of a child, he or she should learn about incest, I do not think such information should be derived from a fairy tale! Since I had found the versions that eliminated it in the retelling, I decided not to include it.

While Huck's verbal text replaces the incestuous father with an ogre, Lobel's visual image explicitly references the incestuous father. Lobel does so by making the image of the ogre in a portrait match the exact image of the father. Lobel makes the incestuous themes in other less reproduced variants of the tale visible and in turn shifts the kinds of graphic knowledge available to adult and child readers.

Similarly, picturebook creators working with the "Little Red Riding Hood" tale, such as Sarah Moon (2002), Beni Montresor (1991), Marjane Leray (2013) and numerous others (see Zipes, 1993 and Beckett, 2014 for additional variants) make decisions about how and what children should learn through a picturebook. These author-illustrators have relied on a different set of metaphors that challenge familiar lessons about gender within the tale, namely a larger "cultural pedagogy tied to discourses about femininity that privilege obedience and sexual innocence" (Marshall, 2004: 264). Take, for instance, Sarah Moon's (2002) black-and-white photograph (in her picturebook version of Perrault's *Little Red Riding Hood*), of empty and tussled bed sheets to symbolize sexual assault and violence. To this collection of fairy tale picturebooks that make explicit the violent and sexual material in the oral tales, American author Aaron Frisch and Italian illustrator, animator, and advertising artist, Roberto Innocenti (2012), contribute *The Girl in Red*. Author and illustrator make explicit the ways in which the commercialized landscape of contemporary capitalism harms and genders children (Figure 8.1).

FIGURE 8.1 *The Girl in Red* (Innocenti & Frisch, 2012).

The Girl in Red

Roberto Innocenti is a self-taught artist with a long career in children's literature that includes illustrating a series of informational books on airplanes and trains in the late 1970s (Reit, 1978). He is perhaps best known for his controversial Holocaust picturebook *Rose Blanche* (Innocenti, 1985). He has also illustrated other classic fairy tales, such as the 1983 *Cinderella* based on Charles Perrault's variant.

For the purposes of this chapter, I define *The Girl in Red* as a "fusion text." Janet Evans defines such texts as "the evolving multifaceted and multimodal close relation of comics and graphic novels and their characteristics show a merging of features from comics and graphic novels with those from picturebooks" (2013: 239). Innocenti fuses the picturebook format with conventions of comics as he visualizes the story through a series of different sized panels. His detailed illustrations are replete with display lettering, graffiti and other symbols, gutters between panels as well as large white spaces that slow down time and invite the reader to linger at certain points in the book.

The challenge of this picturebook lies in Innocenti's decision to include images and references to sexuality and violence. Readers familiar only with the Grimms' variant in which a huntsman saves an innocent young girl, will find Frisch and Innocenti's reference to other variants in which predatory men/wolves eat and metaphorically violate Little Red surprising. Indeed, as Sandra Beckett (2014: 5) rightly points out: "Charles Perrault penned the first literary version of the tale to warn girls and women against predatory males. Today 'Little Red Riding Hood' can be seen as the archetypal tale of child abuse and rape." *The Girl in Red* explicitly addresses sexual violation through its visual references to hyper-sexualized women and girls.

The Girl in Red begins in a bleak post-apocalyptic classroom or a day care facility *before* the title page. The first panel reads: "Draw close, children, and I will weave you a tale." The next, "Toys can be fun. But a good story is magic. And there is no better time for one than when rain is tapping at your window" (Innocenti, 2012: unpaginated). The colour gray dominates the initial image of a group of children gathered around a large brown table.

About the use of colour in picturebooks, Perry Nodelman (1988: 61) writes: "Gray, the color we attach to characterless people, often suggests bleakness, lack of intensity, a cool detachment." In *The Girl in Red* Innocenti uses gray to depict a cheerless atmosphere as children sit around a big brown table and are dressed in a range of muted colours that feature representations of corporate logos. Books, wooden toys, spinning tops, horns that symbolize childhood innocence are juxtaposed with children's toys that signal violence, such as a toy soldier with a machete (Figure 8.2). A deflated Punch-like character hangs out of the puppet theatre and the violence associated with this character, known for beating his wife and child, parallels the violence of the narrative.

Clad in glasses and a blue headscarf, an old woman sits on a table knitting a yellow and orange scarf. A glowing light emanates from her skirt. This is a twenty-first century Mother Goose, who is coolly detached from the children that surround her. The first narration box reads: "Draw close, children, and I will weave you a tale." The big brown table at which the children sit implies security. However, chaos reigns underneath as a train track goes only half way around the table. A scantily clad doll lies on the tracks—in direct line of the oncoming train. Commercially produced toys as well as the violence of children's play define the visual representation of childhood, suggesting that innocence and childhood are, at best, precariously fused together.

This instability is further emphasized as the reader turns to a page that reads: "Know this, though children: stories are like the skies. They can change, bring surprises, catch you without a coat. Look up all you want, but you never really know what's coming" (Innocenti, 2012: unpaginated). The story to be told—a fairy tale—transcends time and location, and the gap between the story frame and the beginning of Sophia's adventure allows the reader to adjust that time, to delay or return to the contained space of childhood, however bleak.

Into the woods . . . or the city?

In *The Girl in Red* the heroine is a prepubescent girl named Sophia, who lives in a high-rise building with her single mother and her little sister. Dressed in red, Sophia leaves the house to take biscuits, honey, and oranges to her sick nana on the other side of the forest. Her mother tells her to "Stay on the main trail all the way."

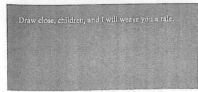

FIGURE 8.2 *The Girl in Red*: "A twenty-first century Mother Goose."

The text assures the reader that while the walk will be a long one; "Sophia is a good girl."

Innocenti replaces the fairy tale forest with a contemporary cityscape. An anonymous reviewer for *Publishers Weekly* suggests that *The Girl in Red* reflects, "the bleak commercial dystopia of *Blade Runner*" (*Publishers Weekly*, 2012: unpaginated). Indeed, the landscape that surrounds Sophia is packed full of global corporate advertisements, people, cars, and inanimate objects, such as garbage, that crowd the city streets as well as the mall through which Sophia will travel.

As Sophia begins her journey, street signs point in the direction of "Il Bosco" or "The Wood"—a shopping mall. One half of one page includes a small gray narration box that takes up the top quarter of the panel. The rest of the page is white space and invites the reader to slow down, and to look closely to find Sophia in the chaotic and commodified landscape. As she travels, Sophia is often lost to the viewer in the vast and busy landscape creating a "Where's Waldo" kind of effect. A full colour panel takes up the remaining one and a half pages. The street sign for Il Bosco points to the right while a green arrow directs drivers (and the reader) to the left. Two circular road signs with a white line through them signifying "wrong way," alert the reader that Sophia chose the wrong path and missed the signs that tell her which way to go.

This dystopian cityscape and the advertisements that surround her foreshadow a violent encounter with the hunter/wolf. Specifically, images of sharp teeth appear on the front of cars; in the mouth of a male driver; in the form of a dog's predatory growl; and as the doorway to a boutique, suggesting sexual appetite and danger. These visual cues also underscore Sophia's naïveté and her inability to interpret the landscape and signs of danger that surrounds her.

Innocenti's images capture what Brian McNair (2002), Feona Attwood (2009) and others define as an expanding "pornosphere" or "striptease culture" (McNair, 2002: 81) that infiltrates public life. Innocenti uses this visual language of contemporary advertising and its reliance on soft-core heteroporn in the streetscape through which Sophia travels. For instance, on one page a woman gazes directly at the viewer, her mouth and nose cut off by a black lace fan; a woman's mouth, with glossy red lipstick speaks into a phone; behind some scaffolding a circular blue street sign with a white arrow points at a woman's bottom in tight jeans wearing thong underwear. *The Girl in Red*, however, is more "porno chic" (McNair, 2002) than actual porn as no one engages in any sex acts, unlike more explicit versions as noted by Orenstein (2002).

Further into the wood

Sophia heads to The Wood, a mall. In neon lights the words lingerie and toys appear on the façade of the building to further emphasize the slippage between adult and child. The fairy tale picturebook format, a genre generally associated with childhood, is consistently ruptured by images of hyper-sexualized girl dolls and by representations of adult women who appear in images of advertisements as fragmented body parts, including lips, legs, breasts, and buttocks. Feminist media scholar, Rosalind Gill (2007: 80) writes that these fragmented representations, "deny women's humanity, to present them not as whole people but as fetishized, dismembered 'bits'." In the context of *The Girl in Red*, the images of the dismembered parts of women's bodies foreshadow the wolf's desire to devour Sophia into bits and pieces.

Unlike more risqué versions of "Little Red Riding Hood" (see Beckett, 2014; Orenstein, 2002; Zipes, 1993), Sophia remains fully dressed in this picturebook variant. However, in the visual images Innocenti consistently invites the reader to imagine Sophia as a sexualized object as he makes visual links between Sophia and the adult women that surround her. Sophia wears a red coat, black leggings and pink shoes. The colour red is often associated with visual codes of pornography.

As Leena-Maija Rossi (2007: 134) argues, "The red background of the images constituted, together with the black underwear, a color combination which media imageries have taught us to associate with environments of sexual consumption: brothels and striptease-joints, or more mundane but 'naughty' bedroom scenes." Numerous references to these media imageries appear throughout the book and link adult women to the child Sophia. For example, in the mall the woman, dressed in red and wearing a black garter, advertises a lottery, and in the visual economy of the streetscape, Sophia's red jacket serves as a sign that she is available for consumption.

Innocenti borrows a familiar visual tactic used in advertising in which adult women are made childlike and girls made to look like sexualized adults. Women are infantilized through childlike poses and young girls made more mature through sexualized images across the seemingly disparate visual cultures of advertising and children's picturebooks. Here the images that children and adults see every day on the street, on subways, in magazines and newspapers, and on television seem incongruous and controversial in a children's picturebook.

Lost! Danger in the woods

Sophia loses her way when she stops to window shop at her favourite place, the "window of wonders." Through the glass, Sophia window shops and looks longingly at a set of gendered toys, such as ballerinas, sexy dolls, guns, and hyper-masculine action figures. The text reads, "Sophia stops and gets to dreaming. Before her are monsters, princesses, dark fates, and happily-every-afters. Images of the past and of the future" (Innocenti, 2012: unpaginated). Sophia's desire for commodities derails her; and, after she stops to act on her own longing, she gets lost. Sophia takes a wrong exit out of The Wood and finds herself trapped in an alley surrounded by a gang of adolescent men on motorbikes. Horizontal lines hold Sophia in as the bricks press against her back, and barbed wire prevents an escape over the wall. "A smiling hunter" saves her (Figure 8.3) (Plate 27); the text reads, "What big teeth he has. Dark and strong and perfect in his timing. Sophia tells him of her grandmother and her little home. Of the biscuits and honey" (Innocenti, 2012: unpaginated).

The hunter offers Sophia a ride on his motorcycle. He only takes her part of the way, and the reader supposes that he is heading to Nana's house. Sophia makes a solitary and final approach to Nana's trailer on the outskirts of the forest. A cloudy sky and a stack of old tyres frame the background. The next panel references the opening classroom scene as gray colours predominate again and lightning punctuates the sky as the hunter/wolf enters Nana's house. The reader sees the hunter's motorbike and his coat as he slips into the trailer. Sophia arrives, her back on the viewer and calls out to her nana; we cannot see her reaction. The viewer—adult and child—can only imagine her confusion, fear, and possible desire (Figure 8.4).

We don't see Sophia's sexual violation and/or her murder as it happens in the gutter between panels and the reader must draw on a larger repertoire of graphic knowledge about girls' bodies, public spaces, and sexual vulnerability, to imagine it

Suddenly, lightning splits the sky.

In the wildest parts of the forest, the law of the food chain holds sway. Small creatures give way to large ones. With a clap of thunder, the jackals are gone.

A smiling hunter. What big teeth he has. Dark and strong and perfect in his timing. Sophia tells him of her grandmother and her little home. Of the biscuits and honey.

FIGURE 8.3 (Plate 27) *The Girl in Red*: "A smiling hunter. What big teeth he has."

(Marshall & Gilmore, 2015). The next two pages show the mother waiting for Sophia and the hunter now fully transformed into a wolf leaving the trailer.

The Girl in Red honours the multiple versions of "Little Red Riding Hood," and readers will find two different endings. The first uses Charles Perrault's (1697) variant in which the wolf gobbles up grandmother and Little Red. The second ending retells the familiar variant by the brothers Grimm in which a woodsman saves Little Red and her grandmother. Innocenti envisions a "choose-your-own" adventure ending, complete with reporters, spotlights, and helicopters.

The Girl in Red received a starred review from *Publishers Weekly* and *Hornbook*, and predominately positive reviews in *Kirkus Reviews* and *School Library Journal*. Vicky Smith (2012: 279) writing for *Kirkus Reviews* suggests that, "Children, and perhaps even teens, might find this tale much to their liking; some, however,

Nana is not at the door, as she usually is.

Sophia calls for her.

FIGURE 8.4 *The Girl in Red*: Sophia arrives at Nana's trailer.

might find its darkness a little too unmitigated, despite the closing sign that says 'Happy End.'" In *School Library Journal,* Wendy Lukehart (2013:106) writes that, "By removing the filter of folklore and pulling the archetypal dangers into the present without a sense of safety anywhere, author and illustrator have created a profoundly unsettling narrative." Critics differ on the age of the audience for the book and their recommendations. For instance, *Kirkus Reviews* and *Publishers Weekly* suggest age 8 and up while *School Library Journal* advocates for age 13 and up. Given that adults, such as these reviewers, rather than children, define appropriate content in schools, it is interesting to consider the ways in which teachers respond to the book as a way to begin to understand the mechanisms through which the myth of childhood, as a protracted and protected state of innocence, becomes reaffirmed.

Fear and danger in the classroom: student teachers respond

Teachers are one of the primary markets and audiences for children's literature, and educators are on the front line of advocating for the use of children's literature in the classroom. Numerous education scholars have documented teachers' self-censorship in relation to using controversial texts in the classroom (Freedman & Johnson, 2001; Noll, 1994; Voelker, 2013; Wollman-Bonilla, 1998). As these authors point out, the stakes of selecting and teaching challenging picturebooks are high as educators confront the possibility of controversy within and outside of the classroom (Voelker, 2013).

Given this, it is no surprise that less controversial or challenging fairy tale picturebooks are regularly included as part of the North American language arts curriculum. These sanitized variants are not neutral. The use of any children's literature in the classroom underscores a particular politics, whether intentional or not, and it is important for educators to critically examine the stories they share (or are mandated to teach) in schools.

Setting the scene

Curious about how and when educators decide to use a challenging picturebook in the classroom, I decided to introduce *The Girl in Red* to my pre-service teacher education course on children's literature and critical literacies. This class met eight hours a week for six weeks. The thirty-one students (all female with the exception of one male student) enrolled in the course were in the last semester of a teacher education program and had completed a classroom practice in order to teach children aged 5 to 12. To encourage pre-service teachers to think critically about language arts instruction, the course had an explicit critical literacy orientation and students were asked to consider children's literature and literacy through this lens (Christensen, 2009; Comber, 2001; Janks, 2014; Leland, Lewison & Harste, 2013; Lewison, Leland & Harste, 2010; Luke & Freebody, 1997; Marshall & Sensoy, 2011; Vasquez, 2005, 2010).

For a module on children's literature and censorship in classrooms, the class read chapter nine, "Challenging the Challengers" in *Teaching Children's Literature: It's Critical!* (Leland *et al.*, 2013). When the class met for this session, I read *The Girl in Red* to the whole group and projected the images on a large screen so that the students could offer critical responses to the text. Of particular interest to the class were the scenes where Sophia travels through the vast, pornified landscape of The Wood. Students commented on the hyper-sexualization of girls and women as well as the class dynamics in the images. We addressed critical literacy questions, such as "who is missing?"

Questioning femininity

Given that thirty of the thirty-one students in the room were women, it seemed important to analyse the visual representations of femininity in the text, and so I also added a theoretical perspective drawn from feminist media studies to ask additional questions. As a whole group we did a feminist visual analysis of *The Girl in Red* to discuss the graphic knowledge about gender, especially girlhood, embedded in the text and images. Sample questions included:

- How are the bodies of girls and women visually represented?
- How do we "know" if someone is male or female?
- How are bodies positioned and what gestures (e.g. touching the face) are used in the images to represent gender?
- How are you asked to read/visualize race, class, gender, and sexuality?

This allowed for feminist analyses, such as the representation of young girls as women and women as young girls; the narrative of young girls as being at risk in public spaces; and female bodies as objects or commodities of consumption.

The fear is real: students' concerns

After discussing the book, I asked students to respond to the following prompt, "I would or would not teach this book in my classroom because …".

I read their responses several times for themes and contradictions. All thirty-one students said that they would not share the book in a primary setting (ages 5 to 8), three wrote that they thought the book might be used with 9 and 10-year-olds, and, twenty-four suggested 11 to 12-year-olds as the audience for the book because this age group would best understand the mature issues in *The Girl in Red*. The following student example captures this theme:

> I believe that children should engage in critical thinking when reading a book, but this book is not suitable and appropriate for discussions with young children. The hidden messages require a more mature audience in order to have a meaningful discussion.

Four students unequivocally stated that they would *not* use the book in any classroom. Not surprisingly, these students were concerned about sharing the sexualized and violent material in the book in a public school setting. One student wrote:

> I would not show this book to a class. I do not think children need to see those dark images. Children should not have to be forced to read or look at it. They could get it on their own if they wanted to but they do not need me to show it to them. I was personally disturbed by the images being so dark and having so many creepy images that I would not want to see it again or show it to a class.

What is striking here is not so much the student's contention that she didn't want to expose children to these images, but that she herself was traumatized by the content of the book. Her tolerance for such material as an adult reader limits her ability to see *The Girl in Red* as a possible text to use in the classroom. However, her response also serves as a reminder to teacher educators to consider how challenging picturebooks books might trigger intense emotional responses and/or memories in adults. Another student stated:

> I want to teach primary grades and could not see this book being read to children due to the images that are used. They could be scary for children aged 5-7 and may be a little confused with the alternate ending. I am also aware of the advertising, sexualizing women and ideas given from the images. I wouldn't want young children picking up on that.

This prospective teacher assumes that the child is unsullied by popular culture and must be protected as long as possible from images of sexuality. At the same time, the child is highly susceptible to the sexualized images in the book. Another student reiterates the concern about children being exposed to sexualized material:

> I would not use this book in elementary school or maybe I would use certain pages of it but I don't think some of the images are appropriate such as the prostitutes on the last page.

It is important to note that there are no prostitutes on the last page of the book; rather, female news reporters in tight clothes. Definitions of what is appropriate or inappropriate are intimately tied to the student's own discomfort with Innocenti's images, as the idea of childhood, as she conceives it, clashes with the realities of violence and sexuality. Innocenti and Frisch use a familiar fairy tale to make the point that these hyper-sexualized images are now the norm, that children grow up with these images all around them. As the illustrations in *The Girl in Red* make clear, children come to know about violence and sexuality outside of the school and outside of textual encounters.

Fear of controversy

At least two students admitted to a fear of using controversial books in the classroom. One student wrote:

> I would not use this because it has a lot of different issues that are not appropriate for children and it sexualizes young girls . . . As a new teacher I think it might be more difficult for me to use this in a classroom because I don't yet have experience with teaching controversial topics.

And another:

> As a new teacher, I don't feel secure enough in my qualifications and my position in school districts to bring this book in at present but it is something I would work towards and perhaps with other pieces of literature first.

These two future teachers speak honestly about the dangers of using challenging books in the classroom. Like the heroine of "Little Red Riding Hood" it is safer for teachers to stick to the path of mandated curriculum.

I had envisioned using *The Girl in Red* in our class session as just one of many activities in the class. However, I was surprised to find that it served as a pivotal moment for some of the students in their ideas about using a critical approach to teaching language arts through children's literature.

At the end of the six-week course in which countless children's picturebooks were read and introduced, I asked students to write a brief one to two-page summary about any aspect of the class. Nine students returned to Innocenti's book as a salient moment in the course. One student wrote:

> Thinking back to the book that was a modern day version of Little Red Riding Hood. I originally said I would not bring that book into my classroom as I felt it was not appropriate for the classroom. It seemed to portray some negative images throughout and didn't seem good for a school setting . . . I think it had more to offer than I first thought and could be taken a number of directions within the classroom. This was one of the turns in my thinking about language arts. Not being afraid to take risks is something that I want to be comfortable doing.

Another student pointed out that although she was aware that sensitive social issues, even those that students' experience, have a place in the classroom, she was still hesitant to bring a text like *The Girl in Red* into the classroom. She wrote:

> In my practicum, I was hesitant to address sensitive social issues when picture books brought them up in class even though I knew they were present in children's lives. Our class discussion on Innocenti's *Girl In Red*, was a powerful moment for me as it demonstrated just how prevalent these issues are in children's lives as they are exposed to them through books, television, music, toys, and social interactions.

A different student reflected:

> The read-aloud of "The Girl in Red" was an interesting way to have us discuss as a class reasons for bringing in controversial literature to the classroom. At first I was so certain I would never introduce a book like that to my class but after the discussion I reflected on some of the reasoning that other students had and I began to think about where there is a place for controversial literature in classes.

Others remained fearful of using the book in the classroom. One student wrote:

> Although I would like to one day read controversial books like this in my classroom, I still have questions around how to discuss this book with concerned parents, and at what grade level would this book be appropriate to read for.

Becoming more critical

Finally, at least one student actively took up the critical literacy perspective and found the book to be an important "counter narrative." She wrote in her reflection:

> We were introduced to the book *The Girl in Red*. This story was inspiring to me in its ability to provide a completely different perspective to the traditional "Little Red Riding Hood." As a result, as an educator I saw this book as an incredible counter narrative that allowed the reader to critically analyze deeper issues.

This student was on her way to using controversial children's literature in the classroom and by the end of the term had bought copies of several provocative picturebooks for her classroom collection, including *The Girl in Red* (Innocenti, 2012), *10,000 Dresses* (Ewart, 2008), *This Land is My Land* (Littlechild, 1997), and *Duck, Death and the Tulip* (Erlbruch, 2011).

Conclusion: conceptualizing childhood through a controversial text

In summary, *The Girl in Red* proved to be an important text to use with aspiring teachers to surface their assumptions about childhood. Controversial and challenging picturebooks like this one confound simple categorizations of child or adult audience. This picturebook challenged the viewers in my course because it breached their assumptions about children's picturebooks as sites of innocence, and children as in need of adult protection.

It is adults that wish to protect children through proxies, such as the wolf. How children might respond to *The Girl in Red* will depend on their own tolerances, memories, and experiences. Similarly, we know from research on response that children will bring varied responses and commentaries to the book.[1] As scholars, such as Bragg and Buckingham (2009) point out, children are not likely to be fixated on or harmed by the suggestive images in the book. For me, the more essential issue here is access to the book and the ideas about the child that drive whether or not an adult shares this book with children. These responses suggest we ask critical questions about the assumptions teachers make about children, such as "How do educators define 'the child' and childhood?"

To add another layer to this analysis, even as *The Girl in Red* attempts to raise awareness about the sexualization and commercialization of childhood, the story is ultimately a traditional retelling "tied to a didactic tradition that seeks to school young readers into appropriate masculine and feminine behaviours" (Marshall, 2004: 269). The visual/verbal representation of Sophia draws on a long tradition of presenting young girls as naïve victims (Walkerdine, 1997). As Jack Zipes (1993: 10) suggests, "Whether sexed or sanitized object, Red Riding Hood is compelled to assume responsibility for the 'predatory acts' of her creators themselves and the assortment of wolves created in illustrations and narratives that are only too willing to eat her." In this case, *The Girl in Red* offers provocative visual/verbal retelling and at the same time carries with it normative ideas about gender and sexuality. Readers, too, often resist our attempts to use picturebooks to intervene in discussions about social issues and/or our efforts to make texts "critical." As researchers have demonstrated (Davies, 1989; Marshall, 2009; Trousdale & McMillan, 2003) adults and children alike often revise a text's message to fit their own ideas about the world.

The Girl in Red challenges adult conceptions about childhood through its use of sexualized imagery and violent scenes only to reassert the figure of an innocent female victim. This innocent and unknowing child—like Sophia herself—mirrors the imaginary child at the centre of the school curriculum in ways that seek to protect rather than empower, to discipline girls' desires rather than support them. *The Girl in Red* offers a forum for thinking about how graphic knowledge about gender and sexuality operates, and a challenge to confront unsettling truths about how children and adults come to know about sexuality and violence.

Note

1   My own informal reading of *The Girl in Red* with a few 7- to 8-year-olds supports this contention. The children I read with noted that some of the images were "inappropriate" and this response could well reflect a performance of the kind of reading that the child thought was expected when reading such material with an adult. However, the children found other aspects of the illustrations much more intriguing. For instance, one child found it funny that Santa Claus was visually portrayed as a thief. On the full-page spread of The Wood, a man dressed as Santa Claus slinks through the mall, wearing dark sunglasses and clutching a bag. In short, younger children have no problem with Santa Claus wearing sunglasses and carrying a bag.

Academic references

Attwood, F. (ed.) (2009) *Mainstreaming Sex: The Sexualization of Western Culture*. London: I.B. Tauris.

Bacchilega, C. (1997) *Postmodern Fairy Tales: Gender and Narrative Strategies*. Philadelphia: University of Pennsylvania Press.

Beckett, S.L. (2014) *Revising Red Riding Hood around the World: An Anthology of International Retellings*. Detroit, MI: Wayne State University Press.

Bottigheimer, R. (1987) *Grimms' Bad Girls and Bold Boys: The Moral and Social Vision of the Tales*. New Haven, CT: Yale University Press.

Bragg, S. & Buckingham, D. (2009) Too Much Too Young?: Young People, Sexual Media and Learning, in Attwood, F. (ed.) *Mainstreaming Sex: The Sexualization of Western Culture*. London: I.B. Tauris, pp. 129–146.

Christensen, L. (2009) *Teaching for Joy and Justice: Re-Imagining the Language Arts Curriculum*. Milwaukee, WI: Rethinking Schools.

Comber, B. (2001) Negotiating Critical Literacies, *School Talk*, 6: 1–3.

Cott, J. (2012) Maurice Sendak, Kind of All Wild Things, reprint of 30 December 1976 interview. *Rolling Stone*, May 8. www.rollingstone.com/culture/news/maurice-sendak-king-of-all-wild-things-20120508.

Davies, B. (1989) *Frogs, Snails and Feminist Tales*. Sydney: Allen & Unwyn.

Evans, J. (2013) From Comics, Graphic Novels, and Picturebooks to Fusion Texts: A New Kid on the Block, *Education 3–13: International Journal of Primary, Elementary, and Early Years Education*, 41(2): 233–248.

Freedman, L. & Johnson, H. (2001) Who's Protecting Whom? *I Hadn't Meant to Tell You This*, A Case In Point In Confronting Self-Censorship In The Choice of Young Adult Literature, *Journal of Adolescent and Adult Literacy*, 44: 356–369.

Gill, R. (2007) *Gender and the Media*. Cambridge: Polity Press.

Huck, C. (1995) *Princess Furball*: The Writing, Illustrating and Response, in Lehr, S. (ed.) *Battling Dragons: Issues and Controversy in Children's Literature*. Portsmouth, NH: Heinemann, pp. 79–86.

Janks, H. (2014) *Doing Critical Literacy: Text and Activities for Students and Teachers*. New York: Routledge.

Jones, C.A. & Schacker, J. (2012) *Marvelous Transformations: An Anthology of Fairy Tales and Contemporary Critical Perspectives*. Peterborough, ON: Broadview Press.

Leland, C., Lewison, M. & Harste, J. (2013) *Teaching Children's Literature: It's Critical!*. New York: Routledge.

Lewison, M., Leland, C. & Harste, J. (2010) *Creating Critical Classrooms: K-8 Reading and Writing with an Edge* (reprint edn). New York: Routledge.

Luke, A. & Freebody, P. (1997) Shaping the Social Practices of Reading, in Muspratt, S., Luke, A. & Freebody, P. (eds) *Construction Critical Literacies*. Cresskill, NJ: Hampton Press, pp. 185–225.

Lukehart, W. (2013) The Girl in Red, *School Library Journal*, 59: 106.

Marshall, E. (2004) Stripping for the Wolf: Rethinking Representations of Gender and Sexuality in Children's Literature, *Reading Research Quarterly*, 39: 256–270.

Marshall, E. (2009) Girlhood, Sexual Violence and Agency in Francesca Lia Block's "Wolf", *Children's Literature in Education*, 40: 217–234.

Marshall, E. & Gilmore, L. (2015) Girlhood in the Gutter: Feminist Graphic Knowledge and the Visualization of Sexual Precarity, *Women's Studies Quarterly*, 43: 96–115.

Marshall, E. & Sensoy Ö (2011) *Rethinking Popular Culture and Media*. Milwaukee, WI: Rethinking Schools.

McNair, B. (2002) *Striptease Culture: Sex, Media and the Democratization of Desire*. London: Routledge.

Nodelman, P. (1988) *Words about Pictures: The Narrative Art of Children's Picture Books*. Athens: University of Georgia Press.

Noll, E. (1994) The Ripple Effect of Censorship: Silencing the Classroom, *The English Journal*, 83: 59–64.

Orenstein, C. (2002) *Little Red Riding Hood Uncloaked: Sex, Morality, and the Evolution of a Fairy Tale*. New York: Basic Books.

Publishers Weekly (2012) Review of *The Girl in Red*, 29 October. www.publishersweekly. com/978-1-56846-223-3

Rossi, L. (2007) Outdoor Pornification: Advertising Heterosexuality in the Streets, in Paasonen, S., Nikunen, K. & Saarenmaa, L. (eds) *Pornification: Sex and Sexuality in Media Culture*. Oxford: Berg, pp. 127–138.

Smith, V. (2012) Review of *The Girl in Red*, *Kirkus Reviews*, 80(22): 279. www.kirkusreviews. com/book-reviews/roberto-innocenti/girl-red/Vicky Smith.

Tatar, M. (1992) *Off with Their Heads! Fairy Tales and the Culture of Childhood*. Princeton, NJ: Princeton University Press.

Trousdale, A.M. & McMillan, S. (2003) "Cinderella Was a Wuss": A Young Girl's Responses to Feminist and Patriarchal Folktales, *Children's Literature in Education*, 34(1): 1–28.

Vasquez, V. (2005). Creating Opportunities for Critical Literacy with Young Children: Using Everyday Issues and Everyday Text, in Evans, J. (ed.) *Literacy Moves On: Popular Culture, New Technologies and Critical Literacy in the Elementary Classroom*. Portsmouth, NH: Heinemann, pp. 83–105.

Vasquez, V. (2010) *Getting Beyond "I Like the Book": Creating Space for Critical Literacy in K-6 Classrooms*, 2nd edn. Newark, DE: International Reading Association.

Voelker, A. (2013) Tomorrow's Teachers Engaging in Unprotected Text, *Journal of Children's Literature*, 39: 23–36.

Walkerdine, V. (1997) *Daddy's Little Girl: Young Girls and Popular Culture*. Cambridge, MA: Harvard University Press.

Warner, M. (1994) *From the Beast to the Blonde: On Fairy Tales and Their Tellers*. New York: Farrar, Straus & Giroux.

Wollman-Bonilla, J. E. (1998) Outrageous Viewpoints: Teachers' Criteria for Rejecting Works of Children's Literature, *Language Arts*, 75: 287–295.

Zipes, J. (1993) *The Trials and Tribulations of Little Red Riding Hood*. New York: Routledge.

Zipes, J. (2012) *The Irresistible Fairy Tale: The Cultural and Social History of a Genre*. Princeton, NJ: Princeton University Press.

Children's literature

Erlbruch, W. (2011) *Duck, Death and the Tulip*. Wellington: Gecko Press.

Ewert, M. (2008) *10,000 Dresses*, illus. Ray, R. New York: Seven Stories Press.

Huck, C. (1989) *Princess Furball*, illus. Lobel, A. New York: Mulberry.

Innocenti, R. (1983) *Cinderella*, illus. Innocenti, R., text Perrault, C. Mankato, MN: Creative Editions.

Innocenti, R. (1985) *Rose Blanche*, story and illus. Innocenti, R., text Innocenti, R. & Gallaz, C,. trans. Creative Education. Mankato, MN: Creative Education.

Innocenti, R. (2012) *The Girl in Red*, story and illus. Innocenti, R., text Frisch, A. Mankato, MN: Creative Editions.

Leray, M. (2013) *Little Red Hood*, trans. Ardizzone, S. London: Phoenix Yard Books.

Littlechild, G. (1997) *This Land is My Land*. New York: Children's Book Press.

Montresor, B. (1991) *Little Red Riding Hood*, illus. Montresor, B., text Perrault, C. New York: Doubleday.

Moon, S. (2002) *Little Red Riding Hood*, illus. Moon, S., text Perrault, C. Mankato, MN: Creative Editions.

Reit, S. (1978) *Sails Rails and Wings*, illus. Roberto Innocenti. New York: Golden Press.

PART III

Creative, critical and philosophical responses to challenging picturebooks

9

WHAT'S REAL AND WHAT'S NOT

Playing with the mind in wordless picturebooks

Sandie Mourao

Beginning with an overview of wordless picturebooks and how they can be interpreted, this chapter shares a small piece of research around the wordless picturebook, Loup Noir, created by the French illustrator Antione Guilloppé. It considers how children's cultural frames of wolves affected their responses to the picturebook. The context and project are described and transcriptions of three groups of children interacting with the picturebook, together with their written stories, support discussion around their response. Discussion highlights the variety of ways these children responded, the creation of opportunities for collaborative talk, and the role our cultural frames play in our interpretations of ambiguous visual narratives.

Wordless picturebooks

Wordless picturebooks are considered a 'distinct genre or sub-genre' (Beckett, 2013: 83) and since the 1990s they have become not only a contemporary publishing trend but also highly sophisticated pieces of literature. The latter has resulted in many wordless picturebooks belonging to the crossover phenomenon and appealing to readers of all ages (Beckett, 2013).

A wordless picturebook has been defined as 'a narrative contained within a book format, essentially based on the sequencing of images (. . .), whereby the page is the unit of sequence' (Bosch, 2014: 71). Nevertheless, no book is completely wordless: Bosch (2012) characterises wordless picturebooks depending on how many words they contain. There are words in the editorial credits, the title and the name(s) of its creator(s), and a wordless picturebook can contain some words on its pages or the covers (an almost wordless picturebook), or it may appear at first glance wordless, but contains any number of words either concentrated onto one page or repeated single words or expressions throughout (a false wordless picturebook).

Wordless picturebooks are usually considered more open to interpretation than picturebooks, as no written text is available to anchor the creator's original meaning (Serafini, 2014), and as Bosch states, 'the more words a *wordless picture-book* has the greater the amount of information the reader receives' (2014: 76), which will subsequently affect the reader's interpretations of the book's sequential visual narrative, thereby restricting its ambiguity. Thus, the title can be highly significant in leading a reader's interpretation of a wordless picturebook, as are the summaries on the back covers. A wordless picturebook is therefore rarely completely wordless; it is dependent upon the sequence of images therein together with the few words it may contain.

Interpreting wordless picturebooks

The reading of wordless or almost wordless picturebooks is considered as challenging, if not more so, than picturebooks with words (Durán, 2002; Nodelman, 1988). Nodelman points out the requisite for 'close attention and a wide knowledge of visual conventions that must be attended to before visual images can imply stories' (1988: 187). These conventions include the significance of media, colour and style, which all contribute to a depiction of mood and atmosphere, as well as the visual grammars of left and right or high and low placed figures or illustrations, indicating not only cause and effect but status amongst and between depicted characters or objects (Kress & van Leeuwen, 1996).

Finding a story from a sequence of images is likened to doing a puzzle (Nodelman, 1988). Ramos and Ramos translate Van der Linden, who believes that:

> [readers leave] the comfort of the spectator of sound and image demanded by a picture story book read aloud and have to take the role of actors and even of 'activators' of a mechanism of a different nature based upon decrypting, setting relationships, inferring, as in all other acts of reading.
>
> *Ramos & Ramos (2011: 327)*

Ramos and Ramos (2011) go on to describe readers entering into a 'productive dialogue' when looking at a wordless picturebook, as they look at the images seen both in isolation and in sequence. In so doing, readers create semantic inferences, which lead to hypotheses and expectations, all based on their personal experiences and understandings of the world at that moment, as well as on the cultural frames and social constructs relevant to any one group. According to Lakoff, 'frames are mental structures that shape the way we see the world'; they form part of our subconscious in such a way that when we hear a word or see an image 'its frame (or collection of frames) is activated in [our] brain' (2004: xv). Gee, similarly, uses the term 'cultural models', defining these as 'descriptions of simplified worlds in which prototypical events unfold (…) they are taken-for-granted assumptions about what is "typical" or "normal"' (1999: 59). If we were to think of a wolf, our cultural frame would activate the image of a fierce, dangerous animal that is more likely to attack a human than befriend one. A taken-for-granted assumption is that a wolf is bad. Upon looking at a picturebook our cultural frames will also influence what we see – socially constructed ideas will contribute to our interpretation of the images.

As the reader moves through a wordless picturebook their interpretations are confirmed or challenged by each image or sequence of images and subsequently adjusted. Jauss describes this as becoming 'aware of the fulfilled form of the [text], but not yet of its fulfilled significance, let alone its "whole meaning"' (1982: 145). The creator of any piece of literature, with words or not, leaves interpretation to the reader, resulting in not just one but any number of interpretations. Meaning is neither given by the text nor the reader but instead is co-created in 'the transactional process of meaning making' (Rosenblatt, 1995: 27). The notion of a textual gap (Iser, 1978) is central to reader response theory, a theory which values the reader in the co-creation of meaning. Pictures and words, in effective picturebooks, interact with each other, either wholly or partially filling each other's gaps or creating their own (Nikolajeva & Scott, 2006). In wordless picturebooks the iconotextual gap is thought to be larger, as the reader elaborates hypotheses without knowing what is significant or what may happen next; it is 'the degree to which readers are expected to actively engage which marks the difference between picturebooks with and without words' (Arizpe, 2013: 163). Wordless picturebooks therefore engage readers to a greater extent based not only on the lack of direction provided by words, but also through the very non-linear nature of the iconic sign, through their very ambiguity.

Loup Noir: a wordless picturebook that challenges cultural frames

In the wordless picturebook *Loup Noir* (*Black Wolf*) Antione Guilloppé (2004), plays with readers' subconscious and the cultural frames we create around wolves. *Loup Noir* is a visual narrative in black and white showing the journey a young boy makes through the woods on a cold, snowy night. As the boy walks he is followed by a wolf, at times the wolf looks menacing and as readers we assume the wolf will harm the boy, especially when we see the wolf leaping towards him in a later spread. Contrary to expectations, the wolf saves the boy from being crushed by a falling tree and they hug as though long lost friends.

Guilloppé very skilfully uses the simplicity of black and white, together with extreme perspectives, to create suspense and fear, knowing that the reader will think the worst of the wolf in his story. However, we see black predator replaced by white saviour in the later spreads. The different emotions evoked by each spread are a result of Guilloppé's skill in positioning the figures, as well as his use of both black and white as colours which evoke fear or calm. As readers we move back and forth between the pages piecing together the puzzle. Our expectations and assumptions change as each page turns and further visual information is added to our interpretations. The reader is led to believe right up until opening 11 that the wolf will harm the boy, and seeing them hug on opening 12 catches us unawares, mainly, I believe, because stereotypical wolves are not creatures we would hug.

FIGURE 9.1 *Loup Noir* (Antoine Guilloppé, 2004).

Guilloppé plays with our subconscious right from the start. The front cover (Figure 9.1) is black except for a pair of slanting eyes, the words of the title *Loup Noir* (*Black Wolf*) and the series name, 'Les Albums Casterman', all in white. If we understand the title we assume the eyes belong to the wolf. Black is stereotypically associated with both fear and death (Pastoureau, 2008), so we are most likely to assume it is a bad, bad wolf.

The back cover, also in black and white, displays the editor's summary written in white on black:

> It's cold, the edge of the wood emerges as a silhouette against the backdrop of the night. The wolf watches, it lurks. The boy walks a little faster. The wolf appears, he leaps . . . A story to make you tremble in bed. [Own translation.]

As noted by Bosch, editorial introductions can 'over-inform and are inclined to reveal too much about the form, content and the way the reader should read a book' (2014: 87). This summary already directs our reading of the pictures. We can expect to see a wolf and a boy. We can expect to see a wolf lurking, a wolf leaping, and finally we can expect to be frightened as we read this picturebook.

The body of the book continues to play with stark black and white illustrations. Sometimes the night sky is black sometimes it is white. Each time it serves as a background to silhouette figures or objects portraying a cold snowy landscape, sometimes scary, sometimes not. Some openings are doublespreads, others are two facing pages interacting cleverly, despite being separate (Figure 9.2).

On the verso page we see the boy from inside the wood, he is standing at the edge, about to enter. The trees and boy are black, the sky is white, and the trees lean inwards creating a menacing feeling, a tension, almost blocking the boy's passage. This feeling of tension is accentuated by the illustration on the recto showing the wolf, black with white eyes and angular branches crossing the lower part of his face. Despite being separate illustrations they interact with each other. The wolf is facing left, looking towards the boy. The boy is looking into the forest, unknowingly at the wolf.

FIGURE 9.2 Opening 2, *Loup Noir.* Recto and verso illustrations interact with each other.

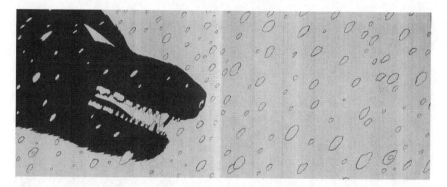

FIGURE 9.3 Opening 7, *Loup Noir.* The wolf's head, black against white.

Guilloppé uses close ups to bond the reader to the boy, as well as to reinforce the reader's fear of the wolf.

In opening 7, we see a close up of the wolf's head, black against white (Figure 9.3). His teeth are white in his open jaws, his eye almost closed and menacing. We can clearly see his fangs and his molars and the falling snow, which is now thicker, could almost be falling teeth outlined in black against the white background. It is a frightening picture and it confirms everything we think we know about wolves. We are indeed made to tremble and fear for the boy's safety.

Black and white are used alternately, the trees, the boy, the wolf, all move from black to white depending on the emotions Guilloppé wants to evoke or what he wants to emphasise. The readers see the moment the wolf becomes white in opening 9 (Figure 9.4). Our hearts are beating fast by the time we reach this opening. We see a stark, mostly white page, divided into top and bottom. White foreground with white tree trunks close together along the top half of the verso. But our eyes are drawn to the black sky in the top centre of the recto page, and the silhouetted figures of a pouncing wolf and a frightened boy, both in white. To their right are more trees and one is leaning precariously to the left. It subconsciously enhances the already high tension. The wolf *is* going to harm the boy.

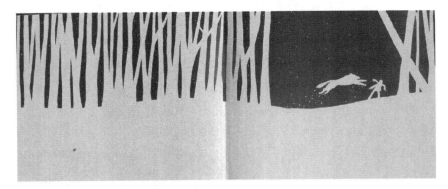

FIGURE 9.4 Opening 9, *Loup Noir*. Black wolf becomes white wolf.

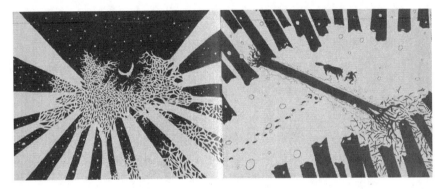

FIGURE 9.5 Opening 11, *Loup Noir*. Different perspectives surprise the reader.

Guilloppé also uses different perspectives to surprise us. The verso of opening 11 (Figure 9.5) shows a worm's eye view of the owl, flying high above the leafless treetops. The trees, in white, tower upwards in an exaggerated perspective, the owl is flying away. The recto is a bird's eye view, looking down upon the wolf and boy, both small and black against the white snow. Is this what the owl sees? As readers, we finally understand that the tree *has* fallen into the path and that the wolf has, though we are still not sure, saved the boy from being crushed. Is this why the owl is leaving, because he knows the boy is safe as the tree did not crush him?

Opening 12 is the surprise (Figure 9.6). A doublespread close up of the wolf being hugged by the boy. Both are smiling. The wolf's eyes are closed, so we have lost the menacing look from previous illustrations, and he is white and fluffy. The boy's hug is heartfelt, so much so his hands dig deep into the wolf's fur. The wolf dominates the opening, in his huge whiteness, pushing blackness out of the illustration – it is seen only in the boy's coat and peeking between the white tree trunks in the background. So what happened? The wolf saved the boy, but were they already friends? Is he a wolf? Could he be a dog?

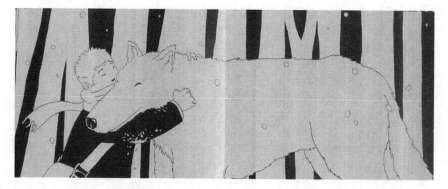

FIGURE 9.6   Opening 12, *Loup Noir.* The surprise.

If we turn this last page we come to the back endpapers, which show the black night and the white snow of the front endpapers, but this time there are white, silhouetted trees at the far left of the verso and a cluster of white squares in the far recto. Could these be the lit windows in blocks of flats at the edge of the forest? Could these flats be where the boy lives?

Guilloppé's French title translates as 'Black Wolf', a nominal title with black as an adjective. Our attention is focused upon the wolf, the bad wolf, even before we open the book. On the other hand, the title could be seen as contradictory, for the wolf is anything but menacing in the final opening, where he is depicted as white as snow. Guilloppé has created a picturebook that makes the reader question what they see. Is the wolf really a wolf?

In comparison to this, if we look at the English translation of this wordless picturebook, it has a very different title, *One Scary Night* (Guilloppé, 2005). This is a narrative title, 'summing up the essence of the story' (Nikolajeva & Scott, 2006: 243): indeed it was a scary night, for the boy and the reader at least. In this case the focus is on the events of the night, and our attention is directed towards the boy's experience. Additionally, this title allows the reader to consider the wolf might not be a wolf at all; he could even be the boy's dog. This title leaves us with fewer questions. Nodelman (1988) reminds us that titles in wordless picturebooks determine our response to them – a title makes a difference.

Contextualising the research

Having read Guilloppé's wordless picturebook, *Loup Noir*, I was left with many unresolved questions. I wondered how children would 'interpret' the book and this led me to use it with a group of children. I wanted to know what they would make of the narrative and how they would respond to Guilloppé's deliberate play on the stereotypical belief that wolves are bad. Thus, with a view to observing how children's cultural frames affected their interpretation of Guilloppé's *Loup Noir*, I set up a small-scale project in a primary school in Portugal. This chapter continues with a description of the children and how I set up the project. It is followed by a discussion around the children's responses to *Loup Noir* and the stories they created from looking at it together.

The children I worked with attended a state primary school in a predominantly low socioeconomic suburb of a city in Portugal. They were Portuguese, aged 8 to 9 years old and spoke Portuguese with me. Their teacher was an enthusiast of authentic texts – unusual in the Portuguese education system where textbooks dominate learning approaches; because of this the children were familiar with picturebooks as a source of pleasure. They were also experienced in talking about their interpretations during shared readings and were able to use picturebook meta-language quite successfully. Prior to reading *Loup Noir* the children had not read any wordless picturebooks with their teacher.

Preparing for the research

I did not know the children; thus to contextualise my visit and the activity, the classroom teacher and I planned a small project that involved all the children in the class. Prior to the activity the children were told that three groups of three children would look at a wordless book, then help each other to write a story for their classmates to illustrate. The final stage was to be the creation of an e-book from each story. In this way the children would together become collaborative authors and illustrators of their own books. The end product, the creation of three illustrated class-made e-books, (which was part of their ongoing class work with the teacher), provided a real reason for giving words to a wordless picturebook. The teacher felt there would be a number of opportunities for the children to work on their writing and illustrating techniques; I would be able to work with a group of children and gather some data; and the children would also benefit from the experience. Additionally, for my purposes, the group writing activity meant that the children's thinking, feeling and reflecting would be more evident as they discussed what they would write. According to Hornsby and Wing Jan (2001), writing also enables children to reflect further by making connections they may not have made before.

Portuguese children are much like children in any Western country; they are led to believe that wolves are wild and dangerous. Through exposure to traditional stories such as *Little Red Riding Hood*, *The Three Little Pigs* and *The Seven Little Kids* they see wolves depicted as baddies. In an endeavour to keep the children's previous cultural perceptions of wolves at bay it was decided to introduce *Loup Noir* with no preparative discussion.

The procedure: working with the children

The nine children were selected by their teacher from the class of 19. Each group of three children, made up of one girl and two boys, worked with me in turn for approximately one hour interacting with *Loup Noir*. Their voices were audio recorded and I took notes on what they did with their hands and bodies as they looked at the book and discussed it together.

The children first looked through the picturebook together without writing anything. This initial 'storybook picture walk' (Paris & Paris, 2001: 4) was adopted with a view to collecting the children's initial impressions of the picturebook and their spontaneous physical and verbal responses. They could not read French, thus the title on the front cover did not initially influence their story interpretations (Nikolajeva & Scott, 2006). Once they had seen the book, they were asked to think of a title and write the story they felt might accompany the pictures. All three groups looked at the picturebook several times before they began writing.

To write their story, the children each selected a role: the director, the scribe, or the editor. It was explained that the story had to be agreed upon by each of them, thus the director's role was to decide what the scribe should write after listening to the other two. The scribe wrote their story and the editor helped the scribe and was also responsible for ensuring everything was written correctly when back in the classroom. During their collaborative creation of the story each group returned to the picturebook many times, moving backwards and forwards through the pages as they argued for certain interpretations, words and expressions and together decided what to write. The children's comments and final written stories have been translated from Portuguese into English.

The children's first encounters with Loup Noir

As the children shared their thoughts and discussed what they wanted to write it was evident that their preconceived ideas about wolves gradually changed from thinking of the wolf as a bad character to a good one.

Responses from Group 1

Upon seeing the book for the first time, Daniel pointed to the eyes on the front cover and exclaimed 'a monster', as the children turned the pages they quietly labelled the illustrations: 'A boy', 'a wolf', 'an owl'. They then moved onto describing action. Here are their utterances from openings 9 to 12:

Opening 9

Daniel: The wolf is trying to catch the boy.

Opening 10

Daniel: The boy fell to the ground.
Berta: And the tree, it almost caught the wolf.
Jorge: The tree fell [pointing to the tree trunk].

Opening 11

Daniel: The boy is trying to escape after being pushed to the ground [pointing to the boy].

Opening 12

Daniel: The boy is …
All: … giving a hug.
Berta: So they were playing?
Jorge: The wolf became the boy's friend.

This excerpt shows that right up to the final page turn, the children believe that the wolf's intentions are to attack and hurt the boy. They notice the fallen tree in the illustrations but do not see any connection between this and the wolf's leap. They conclude that the wolf and boy must have been playing, though Jorge is still not certain that they were already friends.

Responses from Group 2

Like the children in Group 1 these children begin by commenting on the front cover. Carlos says 'Big wolf' and Rui attempts to translate the title into 'Night Wolf', not because he can understand French, but because of the illustration; he also believes that 'noir' must translate into the Portuguese word 'noite', which means night – a logical assumption as the two words share their first three letters. From these initial comments one would think these children were fairly convinced that this story was about a wolf and indeed stereotypical wolf-related observations were scattered through their commentaries and responses. They label the wolf as 'a monster' (opening 2) and 'an angry wolf' (opening 6), and from opening 7 (see Figure 9.3), where the wolf's profile shows bared teeth, they prepare themselves for a terrible ending. The transcription of their responses on these openings follows:

Opening 7

Marta: [She points to the wolf's teeth and counts under her breath] 22 white teeth so he can eat the boy.

Opening 8

Rui: The wolf was furious enough to eat this boy.

Opening 9

Carlos: Oooeee, he's attacking him.
[Surprised and frightened noises]

Carlos: He looks like wolf man.
Rui: Yes he does. It's all black and white.

Opening 10

All: Ahh eee.
Marta: Oh poor thing.
Carlos: The wolf grabbed the man.
Rui: This must be blood [pointing to black shape under their bodies].
Marta: This isn't blood, it's a shadow, the wolf's shadow.
Rui: He's taken him by the throat, like this [dramatically holding his hands around his throat].

Opening 11

Carlos: There's the owl here [pointing at the owl] to save the boy.

Opening 12

Marta: Ahh, so sweet.
Carlos: So it's not a wolf.
Rui: It's a bear.
Marta: No it's not, it doesn't have . . .
Rui: It's a polar bear.
Carlos: Maybe it is.
Marta: So sweet.
Carlos: Polar bears like the snow.
Rui: So in the end he didn't attack the boy, he just wanted affection.
Carlos: That's right, he jumped onto the boy because he wanted affection and that's the end.

We see that these children's certainty of the wolf's intent to harm the boy stays with them right up till opening 12 (see Figure 9.6) where his white goodness challenges the very idea that he is a wolf. On opening 10, Rui thinks the illustration represents blood, a difficulty we all have in interpreting black and white illustrations without the nuances of colour to depict clearly what something is. As a response to his first interpretation, he dramatically enacts the wolf grabbing the boy by his neck. Upon seeing opening 12, the children's cultural frames are so deeply rooted that they no longer believe the creature to be a wolf. Instead they search for other stereotypes. Something sweet and white, that likes the snow and wants affection. It must be a polar bear. This association is one we make with soft toy polar bears, for we know a real polar bear is as dangerous as a wolf in the wild.

Responses from Group 3

These children leapt straight into the main body of the book, seemingly ignoring the cover. They skilfully talked their way through the illustrations, occasionally adjusting what they said to fit a visual sequence or justify a description, all examples of a 'productive dialogue', as mentioned earlier by Ramos and Ramos (2011). Comments from openings 2 to 4 are examples of this.

Opening 2

João: And then he found a forest and saw some white eyes.
David: It looks like a monster.

Opening 3

Luisa: Ah it was a wolf.
David: Yes, it was a wolf, who was walking around.

Opening 4

David: No he didn't know there was a wolf there and so because he didn't know he kept walking.
Luisa: And then what happened?
David: He stopped and looked up and it was snowing.
Luisa: And after?

In opening 3 David responds as though the boy in the book knew it was a wolf all along, but then he adjusts his narrative for opening 4 to allow for the boy to pause to catch snow in his hands. The children responded naturally to each other's narratives.

There were a number of spontaneous 'Oohs', 'Ahhs' and shrieks and Luisa, in particular, made several loud exclamations. On opening 7 (see Figure 9.3), when Luisa sees the wolf's head, she theatrically sucks in air, places her hand on her heart and cries 'Oh goodness'. João accompanies her response with a dramatic narration: 'The wolf opened his mouth, with his big teeth, and started growling'. They quickly turned the next four pages breathlessly relating their story, reaching the climax on opening 11 certain something terrible was going to happen.

Upon seeing opening 12, Luisa questions the illustration, 'And then they became friends?' But the boys continue their spontaneous storytelling, following the visual clues and finish as though it's perfectly normal for a boy to hug a wolf, as the following transcription demonstrates:

Opening 12

David: Yeah, and then the wolf says like this, 'I just wanted someone who loved me'.
João: No the boy said, 'I love you'.
Luisa: 'I'm your friend'.

João: And they lived happily ever after.
David: The end.

Once over, João questions the twist, but David has the answers, as we can see from the next excerpt:

João: Really? The wolf wanted to attack him and then they became friends?
David: No, no he didn't want to attack him.
João: But he jumped onto him.
David: To hug him.
João: [Turns book, looks at cover and points to the eyes] These must be the wolf's eyes.
David: Like this, look [makes his eyes big and wolf-like and opens his mouth then hugs João].
João: Woah, what a wolf.

David not only evidently enjoyed the challenge of justifying his answers but he also used the picturebook as a platform for a dramatic, performative response (Sipe, 2000), pretending to be both a fierce and friendly wolf.

These two groups responded similarly in the sense that their emotions were evident – they experienced a 'lived-through experience' with the book, (Sipe, 2000: 270). The story world and the children's world merge to become one, resulting in unconstrained responses, where the children showed the same fear the boy in the book experienced, as well as the same feeling of happiness, when they realise the wolf, or the bear, will not hurt them.

The children's written responses: a discussion around titles

A title conditions our response to a picturebook; however, the children could not read the French title so nothing was pre-determined for them as such. Additionally, as already mentioned, the French and translated English titles lead the reader into very different stories. The French title, 'Black Wolf', prepares us for a scary wolf; the English one, 'One Scary Night', focuses on the boy's scary experience, which could have involved any creature.

The children agreed upon titles which reflected their response to the wolf changing from bad to good at the end of the story; thus the titles were a direct result of their interpretations of the visual narratives. Group 1 called their story '*The Lost Friends*', a title which is justified by Berta who explains, '(. . .) because the boy could have lost the wolf, and he was his friend, and so one day he went into the woods to find the wolf and he found him'. It is the relationship between the two characters that is important for these children.

The children in Group 2 who thought that the wolf was actually a bear, called their story, '*The Bear in the Night*'. This was a result of both their disbelief that a wolf could save a human and their feeling that words are 'meaningful or important narrative details' (Nodelman, 1988: 186), for Carlos made a connection with the written title, believing that 'noir' must translate into the Portuguese word which means night.

Group 3's final title was narrative, '*The Wolf Who Wanted Company*'. The focus is on the wolf, but the emphasis is on a positive encounter he will have in the story, with someone who will become his companion. The children's experience of the first reading left *each* of them with an idea for the title, which they supported with clear reasoning. David wanted 'Wolf in the snow' because there was a wolf and it was snowing; he showed opening 4 to support his idea. He then suggested that 'The solitary wolf' might also be a good title, justifying that 'Maybe he needed a friend because everyone was afraid of him'. This comment suggests he expects all readers believe wolves are bad. Luisa proposed, 'The wolf who wanted company', because 'he obviously wanted company as he threw himself at the boy to be his friend'.

João also latched onto the written title on the front cover, as Carlos had in Group 2. He too thought that 'noir' must be 'noite', so suggested 'Wolf in the night'. He assured everyone that this was a suitable title as it was night in the story and showed several openings with a black night to support his argument. This led to the children noticing that in fact the night, and even the wolf, was illustrated in both black and white. João's repeated insistence, supported by the possible presence of the word 'night' and the black wolf figure on the cover, did not persuade the others to go for his title. However, the discussion that took place between the children was an excellent example of 'exploratory talk'; that is, talk 'in which partners engage critically but constructively with each other's ideas [and] relevant information is offered for joint consideration' (Mercer, 2000: 98). What supports this kind of talk is the shared 'contextual foundations' – the picturebook and its illustrations – enabling the children to 'reach joint conclusions' (Mercer, 2000: 99).

Negotiating interpretations

All three groups produced stories that were initially more like descriptions of the illustrations rather than being 'real' stories, especially from openings 1 to 8. However, as the children's stories progressed past opening 9, they reflected how each group had interpreted the ending, and structured the narrative associated to these latter openings. The following is an example from Group 1 (see Annex 1 for their final story), where at opening 10 they begin to prepare the reader for the twist. They insert the words 'friend' and 'impulsively', which relates to 'just in time' in opening 11. This connection was the result of a discussion led by Berta who, when deciding what to write for opening 10, admitted she didn't understand the images.

Opening 9

Berta: I don't know why he attacked the boy.
Jorge: He attacked because he didn't know that the boy was his friend.
Berta: Yes, so we write 'The wolf jumped' here. Then here [turns to opening 10] …

Opening 10

Daniel: He jumped on his friend to hug him.
Berta: Daniel, listen to a suggestion. Wolves aren't domesticated.
Daniel: Right, they are wild animals.
Berta: Impulsively. The wolf jumped impulsively onto his friend. How do you spell impulsively?

Opening 11

Daniel: Yeah, then the wolf realised he was his owner. He recognised him right at that moment.
Berta: The wolf recognised his owner just in time.

Opening 12

Jorge: The wolf played with his friend.
Berta: So we don't always start with the wolf, write the boy hugged the wolf.
Daniel: The boy hugged the wolf, he had missed him.

Some interesting negotiation was taking place. Berta resorts to her knowledge of wolves to persuade Daniel that wolves are wild, so they instinctively jump at prey (opening 10). She suggests they use the word 'impulsively' to suit the wolf's wildness. Berta in fact manages very nicely to rephrase parts of the narrative to make it sound better, using 'just in time' and insisting that opening 12 begin with 'The boy' as opposed to 'The wolf'.

This co-creation of the story can be likened to the 'cumulative talk' referred to by Mercer (2000: 30). The children 'build on each other's contributions' as they talk through their interpretations of the visuals. Mercer describes speakers being 'mutually supportive' and 'uncritical' as they co-construct 'shared knowledge and understanding' (2000: 31). The children are doing just this, even if Berta is slightly condescending at times.

Using illustrations to support interpretations

Group 2 had decided their story was about a bear and not a wolf (see Annex 2). However, Marta was not convinced. Their discussion shows their struggles with the decision to call the creature in their story a bear.

Opening 3

Carlos: Now we have to write that the bear went after Pedro.
Rui: A short sentence. He decided to go after the young man.
Carlos: Woah, [pointing to the wolf on the verso] this looks just like a big bad wolf.
Marta: He wants affection.

Rui: It looks like one, but it isn't.

Sandie: Do you still think it's a bear?

Carlos: Yes.

Rui: I think it's a wolf.

Carlos: Here it looks like one, but here, [showing the opening 12] it doesn't.

Rui: Here [pointing to wolf in opening 3] it looks like one because of the shadow.

Marta: [Writing] He decided to go after the young man. OK, it's done. Next picture.

Carlos: [Begins to turn the page]

Marta: Hold it. The wolf is sneaky [points at wolf]. This is just like a wolf, but anyway, no, a bear. Oh boy.

Both Rui and Carlos do their best to justify that it is a bear by making reference to different illustrations, eventually relating the dark outline of the wolf in opening 3 to a shadow. Marta is not convinced as she still insists on calling the creature in the illustrations a wolf. She even shows some concern about their decision by exclaiming 'Oh boy' at the end of the extract. Later on, at opening 9, Rui actually instructs Marta to write, 'Now you can put that the wolf jumps'. Nobody reacted to this and Marta responded, 'Yeah, when the bear was really really close he jumped'. So, despite the children's acceptance that their story was about a bear, they occasionally lapsed into calling the creature a wolf.

Entertaining spontaneous responses

Group 3 were highly entertaining to observe as they created their story. Upon reaching opening 11 (see Figure 9.5) the children decided their story might benefit from including direct speech, and the following excerpt shows the lead up to this decision at the end of their story (see Annex 3):

David: The frightened boy was very still.

João: And the wolf looked at him.

David: And the boy did this [looking scared] 'Huuuu'.

Luisa: [Imitating a frightened boy and recoiling using a squeaky voice] 'Don't hurt me! Don't hurt me!'

David: We could have some speech here, couldn't we?

Luisa: [In a squeaky voice] 'Don't hurt me! Don't hurt me!'

João: Wait what do I write? The frightened boy was very still and then what?

David: And after a dash put 'Don't hurt me! Don't hurt me!'

Luisa: 'Don't hurt me! Help me! I'm still a young boy.'

David: And he said . . . No, he exclaimed 'Don't hurt me! Don't hurt me!'

Luisa: 'I'm still a young boy, I have my whole life in front of me.'

David: 'Don't hurt me! Don't hurt me! Kill me on page 12.'

Luisa: This isn't page 12 it's page 11.

David:	OK. 'Don't let me die on page 11, let me die on page 12, so I get a couple more seconds of life.'
All:	[Laugh]
João:	So don't turn the page, as he hasn't got long left.
David:	So everyone has to die, right?
Luisa:	Die? Yeah.
David:	Everyone has to die when they're old.
João:	But he's not old he's a boy.

It is evident that these children enjoyed this interaction, and it is an excellent example of spontaneous response. They have fun with the direct speech, where the children are seen to merge their identity with the picturebook and become one with it – I liken this to Sipe's aesthetic response which includes 'the desire to forget our own contingency and experience the freedom art provides' (Sipe, 2000: 270). These children literally move in and out of role; first they are storytellers then they become the boy himself. David, in particular, is highly expressive and uses the picturebook as a platform for creative action. He plays around with the idea of prolonging life by not turning the page and obviously expected an 'audience' reaction – on cue we all laugh at his antics.

Concluding remarks

The children's stories are all valid interpretations and as stories in themselves they show that the readers do indeed come to a text with their own expectations and personal experiences. These expectations are culturally framed and affect how the reader and text come together to create a new text. It was evident that children entered into a 'productive dialogue' (Ramos & Ramos, 2011) with the picturebook, which evolved as they read and reread the images and talked together about their interpretations. Many different stories emerged from the rereading(s), which were all influenced by what the children had experienced in relation to what they saw in the picturebook: each reread affected each interpretation and reformed interpretations. This was most evident in Group 2's story featuring a polar bear.

It is of interest to note that none of the groups made the connection between the falling tree, in the visual narrative that runs through openings 9, 10 and 11, and the wolf saving the boy from being crushed. However, during the whole class reading of the picturebook with their teacher, João, from Group 3, noticed the diagonal tree in opening 9 and associated it with the fallen tree in opening 10. He then concluded, 'So the wolf saw the tree was falling and jumped at the boy to save him'. Together the class then reconstructed the sequence, going back further to opening 8 where they thought that the boy, who is looking backwards in this illustration, did not hear the owl or the wolf, but instead the sound of the tree breaking and this was why he began running. They created a fourth story, which ended with the boy thanking the wolf for saving him.

The children used language skilfully to talk collaboratively about their interpretations of these sequential illustrations. The discussion highlights examples of cumulative and exploratory talk, which emerged from their conversations. Exploratory talk, in particular, is a result of people coming together, interacting and thinking collaboratively. Mercer refers to 'interthinking' as being 'joint, co-ordinated intellectual activity which people regularly accomplice using language' (2000: 16), and indeed interthinking was evident in these children's interpretations and discussions. These children's transactional interpretations successfully turned Guilloppé's wordless picturebook into a word-full experience through collaboration and group work. Children were, in Van der Linden's translated words, 'actors' and 'activators' (Ramos & Ramos, 2011) as they decrypted, inferred and created relationships between the boy, the wolf and even the owl.

The children's finished stories are the result of multiple and very creative responses to the wordless picturebook, *Loup Noir*. I have attempted to give some indication of the richness of interpretation and the varying responses that I observed in the three groups of children. In all cases the children's subconscious – their cultural frame in relation to wolves – was challenged. In the case of Groups 1 and 3, the children's cultural frames became fractured as they gave the wolf in the book the opportunity to be friendly and pet-like. However, Group 2 felt so strongly that a wolf could not possibly befriend a human that they insisted the creature was a bear. Their subconscious, socially constructed ideas of what wolves were like completely swamped their interpretations. For these three children ambiguity in this wordless picturebook supported their creation of a narrative quite unlike any that Antione Guilloppé may have originally intended; but this is the right of the reader.

Annex 1

Group 1: The Lost Friends

A century ago, a boy was in a forest in the snow and he was very cold. He saw two strange eyes looking at him. It was the wolf who was following him all the way. It was night when the boy began to catch the snow with his hands. An owl saw some footsteps and then noticed that a boy was there with snow to his knees. The wolf's strange eyes kept watching him. He opened his mouth wide and his teeth were as sharp as knives. The boy heard a noise and looked back. The wolf jumped. He jumped onto his friend, impulsively. Then he recognised his owner just in time. The boy hugged the wolf, he had missed him.

Annex 2

Group 2: The Bear in the Night

One night in the North Pole a young man called Pedro, who was 16 years old, was walking through the forest ... A polar bear was also walking and he heard steps and decided to stop to see. He decided to look from behind some bushes and he saw the young man. He decided to go after the young man. The young man heard steps and noticed it had started snowing. The young man heard an owl, was frightened and started running. As he was running the young man realised he was being chased by an animal. The bear got closer and closer to the young man and he was furious. Pedro ran and looked back to see if he was still being chased. When the bear was very, very close to Pedro, he jumped. A tree fell as the bear jumped, and he fell on top of Pedro.

Pedro was frightened and fell into the snow and saw the bear was friendly. And in the end he gave the bear a big hug and they became the best friends in the world and happy.

Annex 3

Group 3: The Wolf Who Wanted Company

It was night. A boy, who was walking in the snow, became very cold. He kept on walking when suddenly two big eyes appeared from behind a tree. It was a wolf who was walking through the woods behind the boy. The boy looked up and it began to snow and he opened his hands in the shape of a shell. While he was walking he saw two big eyes and he thought they were a wolf's eyes, but when he looked again he saw they were an owl's eyes. He started to run. While he ran, the wolf ran too, watching him through the trees. Then the wolf lost the boy and, sensing danger, he started to sniff looking for him. The boy heard a noise and looked back. And the wolf leapt onto the boy. The wolf grabbed the boy with all his strength and they both fell. And the frightened boy lay quietly and exclaimed, 'Don't hurt me! Don't hurt me!' But the wolf did not want to hurt him, he just wanted a friend.

Academic references

Arizpe, E. (2013) Meaning-Making from Wordless (Or Nearly Wordless) Picturebooks: What Educational Research Expects and What Readers Have To Say, *Cambridge Journal of Education*, 43(2): 163–176.

Beckett, S. (2013) *Crossover Picturebooks: A Genre for All Ages*. New York: Routledge.

Bosch, E. (2012) ¿Cuántas palabras puede tener un álbum sin palabras? (How Many Words Can a Wordless Picturebook Have?), *Revista OCNOS*, No.8: 75–88.

Bosch, E. (2014) Texts and Peritexts in Wordless and Almost Wordless Picturebooks, in Kümmerling-Meibauer, B. (ed.) *Picturebooks. Representation and Narration*. Abingdon: Routledge.

Durán, T. (2002) *Leer antes de Leer (To Read before Reading)*. Madrid: Anaya.

Gee, J.P. (1999) *An Introduction to Discourse Analysis. Theory and Method*. London: Routledge.

Hornsby, D. & Wing Jan, L. (2001) Writing as a Response to Literature, in Evans, J. (ed.) *The Writing Classroom. Aspects of Writing and the Primary Child 3-11*. London: David Fulton Publishers.

Iser, W. (1978) *The Act of Reading*. London: Routledge & Kegan Paul.

Jauss, H.R. (1982). *Toward an Aesthetic of Reception.* Minneapolis: University of Minnesota Press.

Kress, G. & van Leeuwen, T. (1996) *Reading Images: The Grammar of Visual Design.* London: Routledge.

Lakoff, G. (2004) *Don't Think of an Elephant: Know your Values and Frame the Debate.* White River Junction, VT: Chelsea Green.

Mercer, N. (2000) *Words and Minds. How We Use Language to Think Together.* Abingdon: Routledge.

Nikolajeva, M. & Scott, C (2006) *How Picturebooks Work.* Abingdon: Routledge.

Nodelman, P. (1988) *Words about Pictures: The Narrative Art of Children's Picture Books.* Athens: The University of Georgia Press.

Paris, A. & Paris, S. (2001) *Children's Comprehension of Narrative Picture Books* (CIERA Report no. 3-012). Ann Arbor, MI: Centre for the Improvement of Early Reading Achievement. www.ciera.org/library/reports/inquiry-3/3-012/3-012.pdf

Pastoureau, M. (2008) *Noir. Histoire d'une couleur.* Paris: Éditions Points.

Ramos, A.M. & Ramos, R. (2011) Ecoliteracy through Imagery: A Close Reading of Two Wordless Picture Books, *Children's Literature in Education,* 42: 325–229.

Rosenblatt, L.M. (1995) *Literature as Exploration,* New York: Modern Language Association of America.

Serafini, F. (2014) *Reading the Visual: An Introduction to Teaching Multimodal Literacy.* New York: The Teachers College Press.

Sipe, L. (2000) The Construction of Literary Understanding by First and Second Graders in Oral Response to Picture Storybook Read-Alouds, *Reading Research Quarterly,* 35(2): 252–275.

Children's literature

Guilloppé, A. (2004) *Loup Noir.* Paris: Casterman.

Guilloppé, A. (2005) *One Scary Night.* New York: Milk and Cookies Press.

10

WHO'S AFRAID OF THE BIG BAD WOLF?

Children's responses to the portrayal of wolves in picturebooks

Kerenza Ghosh

The wolf has existed alongside humans for centuries, both in reality and through literary and cultural representations. Consequently, the mere mention of the word 'wolf' evokes an immediate response within most people. Stereotypical images of this creature are embodied in traditional stories which have been passed on from one generation to the next. More recently, polysemic picturebooks offer renewed portrayals of the wolf, which challenge and extend the reader's expectations of this character within stories. Such books employ metafictive devices to recast the wolf, encouraging readers to adopt an active approach when interpreting these texts. Beginning with a history of the wolf in literature, this chapter considers how the portrayal of wolves in contemporary picturebooks is often unconventional and thought-provoking. It then goes on to analyse the responses of a group of children, aged 10 and 11, as they read and discussed two polysemic picturebooks featuring the wolf. The children's discussions around these idiosyncratic texts built upon their previous experience of this animal in folktales, fables and in reality. The overall findings demonstrate how such picturebooks provide rich opportunities for the development of reader response, in relation to diverse, sometimes frightening, and often challenging, representations of the wolf.

Why the wolf?

The truth is we know little about the wolf. What we know a great deal more about is what we imagine the wolf to be (Lopez, 1978: 3).

The influence of culture and imagination over our impressions of the wolf is acknowledged by Lopez's statement. This animal has come to be part of our 'collective unconscious' (Jung, 2010: 42), an archetype developed subliminally by society, transcending time and tradition. Throughout their existence, wolves have endured varied treatment from humans. Twentieth-century observations of actual wolves in their natural habitats show them to be exceptionally social and elusive animals, who rarely pose a threat to people (Lopez, 1978). Comparisons have been drawn between the evolution of wolf and man, as both species developed the intelligence to outwit their prey and used their social tendencies to cooperate as a group during the hunt and when caring for their young. Generations of Native Americans have respected the wolf as a lodestar in their tangible and spiritual worlds. However, during the 1600s, American settlers who depended upon domesticated animals for food and work found that wolves were turning to livestock for their food source. Together with this real threat to farmers' livelihoods, religious community leaders exploited images of the wolf within the Old Testament. Jesus' followers were sent out into the world 'as lambs among wolves', and were warned to stay alert to people who may be morally corrupt. Thereby, the Biblical wolf became symbolic of any human threat to the spiritual lives of early Christians. This methodical demonisation of the wolf led to 'lupophobia', not merely fear, but deep hatred towards this creature (Marvin, 2012). Consequently, throughout Europe and America from the Middle Ages onward, wolves have been persecuted by humans and hunted to near-extinction. Only in the 1970s did the wolf become listed as an endangered species in America, after an alarming census reported their dwindling numbers. There has since been a resurgence of wolves in the wild, across North America, Canada and Europe, news which continues to generate debate between conservationists, governments and farmers alike, identifying the wolf as a subject of extreme controversy.

Within the English language, common idioms allude to what is often perceived as the behaviour of real wolves: 'lone wolf', 'wolf it down', 'to cry "wolf"' and 'keep the wolf from the door' suggest isolation, greed and deception, and invoke protection against evil omens (Brewer, 1995). Through the years, adverse opinions of this animal have even extended to the popular playground game, 'What's the time, Mr Wolf?', whereby children are beckoned gradually towards the 'wolf', who suddenly shouts 'Dinner Time!' before chasing the others to catch them. Musically, the wolf has been portrayed as an imposing figure: in *Peter and the Wolf*, composed by Sergei Prokofiev (1936), three French horns perform a grand, ominous refrain to signify his presence. This particular rendition of the wolf has been further developed through stop-motion animation (Templeton & Prokofiev, 2006). However, instead of being captured and taken to the zoo as in Prokofiev's original story, in this animated version Peter shares an affinity for freedom with the wolf, allowing him to escape back into the forest. Alongside this, television documentaries such as David Attenborough's *Frozen Planet* (2011) have given insight to the struggles faced by wild wolves, their intrinsic role in the ecosystem, and the curious, friendly nature of a lone wolf. Peter Hollindale (1999) argues that humankind's relations with the wolf are more complex and intimate than with any other wild creature, making the wolf a robust subject for storytelling. A myriad of stories, from traditional tales to contemporary picturebooks, have contributed in various ways to the wolf's literary image.

A history of the wolf in children's literature

The fables of Aesop, originating around 600 BC, are some of the oldest tales known to associate the wolf with specific character traits. Distinguished by size, hunger and gluttony, the fable-wolf is typically dishonest and cruel. His insatiable appetite reflects danger, and is the source of his actions and the reason for his existence (Mitts-Smith, 2010). Morals reinforce this stereotype: *The Wolf and the Crane* deems him 'wicked'; *The Wolf and the Shepherd* announces the damning indictment, 'once a wolf, always a wolf' (Aesop, 1919). Contrary to popular belief, this animal is not always successful in his ravenous endeavours: *The Wolf in Sheep's Clothing* proclaims him an 'evil doer', yet his tactic to masquerade as a sheep backfires, resulting in his downfall. In *The Wolf and the Kid*, the wolf falls victim to trickery, duped into playing music, then chased by dogs as the kid escapes. *The Wolf and the House Dog* sees him undernourished and dejected, although he does symbolise liberty compared to his cousin, the dog, who is suppressed through domestication. Such lesser-known Aesopian tales can challenge the expectations of the reader who is used to hearing fables of pure wolfish greed and menace.

Folktales likewise tend to represent the wolf in a negative way. Perhaps the most well-known is *Little Red Riding Hood*, said to have originated in Europe during the Middle Ages, a time when wolves were the predominant predator living in close proximity to human beings. This historical period saw much social and political unrest: extreme poverty and hunger meant that violence amongst people was rife, and children were believed to be under constant threat from sinister men, wild animals and the hybrid figure of the werewolf (Zipes, 1993). Widespread superstition and anxiety framed the wolf as a scapegoat for social misfortune, and *Little Red Riding Hood* was told as a cautionary tale to warn about the dangers of life. The classic version by Perrault (1697) tells of a young girl lured into bed by the wolf, wherein he attempts to attack her. Clearly, the desire is sexual as much as nutritional, turning the wolf into a symbol for lustful, seductive men. The Grimms' (1812) retelling, which does not feature the pair in bed together, is widely shared today and continues to inspire contemporary illustrators such as Daniel Egnéus (2011), who uses gothic imagery to encapsulate its horror and romance. For Jack Zipes, the reason for this story's enduring popularity is clear: 'it is because rape and violence are at the core of the history of *Little Red Riding Hood* that it is the most widespread and notorious fairy tale' (1993: xi). It stands out as having been reimagined for readers of all ages in virtually every genre and mode imaginable. Sandra Beckett, in her extensive work on *Little Red Riding Hood*, presents a collection of translated versions, showing how,

> various threads of the traditional tale have been woven together differently to reflect changing times, audiences, aesthetics and cultural landscapes. The number and diversity of these retellings from the four corners of the globe demonstrate the tale's remarkable versatility and its unique status in the collective unconscious and in literary culture, even beyond the confines of the Western world.
>
> *Beckett (2014: 11)*

These works recast this story, from traditional perspectives, to playful versions and innovative approaches focusing on the wolf or wolf-hood.

Myth and legend from other countries have also laid claim to the wolf. In Norse mythology, wolves threaten the Gods, time and life itself. Chariots bearing the sun and moon are pursued by two wolves, setting time in motion and forcing it to move at a vigorous pace. Catching up with their prey will bring about the release of Fenrir, a monstrous wolf whose destiny is to initiate the end of the world. Medieval legends of St Francis of Assisi tell of a frighteningly large wolf which devours livestock and people. In these tales, the wolf's predatory instinct and choice of victims defines his behaviour as fearsome and his character as immoral. Contemporary retelling, *Brother Wolf of Gubbio* (Santangelo, 2000), emphasises the plight of the lone wolf, starving, tired and too old to travel with his pack. He is eventually tamed by the kind treatment of St Francis, who accepts that natural hunger drove this creature to hunt animals; therefore the wolf is without sin. Compared with the original legend, this presents a more ecological depiction of the wolf as a predator (Mitts-Smith, 2010). One tale which holds the wolf in highest regard is *Romulus and Remus*, the legendary founders of Rome, who as babies were protected and nursed by a she-wolf. Since the wolf is so often taken for granted to be male, this female depiction is notable and rare. Naturally, the story of *Romulus and Remus*, believed to have originated around 750 BC, influenced the attitudes of Romans, who viewed wolves favourably. For them the wolf pack embodied characteristics valued in ancient Roman civilisation and military life, including group loyalties and intuitive tactical understanding. Over time and across different cultures, the wolf has recurred as an archetype, creating 'myths, religions and philosophies that influence and characterise whole nations and epochs of history' (Jung, 1978: 68). These ideologies continue to be shared today, through storytelling and adaptations of original tales, demonstrating their continued significance within society.

Deconstructing the wolf in children's literature

Naturalistic depictions of pack animals are found in *The Jungle Book* (Kipling, 1894). In this classic novel, the wolves who are Mowgli's brothers behave similarly to wolf cubs in the wild, offering him loyalty and companionship. Despite these positive portrayals, Hourihan states that 'the effect of the folkloric and literary tradition on living wolves has been catastrophic', and calls for this convention to be deconstructed (1997: 126). Following *The Jungle Book*, other contemporary novels have offered complementary images of the wolf: *Wolf Brother* (Paver, 2004), for example, is the first in a series of books about the bond of friendship and loyalty between a boy and a wolf. However, within literature this animal continues to be conceptualised in diverse and challenging ways. At one extreme the wolf is a male stereotype, deemed to be a purely frightening, hostile force, yet elsewhere the wolf can be naïve, dim-witted, sensitive and even benign. This suggests that the wolf is a social and literary construct, depicted according to whatever may be the intended purpose. Such varied representations indicate that the wolf can act as a metaphor to show that not all human behaviour is wholesome or harmless, but also that humans should develop a sense of empathy for others. The following section explores a range of contemporary picturebooks and considers wolf characters that are stereotypical, parodied, undone, temperamental and reformed, along with female representations of the wolf.

The wolf in contemporary picturebooks

Time and again, wolves have been used allegorically to represent fear, threat and danger. *The Wolf* (Barbalet & Tanner, 1992) is a metaphorical tale about confronting and mastering one's own terrors. The story tells of three children and their mother, whose tranquil life is shattered when a wolf begins to howl forebodingly outside their house. The family members become virtual prisoners, barricading themselves inside their home in an attempt to ward off the beast. Alarmingly, one child wonders whether he should sacrifice his cat, or even himself, to appease the creature. The family gradually realise they must face their fears, and gather the courage to unbar the door and admit the wolf. The fact that the wolf never actually appears in the illustrations intensifies its power as a metaphor, and its influence is evident in the dramatic, realistic portraiture of the characters. A far sinister incarnation of the wolf is found in *The Girl in Red* (Innocenti & Frisch, 2012), wherein this creature manifests itself as a young man, heroic and handsome, yet morally suspicious: 'A smiling hunter. What big teeth he has. Dark and strong and perfect in his timing' (2012: unpaginated). Language and image both draw deliberate comparisons with the folktale wolf, and events later on in the story imply that this man has committed extreme violence against Sophia and her grandmother. The general ambiguity around the characters and plot raises challenging questions about safety and risk, to ensure that this recasting of *Little Red Riding Hood* retains the same impact as the original cautionary tale.

First person narrative can be used to parody the wolf in folktales. *The Wolf's Story* (Forward & Cohen, 2005) and *The True Story of the Three Little Pigs* (Scieszka & Smith, 1991) are each told from the viewpoint of the wolf, presenting him as the ill-fated hero, rather than the villain. Response is encouraged as each narrator addresses the readers directly, imploring them to listen to his side of the story: *The Wolf's Story* begins, 'No, please. Look at me. Would I lie to you?' (Forward & Cohen, 2005: unpaginated). The turns of phrase he uses have double-meanings, implying that his intentions are not wholly honourable: in trying to proclaim his innocence and work ethic, the wolf's pun, 'I won't make a meal of it!', undermines his self-image. *The True Story of the Three Little Pigs* also opens informally: 'You can call me Al. I don't know how this whole Big Bad Wolf thing got started, but it's all wrong' (Scieszka & Smith, 1991: unpaginated). Illustrations of rabbit ears stuffed in burgers are juxtaposed with Al's innocent tone. Reading on, it becomes evident in his use of rhetoric, and through certain unneighbourly behaviour, that Al's version of events may not be entirely truthful. In both of these stories, the combination of a satirical narrator and manipulation of visual viewpoint means that the reader must actively decide whether or not to trust these beguiling wolf-narrators.

In certain stories, the wolf can be undone by those who traditionally fall victim to him. In *Little Red Hood* (Leray, 2010), a fearless young girl is wise to the wolf's gastronomic motives. She skilfully diverts her accoster's attention as he tries to engage her in the familiar exchange about big ears, eyes and teeth. Boldly, she questions the wolf's personal hygiene, offering him a poisoned sweet to freshen his breath. Upon eating this, the wolf dies dramatically, and with cynicism Red denounces him a 'fool!' (Leray, 2010: unpaginated). The witty reversal of traditional roles gives Red the upper hand, conveying an acute sense of power. This subversion harks back to *The Story of Grandmother*, an oral French tale told during the late Middle Ages, in which a clever girl held hostage by a werewolf tricks her captor into letting her go outside to use the toilet (Zipes, 1993). Once out of sight, she is able to make her getaway, thereby foiling the monster's plan and undermining his deceitful persona.

Bruno Bettelheim declares that 'we all refer on occasion to the animal within us, as a simile for our propensity for acting violently or irresponsibly to attain our goals' (1975: 175–176). Bettelheim argues that the metaphoric temperamental wolf, ensconced in the child characters of certain stories, can offer valuable lessons about willpower, since it represents subconscious, disruptive forces. One must learn to conquer such forces though strength of character, as seen in *Where the Wild Things Are* (Sendak, 1963). Dressed in a wolf costume, Max makes mischief. He is banished to his bedroom and in retaliation sails away to the land of the Wild Things. Max's temper, his inner wolf, is signified by the creatures that live there; once he has gained control over them he is ready to return home. The act of taming an upset mood is also explored in *Virginia Wolf* (Maclear & Aresnault, 2012). Awaking one morning in a rage, Virginia, a young girl, skulks around the house, growling and howling, her silhouette revealing lupine ears, teeth and tail. Thanks to her sister's artistic efforts, Virginia's anger gradually fades, her wolf ears become a decorative hair bow and harmony is restored. Taking inspiration from the life of modernist writer Virginia Woolf, who suffered with depression, the story sensitively addresses the complexities of melancholia. In both picturebooks, transformation from wolfish to serene enhances the drama and its resolution. Such characterisation of the wolf may introduce children to the intricacies of human behaviour and emotion, enabling them to manage their own actions and deal with the conduct of others.

Some stories see the wolf himself reformed. On the way, he often suffers humiliation rather than harm: upon drinking large quantities of ginger beer in *Little Red: A Fizzingly Good Yarn*, the wolf lets out 'an enormous burp' causing Grandma to fly out of his mouth (Roberts & Roberts, 2005: unpaginated). In return for promising not to eat anyone else, Little Red provides the wolf with a continuous supply of ginger beer, which he quaffs eagerly despite its embarrassing after-effects. Though he remains a glutton, this newly vegetarian wolf is a comedy figure and far less threatening. Alongside improvements to dietary habits, becoming literate is another route to rehabilitation, as seen in *A Cultivated Wolf* (Bloom & Biet, 2001). The farmyard animals, whose peace and quiet is disturbed by lupine howling, will not tolerate such aggressive, antisocial behaviour. To be accepted, the wolf must prove himself a good influence on those around him. This he accomplishes by learning how to read. His positive transformation is confirmed in the final endpapers, which show him reading happily to a group of children: he is now a fully integrated, cultivated member of society. Reformed wolves carry 'human attributes and values, creating characters which share our concerns and behaviours. In this way, the wolves of children's books mirror and model the lives of their audience' (Mitts-Smith, 2010: 3), demonstrating contemporary values and exploring the challenges that arise from social relationships.

The imposing masculine figure of the Big Bad Wolf, with his wily ways and voracious appetite, appears to have damaged the reputation of *Canis lupus*. Through consideration of gender, modern reversions of *Little Red Riding Hood* can offer more positive representations. *Little Evie in the Wild Wood* (Morris & Hyde, 2013) is one such retelling. References to the classic tale are clear: the wild wood signifies danger, and Evie stands in a vivid red dress against the dark, silhouetted wolf. Familiar descriptions of the wolf emphasise Evie's vulnerability: 'Great eyes, the better to see her with. Great ears, the better to hear her call. Sharp teeth like daggers' (Morris & Hyde, 2013: unpaginated). The similarity ends here, as the traditionally male beast is reimagined as female, and Evie presents her with a basket of jam tarts, baked by Grandma as a gift. Poetic images reflect the benevolence of this she-wolf: her velvet ears and warm body are a comfort in the chill of the night, and she returns Evie safely home to her mama. Themes of domesticity and nurture evoke those maternal instincts of the mother wolf in *Romulus and Remus*, challenging traditional gender stereotypes. Conscious decisions about gender are also found in picturebooks featuring more realistic, factual portrayals of wolves. Readers of *Walk with a Wolf* (Howker & Fox-Davies, 1997) follow the story of a female animal, the effect of which is to 'naturalise the wolf as a wild fellow-spirit, a fierce but unthreatening presence in the child's imaginative world' (Hollindale, 1999: 106). This suggests that, compared with the male of the species, the female is benign and offers a fresh perspective of the wolf.

Aims and approaches to the research

In previous reader response research carried out with 7- to 11-year-old children, I noticed that the wolf and various wolf-related characters feature greatly in children's literature. In particular, it was whilst focusing on Pennac's (2002) novel *Eye of the Wolf*, which tells the sympathetic story of a wolf in captivity, that I realised the potential richness of the wolf as a character. Given this, I wanted to discover how children would respond to two picturebooks that depict wolves in quite different ways. Research by Arizpe and Styles demonstrates 'the pleasure and motivation children experienced in reading [picturebooks], and the intellectual, affective and aesthetic responses they engendered in children' (2003: 223). In light of this, the central aim of my research was for the children involved to engage with complex, at times, challenging picturebooks, to share their responses to the texts, and for them to develop as confident, autonomous and reflective readers willing to take risks as they responded to the texts. Louise Rosenblatt's transactional theory states that readers continually make connections between their current reading, prior experience and sociocultural issues, bringing word and image to life: attention given to a text activates 'certain reservoirs of experience, knowledge, and feeling' in the reader (1978: 54). Given this, I hoped the children would share any existing experience and understanding of the wolf in folktales, fables, myths and legends, and their opinions of real wolves, alongside reading the chosen texts. I was interested to see how the children would draw on this knowledge in their discussions, and if their view of wolves might then change depending on representations encountered in the chosen picturebooks.

My research was carried out in a multi-ethnic primary school in Greater London. The participants were a group of six children (three boys and three girls) aged 10 and 11. They were chosen by the class teacher and identified as keen and competent readers, skilled in responding to a range of texts and able to make good use of inference and deduction. Each child was given their own copy of the picturebooks, which they took turns to read aloud to each other. I felt it was important for the children to spend time on sustained, close reading of the text, so as to enable active, critical interpretations. As they read, they were invited to comment on anything that interested them and discussion was encouraged by means of 'literature circles' (Short, 1997), whereby dialogue is used to orchestrate a community of enquiry and enthusiasm around books. Aidan Chambers states that 'The art of reading lies in talking about what you have read' (1985: 138), and conversation was further guided by the use of Chamber's 'tell me' approach (1993), which encouraged the children to consider the books in more depth. Evans also states, 'It isn't enough to just read a book, one must talk about it as well' (2009: 3). These shared response methods would enable children to take a joint, active and reflective role in developing their responses to picturebooks featuring the wolf.

Polysemy and counterpoint

The two picturebooks discussed by the children were *Wolves* (2005), by award winner Emily Gravett, and *Guess Who's Coming for Dinner?* (2004), by John Kelly and Cathy Tincknell. They were chosen for their polysemic nature, since they offer multiple opportunities for meaning-making. Sylvia Pantaleo explains how polysemy is brought about by 'metafiction', which 'draws the attention of readers to how texts work and to how meaning is created' (2005: 19). Metafictive devices in these picturebooks include: intertextuality; multiple narratives; illustrative framing; indeterminacy; and unconventional design and layout. Both picturebooks tell their story through counterpointing interaction, explained by Nikolajeva and Scott who state, 'dependent on the degree of different information presented, a counterpointing dynamic may develop where words and images collaborate to communicate meanings beyond the scope of either one alone' (2000: 226). This has an especial effect in engaging the reader's imagination and eliciting various interpretations. In *Wolves*, the verbal text consists of facts about grey wolves, whereas the visual text simultaneously shows a rabbit's experience of reading a book, whilst being unwittingly stalked by a wolf. A similar predator–prey relationship unfolds through counterpointing interaction in *Guess Who's Coming for Dinner?*. The words tell the story of the Pork-Fowlers, a pig and a goose, who accept a mysterious invitation to a weekend of fine dining. Unbeknown to them, they *are* the gourmet food: the reader can see their host, who happens to be a wolf, spying upon the unsuspecting couple, visible in each illustration but not mentioned by the text. In these polysemic picturebooks, readers are expected to provide meanings that are not directly conveyed by the words and images, but are merely implied. For reader response theorist Wolfgang Iser, this active engagement is at the centre of the reading experience, since there are gaps in the text which must be filled by the reader: 'it is the gaps, the fundamental asymmetry between text and reader that give rise to communication in the reading process' (1978: 167). Such gaps are particularly evident in picturebooks featuring counterpoint, because once words and illustrations are juxtaposed on the page they begin to influence and interact with each other. Iser's (1978) notion of the 'implied reader' refers to one who can accept those invitations offered by the text, to participate in meaning-making. In my research, it was essential for children to take up the role of the implied reader so as to respond fully to these picturebooks.

Exploring children's responses to *Wolves*

Emily Gravett has created a polysemic picturebook, which at face value tells a simple story of a rabbit reading a library book and being eaten by a wolf (Figure 10.1). Visual depictions of the wolf pack shift between anthropomorphic and realistic, so the portrayal of these animals is humorous, yet unsettling and sinister. Tension builds as the wolf steadily closes in on his unsuspecting victim, until launching the final brutal attack. It is through the reading event that the complexity of *Wolves* is revealed, as it explores boundaries between fantasy and reality, bringing attention to the text not just as a secondary world but as a real artefact in the reader's hands. The ingenuity in the presentation of the story means that rabbit and the reader are drawn into the tale, while the wolf is drawn out. Gravett blends narrative and non-fiction, to play further with readers' interaction and transaction with the text. The children began to interpret some of these complexities in the opening pages of *Wolves* (Figure 10.2).

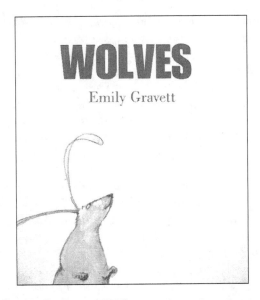

FIGURE 10.1 *Wolves* (Emily Gravett, 2005).

FIGURE 10.2 *Wolves*: 'They can survive almost anywhere: from the Arctic Circle ...'

James: The wolves look mean, with sharp teeth and really angry eyes. They're growling ...

Oliver: At the rabbit, because they're growling *that* way!

Emma: They've made the idea of packs literal. It says 'they live in packs' and they're in a box. It's a pack of wolves ... in a pack!

James: Although the writing is factual, the story seems unrealistic because there's a rabbit getting a book from the library ...

Matthew: [Turns the page] It's facts, but there's something different going on in the pictures ... the wolves are sneaking up on rabbit. They probably want to eat him!

Irayna: It looks like they're spying on him.

Matthew: The wolves have probably come alive. They've made a snow-bunny to hide behind. I think rabbit will outsmart them! He'll act like he doesn't know ... but really he does!

Emma: Maybe it's part of their plan to attack rabbit ... and when the snow-bunny melts, that's when ... well, they hope by the time it melts they'll have killed rabbit!

Oliver: It's a count down!

Hannah: Maybe they're trying to hide behind the snow-bunny so the rabbit thinks it's really *another* rabbit and doesn't get afraid.

Recurrent motifs of the wolf as fierce and threatening aligned with the children's existing shared awareness of a common cultural archetype. Previous discussions had reflected their awareness of stereotypes of the wolf, both in folktales and reality, which the children had described as 'sly predators, working systematically as a team' and 'wild creatures, living in forests, where they can be sneaky and hide easily'. The children had also discussed commonplace idioms featuring the wolf as being representative of trickery and isolation. They had suggested that 'wolf it down' makes reference to the wolf rather than any other animal because 'that's what wolves are like, starving hungry and ravenous: they eat quickly'. Their experience of idiomatic phrases shows how everyday language reinforces typecasts, to the extent that these depictions are taken to be the true behaviour of wolves. The children's familiarity with stereotypes and idioms encouraged them to interpret the 'snow-bunny' as symbolic of the wolves' calculated plan to pursue rabbit. This influenced their reading as they interpreted gaps in the text to predict the wolves' intentions and the inevitability of rabbit's situation.

Oliver: The wolf might be coming out of the book, in the book.

Irayna: Here he's dressed a bit like the wolf that eats Red Riding Hood's grandma, like he's in disguise.

James: I think he's dressed like Red Riding Hood, because of the cape.

Hannah: Maybe there are loads of different wolves from other fairy tales in this book, and they'll come out and try to get rabbit.

Matthew: Yeah, the wolf jumped out of *Little Red Riding Hood* and now he's in this one! Maybe he's eaten an old woman and put her clothes on to disguise himself, so rabbit won't know.

As the wolf pack begin to materialise from the pages of rabbit's book, the children appreciated the ways in which visual and verbal texts were manipulated to convey meaning. Illustrations and context inspired references to traditional tales, bringing further preconceptions and ideals to the story. Gianni Rodari (1996) describes this intertextuality as 'Fairy Tale Salad', in which familiar folktales can be re-imagined in new and unexpected ways. This presupposes active participation in the reading process, because the reader must be the one to make such intertextual links, to develop the meaning of the story. The children's impulse to distinguish between fiction and non-fiction was challenged by 'counterpoint in genre', as boundaries between text types were deliberately blurred (Nikolajeva & Scott, 2001: 24). Despite this, the nature of their discussion shows their desire to make sense of what they were seeing and to piece together a plausible narrative, and demonstrated that they were becoming more autonomous in their responses.

Rabbit meets his end . . . or does he?

As the reader progresses through the book with rabbit, the wolves physically make their escape from the confines of the pages and take form in the world that rabbit occupies. Eventually, the reader is presented with one wolf, so huge that just his tail or legs occupy the entire page, and the reader can only imagine the actual size of this creature. This is achieved through the illustrative technique of frame-breaking, which allows the wolves to escape from the book, whilst inviting the readers 'to step into the image and become an active part of the story' alongside rabbit (Nikolajeva, 2008: 64). Tension grows, as certain images show the wolf to be particularly threatening, though rabbit is oblivious to the fact that he is being tracked. Thereby, the illustrations intruded into the children's visual space, and consequently they felt they were being placed in rabbit's position (Figure 10.3).

Hannah:	Because rabbit is reading the library book, and we see the same book when we're reading, it's like we *are* rabbit. A bit frightened!
James:	[Turns the page] The wolf is really big! He takes up the whole page, looking right at you, close-up.
Irayna:	Even though you can't see all of the face or the body, you can tell he's angry. It's his eyes and maybe he's licking his lips because rabbit is right there!
Oliver:	[Reads 'They also enjoy smaller mammals, like beavers, voles and …'] It's going to say 'rabbits'! [Turns the page] Oh, my goodness! What's happened?! It's Red Riding Hood!
Irayna:	Oh … the book is torn! The wolf's probably eaten rabbit! There's a small piece of paper with the word 'rabbit' on it. . . . The book is shredded. The wolf probably did that.
Hannah:	The book is red, meaning 'danger' for poor rabbit.
Oliver:	And red like Red Riding Hood's cape. Because she got away but rabbit hasn't, in a way, it's like Little Red Riding Hood is dead.

An adult wolf has 42 teeth. Its jaws are twice as powerful as those of a large dog.

FIGURE 10.3 *Wolves*: 'An adult wolf has 42 teeth.'

This episode centres on 'the drama of the turning page' (Bader, 1976: 1), which built anticipation as the children watched rabbit's predicament unfold, filling in the gaps between these pages to ascertain what had happened. Frame-breaking and the realistic image of rabbit's book, ripped up, enhanced this dramatic moment in the story and caused the children to feel vulnerable and empathetic. Observing events from rabbit's perspective invited them to interpret the episode as a metaphor for the fate of Little Red Riding Hood, who is usually saved by the huntsman. Their responses show how folktale symbolism can be reshaped and redeployed by both author and reader, to engender a fresh but still menacing view of the traditional wolf story.

An alternative ending: making a choice

Having seen rabbit meet what seems to be a rather gruesome end, Emily Gravett presents an alternative ending 'for more sensitive readers' (2005: unpaginated), in which rabbit is not eaten. Instead, he and the wolf supposedly become friends and live happily ever after. The book continues to work in a contrapuntal way so that the reliability of this conclusion is ambiguous and the choice of two endings challenges readers. Lawrence Sipe and Sylvia Pantaleo state that in such cases, 'readers are invited to generate multiple, often contradictory interpretations and to become co-authors' (2008: 4), and I was interested in how far the children were able to assume this position, as they discovered and attempted to make sense of this second ending (Figure 10.4) (Plate 28).

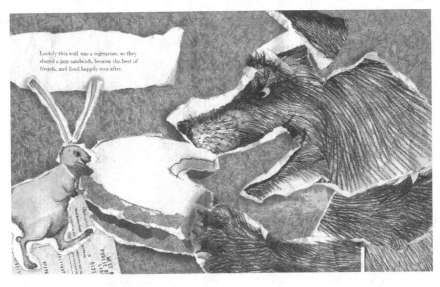

Luckily this wolf was a vegetarian, so they shared a jam sandwich, became the best of friends, and lived happily ever after.

FIGURE 10.4 (Plate 28) *Wolves*: 'They shared a jam sandwich.'

Emma: Phew! The wolf's teeth have gone! No need for sharp teeth now he's vegetarian.

James: I think he actually does have teeth; see the white. But instead of pointy, they're smooth because he's vegetarian . . . I don't think that bit about the jam sandwich is true, because rabbit's neck is cut in half.

Emma: You know how the wolf came out of the book to eat rabbit . . . well, maybe the wolf went back inside just before book got destroyed, so he's stuck in there and can't get out again.

Matthew: Look, the next page! There's a letter from the library . . . and loads of letters for rabbit. He hasn't got them, because he's dead! Oh!

Irayna: It looks like the wolf destroyed rabbit, and because the book got destroyed, he got destroyed too. So they put the pieces back together like it was before. Then they ate a sandwich!

Matthew: Sometimes, when you read a book and you know what's going to happen, you want to tell the character to do the right thing! I wanted to read on because I thought rabbit would do something smart to survive, like a karate chop!

To comprehend the finale, the children needed to suspend their commitment to either of the two endings until their relative credibility could be judged. This was somewhat unsettling, as they were not entirely sure what had occurred or which version of events to take as true. In attempting to figure out the actual fate of rabbit and the wolf, they considered the world within and outside of the library book, offering explanations for the blurring between the represented realms of fantasy and reality. The alternative endings invited the children to predict, invent and even wish for other outcomes, and their comments reflect their vested interest in the characters and plot.

James: At the start, when rabbit is in the library, there's a bookshelf with a rabbit book sticking out. It's as if the wolf has been there and maybe borrowed a book about rabbits.

Irayna: Maybe the wolf took it, to find out about rabbits. Then he put it back.

Oliver: Perhaps the wolf made the *Wolves* book poke out a little bit, so the rabbit would take it, and then the wolves could come out and get him!

Matthew: Here's one of those borrowing cards you get in library books. There are loads of dates . . . it's a popular book!

Hannah: Because this book has been borrowed loads, the wolf must have eaten a lot of rabbits!

Perry Nodelman argues that each text calls for an 'implied viewer', who can attend to the 'apparently superfluous pictorial information [that] can give specific objects a weight beyond what the text suggests' (1988: 106). On rereading, the children noticed such details in the illustrations at the very beginning of *Wolves*, inviting them to embellish the story. It was only having read the whole book that the children could revisit and interpret these supplementary details, to create possible events not actually mentioned in the text. The children's ideas reinforced their interpretation of Gravett's wolves as unremitting predators that had set into action a plan to catch rabbit before the story itself had even started. The appeal of *Wolves* as a physical artefact prompted them to interpret the library docket and date stamp sheet: Hannah's sincere yet whimsical suggestion, that the wolves had been around a long time and had already devoured several other rabbits, uses metafictive devices to take the story beyond the page. Such engagement with the text shows how development of reader response enables children to understand and critique literature.

Exploring children's responses to *Guess Who's Coming for Dinner?*

Having read *Wolves*, which centres on archetypes of the wolf as a successful predator, the same children then read *Guess Who's Coming for Dinner?* (Figure 10.5). Elements of this picturebook echo the classic version of *The Story of the Three Little Pigs* (Jacobs, 1843), wherein a wolf successfully preys upon two pigs but is ultimately undone by the third little pig, into whose cooking pot he falls and is himself turned into supper. Similarly, in Kelly and Tincknell's picturebook the

FIGURE 10.5 *Guess Who's Coming for Dinner?* (Kelly & Tincknell, 2004).

wolf's potential victims are a pig and goose. Their predator, Hunter, builds an elaborate contraption designed to ensnare and cook his dinner, but through a series of mishaps it is he who ends up baked in a pie and eaten by his fellow pack mates. Such traditional themes offer children renewed perspectives of conventional stories. Despite his namesake, Hunter is flawed, and his supposed status as an evil genius establishes this story as a spoof of the mystery genre. This plot development takes place gradually; to begin with the wolf is conventionally cunning and devious. In reading Hunter's note to the Pork-Fowlers, the children recognised clues in the language which enabled them to appreciate the underlying meanings and ironic tone (Figure 10.6).

Emma: It says 'meat' as in the meat you eat, instead of 'I will *meet* you personally'.

Hannah: And, 'Your very special *fiend*' instead of 'friend'.

Irayna: Like he's the enemy!

Matthew: The wolf is *good* with his spelling. He's doing it on purpose . . . very sneaky!

Irayna: But the Pork-Fowlers think Hunter 'can't spell for toffee'.

Emma: It's a huge clue!

Irayna: It says 'eat, drink and be merry', so he's telling them to eat more, but that's just so they'll get fatter and he'll have more meat.

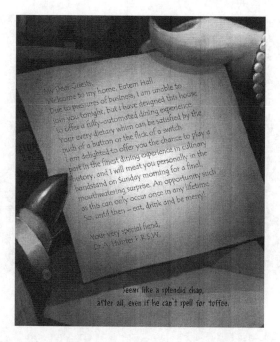

FIGURE 10.6 *Guess Who's Coming for Dinner?*: A note from Hunter.

As children engage with texts, they discover more about language as 'a rich and adaptable instrument for the realisation of . . . intentions' (Halliday, 1969: 27). Metafictive features such as this note from Hunter offer readers the opportunity to see how language can be manipulated according to audience, purpose and context. A few pages on, the children saw Horace Pork-Fowler visit the kitchen for a midnight snack (Figure 10.7). Their comments show their ability to read the pictures and the words, both separately and together, so as to engender thoughtful interpretations.

James:	In the background there are two diagrams of a pig and goose, like in a butcher's shop. It's the best parts of meat!
Emma:	Hunter has been reading all these cookery books, preparing to cook the pig and the goose!
Matthew:	Yeah, 'Cook your Goose' . . . They're definitely in trouble. Their goose is cooked!
Oliver:	'Meals that Squeal' and 'Get Stuffed'!
Irayna:	They're funny; quite cheeky. A lot of them rhyme . . . 'Let's Talk Pork'!
James:	'Fattening Friends'! On the other page there was a poster saying '*Pie Feast this Sunday: Wolf it down!*', so I think the wolf will kill the fattened pig and goose, then he'll put them in a pie and eat them!
Matthew:	He likes only the best meat. Gourmet food!
Hannah:	It says 'no power in the kitchen', but the fridge is working …

FIGURE 10.7 *Guess Who's Coming for Dinner?*: Horace Pork-Fowler's midnight snack.

Irayna: There has to be some light otherwise the pig wouldn't be able to see clearly . . . all that food!

Oliver: Oh, I know what the wolf's done! The main light is not on because there might be loads of secret stuff about how to cook the pig and goose, which the wolf doesn't want them to see, but he *does* want the pig to find the fridge and eat more. So the *fridge* has been lit up.

Matthew: Like heaven . . . Food heaven!

The children took pleasure in reading aloud Hunter's cookery book titles, appreciating how alliteration, pun and rhyme contributed to humour. Language thereby became a source of play. The children noted the relevance of these recipes to the characterisation of the wolf as a voracious yet comical villain, as the books pointed openly at his scheme to prepare a pie feast. Through shared dialogue, they reasoned beyond the text, interpreting the illuminated food store to be part of Hunter's elaborate plans. Margaret Meek states, 'When we want to make new meanings we need metaphor . . . the words *mean more than they say*' (1988: 16). Matthew's own use of the metaphor, 'food heaven', showed his understanding of the pig's disposition, for whom a full fridge really is heavenly, and affirmed his awareness of the wolf's intentions. Vocabulary encountered elsewhere in the book, such as the word 'gourmet', filtered into the children's discussion, and their responses to familiar idioms including 'wolf it down' reinforced stereotypes of the wolf as a carnivore and a glutton. The story contributed significantly to the children's linguistic development, enabling them to appreciate subtleties in vocabulary and to use language with dexterity and playfulness.

Reviewing and rereading plus a serving of wolf pie

Lawrence Sipe observes how reviewing and rereading picturebooks allows children to have 'multiple experiences as they engage in creating new meanings and constructing new worlds' (1998: 107). This continued meaning-making shifts between words and pictures as the reader assimilates new information, a process that Sipe (1998) refers to as 'transmediation'. Visual and verbal texts are of equal significance in this process, seen in the children's discussion as they revisited certain pages to make sense of events in *Guess Who's Coming for Dinner?*

James: In the picture you can see pie-crust under the top of the bandstand.
Irayna: Didn't we see a model of that bandstand before, and a miniature goose and pig inside it?
Matthew: I think something will release, and the roof will drop down on those two.
Oliver: No, I think actually what's happening is . . . look . . . it's dropping on the wolf.
Emma: Oh! Hunter is being cooked, because see this picture . . . he's going up the ladder into the tin. Then the contraption works . . . but instead of the pig and goose being caught, it's Hunter!
Oliver: Yeah, it says 'searched for Hunter but couldn't find him' . . . He was trapped underneath!
Irayna: But the pig or the goose don't even realise what's happening . . . No, not a clue! It shows you what's happening to the wolf in the pictures. Without the pictures it would be a very different story, because we wouldn't know what's really happening!

On rereading, the children benefitted from looking back and forth through the book autonomously and talking through their ideas as a group. Details within the pages thereby gained fresh relevance and contributed to a fuller understanding of the wolf's scheme. Even though the various characters were clueless as to what was really happening to one another, the children were in the know, which empowered them as they explained the consequences of Hunter's misdemeanours (Figure 10.8).

Hannah: On one of the earlier pages there's a 'Bed-o-Scales' to show if the pig is heavy enough . . . if he's ready to eat!
Oliver: And here, the wolf is hiding under the trap door . . . looking at that arrow on the 'Bed-o-Scales'!
Emma: The dial is *just* on the line of being too heavy . . . it says somewhere . . . here, on the wolf's blueprint, 'DANGER! Filling should not exceed recommended weight'.
Irayna: Oh no, the arrow is near the red! Unless the wolf eats him soon, he might be too heavy. He'll need to go on a diet!
Matthew: But the pig ate too much food, so the machine broke!

FIGURE 10.8 *Guess Who's Coming for Dinner?*: Hunter's surveillance room.

Irayna: His plan didn't work because the Pork-Fowlers were too smart for him.

Matthew: No, they didn't know . . . the Pork-Fowlers just walked off by accident.

Hannah: They left a bit earlier than the wolf expected.

Emma: The pig and goose ate more than they were supposed to . . . and Hunter didn't know!

James: [Reads] 'I wonder what sort of pie they're having?'

Matthew: Wolf pie! Look, there's an empty seat for him! I think that's the wolf's family, the rest of his pack.

Hannah: They're eating the pie, but they don't know Hunter is inside!

Irayna: Poor wolf . . . I've realised he's not going to get what he wants . . .

Oliver: Hunter was clever because he tricked the Pork-Fowlers into eating loads of food. But he's not *so* clever because he's been turned into a pie by his own machine!

The children had the confidence to experiment with genre-specific vocabulary ('machine', 'contraption', 'blueprint') and adopted unusual concepts from the book in their responses ('Bed-o-Scales', 'wolf pie'). They assumed the perspective of the characters, even going into role to imagine what the wolf pack might be thinking as they watched their dinner disappear. Hunter's incompetence and ultimate undoing generated real sympathy, perhaps partly evoked through the metaphorical subversion of his traditional-wolf counterpart, who at least tends to get a decent meal before meeting his end. The children followed the irony generated through counterpoint in perspective: the verbal text that chronicles the Pork-Fowlers' weekend retreat emphasised the naïvety of these characters, while the illustrations quite literally showed the wolf's vantage point, through binoculars, periscopes and CCTV footage. Despite his well-laid plans and self-portrayal as a criminal master-mind, the children knew that Hunter was never a serious threat, because his plot to eat his guests was wholly exaggerated and the source of much humour. Pantomime features such as these ensure significant collaboration between reader, author and illustrator, and the children's responses articulate their appreciation of the different meanings derived from the written text and the pictures.

Conclusion: reflections on the reading process

Wolves and *Guess Who's Coming for Dinner?* are powerful examples of the function of literature to provoke, puzzle and challenge, as they each portray wolves in very different but thought-provoking ways, challenging the reader to talk beyond the page (Evans, 2009). By deliberately contradicting the information and viewpoint provided by the text, the pictures create intensely dramatic situations, to convey the climax of the hunt in one story, and the wolf's theatrical undoing in the other. The children's growing awareness of this ironic dissonance between words and pictures was evident, as they willingly engaged in playful re-negotiation of meaning. Since these texts demand a substantial degree of openness, flexibility, and cognisance in their audience, time spent on sustained, close reading was essential for encouraging active and critical interpretations. Drawing on the children's knowledge of stories brought to light a shared cultural heritage, founded on archetypes of the wolf within traditional tales. These enriching aspects of the children's prior experience proved to be beneficial when reading the picturebooks, as the recasting and subversion of familiar characters and themes revived the children's interest in folktales, challenged stereotypes and invited them to make intertextual links. The children realised that although both stories were propelled by the wolf characters' intentions to hunt and eat, these creatures had different characteristics and their endeavours resulted in varied degrees of success. Depending on which picturebook representation they encountered, the children's initial impressions of the wolf as a fearsome beast did change. Responses to Gravett's wolves and then to Hunter, ranged from fear to sympathy, although a sense of humour was always evident both in the texts themselves and the children's discussions. Empathy for certain characters deepened the children's involvement with the stories, as seen in their reactions to rabbit's predicament and Hunter's demise.

Wolfenbarger and Sipe identify three main impulses that guide children's responses to polysemic picturebooks: the 'hermeneutic impulse' or the desire to interpret the text; the 'personal impulse', which connects stories to one's own life; and the 'aesthetic impulse', which 'pushes reader's creative potential to shape the story and make it their own' (2007: 277). As my research shows, each of these impulses was evident within the children's responses, as metafictive devices enhanced their experiences as readers of polysemic picturebooks. Further to this, it was the richness of the context, the wolf itself, which enabled children to reflect so thoughtfully upon their interpretations, and consequently on the act of reading. Since our relationship with the wolf is steeped in history and culture, diverse, unexpected and controversial representations of this animal will continue to challenge children to read at abstract levels of understanding. For renowned wolf biologists David Allen and L. David Mech, hearing the wolf pack howl is 'a mass chorale of resounding splendour . . . the grand opera of primitive nature' (1963: 202). Conversely, Peter Hollindale (1999) notes that the sound of wolves is shorthand for terror in stories for children, their howls frequently sending a shiver up the reader's spine. Whichever view is favoured, wolves still abound in contemporary children's literature, as authors and illustrators continue to create polysemic, challenging picturebooks that affirm this creature's enduring hold on the imaginations of both children and adults.

Academic references

Allen, D.L. & Mech, L. D. (1963) Wolves Versus Moose on Isle Royale, *National Geographic*, 123(2): 200–219.

Arizpe, E. & Styles, M. (2003) *Children Reading Pictures: Interpreting Visual Texts*. London: Routledge.

Attenborough, D., Berlowitz, V. & Fothergill, A. (2011) *Frozen Planet* [Documentary] BBC and The Open University. www.bbc.co.uk/nature/life/Gray_Wolf

Bader, B. (1976) *American Picture Books: From Noah's Ark to the Beast Within*. New York: Macmillan.

Beckett, S.L. (2014) *Revisioning Red Riding Hood Around the World: An Anthology of International Retellings*. Detroit, MI: Wayne State University Press.

Bettelheim, B. (1975) *The Uses of Enchantment*. London: Penguin Books.

Brewer, E.C. (1995) *Brewer's Dictionary of Phrase and Fable*. London: Cassell Publishers.

Chambers, A. (1985) *Booktalk: Occasional Writing on Literature and Children*. London: The Bodley Head.

Chambers, A. (1993) *Tell Me: Children, Reading and Talk*. Stroud: Thimble Press.

Evans, J. (2009) *Talking Beyond the Page: Reading and Responding to Picturebooks*. London: Routledge.

Grimm, J. & Grimm, W. (1812) 'Little Red Cap', in Zipes, J. (ed.) (1993) *The Trials and Tribulations of Little Red Riding Hood*. London: Routledge.

Halliday, M.A.K. (1969) Relevant Models of Language, *Educational Review*, 22(1): 26–37.

Hollindale, P. (1999) Why the Wolves Are Running, *The Lion and the Unicorn*, 23(1): 97–115.

Hourihan, M. (1997) *Deconstructing the Hero*. London: Routledge.

Iser, W. (1978) *The Act of Reading*. London: Johns Hopkins University Press.

Jacobs, J. (1843) The Story of the Three Little Pigs, in Tatar, M. (2002) *The Annotated Classic Fairy Tales*. New York: Norton and Company.

Jung, C.G. (1978) *Man and his Symbols*. London: Picador.

Jung, C.G. (2010) *The Archetypes and the Collective Unconscious*. London: Routledge.

Lopez, B.H. (1978) *Of Wolves and Men*. New York: Scribners.

Marvin, G. (2012) *Wolf*. London: Reaktion Books Ltd.

Meek, M. (1988) *How Texts Teach What Readers Learn*. Stroud: The Thimble Press.
Mitts-Smith, D. (2010) *Picturing the Wolf in Children's Literature*. New York: Routledge.
Nikolajeva, M. (2008) Play and Playfulness in Modern Picturebooks, in Sipe, L.R. & Pantaleo, S.J. (eds) *Postmodern Picturebooks: Play, Parody, and Self-Referentiality*. New York: Routledge.
Nikolajeva, M. & Scott, C. (2000) The Dynamics of Picturebook Communication, *Children's Literature in Education*, 31(4): 225–239.
Nikolajeva, M. & Scott, C. (2001) *How Picturebooks Work*. New York: Routledge.
Nodelman, P. (1988) *Words About Pictures – The Narrative Art of Children's Picture Books*. Athens: University of Georgia Press.
Pantaleo, S. (2005) Young Children Engage with the Metafictive in Picture Books, *Australian Journal of Language and Literacy*, 28(1): 19–37.
Perrault, C. (1697) 'Little Red Riding Hood', in Zipes, J. (ed.) (1993) *The Trials and Tribulations of Little Red Riding Hood*. London: Routledge.
Prokofiev, S. (1936) *Peter and the Wolf* [Music]. USA: RCA Victor.
Rodari, G. (1996) *The Grammar of Fantasy: An Introduction to the Art of Inventing Stories*. Translated from French by Zipes, J. New York: Teachers and Writers Collaborative.
Rosenblatt, L. M. (1978) *The Reader, the Text, the Poem: The Transactional Theory of Literary Work*. Carbondale, IL: Southern Illinois University Press.
Short, K.G. (1997) *Literature as a Way of Knowing*. Portland, ME: Stenhouse Publishers.
Sipe, L.R. (1998) How Picture Books Work: A Semiotically Framed Theory of Text-Picture Relationships, *Children's Literature in Education*, 29(2): 97–108.
Sipe, L.R. & Pantaleo, S.L. (eds) (2008) *Postmodern Picturebooks: Play, Parody, and Self-Referentiality*. New York: Routledge.
Templeton, S. & Prokofiev, S. (2006) *Peter and the Wolf* [Film]. Warsaw: Breakthru Films.
Wolfenbarger, C.D. & Sipe, L.R. (2007) A Unique Visual and Literary Art Form: Recent Research on Picturebooks, *Language Arts*, 84(3): 273–280.
Zipes, J. (1993) *The Trials and Tribulations of Little Red Riding Hood*. London: Routledge.

Children's literature

Aesop (1919) *Aesop's Fables for Children*. Chicago, IL: Rand McNally & Company.
Barbalet, M. & Tanner, J. (1992) *The Wolf*. New York: Macmillan Publishing Group.
Bloom, B. & Biet, P. (2001) *A Cultivated Wolf*. London: Siphano Picture Books.
Egnéus, D. (illus.) (2011) Grimm, J. and W. (unabridged text) (1812) *Little Red Riding Hood*. New York: Harper Design.
Forward, T. & Cohen, I. (2005) *The Wolf's Story: What Really Happened to Little Red Riding Hood*. London: Walker Books.
Gravett, E. (2005) *Wolves*. London: Macmillan.
Howker, J. & Fox-Davies, S. (1997) *Walk with a Wolf*. London: Walker Books.
Innocenti, R. (2012) (translator Frisch, A.) *The Girl in Red*. Mankato, MN: Creative Editions.
Kelly, J. & Tincknell, C. (2004) *Guess Who's Coming for Dinner?* Dorking, Surrey: Templar Publishing.
Kipling, R. (1894) *The Jungle Book*. London: Macmillan Publishers.
Leray, M. (2010) (translator Ardizzone, S.) *Little Red Hood*. London: Phoenix Yard Books.
Maclear, K. & Arsenault, I. (2012) *Virginia Wolf*. Toronto: Kids Can Press.
Morris, J. & Hyde, C. (2013) *Little Evie in the Wild Wood*. London: Frances Lincoln Children's Books.
Paver, M. (2004) *Wolf Brother: Chronicles of Ancient Darkness*. London: Orion.

Pennac, D. (2002) (trans. Adams, S.) *Eye of the Wolf*. London: Walker.

Roberts, L. & Roberts, D. (2005) *Little Red: A Fizzingly Good Yarn*. London: Pavillion Children's Books.

Santangelo, C.E. (2000) *Brother Wolf of Gubbio: A Legend of Saint Francis*. New York: Handprint Books.

Scieszka, J. & Smith, L. (1991) *The True Story of the Three Little Pigs*. London: Puffin.

Sendak, M. (1963) *Where the Wild Things Are*. New York: Harper and Row.

11

FILLING THE GAPS

Exploring the writerly metaphors in Shaun Tan's *The Red Tree*

Sylvia Pantaleo

Shaun Tan's The Red Tree *(2003) can be described as a writerly text (Barthes, 1970) as readers are positioned as co-authors. The indeterminate nature of the metaphorical artwork and symbols in* The Red Tree *requires readers/viewers to become more engaged in experiencing, understanding, and interpreting Tan's polysemous picturebook. The small group discussion excerpts featured in this chapter reveal how 9-year-old children actively filled in the verbal and visual gaps in Tan's writerly picturebook. Indeed, the artwork and phrases in* The Red Tree *challenged the children positively and constructively in ways that involved emotional and cognitive stimulation, excitement, and thoughtful contemplation.*

> *I also like how the author makes imaginary pictures so that you have a better idea of what the girl is feeling.*
>
> Lawson

The above sentence from 9-year-old Lawson's written response to Shaun Tan's *The Red Tree*[1] (2003) communicates his recognition and appreciation of the surreal artwork in this sophisticated picturebook. Allegorical in nature, the evocative paintings and minimal text in *The Red Tree* capture and convey the power of depression. The intricate detail in the complex and collage-like illustrations necessitates and rewards both multiple viewings and close analysis, as much of the artwork encapsulates subtle symbolism and metaphors. Indeed, Tan has explained that the illustrations in *The Red Tree* "are as open to personal interpretation as I could get them, largely through a healthy dose of surrealism" (n.d.: para. 24). Thus, Tan purposefully invites and expects various interpretations of his artwork, thereby intentionally positioning readers in a co-authoring role.

The Red Tree was one of several picturebooks used during a study with Lawson and his peers. The classroom-based research project explored developing young children's visual meaning-making skills and competencies through a focus on particular visual elements of art and design in picturebooks, graphic novels, and magazines. Subsequent to the discussion of the multimodal nature of picturebooks, a description of *The Red Tree*, and a consideration of the topics and issues addressed in some contemporary picturebooks, I review the theoretical frameworks that guided the research, and provide an overview of the research context and the instructional unit. I then present excerpts from three small group discussions that reveal how six children were actively involved in filling the gaps and "producing" the text of Tan's writerly picturebook. As is described below, Barthes (1970) describes writerly or scriptible texts as those that necessitate readers to draw inferences, pose questions, generate connections, fill in gaps, make interpretations, and formulate hypotheses. The chapter ends with a consideration of the importance of affording children with opportunities to orally share their aesthetic responses to and interpretation of picturebooks.

Picturebooks as multimodal and writerly texts

As an art form, the illustrations in picturebooks have become increasingly more sophisticated over the years; changes in printing technology have also affected the range of artwork represented in these multimodal texts. Although picturebooks have always been multimodal in nature, there seems to be an augmentation in both the awareness of and appreciation by contemporary scholars and practitioners about the importance of reading/viewing the artwork in these "visual-verbal" entities (Marantz, 1977: 150). Scholars who have worked with children of varying ages, academic achievement, and linguistic and cultural backgrounds, have written about these children's insightful interpretations of the artwork in picturebooks (e.g. Arizpe & Styles, 2003, 2008; Evans, 2009; Kiefer, 1995; Pantaleo, 2008; Sipe, 2008; Walsh, 2003).

Numerous metaphors, concepts, and taxonomies have been developed to describe the synergistic relationship between the artwork and words in picturebooks (Lewis, 2001; Pantaleo, 2008; Sipe, 2008, 2011). Picturebooks have always required readers to fill in gaps and generate predictions on multiple levels, as readers must move back and forth between text and artwork (except in wordless texts). However, some picturebooks, such as *The Red Tree*, demand a higher level of sophistication and complexity with respect to gap-filling (Iser, 1978). These picturebooks can be considered writerly texts, as they require readers to adopt a co-authoring role in producing the text (Barthes, 1970).

According to Barthes (1970), readerly texts are unambiguous and can be described as didactic, as they impose an invariable meaning on readers. Readerly texts position readers as "consumers" who are neither expected nor invited to make any contributions to the meaning (Barthes, 1970). In contrast, writerly texts position readers as imaginative interpreters of texts who "write" while reading, by filling in the textual gaps that induce and guide a "reader's constitutive activity" (Iser, 1989: 39). By embracing their roles as co-authors and co-producers of meaning, readers are actively involved in the reading process. In writerly texts indeterminate sections or gaps "are a basic element for the aesthetic response" (Iser, 1989: 9). Indeed, writerly texts achieve plurality of meaning because each reader brings a unique repertoire of literary and life experiences to each unique reading event. The indeterminate nature of the metaphorical pictures and symbols in *The Red Tree* adds deeper meaning to the work and requires readers/viewers to become more engaged in experiencing, understanding, and interpreting the polysemous picturebook.

The symbolic nature of Tan's writerly paintings in *The Red Tree* requires readers to thoughtfully consider the denoted (i.e. what is signified directly or literally) and the connoted (i.e. what is signified indirectly, or the associations or meanings that are suggested or implied or evoked) in the artwork. Readers must infer from what they observe—the subject matter represented as well as Tan's use of visual elements of art and design. Additionally, readers must contemplate the phrases that accompany the paintings as they work to understand and analyse each opening in the picturebook.

Shaun Tan's picturebooks

Communicated in Shaun Tan's picturebooks, essays, acceptance speeches, interviews, and conference presentations is his attraction to "ideas of belonging, difference, and the conceptual boundary between what is familiar or 'normal', and what is exotic, or 'weird'" (Tan, 2012: para. 4). When asked why his illustrations "often deal with dark subjects—death, disaster, depression, and the like," Tan explained that "such things are more thought-provoking than something light or harmonious" (n.d.: para. 21). Another characteristic of Tan's multilayered and sophisticated picturebooks is his expectation that readers are "co-creators" of his work. Tan has stated that readers must "invest meaning into [his] illustrated stories that are really half-finished, deliberately incomplete" (2012: para. 29). Indeed, as is evident by the description of *The Red Tree* below, this writerly text requires readers to actively engage in asking questions, drawing inferences, making connections, and generating interpretations about the multi-faceted indeterminacies in the picturebook.

The Red Tree[2]

The identical dust jacket and hard cover of *The Red Tree* (Figure 11.1) feature a young girl with orangey-red hair afloat in a paper hat/boat. Compelling thoughts and emotions are stimulated by the text on the hat/boat and the nature of the reflection of the girl and her craft, including the image of a single red leaf. The mottled grey front endpages, featuring a single brown leaf, establish the atmosphere for Tan's thought-provoking picturebook. On the first frontispiece, the young girl is situated in a field, standing on a stool, with disorderly letters spewing from a megaphone that is raised to her mouth. The second frontispiece depicts a framed illustration of a grandfather clock in a field with letters from the previous page scattered about in the bottom one-third of the page. The face of the timepiece,

FIGURE 11.1 *The Red Tree* (Shaun Tan, 2001).

comprised of one red leaf (at the top) and seven brown leaves, features a single hand poised to strike the hour of the red leaf.

The recto of the first opening depicts the girl awakening to brown leaves descending into her bedroom. On the wall above the girl's bed is a framed picture of a single red leaf. The text on this page reads, "sometimes the day begins with nothing to look forward to" (unpaginated). A page turn reveals the girl's room nearly half full of brown leaves. She exits her bedroom and over the next 11 openings the girl wanders through imaginary and dreamlike landscapes that portray despondency and isolation. For example, double-page spreads show the girl followed by a massive repulsive fish with bloodied-eyes, enclosed in a glass bottle wearing a scuba diving helmet, and counting aimlessly on the surface of a giant snail. The girl is overwhelmed by feelings of despair and melancholy. As well as conveying emotions and thoughts associated with depression, the minimal text featured throughout the book communicates sophisticated themes such as search for identity, overload of information, pressure to conform, and lack of control of one's destiny. However, a red leaf depicted in each of Tan's mixed-media visual compositions seems to represent hope, even in the darkest moments of misery and loneliness.

At the end of the day when the girl returns to her bedroom, a red leaf has taken root on the floor and is "quietly waiting" for her. A page turn reveals the girl smiling at the luminous red tree that has blossomed from the single red leaf. Readers are reminded of the power of regeneration and encouragement. The final endpapers have the same marbled appearance as the beginning endpapers but red is the dominating colour of these closing pages.

The content of "unconventional" picturebooks

Although some adult readers have questioned the suitability of *The Red Tree* for children, stating that the picturebook is "just plain depressing and inappropriate for children" (Tan, 2011: 10), picturebooks that explore depression and hopelessness "reflect current efforts to rethink, revalue, and refashion what childhood is and how it is experienced" (Reynolds, 2007: 91). Indeed, "adults do not have the monopoly on powerful negative emotions or suffering" (Reynolds, 2007: 89) and according to Clarke, the rate of "the diagnosis of depression in children" has grown (2011: 53).

Reflecting Bader's assertion that a picturebook is "a social, cultural, historic document" (1976: 1), many current authors and illustrators have questioned and confronted traditional assumptions about childhood and the "appropriateness" of content for children's picturebooks by responding to and representing issues and events in our contemporary world. Postmodernism and Radical Change theory (Dresang, 1999) are two conceptual frameworks that have been proposed to explain the changes evident in contemporary children's and young adult literature (Pantaleo, 2008, 2009). A discussion of Radical Change theory and Postmodernism are beyond the scope of this chapter; however, a few basic tenets of Dresang's Radical Change theory assist in contextualizing the expanding topics and themes evident in some contemporary picturebooks such as *The Red Tree*.

According to Dresang (1999), the changes in many contemporary handheld books for children and adolescents reflect the underlying principles of the digital age: interactivity, connectivity, and access. She identifies three types of fundamental changes: changing forms and formats, changing perspectives, and changing boundaries. Dresang states that books that reflect Type Three Radical Change, changing boundaries, incorporate characteristics such as "subjects previously hidden, settings previously overlooked, characters portrayed in new complex ways, new types of communities, [and] unresolved endings" (1999: 26). *The Red Tree* can be described as a picturebook that reflects characteristics of Dresang's Type Three Radical Change as childhood despair and depression are explored in Tan's picturebook.

As stated by Tan, and as is evident by the brief description of *The Red Tree*, the compellingly surreal artwork and minimal text in the picturebook invite personal interpretation. Tan has described how readers will experience and interpret his artwork in their own unique way. According to Tan, "the question of meaning must remain open, carefully passed to the reader intact" (2011: 10). However, some readers may resist and be uncomfortable with the indeterminacy of meaning of both the paintings and narrative text in *The Red Tree*. In this chapter, rather than using the word "challenge" to mean affront, oppose or attack, I use the word "challenge" positively to mean to "invite, arouse, stimulate, inspire" or excite (Rodale, 1978: 157) when describing the children's stance to the picturebook. The children's transcript excerpts featured below reveal how they embraced the challenging openness of the visual and verbal texts in *The Red Tree*, how they were provoked by the paintings and textual phrases, and how they accepted Tan's invitation to use their imaginations as they worked to fill in the multiple gaps "to make sense of the 'unfinished' stories" (n.d.:para. 25) in the picturebook.

Situating the research theoretically and conceptually

The classroom-based research conducted with 8- and 9-year-old children was informed by the theoretical and conceptual frameworks to include: transactional theory, sociocultural theory, and multimodality, social semiotics, and visual literacy.

Transactional theory

During the study, the children were both encouraged and expected to adopt an aesthetic stance to the literature they read and responded to orally and in writing. Rosenblatt (1978) adopted Dewey's term 'transaction' to describe the reciprocal relationship between reader and text. Respecting the unique nature of each reader's background experiences and knowledge and each reading event, Rosenblatt wrote about the particularity of readers' evocations and the diversity of their responses. According to Rosenblatt, the poem, the lived-through "work," is what readers "respond to" "as it is being called forth during the transaction, and as it is reflected on, interpreted, evaluated, analyzed, criticized afterward" (1986: 124). Although readers can make various defensible interpretations of their evocations, Rosenblatt explained that a "shared criteria of validity of interpretation in a particular social context, recognizes that some readings may satisfy the criteria more fully than others" (1994: 1079).

An essential tenet of Rosenblatt's theory of the reading process was her assertion that any text can be read from either a *predominantly* aesthetic or efferent stance, with most reading events falling somewhere along the aesthetic/efferent continuum. An aesthetic stance refers to a reader adopting "an attitude of readiness to attend to what is being lived through during the reading event" (Rosenblatt, 1988: 74), and thus a reader's attention is directed more to the private and emotive elements of meaning. With the adoption of a predominantly efferent stance, a reader's "attention is focused primarily on what will remain as the *residue* after the reading" (Rosenblatt, 1978: 23), and consequently he/she focuses mostly on the public referents of meaning. Other key elements of Rosenblatt's (1994) transactional theory include the following: any text can be read from either a predominantly aesthetic or efferent stance; a reader's stance may fluctuate as she/he reads; and the adoption of a reader's stance toward any one text is affected by the synergistic relationship among various reader, textual, and contextual factors.

Sociocultural theory

Throughout the study, a significant amount of time was allocated for the children to talk about the texts featured during the research. A sociocultural perspective on teaching and learning in classrooms, which draws heavily on Vygotskian (1978) theory, is conceptually consistent with Rosenblatt's emphasis on the importance of children being provided with opportunities to discuss and write about their transactions with literature. The tenets of sociocultural theory acknowledge both the personal and the social nature of learning environments, and recognize how children's engagement with particular kinds of texts is mediated by social interactions, discourses, and experiences in specific contexts.

Multimodality, social semiotics, and visual literacy

The research was also informed by multimodality, social semiotics, and visual literacy. A social semiotic approach to the analysis of multimodal texts such as the picturebooks used in the research focuses on a sign-maker's choices and uses of available semiotic resources, and explores how the deployment of these modal resources "gives particular shapes to meaning" (Mavers, 2009: 264). With respect to the mode of image, the children's abilities to "see" and interpret visual images were greatly influenced by the multiple opportunities they had to develop their knowledge about the visual qualities of artwork throughout the research. Making "critical the role of visual analysis significantly implicates the textmaker and the viewer as active and critical makers and readers of visual texts" (Albers, Vasquez & Harste, 2011: 200). However, the latter requires sign-makers and sign-readers to be visually literate, and learning about the artwork of picturebooks can afford readers with rich opportunities to develop their visual literacy competencies.

Contextualizing the classroom-based research

The study took place in an independent school for 5- to 10-year-old children, located in a city in western British Columbia, Canada. For approximately 10 weeks I worked with 8 girls and 12 boys, aged 8 and 9, and their teacher, during the Language Arts/Literacy teaching block. The ethnic backgrounds of the 20 children were: European-Canadian (14), Chinese (2), Korean (1), South Asian (1) and biracial (2).

Although the research study began at the end of September and finished in mid December 2011, scheduling restraints resulted in the children being inter-viewed about their culminating projects at the commencement of the January 2012 term.

The children's 2011 December report card marks for Language Arts/Literacy reflected a range in academic achievement from "exceeding" to "minimally meeting" the children's age level expectations.

Although the research was guided by several overarching purposes, the objectives most relevant to this chapter were to develop the children's visual meaning-making skills and competencies by focusing specifically on visual elements of art and design in picturebooks, graphic novels, and magazines; and to explore their comprehension, interpretation, and analysis of multimodal texts.

An overview of the teaching unit

The lessons were approximately 60–70 minutes in duration, and generally the children read silently for 15–20 minutes before the commencement of each day's lesson. Initial teaching focused on constructing a communal understanding of the characteristics of "successful" small group discussions and developing the children's understanding of personal response to literature. As stated previously, the children were expected to approach the literature from an aesthetic stance, and to thoughtfully explore multiple interpretations of texts. Consistent with criteria explicated in provincial curriculum documents (British Columbia Ministry of Education, 2009: 125), a "good aesthetic response" was defined as one where the children expressed their thoughts, opinions, and emotions about a text and provided supporting reasons/explanations.

During the teaching unit the children were introduced to a selection of picturebook peritextual features (e.g. dust jacket, front and back cover, title page, frontispiece, copyright page). In addition, a sequence of lessons introduced the children to the six visual elements of art and design that were the focus of the study: colour, line, typography, point of view, framing, and perspective (see Pantaleo, 2013a, b for further information).

The five picturebooks and three graphic novels used during the research were read in the following order: *Re-zoom* (Banyai, 1995), *Flotsam* (Wiesner, 2006), *The Red Tree* (Tan, 2003), *Voices in the Park* (Browne, 1998), *Don't Read This Book!* (Lewis & Allwright, 2009), *The Arrival* (Tan, 2006), *Babymouse: Queen of the World* (Holm & Holm, 2005), and *Amulet Book One: The Stonekeeper* (Kibuishi, 2008). The children read each book independently; completed a written response for each selection of literature; engaged in small group, peer-led, and digitally recorded discussions of the literature; and participated in whole-class discussions about each book.

The small group discussions were guided by focus questions/discussion prompts that encouraged adoption of an aesthetic stance to the texts and that concentrated on pertinent visual elements of art and design.

Reading, talking and writing about The Red Tree

Although all of the visual texts invited creative and critical discussion, it was *The Red Tree* which was chosen for closer study. It was the third picturebook which was read and discussed. Once individual copies of the book had been distributed, the children were instructed to carefully view the dust jacket and to share their observations and thoughts. We used open-ended questions to engage the children in conversation about the endpages and the two frontispieces. The children were encouraged to interpret Tan's images, to consider not only the content of the images but also his use of colour, line, perspective, and point of view. The children were told that it was "okay to be uncertain, puzzled" (Tan, 2011: 9) and that multiple expressions of meaning were encouraged and indeed expected. The children enthusiastically shared their ideas and opinions. Subsequent to this whole-class discussion, we reminded the children to think deeply about the possible meanings of each double-page spread or single page as they worked their way through the picturebook. Once they had finished reading *The Red Tree*, the children wrote a personal response. Before engaging in their small group discussions, the children used post-it notes to identify two openings to talk about with their peers.

Small group discussions: filling the gaps

The digitally recorded discussions of the children (six groups of 3, and one group of 2) varied in length from 25 to 30 minutes. The discussion prompts for *The Red Tree* directed the children to talk about the meaning/significance of the following: the colours and images on the endpages and the frontispieces, the absence of a mouth on the girl throughout the picturebook except for the last opening, the overall meaning of the picturebook, and each child's two previously chosen openings (although all seven groups talked about more than the required number of openings).

Double-page openings 4, 8, and 10 are featured below because analysis of the children's transcripts revealed that each of these particular openings was discussed by six of the seven small groups. Although all of the children engaged in thoughtful collaborative and exploratory talk (Barnes, 1992, 2008) about the picturebook, this chapter features transcript excerpts from only two groups because the nature of the discourse of these six children was particularly insightful and sophisticated as they worked to fill the multifaceted gaps in *The Red Tree*.

Opening 4 (Figure 11.2) features the girl wearing a large scuba diving helmet and sitting at the bottom of a narrow-necked glass bottle. The bottle, which contains a small amount of water, sits on a rocky beach. The fragment of text reads, "nobody understands." In the excerpt below, Calvert, Myca, and Barth talk about the multiple meanings of this opening—how the artwork and text synergistically communicate the girl's overwhelming feelings of desolation and vulnerability.

Calvert: In this book it's really cool because instead of making her look more sad, the illustrator actually has her look the same. Like he makes more things go into the picture, which is like her feelings pretty much.

Myca: Yeah. So, Calvert, what was your first choice?

Calvert: My first choice is the page where she's like in a bottle. And I think that she's in, um, the old beer bottle because she's like . . . it says, "nobody understands." So nobody understands—she's alone in her own fate.

Myca: It's just like that feeling—when you feel like you're sinking.

Barth: Yeah.

Myca: I bet she feels like she's sinking and so she's . . .

Barth: Especially when she's in a scuba diving suit.

Myca: Mm-hm. She just feels it's like she's drowning and so she made herself drown.

FIGURE 11.2 *The Red Tree*: "... nobody understands."

Calvert: She's drowning in the bottle. I think it's really powerful because it's just like it says "nobody understands" so she's like believing in your own faith that nobody will believe in it with her so she's like all alone, and ...

Myca: I think it's getting, the bottle is getting filled up by the rain because ... and as you can see over in the corner there's all the sun in the nice beautiful sky and then right above her it's raining. It's like she has her own rain cloud following her.

Calvert: Just like she's all alone, which she is.

Barth: For miles, and miles.

Calvert: Like I said a couple of times, she's like alone in her own faith stuck in her bottle.

The discussion passage reveals how the children engaged in exploratory talk as they considered multiple meanings of the painting, hypothesized the emotions and circumstances of the girl, as well as inferred the meaning of her overall condition. The children's conversation includes consideration of the significance of particular details in the painting: the diving helmet, the rain, and the dark clouds. As they collaborated to interpret Tan's metaphorical artwork, Calvert, Myca and Barth made reference to the feelings of sinking, drowning, and loneliness, and the concepts of faith and fate. The children's discourse reveals how they interpreted many aspects of the artwork as embodying underlying emotional and psychological meanings.

The double-page spread of opening 8 (Figure 11.3) depicts the girl crouched in a tiny boat adrift amongst surging waves and colliding massive ships. The girl's vulnerability against the forces and power of machines and nature is accentuated by the size differentiation of her boat. The text, arranged in a slight arch on the verso, reads "then all your troubles come at once" with the typography of the word "troubles" larger in size. In the passage below, the children's conversation reveals the visual metaphors that they inferred from Tan's artwork.

Jorgen: It kind of makes you feel like all the troubles are coming at once and it's not fair.

Anike: Yeah, like all these ships are about to smash into her and she's in this tiny little ship.

Jorgen: It's like, those are what's supposed to happen in her life like her whole life but they come every day in vast numbers so she just feels like the world is unfair and the ships kind of describe what she's feeling. Like huge ships, just huge problems, small problems of all sizes just come at you. What do you think, Seward?

Seward: Well I think these [portholes on ship] are like her parents crying because of those eyes, I mean those dots that look like eyes. They're crying because of how bad their daughter is feeling but they don't know how to help.

Jorgen: Yeah and then I wonder how ... notice the colours ...

Anike: Yeah, just her ship is the only red part and then the rest is like grey and white with all those kind of the little splotches of pink to make it look kind of ...

FIGURE 11.3 *The Red Tree*: "... then all your troubles come at once."

Jorgen:	The ships' lines kind of lead you to where her water road is.
Seward:	They all do. You know you're right. And then look at this one. This is the main line, the highway for your eyes, even this one, it leads there, that one leads there, and that one leads there.
Jorgen:	Yeah. What do you think, Anike?
Anike:	Um, this really small leaf here maybe before it was larger but then it feels like her hope is kind of like ebbing, ebbing away, and then it's like . . . you feel like you're kind of standing on one of the ship's deck on one of these ship's decks almost as if you were like her parents and you don't know how to help her.
Jorgen:	It's almost as if this is like a barge. This is like a barge in between that has a good life moving away and she can't, she's trying to get to it almost. But she wants to get her hope back before she gets to it but it just charges past her. She's left alone with everybody else who's sad or that's evil maybe or something.
Anike:	It's kind of like it's two hard decisions. It's like her life that she has right now and the life she's going to get. It's kind of a really hard decision that she's going to make.

The above excerpt is an excellent example of interthinking (Mercer, 2000)—of people using talk to think collectively, to engage with others' ideas through oral language. Jorgen, Anike and Seward collaboratively interpret the symbolism of the ships in the artwork. They conjectured that the ships represent the girl's problems and the size and placement of the ships communicate the girl's emotional state and circumstances. The children's exploratory talk includes consideration of colour, as well as contemplation of how the bows of the ships act as illusionary lines leading readers' eyes to the girl. Jorgen, Anike and Seward were the only group to hypothesize the symbolic presence of the girl's parents in this painting. The children talked about how the parents felt powerless to provide the girl with assistance. Finally, although briefly, the children explore how the girl needs to make a decision with respect to her life—to remain on her course feeling alone and hopeless or to follow the path of the red leaf that represents a "good life" and hope.

The artwork for opening 10 (Figure 11.4) (Plate 29) resembles a "board game" and features a "big wolf thing" (Laird) or "dragon" (Anike) dangling an hourglass and the girl holding a single die with peculiar numbering. Below, Jorgen, Anike and Seward collaboratively construct their interpretations of the numbering on the die, the structure of the board game, and the hourglass framed by the forelimbs of the mechanical beast.

Jorgen:	And in the end I realized her life must be like, see on page, the one that I chose with a sticky, see on the dice it's all sixes on all sides. That means her life is a repeat. It's a game that just repeats. This is like her life, she just goes like this, falls asleep, goes again, every day, same thing, it's a repeat and it's a game.

FIGURE 11.4   (Plate 29) *The Red Tree*: "... terrible fates are inevitable."

Anike: Yeah, that's why it says six on every side.

Jorgen: Yeah. It's kind of like the dice is cheating or something because it doesn't want ... because her life is just like every day it's the same life going to the same thing.

Seward: Yeah. The giant-like robotic thing. It's almost as if these [eyes in borders] are, those are like her parents', one of her parents' eyes or something like that but they don't know how to help her get through.

Anike: These different buildings are probably ... they could be like events in her life and then if she starts over here she walks down and then she goes to sleep and then she wakes up.

Jorgen: These are kind of like rough roads.

Anike: And kind of like this is like her fate or something. Then that's her dice which is like kind of like part of her fate, everything keeps repeating for her.

Seward: What do you think Jorgen about this?

Jorgen: I think it's kind of like spikes and stuff because it's a really rough road that she's taking every day and she doesn't want to do that every day. She wants to just sit down and relax one day but she kind of can't—it's part of her fate.

Seward: I kind of think that the wall-looking-like thing is a city because you see those kind of building-looking chimneys.

Anike: It made me kind of think that she was walking through a junkyard and then this is kind of like a house, not really her house but just ... like the contents of the junkyard kind of made up into like some sort of her fate sort of. There's a path leading up to this.

Jorgen:	What I'm thinking is maybe this is a really long wall separating the nice fun world from the evil world and this guy [robotic beast] is trying to take over the good world which might be over here.
Anike:	Or maybe the other path and she chose the wrong path.
Jorgen:	And she's so sad that she's trying . . . she's almost like being torn in two.
Anike:	So she like chose the wrong path.
Seward:	Like the water pipe is already dried up so there's no water and sadness and everything and it looks like her time is like . . . her life's running out.
Jorgen:	Oh, yeah. Notice this like little time glass here and it's like . . .
Seward:	Yeah, see the hourglass is almost like the clock [on the frontispiece] but an eviler way of showing it.
Anike:	Her hope is running out. [Conversation continues about opening 10.]

The above excerpt is another outstanding example of exploratory talk, revealing how Jorgen, Anike and Seward were "thinking aloud," how they talked their way through and into ideas (Barnes, 1992, 2008). The children not only described details in the painting, but they provided hypotheses to explain their conjectures, and reasons to support and justify their interpretations of Tan's artwork. Jorgen, Anike and Seward considered the symbolic nature of the die, the buildings and content of the junkyard, the paths, and the hourglass. They introduced the notion of the girl's fate as they deliberated the meaning of the unusual numbering on the die. Once again, Seward inferred the presence of the girl's parents and their inability to assist their daughter. Similar to their conversation about opening 8, the trio discussed how the girl must make a decision and that ultimately she desires hope and happiness.

Discussion

Iser (1989) writes about the participatory invitation of indeterminacies or blanks or gaps in texts. Indeed, indeterminacy brings about "an intensified participation that will compel the reader to be that much more aware of the intention of the text" (Iser, 1989: 22). The children's discussions reflect how they embraced the visual indeterminacies in *The Red Tree*, how they positioned themselves as active readers who looked closely at, and thought deeply about, the intentionality and deliberate indeterminate meaning of Tan's sophisticated and metaphorical paintings. The children's discourse also reveals that although they adopted a co-authoring role as they interpreted the emotional landscapes and phrases in the picturebook, they were comfortable sharing their uncertainty of "the" particular meaning of individual openings, and entertained and welcomed plurality of meaning as they engaged with Tan's writerly metaphors. Indeed, the children did not discuss what they believed the book to "really mean" or express any disquiet for how Tan chose to convey meaning through his visual and verbal texts. Thus, the children did not challenge *The Red Tree* through resistance, opposition, or criticism. However, as is evident by the transcript excerpts featured above, the artwork and phrases in the picturebook challenged the children positively and constructively in ways that involved both emotional and cognitive stimulation, excitement, and thoughtful contemplation. Tan has conveyed how the text in *The Red Tree* is "consciously minimal and prosaic so as not to get in the way of the mysterious invitation offered by each painting to the reader" (n.d: para. 23). The children readily accepted Tan's invitation to be positioned as co-authors. Indeed, the children engaged in conversations both about and with the picturebook as they considered various meanings and interpretations of the writerly metaphors.

Consistent with the tenets of sociocultural theory, the excerpts also demonstrate the fundamental role of talk as process, showing how the children engaged in exploratory talk, co-reasoning, building knowledge, and sharing jointly constructed meaning. Together, the children's observations and talk resulted in them collectively identifying and filling in gaps in the picturebook. The children's discourse reveals how they interpreted the metaphorical and symbolic artwork in *The Red Tree* and how they contemplated both the denoted (i.e. what is signified openly or factually) and the connoted (i.e. what is signified implicitly, or what is intimated or stimulated) in the writerly paintings. The children expressed mature responses and interpretations of the serious subject matter represented in and evoked by the paintings. The children conjectured about the underlying emotional and psychological meanings of the artwork and their inferences were both logical and empathetic in nature.

During the whole-class discussion of *The Red Tree*, each group shared the opening that they thought conveyed or expressed the girl's emotions or ideas in the most powerful way. This sharing afforded teacher and myself with opportunities to question the children further about their interpretations and to explore and guide the conversations about depression in a respectful and compassionate manner. Some children conveyed empathy for the girl's emotions, expressing how they too had experienced feelings of isolation, lack of understanding, and loneliness. Picturebooks such as *The Red Tree* that "display literary and aesthetic quality" and that respectfully and thoughtfully explore topics that "challenge the status quo" (Mickenberg & Nel, 2011: 445) such as childhood depression provide opportunities for children to encounter such realities and their accompanying emotions. According to Reynolds, "these works are not only reshaping children's literature, but also creating opportunities for young people to gain insights into themselves and those around them that may have positive long-term social and emotional benefits" (2007:89).

Conclusion

Children need opportunities to share their understandings and interpretations of all literature, to use oral language to think together, but especially so with picturebooks that address challenging and controversial topics about the human condition. Although the value and effectiveness of discussion-based approaches in school has been documented by research, Mercer notes that, "in most classrooms, the range of opportunities for learners to contribute to talk is quite narrow and the amount of talk they contribute is relatively small" (1995: 60). Further, research has shown how children need instruction about the pragmatics of engaging in productive discussions in order to benefit from the opportunities afforded by group work. As described previously, instructional time and effort was devoted to children "talking about talk" and to the development of discussion etiquette at the beginning of the research. It was fundamental to create a classroom environment where the children felt safe and supported in sharing their ideas and opinions. On numerous occasions and in various ways, the teacher and myself conveyed to the children that we respected and were genuinely interested in their meaning-making, opinions, responses, and interpretations.

Finally, as noted earlier the children had abundant opportunities to develop their visual literacy skills as they participated in activities that focused on visual elements of art and design, and how these elements are used deliberately by sign-makers in multimodal texts. My research experiences have revealed how children's comprehension, analysis, and interpretation of picturebooks can be informed when they develop their ability to "see" and understand the artwork in these aesthetic objects—when they understand some of the visual elements of art and design, and recognize and appreciate the intentionality of art. The artwork of Shaun Tan that depicts childhood depression in *The Red Tree* respectfully explores the human condition and broadens our notions of "appropriate" literature for children.

Notes

1 *The Red Tree* and two other picturebooks by Tan have been collected into one volume called *Lost and Found* (Tan, 2011). This 2011 publication of three picturebooks includes additional artwork and notes by both Shaun Tan and John Marsden.
2 Some of the content of the description of Tan's picturebook was first published in a review I wrote of *The Red Tree* and also appears in Pantaleo, 2012.

Academic references

Albers, P., Vasquez, V. & Harste, J. (2011) Making Visual Analysis Critical, in Lapp, D. & Fisher, D. (eds) *Handbook of Research on Teaching the English Language Arts.* New York: Routledge.
Arizpe, E. & Styles, M. (2003) *Children Reading Pictures: Interpreting Visual Texts.* London: RoutledgeFalmer.
Arizpe, E. & Styles, M. (2008) A Critical Review of Research into Children's Responses to Multimodal Texts, in Flood, J., Heath, S. & Lapp, D. (eds) *Handbook of Teaching Literacy Through the Communicative and Visual Arts: Volume II.* New York: Lawrence Erlbaum.
Bader, B. (1976) *American Picturebooks from Noah's Ark to the Beast Within.* New York: Macmillan.
Barnes, D. (1992) *From Communication to Curriculum* (2nd edn). Portsmouth, NH: Boynton/ Cook Publishers.
Barnes, D. (2008) Exploratory Talk For Learning, in Mercer, N. & Hodgkinson, S. (eds) *Exploratory Talk in School.* London: Sage Publications.

Barthes, R. (1970, trans. 1974) *S/Z: An Essay.* New York: Hill & Wang.

British Columbia Ministry of Education (2009) *BC Performance Standards: Reading: Revised 2009.* Victoria, BC: Author.

Clarke, J.N. (2011) Childhood Depression and Mass Media Print Magazines in the USA and Canada: 1938–2008, *Child and Family Social Work*, 16(1): 52–60.

Dresang, E. (1999) *Radical Change: Books for Youth in a Digital Age.* New York: H.W. Wilson Company.

Evans, J. (2009) Reading the Visual: Creative and Aesthetic Responses to Picturebooks and Fine Art, in Evans, J. (ed.) *Talking Beyond the Page: Reading and Responding to Picturebooks.* London: Routledge.

Iser, W. (1978) *The Act of Reading.* Baltimore, MD: Johns Hopkins University Press.

Iser, W. (1989) *Prospecting: From Reader Response to Literary Anthropology.* Baltimore, MD: Johns Hopkins University Press.

Kiefer, B. (1995) *The Potential of Picturebooks: From Visual Literacy to Aesthetic Understanding.* Englewood Cliffs, NJ: Merrill.

Lewis, D. (2001) *Reading Contemporary Picturebooks: Picturing Text.* London: Routledge.

Marantz, K. (1977) The Picture Book as Art Object: A Call for Balanced Reviewing, *Wilson Library Bulletin,* 52(2): 148–151.

Mavers, D. (2009) Image in the Multimodal Ensemble: Children's Drawing, in Jewitt, C. (ed.) *The Routledge Handbook of Multimodal Analysis.* London: Routledge.

Mercer, N. (1995) *The Guided Construction of Knowledge: Talk Amongst Teachers and Learners.* Clevedon, UK: Multilingual Matters.

Mercer, N. (2000) *Words and Minds: How We Use Language to Think Together.* London: Routledge.

Mickenberg, J. & Nel, P. (2011) Radical Children's Literature Now! *Children's Literature Association Quarterly,* 36(4): 445–473.

Pantaleo, S. (2008) *Exploring Student Response to Contemporary Picturebooks.* Toronto: University of Toronto Press.

Pantaleo, S. (2009) Exploring Children's Responses to the Postmodern Picturebooks *Who's Afraid of the Big Bad Wolf,* in Evans, J. (ed.) *Talking Beyond the Page: Reading and Responding to Picturebooks.* London: Routledge.

Pantaleo, S. (2012) Exploring Grade 7 Students' Responses to Shaun Tan's *The Red Tree, Children's Literature in Education,* 43(1): 51–71.

Pantaleo, S. (2013a) Paneling "Matters" in Elementary Students' Graphic Narratives, *Literacy Research and Instruction,* 52(2): 150–171.

Pantaleo, S. (2013b) Revisiting Rosenblatt's Aesthetic Response Through *"The Arrival",* *Australian Journal of Language and Literacy,* 36(3): 125–134.

Reynolds, K. (2007) *Radical Children's Literature: Future Visions and Aesthetic Transformations in Juvenile Fiction.* London: Palgrave Macmillan.

Rodale, J.I. (1978) *The Synonym Finder.* New York: Warner Books.

Rosenblatt, L. (1978) *The Reader, The Text, The Poem: The Transactional Theory Of The Literary Work.* Carbondale, IL: Southern Illinois University Press.

Rosenblatt, L. (1986) The Aesthetic Transaction, *Journal of Aesthetic Education,* 20(4): 122–127.

Rosenblatt, L. (1988) The Literary Transaction, in Demers, P. (ed.) *The Creating Word.* Edmonton: University of Alberta Press.

Rosenblatt, L. (1994) The Transactional Theory of Reading and Writing, in Ruddell, R., Ruddell, M. & Singer, H. (eds) *Theoretical Models and Processes of Reading* (4th edn). Newark, DE: International Reading Association.

Sipe, L. (2008) *Storytime: Young Children's Literary Understanding in the Classroom.* New York: Teachers College Press.

Sipe, L. (2011) The Art of the Picturebook, in Wolf, S., Coats, K., Enciso, P. & Jenkins, C. (eds) *Handbook of Research on Children's and Young Adult Literature*. New York: Routledge.

Tan, S. (n.d.) *Picture Books: Who Are They For?* Accessed 1 February 2009 from www.shauntan.net/comments1.html

Tan, S. (2011) Lost and Found: Thoughts on Childhood, Identity and Story, *The Looking Glass: New Perspectives on Children's Literature*, 15(3): 1–13.

Tan, S. (2012) Strange Migrations. Keynote speech at IBBY Conference London. Accessed 30 April 2014 from www.shauntan.net/comments1.html

Vygotsky, L. (1978) *Mind in Society*. Cambridge, MA: Harvard University Press.

Walsh, M. (2003) "Reading" Pictures: What Do They Reveal? Young Children's Reading of Visual Texts, *Reading: Literacy and Language*, 37(3): 123–130.

Children's literature

Banyai, I. (1995) *Re-zoom*. New York: Puffin Books.

Browne, A. (1998) *Voices in the Park*. London: Picture Corgi Puffins.

Holm, J. & Holm, M. (2005) *Babymouse: Queen of the World*. New York: Random House.

Kibuishi, K. (2008) *Amulet Book One: The Stonekeeper*. New York: Scholastic Inc.

Lewis, J. & Allwright, D. (2009) *Don't Read This Book!* London: Egmont Ltd.

Tan, S. (2001) *The Red Tree*. Melbourne: Lothian.

Tan, S. (2006) *The Arrival*. Melbourne: Lothian.

Wiesner, D. (2006) *Flotsam*. New York: Clarion Books.

12

COULD THIS HAPPEN TO US?

Children's critical responses to issues of migration in picturebooks

Janet Evans

This chapter looks at the concept of migration as dealt with by a text set of picturebooks. It is child focused and includes the thoughts and responses of a small group of 9-year-old children working collaboratively as part of a community of learners over a 4-day period. The children talked about migration and some related issues, prior to responding to one particular picturebook, Home and Away *written by John Marsden and illustrated by Matt Ottley. The children finally considered what it would be like if, because of war, they found themselves refugees and migrants in a strange land away from those they love.*

There are those who chase their dreams and there are those who are chased. Many people leave the land of their birth to re-exist in another place and yet it is not always easy for them to see that new and different place as home. For some the word migration is an alluring word, it can be synonymous with courage, hope and future, whilst for others it can mean despair, sadness and a longing for times gone by and for places long lost.

Many picturebooks, in focusing on issues related to migration, 'show and tell' (Bearne, 2004; Kress, 2003) of *migration, loss, separation* and *belonging* from a personal point of view. Some take an individual point of view, where the narrator of the book may be the person who has experienced these emotions, as with:

> *Grandfather's Journey* by Allen Say
> *Home of the Brave* by Allen Say
> *The Arrival* by Shaun Tan
> *The Lost Thing* by Shaun Tan
> *Lost and Found* by Oliver Jeffers
> *The Island* by Armin Greder
> *Caja de Carton* (*Cardboard Box*) by Txabi Arnal and Hassan Amekan
> *Refugees* by David Miller

A True Person by Gabiann Marin, illus. Jacqui Grantford
Home and Away by John Marsden, illus. Matt Ottley

. . . whilst other picturebooks look at migration from a group/society point of view, as with:

The Rabbits by John Marsden and Shaun Tan
Migrando (*Migrating*) by Miriana Chiesa Mateos
Sapore Italiano (*Italian Flavour*) by Valerie Losa
Underground: Finding the Light to Freedom by Shane W. Evans

All of these picturebooks deal with powerful themes that are at times challenging, controversial and extremely unsettling, often making us question who they are written for and the suitability of the subject matter for children if they are the intended audience (Evans, 2009). They also require us to read critically, to look at bias, different points of view, and different 'sides' being portrayed, often within the same book. They demand that we ask questions such as:

- Who is affected, who is telling the story?
- Why are some people moving from one particular place to another?
- Are they moving by choice or being made to move?

These are complex questions which most adults find difficult to answer. For the most part they are inextricably linked to international, national and regional issues of politics, power, religion and the economics of any particular country. Prior to reading the books and in an attempt to understand some of the underlying issues being alluded to, the children considered some of the basic terminology and looked up meanings of the words:

What is migration?

Migration is usually seen to be the movement of people from one place to another. The reasons for this movement are many and multifaceted and include economic, social, political or environmental or sometimes a blend of these factors. The act of migrating almost always has an impact on the people whose lives are often totally disrupted and changed for ever.

What is a migrant?

A migrant is a person (or animal) who goes to live or work in another place or another country.

What is a refugee?

A refugee is a person who has fled his/her country because of danger or some problem such as war or political unrest. Refugees are forced to flee their country.

Searching for these definitions led to more in-depth questions, some of which the children considered in their discussions. It is evident that these deeply complex, at times philosophical, issues do not have straightforward solutions ...

- Do migrants feel free? What is freedom?
- When migrants go to another place do they gain or lose independence?
- Do migrants experience a loss of identity or just take on a new/different identity?
- Are refugees the same as migrants and do some people migrate because they have to escape their own countries because of war or conflict?

Viewing texts from a critical perspective

All texts are constructed from a particular stance and there is no such thing as an innocent text. When children read from a critical perspective they see beyond the text, question the author's intent, and seek to understand how they are influenced by the author's message. In other words they see how books are produced and how they position readers by conveying messages in particular ways (Comber & Simpson, 2001; Fehring & Green, 2001; Knobel & Healy, 1998; McLaughlin & DeVoogd, 2004; Vasquez, 2004; Vasquez *et al.*, 2003).

Picturebook authors/illustrators portray migrants, immigration and associated issues in a variety of different ways. Ommundsen focused on the way picturebook creators portray immigration from the point of view of the immigrants themselves and maintained that over the years:

> migration has provided a rich source of myth throughout human history. It engenders dreams, fears and memories in both migrant and resident populations; giving rise to hope for a new start and a bright future, feelings of exile and alienation, nostalgia for lost homelands, dreams of belonging and entitlement, fears of invasion, dispossession and cultural extinction.
>
> *Ommundsen (2009: 220–226)*

Taking a different viewpoint Cornell (2010) stated that picturebooks about immigration and citizenship rarely portray the issues that children from immigrant families face every day. She noted that although many books deal with issues such as border crossings, very few address issues of documentation and unequal access to citizenship in any meaningful way. She also noted that, although many picturebooks feature Asian and Latin American immigrants, there are not many featuring immigrants from countries such as those in Africa or the Middle East. Cornell feels that immigrant children need exposure to books that portray other immigrant children facing similar experiences in order that they may realise they are not the only ones facing adversity.

Yoshikawa (2011), in the academic book *Immigrants Raising Citizens: Undocumented Parents and their Young Children*, considered how undocumented migrants are faced with disadvantage at every single stage in their lives. Yoshikawa noted that there were 4 million children born in America who have undocumented immigrant parents; these parents, without legal status, are fearful of being discovered and are raising their children under 'stressful work and financial conditions'.

In their book *Visual Journeys Through Wordless Narratives*, Arizpe, Colomer and Martínez-Roldán (2014) focus on the responses of children from different parts of the world (the United Kingdom, Spain, Italy and the USA), to Shaun Tan's wordless picturebook, *The Arrival*. Their enquiry highlights the potential of wordless picturebooks to support immigrant children as learners and meaning-makers, and in studying the challenging issues raised by migration and literacy education they 'provided paths for the children to "cross the border" into the picturebooks'. In the foreword to this book Shaun Tan shares some of his thoughts that allow us to try to understand how immigrants might feel:

> In my book, *The Arrival*, I was not so much interested in imagining the life of a migrant, as much as looking at how a migrant must imagine life. How we make sense of the world, how we ask questions, how we make connections: this is more important than knowledge.
>
> *Tan (2014: xiv–xv)*

We are all born free and equal

Many of the picturebooks featuring issues of migration and immigration depict in detail what it must be like to live a life in a different country without documentation, help, support and the rights normally afforded to the indigenous citizens of that country. We are all born free and equal and have an entitlement to basic human rights. The Universal Declaration of Human Rights looks after us, no matter who we are or where we live. Thirty rights were proclaimed by the United Nations in December 1948, in reaction to the atrocities of World War 2, and in an attempt to say 'never again' to those atrocities. World governments promised they would inform people of these rights and try their best to uphold them.

Our rights are part of what makes us human and no one should take them away from us. Amnesty International, which is made up of ordinary people across the world, endorses the values contained in the Universal Declaration of Human Rights and works to promote our human rights, protecting individuals, wherever justice, fairness, freedom and truth are denied (Amnesty International, 2008). Notwithstanding the strength of this organisation and the evident 'moral rightness' of the thirty human rights, things don't always go as they should and many millions of human beings now have their rights denied and are fighting for their lives and their survival in war-torn countries across the world; conflict, famine and natural disasters are taking these rights away.

Home and Away

Home and Away by John Marsden and Matt Ottley was nominated Children's Book Council of Australia (CBCA) Honour Book 2009: Picturebook of the Year (Figure 12.1) (Plate 30). It considers what it would be like to lose one's rights and to be forced to leave one's home country because of conflict. It then looks at the subsequent breakdown of family life for the individuals concerned.

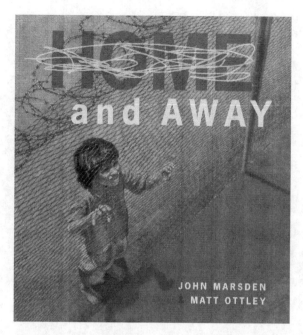

FIGURE 12.1 (Plate 30) *Home and Away* (John Marsden & Matt Ottley, 2008).

Everyone wants a place of safety, a place to share with the people they love. A place to relax. A home. Right now, more than a billion people don't have a home - that's one in seven of the world's population. There are only two places you can be in life: home or away.

Home and Away *(Back cover synopsis)*

Home and Away depicts a family living a normal, ordinary life that suddenly has their world completely shattered by war. Molly's illustration from the book depicts a family photograph before the war (Figure 12.2). The family members try to stay alive, they are shown searching for food, trying to keep healthy, and eventually looking for a way to escape. They find space on a rusty, unsafe boat which they think is going to a safer place. However, when the family arrives at the 'safe place', the sanctuary they had hoped for is denied them and instead they find themselves imprisoned and treated like criminals. Their hope is gone and there are too many memories of death and dying, including members of their own family.

The CBCA Honour Book 2009 description states:

> Marsden and Ottley put Australian faces to the refugee experience, challenging the reader to walk in the shoes of those incarcerated in detention centres. The reader feels the desperation, the terror, the confusion, the grief of those forced from their homes by war and hunger, only to be welcomed in a new land by guns and anger.

FIGURE 12.2 Molly's portrayal of a family photo before the war.

The description continues:

> Ottley's mixed media illustrations echo the graphic work of child refugees, interspersed with haunting images of a family badly affected by hunger and illness. Poignant, realistic details such as skin infections and ungroomed hair add a stark subtext about how easily it could be the 'safer' societies to whom this happens [Figure 12.3].

The description ends with a warning: 'may distress sensitive readers; supervised reading best for 9–12 yrs'. It also notes that this book makes, 'A powerful plea for compassion, empathy and generosity, this is a disturbing and memorable picturebook for older readers'.

With *Home and Away,* Marsden and Ottley have created a picturebook that is both challenging and controversial. It obliges the reader to ask:

> What would happen if a typical Australian family found themselves refugees?

… or more specifically:

> What would happen if *you and your* family found yourselves refugees?

It is clear that *Home and Away* is set against the historical/political backdrop of the late 1970s, with the mass departure of Vietnamese boat people from Communist-controlled Vietnam following the Vietnam War. Marsden depicts the devastating effects of displacement linked to the boat people; it is an episode in history that still resonates with political migrants trying to flee their war-torn home lands. It was the

FIGURE 12.3 Harriet's portrayal of the sister with skin infections and ungroomed hair.

concept of 'boat people' which influenced Marsden when he wrote the book. Boat people is a term that usually refers to refugees, illegal immigrants or asylum seekers who emigrate in large numbers in boats that are sometimes old, crudely made and unsafe. These boats were not intended for sailing in open waters, and would typically head for busy international shipping lanes. Some lucky boat people would be rescued by freighters or reach shore a couple of weeks after departure. The unlucky ones continued their perilous journeys suffering from hunger, thirst, disease and the threat of pirates, before finding safety, often after several months at sea.

Pre-reading responses

Prior to reading the picturebook, a group of 9-year-old children were shown the book cover and asked to predict what they thought it would be about. Charlotte and Emily's predictions showed the influence of their previous experiences, both in the form of an Australian TV soap opera. At this point none of the children knew the book was set in Australia.

> *Home and Away* is a TV programme from Australia. I think the book is about a boy that wants to get away from his home and one day he does manage to get away from his home. I think this because on the front cover the boy is holding onto a gate which is blocking him from getting away. Maybe he doesn't like his parents or he might dream of living in America.

> I think 'Home' is scrubbed out because maybe his home and his brain is a mess. Maybe he doesn't even have a home to live in. I was influenced by the barbed wire because it looked like he was trapped.
>
> *Charlotte*

> The boy has run away from home and he has gone to an army base in Australia. I thought it was an Australian TV series. The boy has no money and he is poor. His parents have chucked him out of the house because he is very horrid or they can't look after him any more. The army troops let him stay there and his parents come back and find him and he goes back home. He has brothers and sisters at home and everything is tangled and everybody is angry, family members have died. He hates life at home but loves being away. Home is a struggle. Nothing ever seems to go his way. There is a barrier to get out of his town.
>
> *Emily*

First reading responses

The book description stated that *Home and Away* may upset sensitive readers and this was what initially happened. Straight after reading the book two of the children cried and all of the group members were silent and obviously very moved. The impact of the book was huge, however; the children immediately began to think about how *Home and Away* had made them feel and what they thought about it. Three of the children's written responses reflected the views of the other group members. Patrick felt that it might bring back bad memories (Figure 12.4).

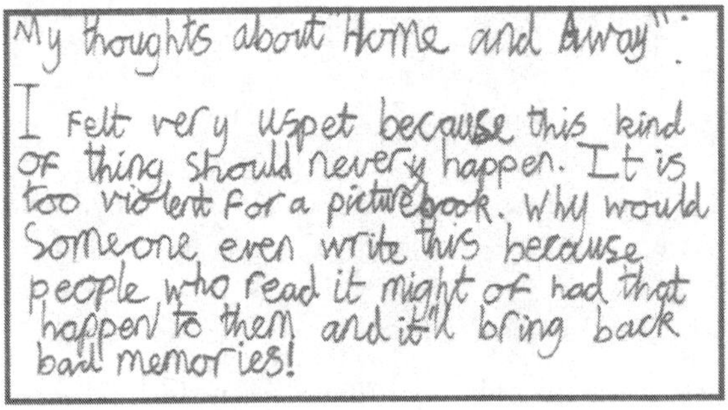
My thoughts about "Home and Away":
I felt very upset because this kind
of thing should never happen. It is
too violent for a picturebook. Why would
Someone even write this because
people who read it might of had that
happen to them and it'll bring back
bad memories!

> I felt very upset because this kind of thing should never happen. It is too violent for a picturebook. Why would someone even write this because people who read it might have had that happen to them and it will bring back bad memories!
>
> *Patrick (Figure 12.4)*

FIGURE 12.4 Patrick's thoughts about *Home and Away*.

Edward felt the book was shocking and clearly pointed out how terrible war really is (Figure 12.5), whilst Caroline clearly thought that the book wasn't suitable for children (Figure 12.6).

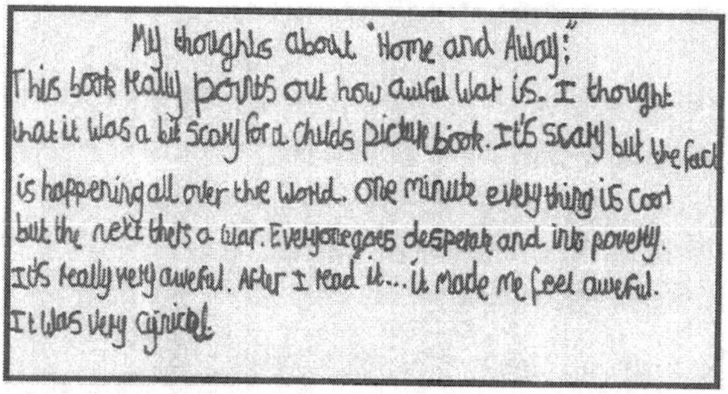

My thoughts about "Home and Away":
This book really points out how awful war is. I thought
that it was a bit scary for a childs picture book. It's scary but the fact
is happening all over the world. One minute everything is cool
but the next there's a war. Everyone goes desperate and into poverty.
It's really very aweful. After I read it... it made me feel aweful.
It was very cynical.

This book really points out how awful war is. I thought it was a bit scary for a child's picturebook. It's scary but the fact is, it's happening all over the world. One minute everything is cool but the next there's a war. Everyone goes desperate and into poverty. It's really awful. After I read it . . . it made me feel awful. It was very cynical.

Edward (Figure 12.5)

FIGURE 12.5 Edward's thoughts about *Home and Away.*

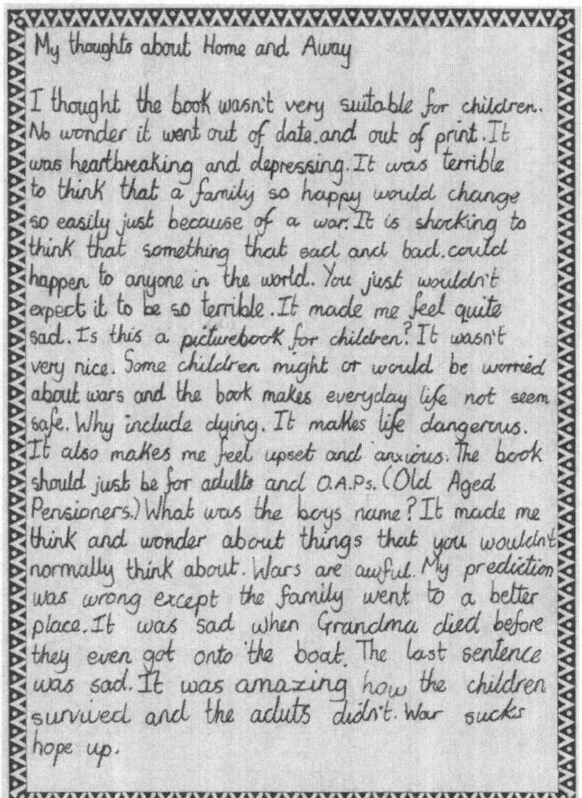

My thoughts about Home and Away

I thought the book wasn't very suitable for children.
No wonder it went out of date and out of print. It
was heartbreaking and depressing. It was terrible
to think that a family so happy would change
so easily just because of a war. It is shocking to
think that something that sad and bad could
happen to anyone in the world. You just wouldn't
expect it to be so terrible. It made me feel quite
sad. Is this a picturebook for children? It wasn't
very nice. Some children might or would be worried
about wars and the book makes everyday life not seem
safe. Why include dying. It makes life dangerous.
It also makes me feel upset and anxious. The book
should just be for adults and O.A.Ps. (Old Aged
Pensioners.) What was the boys name? It made me
think and wonder about things that you wouldn't
normally think about. Wars are awful. My prediction
was wrong except the family went to a better
place. It was sad when Grandma died before
they even got onto the boat. The last sentence
was sad. It was amazing how the children
survived and the aduts didn't. War sucks
hope up.

FIGURE 12.6 Charlotte's thoughts about *Home and Away.*

Asking and responding to 'big' questions

We read the book once again and the children asked some 'big' questions:

- Why would anyone want to write this book?
- Is it a real story? Does this sort of thing really happen?
- Would it be worth living a life in war?
- Who is the audience for this kind of book?

. . . they also made some very sensitive and pertinent comments:

- War sucks up all our hope.
- The dark, double-page supper meal reminds me of 'The Last Supper' before Jesus died, especially the light on their faces (Figure 12.7).

In the ensuing discussion the children considered who the book was for. In interview John Marsden had also been asked this same question, who was the target audience for *Home and Away*? He stated that it wasn't a book he would give to young children and felt it was for 10 or 11 years and older. When further asked what he wanted readers to take away from the book? He answered, 'I would hate to think I'm coming from a "What people need to understand is ..." approach, but I can't deny that this book is didactic. So I would say an increase in empathy.'

FIGURE 12.7 Harriet's portrayal of the family's last supper.

The children began to wonder how they might feel if they were in a similar situation. They considered the concept of empathy (having initially looking up the definition) and in response to the question, 'Could we empathise with the family?' Patrick stated, 'No, because we haven't experienced it (war) – you have to experience something to know about it for real.'

Returning to the book the children considered what words could be used to describe how they might feel if they were in war. They each drew a picture of themselves and wrote the words that represented their feelings. Their chosen words were apposite and sensitive and showed a real awareness of how a conflict situation might make them feel (Figure 12.8).

FIGURE 12.8   Megan's thoughts: 'How would I feel if I was in war?'

Children's critical thoughts, responses and discussions

The book was read several more times over a period of 4 days and the children began to think in more detail about the concepts of immigration, migration, migrants, refugees, illegal immigrants and asylum seekers. They had already looked up the meaning of these words but it was a documentary news item, broadcast on the BBC Radio 4 *Today* programme, addressing the question of who should have jobs in Britain, newly arrived immigrants or born and bred indigenous British citizens, that was the catalyst for a spontaneous and at times rather heated discussion

The news item gave the children the opportunity to discuss some of the issues and showed very clearly that they all held quite strong viewpoints regarding immigrants and the question of jobs in this country.

Molly: Immigrants always get jobs as opposed to the British.

Patrick: Immigrants come just to get jobs.

Edward: Yeah, but they probably come here to get jobs because there are no jobs in their countries.

Molly: But then we have to move to get jobs for us.

Patrick: Yeah, we wouldn't have jobs because there wouldn't be enough jobs for us. They come to take our jobs, they have to move and we have to move.

Emily: We have to create jobs.

Megan: We have to create jobs for everyone.

Edward: You can't just create jobs.

Megan: They (people making jobs) try to make jobs for people but they can't afford it.

Molly: 'They' are the government.

Patrick: None of this would have happened if they had their own jobs.

Megan: They might have had to flee their own country – not just for war, for food or for health but maybe just because theirs is not a nice country.

Patrick: Yes true, but the main cause is war though.

Megan: A quarter of them are immigrants.

Patrick: Yeah, but it would still be for war.

Megan: . . . like Jamaica.

Teacher: So what is an immigrant?

Molly: Someone who comes to a country from another country.

Patrick: To make money.

All: Not necessarily.

Megan: Three-quarters are here for something to do with war.

Molly: They are here to take our jobs.

Teacher: Sometimes born and bred British people are not interested in the ordinary, down to earth jobs that are available in our country, they want more prestigious, higher paid jobs so someone has to do the ordinary jobs and immigrants very often take the jobs that other people don't want.

Molly: I agree with you but they should be for 'UK-'uns' first, then, if they don't want the jobs, anyone else could have the jobs. British people should get the job chances first then other people after.

Patrick: British people had the chance to shoot but didn't score.

Emily: What does that mean?

Patrick: I've just made it up. It means British people had the chance to shoot and score a goal but they didn't take the chance to shoot. I mean they had the chance to have a job but they didn't apply.

Megan: Another reason why people are coming to our country from Poland is if something happened to their street, say a big fire or earthquake.

Molly: Yeah, but why couldn't they move to somewhere else in their own country?

Megan: Fire and earthquake and things like that could be in their country.

Molly: I see what you're saying, that they might want to come here because we don't have earthquakes etc. but they *still* shouldn't get the first chances to get a job.

Megan: We should take it turns to get jobs.

Molly: No, we should have the first chance to get jobs in our country.

Patrick: Do we (Britain) usually get the most migrants? ... they should be given some kind of hostel.

Molly: It seems that immigrants get the jobs first. They come into our country and are given jobs straightaway. The government says, 'Here you are, have a job', and someone from our country could be waiting for ages.

Patrick: They should have to get qualifications and things to get jobs.

Megan: If you think about it, to be a business man you don't need many qualifications.

Patrick: British people need to get qualifications to get jobs but immigrants come over and get the jobs straightaway.

Molly: Say for example Charlotte is an immigrant and I am British and there is a job and I have been waiting a year and Charlotte's been waiting two days. She could walk in and 'they' would give her the job because she's from a different country and has had a hard time so they give her the job.

Patrick: The problem with this is that there are two different points of view:

The first point of view is that it is unfair to British people because they have been waiting for jobs for ages and they should get the jobs.

The second point of view – say like an immigrant has no way to make money and the British person has a way to make money and already has a job, the immigrant should get the job. If the immigrant has no job then maybe they should get the job first so they can make money.

Emily: I think the English should get the jobs because they're English and we need to look after the English people first.

This incredibly hard hitting and profound discussion was stopped in full flow by the school lunchtime bell! Despite their young age these children were very

FIGURE 12.9 Patrick's illustration: 'Go away you are not welcome.'

aware of the critical, national issues surrounding the issue of immigrants and immigration and were not frightened of offering an opinionated viewpoint in relation to a fairly controversial issue.

The children read the book once again. They were deeply affected by Matt Ottley's illustration, made to look like a child's drawing, of a small refugee boat which held the family members as it was confronted by the large navy boat which they hoped would rescue them. The children were upset and moved because of the way in which the family's hope so quickly turned to despair as the navy boat's crew members shouted at them to turn round and go away as they were not welcome. Patrick illustrated the boat being turned away (Figure 12.9).

The children were even more moved as they talked about their own family members in relation to the family members in the book. At the end, gran had died, dad had died, mum had died, 12-year-old Claire was in a psychiatric hospital, 6-year-old Toby was self-harming and diagnosed as schizoid. The 16-year-old narrator tells:

> The government says there's no room for us. The Prime Minister says that if they let us stay, it will encourage more illegal immigrants. The Deputy Prime Minister says we're not genuine refugees, we just came here to try and make money. The Minister for Immigration says that we should have gone through the proper procedures. Apparently there was a list or something, and we should have found their office and put our names down.
>
> *Marsden & Ottley (2008: unpaginated)*

The young narrator goes on to tell how he has given up on all his dreams:

> As for me, well, I've given up on being a vet. If I could get Clare and Toby together and out of here, maybe I could wash cars or something. Whatever it takes, to keep us together. That's what mum and dad would have wanted.
>
> *Marsden & Ottley (2008: final page)*

My family and war – written responses to *Home and Away*

Home and Away enabled the children to empathise with the family in the book and to consider what it might feel like if their family were involved in war. Each child in the group wrote a piece showing how their family would cope if they were at war. Emily's piece reflected the views of the other group members.

The war arrived everybody suffers

Hope has gone, never to be found again. Me, my mum and dad and the family's house have been blown up. I get shot at every day, I feel weak and helpless, nothing is going the way we want it to. It's not fair. We are a genuine family. My mum and my dad work. We are good children. We want to learn.

Scared to death, we fall apart, nothing left just a hole in our relationship and our hearts. Children scream as their parents panic as the bombs fall. Darkness falls on us like a rain cloud. I feel lost in a world of war, food is scarce and we become just bones. The emotions get more unbearable every minute of the day. We are petrified as the planes fall on our gardens and they loot us of all we own. Helpless, as we wander the streets, distraught as we see the dead bodies of our friends. We cry together. Then we realise we have to migrate to another country. We had a long trip to the port to beg for a boat to let us go to *Hollania*. Finally, after hours of begging we found a man who would let us ride but we had to sell everything we owned. All we had left was 50 grams of rice and three green beans.

The boat ride took 10 days. The minutes crawled by like hours and the hours crawled by like years. We finally saw the light of land we saw people on the beach cheering and we cheered too but as we got closer we saw they were telling us to go away. We explained everything but they wouldn't listen. They hit me, beat me up, and then the next thing I know I'm in prison.

Dad dies of sickness and stress, just me and mum left.

A year on mum died of starvation, only me left, I escaped in the nick of time, I went into care then I got a home. Was it worth losing everything?

I don't think it was worth losing everything. You should stay and face the problems rather than running away thinking everything will get better. It doesn't always happen.

Emily

Thoughts and conclusions

Focusing on a text set of picturebooks dealing with migration in general, then *Home and Away* in particular, enabled the children to think about migration as an ongoing issue affecting each and every one of us in society. It gave them a platform from which to share their developing critical viewpoints about what is happening regarding migration in Britain and in the rest of the world. They looked at the book, *We Are All Born Free: The Universal Declaration of Human Rights in Pictures* (Amnesty International, 2008). They recognised that all of the thirty rights are crucial but felt that some of the rights more precisely summed up what they had been considering in relation to *Home and Away*:

- We all have the right to life, and to live in freedom and safety. Article 3
- Nobody has the right to put us in prison without a good reason, to keep us there or to send us away from our country. Article 9
- If we are frightened of being badly treated in our own country, we all have the right to run away to another country to be safe. Article 14

It was, however, Article 15 that seemed to best sum up their thoughts and responses to *Home and Away*: 'We all have the right to belong to a country'. This resonates with John Marsden's point, 'There are only two places you can be in life: home or away'.

At the end of this piece of small-scale, reader-response work the children were asked if reading some of these books had changed their opinions and points of view in relation to migration and immigrants and if anything like this was happening in the world now. They mentioned conflict in Iran, Afghanistan, Syria and other parts of the world but it was a statement by Charlotte that clearly summed up what many immigrants are currently trying to do, '... *never give up hope*'.

Academic references

Arizpe, E., Colomer, T. & Martínez-Roldán, C. (2014) *Visual Journeys through Wordless Narratives: An International Inquiry with Immigrant Children and* The Arrival. London: Bloomsbury Academic.

Bearne, E. (2004) Multimodal Texts: What They Are and How Children Use Them, in Evans, J. (ed.) (2004) *Literacy Moves On: Using Popular Culture, New Technologies and Critical Literacy in the Primary Classroom.* London: Routledge.

Comber, B. & Simpson, A. (eds) (2001) *Negotiating Critical Literacies in Classrooms.* Mahwah, NJ: Lawrence Erlbaum Associates.

Cornell, G. (2010) Who Can Stay Here? Confronting Issues of Documentation and Citizenship in Children's Literature, *Rethinking Schools*, 25(1): 32–37.

Evans, J. (ed.) (2009) *Talking Beyond the Page: Reading and Responding to Picturebooks.* London: Routledge.

Fehring, H. & Green, P. (eds) (2001) *Critical Literacy: A Collection of Articles from the Australian Literacy Educators' Association.* Newark, DE: International Reading Association & Australian Literacy Educators' Association.

Knobel, M. & Healy, A. (1998) *Critical Literacies in the Primary Classroom*. Newtown, NSW: Primary English Teaching Association.

Kress, G. (2003) *Literacy in the New Media Age*. London: Routledge.

McLaughlin, M. & DeVoogd, G. (2004) *Critical Literacy: Enhancing Students' Comprehension of Text*. New York: Scholastic.

Ommundsen, W. (2009) Brave New World: Myth and Migration in recent Asian-Australian picture books, *Coolibah*, 3: 220–226.

Tan, S. (2014) *Foreword* in Arizpe, E., Colomer, T. and Martínez-Roldán, C. (2014) *Visual Journeys through Wordless Narratives: An International Inquiry with Immigrant Children and The Arrival*. London: Bloomsbury Academic.

United Nations (1948) *The Universal Declaration of Human Rights*, December 1948.

Vasquez, V. (2004) *Negotiating Critical Literacies with Young Children*. Mahwah, NJ: Routledge.

Vasquez, V. with Muise, M., Adamson, S., Hefferman, L., Chiola-Nakai, D. & Shear, J. (2003) *Getting Beyond 'I Like the Book': Creating Space for Critical Literacy in K-6 Classrooms*. Newark, DE: International Reading Association.

Yoshikawa, H. (2011) *Immigrants Raising Citizens: Undocumented Parents and Their Young Children*. New York: Russell Sage Foundation.

Children's literature

Amnesty International (2008) *We Are All Born Free: The Universal Declaration Of Human Rights In Pictures*. London: Frances Lincoln Children's Books.

Arnal, T. & Amekan, H. (2010) *Caja de Carton*. Pontevedra: OQO Editora.

Evans, S.W. (2011) *Underground: Finding the Light to Freedom*. New York: Roaring Brook Press.

Greder, A. (2007) *The Island*. Crows Nest, NSW: Allen and Unwin.

Jeffers, O. (2007) *Lost and Found*. London: Harper Collins.

Losa, V. (2010) *Sapore Italiano*. Reggio Emilia: Zoolibri.

Marin, G. & Grantford, J. (2007) *A True Person*. Frenchs Forest, NSW: New Frontier Publishing.

Marsden, J. & Ottley, M. (2008) *Home and Away*. Melbourne: Lothian Children's Books.

Marsden, J. & Tan, S. (1998) *The Rabbits*. Melbourne: Lothian Books.

Mateos, M.C. (2010) *Migrando*. Lisbon: Orfeu Negro.

Miller, D. (2003) *Refugees*. Melbourne: Lothian Books.

Say, A. (1993) *Grandfather's Journey*. New York: Houghton Mifflin.

Say, A. (2002) *Home of the Brave*. New York: Houghton Mifflin.

Tan, S. (2000) *The Lost Thing*. Melbourne: Lothian Books.

Tan, S. (2006) *The Arrival*. Melbourne: Lothian Books.

PART IV

Thoughts from a children's book publisher

13

THE LEGENDARY KLAUS FLUGGE

Controversial picturebooks and their place in contemporary society

Klaus Flugge in conversation with Janet Evans

It has been said that in the world of children's book publishing, there are certain people that '... everyone likes to keep an eye on. Willing to take risks, outspoken, with a clear vision of what children's publishing should be, they challenge, provoke, arouse admiration, respect, surprise and controversy' (Triggs, 1984).

Klaus Flugge is one such person!

Klaus was born in Hamburg in 1934 and after training as a bookseller in Leipzig he was involved in the world of books and book sales right from the beginning of his career. He initially came to England to build up the British branch of Abelard-Schuman. In 1976 he started his own publishing company, Andersen Press, in tribute to Hans Christian Andersen, in order to concentrate on high quality books for children, with authors and illustrators such as Quentin Blake, Michael Foreman, Leo Lionni, Max Velthuijs and David McKee.

Klaus's love for children's books made Andersen Press a highly respected publisher, which quickly became internationally known for quality picturebooks with an idiosyncratic, unconventional, often alternative, 'look'. He made frequent visits to book fairs in New York, Frankfurt, London, and of course, the now internationally famous Bologna Children's Book Fair. Klaus has attended all fifty-one Bologna fairs and at the 50th Anniversary in 2013, he was awarded the honorary citizenship of Bologna for his remarkable commitment in the field of children's books and to the Fair. Prior to this, in 1999, Klaus received the Eleanor Farjeon Award for outstanding contribution to children's books and in 2010 he became only the second publisher ever to be awarded honorary membership of the Youth Libraries Group.

Klaus stated, 'I have always tried to discover and nurture texts that contributed new ideas and were challenging to children and adults alike, not all of which found immediate approval with the general public or even librarians' (personal correspondence, May 2013).

Klaus very kindly agreed to be interviewed and to answer some questions about controversial picturebooks and their role in contemporary society, however, our interview very quickly turned into a wonderfully informal conversation. This chapter shares the results of that conversation.

Janet: Klaus, you truly are a legend in the field of children's books and publishing and have been involved in the area for nearly 60 years. Your knowledge and passion for your work is known internationally and your expertise in the field is beyond compare. **What initially sparked your interest in children's literature with a particular focus on picturebooks?**

Klaus: I trained as a bookseller in East Germany and became a political refugee in 1953, returning to Hamburg where I continued in bookselling, emigrating to the US in 1957. The then owner and publisher of Abelard-Schuman, Lew Schwarz gave me the chance of entering the world of publishing both adult books and children's books. In 1961 I accepted the job of managing director for Abelard-Schuman in London where I published adult books and more and more picture books, increasingly illustrated by the most talented British artists of the day, including Charles Keeping and John Vernon Lord. In 1976 I started Andersen Press, having discovered the brilliant Tony Ross and being joined by David McKee.

Janet: But why picturebooks, why were you particularly interested in picturebooks?

Klaus: I always liked illustrated books, art books and of course adult books. Illustrated adult books were difficult to sell then however, when I published picturebooks I tended to be quite successful selling co-productions and having a list of pretty outstanding books by people like Quentin Blake, Michael Foreman, David McKee and Tony Ross. Some I took over but others are no longer with us like Leo Lionni for instance. I initially published quite a number of his books. His work was considered old-fashioned but now retro art seems to have become fashionable again. In fact I've just re-issued and republished two of his books. We will see what happens.

Janet: The title of this book is Challenging and Controversial Picturebooks. *There are other words that might be used to describe these kinds of picturebooks, such as, strange, ambiguous, unsettling and unconventional.* **How would you define a challenging/controversial picturebook?**

Klaus: Well first of all I like unusual texts. There are too many boring texts and we try not to do those at Andersen Press. The problem is always to find original picturebook texts that have something different to offer. There are of course examples that were controversial when I first published them like, *Not Now Bernard* (David McKee). I had several letters from important librarians saying, 'How dare you publish a book like that? I shall never buy another book published by Andersen Press'. There are also other books, like *Angry Arthur* on the subject of anger [Figures 13.1a and 13.1b]. It was written by Hiawyn Oram and I gave the text to Satoshi Kitamura, then a young illustrator who was fed up and angry with publishers' reactions to his unusual, quirky illustrations and who was on the verge of going back to Japan. This was a fantastic example of creative publishing as Satoshi won the Mother Goose Award in 1983 for the most promising artist newcomer to picturebooks and we went on to publish more of his unusual picturebooks.

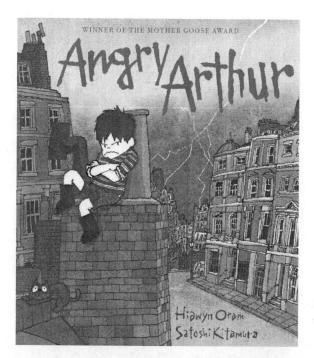

FIGURE 13.1A *Angry Arthur* (Hiawyn Oram & Satoshi Kitamura, 1982).

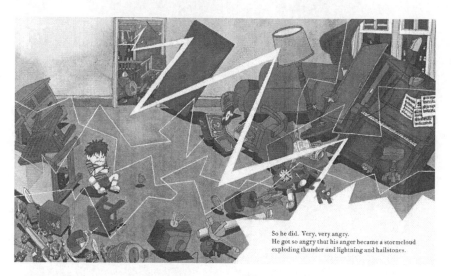

FIGURE 13.1B *Angry Arthur.* Arthur got very, very angry.

Very often it was the endings of some of the books that made them controversial. *Tadpole's Promise* is one of the more recent ones that some people disapproved of because of the sad or terrible, some would say funny, ending but I think children can deal with this much more than overprotective parents. In fact the book has a message that children will not forget as easily as some of the happier endings that apply to many children's books these days. We do have other examples of controversial picturebooks but these were the books that created some criticism when they came out. In the end they became classics, like *Not Now Bernard* [Figures 13.2a

FIGURE 13.2A *Not Now Bernard* (David McKee, 1980).

FIGURE 13.2B *Not Now Bernard*: 'The monster bit Bernard's father. "Not now, Bernard," said Bernard's father.'

and 13.2b] which was heavily criticised in some quarters and yet 10–15 years later it was put on the National Curriculum.

Janet: Not Now Bernard is a brilliant example of a picturebook with 'gap' (Iser, 1978) that can be read by children and adults alike. You publish many picturebooks like this.

Klaus*:* We have a lot of artists who find it difficult to write texts and it isn't easy to find texts from people who are good writers. The most brilliant one we have is a lady called Jeanne Willis who has consistently come up with outstanding picturebook texts that are provocative, in fact not just provocative but funny as well. Her books often have a message that is easily understood by both adults and children. One of the satisfying things about good picturebooks is that both adults and children can appreciate them and of course ideally share them and that makes a really good picturebook I would have thought.

Janet: As soon as writers and illustrators inject humour into their picturebooks unsettling feelings of unease often begin to dissipate and adults start to think they are more suitable for children. That is perhaps why the humorous picturebooks of Jeanne Willis and Tony Ross have made them such a successful partnership.

Klaus*:* You could be right. The most recent book by Jeanne Willis and Tony Ross is *Chicken Clicking*, a very timely, cautionary tale about the perils of using the internet. It has been rejected by a number of people (and international publishers) because of its perilous ending but it is now getting great reviews because of its humorous style, its relevance to today's society, and the concerns and potential dangers of online communicating. A first glance at the cover indicates a book that is likely to be simple and innocuous but in fact it is thought-provoking and challenging as the last couple of pages show [Figures 13.3a and 13.3b].

FIGURE 13.3A *Chicken Clicking* (Jeanne Willis & Tony Ross, 2014).

She put her photograph online
She gave her name and age.
CLICK! Another chick appeared
Upon the friendship page.

CLICK! They started chatting.
Chick had found the perfect chum
And off she went to meet her
Without telling Dad or Mum

FIGURE 13.3B *Chicken Clicking*: 'She put her photograph online. She gave her name and age.'

Janet:You founded Andersen Press in 1976. **Do you think challenging and controversial picturebooks were the same then as they are now?**

Klaus: I would have thought so. As you know, over the last few years there have been dramatic cuts in library spending in addition to the closing of libraries. Librarians were always our most important customers, in fact, very often *the* most important customers. And 20–30 years ago library suppliers were of the utmost importance and we could at times subscribe to 2–3 thousand or more copies of a hardback picturebook. This hardly happens anymore unless it's a classic like *Elmer* the patchwork elephant. There was a time, when I started at Andersen, when there were more demanding, and I think more beautiful, picturebooks coming on the market.

Janet: So were readers more accepting of these types of picturebooks 25 years ago than they are now?

Klaus: Yes but also librarians were responsible for buying a substantial part of the first and even the second editions of a book and once it was on the library shelves it was reordered and it had a much longer life.

Janet: So this kept challenging and controversial books in the public domain more than now?

Klaus: Yes.

Janet: So have the books had to change because of the audience?

Klaus: I suppose we now have more light entertainment and books that are easier to digest. Publishers are also aware of the fact that libraries are not such an important market any more. Plus they have to sell the books not just to booksellers such as Waterstones but also to supermarkets such as Sainsbury's and Asda and so the general level is going down a bit.

Janet: In 1984, when Andersen Press was 8 years old, you said, 'We are now doing well enough to publish books that are not successful. I will always go on publishing books that are not successful.' **That was a very unusual statement. What exactly did you mean by it and have you been able to keep to your intent?**

Klaus: If you manage to sell several co-productions you don't have to rely on the UK so much. This applies to most publishers. However tough the Finance Director may be, there are some books that just *have* to be published because they are brilliant. This probably applies to some publishers more than others but because I am the boss at Andersen's I can make the decisions without having to defer to the publishing committee or the Finance Director.

Janet: So you have been able to keep to your intent?

Klaus: Yes, we will always do that. We don't necessarily know in advance if a book will make money. Sometimes we have published books that we didn't expect to make money but simply because they were lovely books that just had to be published. Often we have been pleasantly surprised if they make money. For example, with *Tadpole's Promise* by Tony Ross and Jeanne Willis. We thought it would be criticised and people would shy away from it but in the end it became a little cult [Figure 13.4].

Janet: You once stated that, 'we underestimate the capacity for young children to appreciate a more demanding book. Picturebooks are not only for three or four year olds, they are even more important for six and seven year olds and yet publishers find again and again that only simple books will sell' (Flugge, 1994: 212).

Do you think this is still the case and how does this affect the picturebooks on the Andersen list?

Klaus: We *do* have books that a sales director would consider difficult to sell, maybe because the text is too long or complicated. What they ideally want in the

FIGURE 13.4 *Tadpole's Promise* (Jeanne Willis & Tony Ross (2003).

sales department is a picturebook that is cute, funny and has a very short text. Very often as in the case of *Elmer* for instance, people say the text is too long, but they just have to make a bit more of an effort to read a text that is not just 200 or 400 words long but more like 2,000 words. That's something that we will always do. If the text is good and needs to be a certain length, then we will make it a certain length!

Janet: Tony Ross was one of your first artists who, in 1976, had an unconventional style of illustration which didn't hide or soften the sometimes gruesome parts of a traditional tale. You were content with this, stating that children 'don't need a straight story; they don't need things explained. They love to be mystified and to discover; and they are a lot more intelligent than some parents or teachers give them credit for' (Triggs, 1984).

Klaus: Did I actually say that?

Janet: Yes you did, in 1984. Now, over 30 years later, children very often read and respond to challenging and controversial picturebooks in a practical, down to earth, accepting manner. **It seems to be adults and parents who find such books problematical often censoring them before children can read them. Why do you think this is the case? Why are parents censoring these books?**

Klaus: They are overprotective of little ones and I think they underestimate the capacity of small children to understand new concepts. They often accept a child's existing vocabulary but don't always consider their expanding mind. As a result parents very often don't give enough credit to young children.

Janet: I totally agree with you Klaus . . . what concerns me is that parents often don't or won't give their children access to these kinds of books and yet the same overprotective parents allow their children to sit in front of a television watching international news reports about conflict, with killing, death and dying in war-torn countries such as Syria and Afghanistan. They see detailed images of dead and injured bodies with blood, gore and often fatal wounds. In relation to this I often wonder what can be better than parents or carers sharing a challenging picture-book and talking about it with their child. It seems to me crazy!

Klaus: Hmm, yes.

Janet: In the introduction to my last book, Talking Beyond the Page: Reading and Responding to Picturebooks, *I stated, 'It isn't enough to just to read a book, one must talk about it as well' Evans (2009:3). You too have pointed out that children often require the help of an adult to extend the range and sensibility of a child's imagination when dealing with demanding picturebooks.* **Do you think it is a certain kind of adult or parent who would choose to read and share challenging picturebooks with children?**

Klaus: Yes unfortunately it is the case that there are parents who seem to have less and less time for their children. Yet there is a certain section of the population where the parents really care for the mental and intellectual development of their children and of course one of the most important things to do with a small child is to read a bedtime story and if you read a bedtime story every day, which you should, really, in my humble opinion, not just as a publisher but also as a parent, then you need a variety of books. You can't just read the same old story that has been republished for the last 50 to 100 years! There is good reason to read Beatrix Potter but there's also good reason to read David McKee for instance, or Jeanne Willis, or Michael Foreman, or Quentin Blake for that matter. Quentin Blake became very famous because of Roald Dahl and yet not all of his individual picturebooks sell that well even though he is an absolute master in the world of picturebooks. Additionally, we have librarians with fewer books and less time, also teachers with less time who often seem unable to prioritise children reading in class. I believe Michael Rosen has recently talked once again about this perceived lack of time to read in the class-room and the lack of emphasis placed on reading aloud.

Janet: So how do you as a publisher 'target' these adults?

Klaus: We target them in the same way as most publishers but it is not easy. Independent booksellers have problems too and some of them have recently been closing down. I remember one of my favourite booksellers, *The Lion and the Unicorn*. It was situated in a middle-class neighbourhood and yet it still couldn't make a go of it. In London there is a good selection of larger bookstores but now there are no specialist children's bookshops.

Janet: It was in 1984 that you published Badger's Parting Gifts *by Susan Varley. At the time this was a very controversial picturebook as it dealt with the subject of death, still rather a taboo subject.* **Was it a difficult decision to publish this book at the time?**

Klaus: No! Well, the subject of death is never very popular and some people shy away from it. In fact books on the subject of death can be heavy and didactic and yet if you look at *Frog and the Birdsong* [Figure 13.5] and of course *Badger's Parting Gifts*, two of our books on this subject, you will find that they have been created with lightness of touch and yet don't shirk the subject. It is not easy to do a book on this subject.

Janet: I very much like your phrase, 'lightness of touch'. It says such a lot.

Klaus: The story linked to *Badger's Parting Gifts is* interesting because Tony Ross was a lecturer at the Manchester College of Art and he was one of Susan Varley's teachers. Susan is one of those artists who find it very difficult to write a text, it's not that unusual but in her case she was really stuck and then a sad thing happened . . . Tony's father died and Tony practically gave her the text, he half wrote it for her and she illustrated it. He somehow felt that he couldn't illustrate it himself which is understandable but he thought very highly of her and so do we because we've gone on publishing her work. In fact she has just finished illustrating a book, on the subject of Alzheimer's disease, written by Julia Jarman. This is easier to illustrate with animals than humans, so it's a story of an old lion who starts forgetting things. I think it is an important subject, after all Alzheimer's is now more and more prevalent. I'm glad I found this story. It will be a very thought-provoking story.

"We must bury him," said Hare, "over there, at the bottom of the hill."

Together, they made a stretcher and carried the bird into the meadow.

FIGURE 13.5 *Frog and the Birdsong* by Max Velthuijs (1991): "'We must bury him,' said Hare.'

Janet: Some picturebooks are very disturbing, unsettling and controversial, often dealing with taboo subjects such as suicide, drugs, death, war and conflict? **Do you think there is a need for these kinds of books and who do you think is their intended/implied audience?**

Klaus: I'm not sure. The subjects you've just mentioned are subjects I would shy away from. I mean suicide, what can you do with that? Unless you are aiming for young adults, you're not likely to find a book on the subject for the picturebook age; well, I suppose the audience for picturebooks could start with 3 year olds and go to 83 year olds but the main age group for picturebooks is still seen as 3 to 7 year olds.

Janet: So how does that fit in with what you just said about Susan Varley illustrating one on Alzheimer's disease? The analogy is the same; that is, could you not say that a book on Alzheimer's is as threatening and/or controversial as one on suicide?

Klaus: It all depends on the way you treat it. In the book that Susan illustrated, *Lovely Old Lion*, the reader sees the slow deterioration of the old lion and so children can identify with their grandfathers, great-grandfathers and other relatives who have this affliction, this illness, and they can relate to it [Figure 13.6].

Janet: Do you have any picturebooks on drugs?

Klaus: No. People did say that when David McKee came up with *Elmer*, the multicoloured elephant in 1989 he must have been hallucinating. That didn't occur to him and as far as I know he has never taken hash or anything, so *Elmer* was nothing to do with drugs. Actually, when he wrote *Elmer* he was inspired by the art of Paul Klee.

Janet: So people suggested that David McKee was on LSD when he did the book?

Klaus: There have been people who said that, yes.

One morning, Lenny found his grandpa's crown in the bin with some other things that shouldn't have been there.

King Lion kept getting muddled. He even mixed up day and night.
He would say, "Goodnight, er . . . cub."
Then he would get into bed when the sun was shining!

FIGURE 13.6   *Lovely Old Lion* by Julia Jarman and Susan Varley (2014): 'King Lion kept getting muddled. He even mixed up day and night.'

Janet: You once stated that Andersen Press has a number of 'demanding' books.

Klaus: I shouldn't call them demanding, maybe irresistible rather than demanding . . . demanding means not easy to read so I think maybe we should use another word for them.

Janet: You gave me the word demanding.

Klaus: Did I?

Janet: Yes in an email . . . and I would say that even though a book is easy to read the content can be demanding.

Klaus: That's true so maybe unusual and strange are better words to use than demanding . . . maybe it was the mood I was in when I wrote it!

Janet: I think David McKee's books fit this description. As one of your original author/ illustrators and the creator of the internationally famous, Elmer *the Elephant and the teasingly ambiguous,* Not Now Bernard, *McKee was once criticised for his book,* I Hate My Teddy Bear *which was said to be, 'difficult', 'surreal' and 'indulgent'. McKee has since created many such picturebooks, one of his more recent ones being* Denver, *an unsettling yet profound picturebook about a rich but charitable capitalist and the effects of others' jealousy and discontent on his life [Figures 13.7a (Plate 31) and 13.7b]. I know that you have worked with David McKee for a very long time and that you know him personally.* **Would you share some of your thoughts about David McKee's 'demanding, strange and yet irresistible' picturebooks?**

Klaus: Yes I have known him for 50 years and we just had a wonderful exhibition at *The Illustration Cupboard* in London that celebrated 25 years of *Elmer* and 25 years of David McKee at Andersen Press. Of course he did books before that. His first published picturebook was called *Two Can Toucan,* about a toucan who was no good at anything. He went to the city to get a job but he was useless until, thanks to his beak, he was able to carry two cans; that is why he was called *Two Can Toucan.* Well that was his first book; *Elmer* became successful much later. He did books like *Melrick the Magician* and *The Sad Story of Veronica Who Played the Violin,* wonderful books full of detail and exuberance but then he also did books, as you said, that are more demanding. *I Hate My Teddy Bear* is not in print at the moment but there are other books that are in print like *Two Monsters* which won a few prizes, and *Three Monsters.* *Charlotte's Piggy Bank* is a fascinating example of a book for classroom discussion because children might disagree with the basic tenor of the story. It sometimes needs a teacher to discuss what the story is about and help the children see other aspects of the book. This is something that fascinates David and of course thank God he still comes up with one *Elmer* book every year, which is a very important part of Andersen's well being, not just because of the books but also because of the supporting merchandise. The book is well

Denver was rich. Very rich. Very, very rich.
He lived in a big house called Berton Manor.

FIGURE 13.7A (Plate 31) *Denver* by David McKee (2010): 'Denver was rich. Very rich. Very, very rich.'

One day a stranger came to Berton.

"Why should Denver have so much money and you so little?" he asked the villagers. "It isn't right."

FIGURE 13.7B *Denver.* 'One day a stranger came to Berton.'

known . . . every child in Japan, in France and now also in Spain and Italy knows *Elmer*. It has been absolutely incredible . . . the conquest of the world by this adorable animal . . . this wise elephant. Anyway, that's not what you wanted to know.

"I hate my teddy bear," said John.   "I hate my teddy bear," said Brenda.

FIGURE 13.8 *I Hate My Teddy Bear* (David McKee, 1982).

Janet: I Hate My Teddy Bear *is not a book that I have. I must admit I find it a bit, discordant, rather surreal and very postmodern. Indeed I would call it quite challenging [Figure 13.8].*

Klaus: It is a book that I will re-issue one of these days, no question about that. It is one of those books that you only expect to have small sales but it deserves to be republished especially for classroom use.

Janet: Ah, so it comes under the category of books that may not make a lot of money but they deserve to be published? Another of David McKee's books that I think is quite demanding is *Tusk Tusk*.

Klaus: Yes, well, we had criticisms about that you know, especially the ending with the big ears and the small ears elephants that gave each other funny looks [Figures 13.9a and 13.9b]. You assume after the first battle there is another one looming ahead. It's about racism and intolerance. This is a subject that is very close to my heart. You know I am a refugee from communist Germany so that may have had something to do with it and I grew up in Nazi Germany but nevertheless there are subjects that apart from friendship and truth and beauty and wisdom that we know are very important. More important than ever in fact because you just open the newspaper and, as you said before, even little children are exposed to what goes on in Syria and Afghanistan and other war-torn places.

Janet: Yes, children are exposed to violence even on our doorstep. Here in London with the off-duty soldier who was hacked to death in cold blood in June 2013. Children were seeing those reports on television and they were seeing the men with blood on their hands and blood

FIGURE 13.9A   *Tusk Tusk* (David McKee, 1978).

But recently the little ears and the big ears   have been giving each other strange looks.

FIGURE 13.9B   *Tusk Tusk:* 'Recently the little ears and the big ears have been giving each other strange looks.'

on the road. Despite this there are still certain adults who don't want their children to read books that deal with difficult and challenging subjects. This seems to be a contradictory way of seeing things.

Klaus: Yes it does.

Janet: You once noted that whenever the subject and style of illustration are more demanding or sophisticated, the sales drop considerably (Flugge, 1994). Some picturebooks can certainly seem very sinister depending on the illustrations. For example, one version of a traditional fairy story such as Little Red Riding Hood can seem innocent and benign because of the simple, non-threatening illustrations, whilst the written version of the same story could be seen as extremely sinister and frightening because of the illustrative style used. **What are your thoughts on this text – image relationship with regards to challenging picturebooks?**

Klaus: It's an interesting question: for instance if you have a picturebook by Hans Christian Andersen you expect a text to be reproduced faithfully, whereas if you take a Grimms' Brothers fairy tale like *Little Red Riding Hood* you can play around with it and give it a new meaning if you like because the Grimm fairytales were not written down. The Grimm brothers went around Germany collecting and telling these stories, which changed every time someone else told them. You can change their stories and children get great pleasure from having funnier and different interpretations. Tony Ross has done some of this.

Janet: Yes, despite many of their stories being quite threatening and upsetting, today's parents often accept them and share them with their children!

Klaus: Yes, yes.

Janet: In the USA there is an annual Banned Books Week, which celebrates the freedom to read anything and to express ideas, even those which may be considered unorthodox or unpopular by some. Picturebooks too are censored. By not translating extremely controversial books publishers are in effect censoring them on behalf of the reader; that is, the reader doesn't even get the chance to read them and make their own decision because they are not in their language. **Do you think publishers and translators contribute, albeit unknowingly to the censorship of picturebooks?**

Klaus: In as much as the publishers know the marketplace. If they think there is no market for certain books as they do in America (more than here), then certain books simply won't get published. Don't forget, publishing is a business! And a businessman will not come out with a product that will not sell, however idealistic it may be.

Janet: So are publishers and translators responsible for the censorship of some picturebooks?

Klaus: I guess so to some extent. In America certain books do not get published simply because there isn't a market or the book might be banned. Consider some of Maurice Sendak's picturebooks, they were banned simply for showing bare bottoms.

Janet: Why are certain picturebooks censored and who decides? What factors are in play when these decisions are made?

Klaus: I think Britain is a free country in relation to censorship. However, you wouldn't dream of publishing books about paedophilia or perverted subjects, so there is evidently censorship by publishers. I think you are talking about censorship of books that deserve to be published and I think that in Britain we're pretty lucky regarding this. In America, as you said before, there is a certain censorship applied by librarians who are a real force. In certain states which are either conservative or puritanical or both, they wouldn't dream of having a book on the subject of homosexuality. This situation is something that is still prevalent in America, things have improved but we are always conscious of the fact that there are certain books that will not sell in America. *But*, if it is good, it's *got* to be published. Andersen for instance would never decide not to publish a book just because it might be rejected by the Americans.

Janet: I think this is exactly why so many people really respect you, Klaus, because of your strong philosophy in relation to exactly which books should be published regardless of what people think.

Klaus: Luckily, I didn't have to worry too much about things like that until recently.

Janet: No, exactly.

Janet: In 1994 you wrote an article entitled, Crossing the Divide: Publishing Children's Books in the European Context *in which you referred to a quote by Aidan Chambers who stated, '… the British are becoming more and more insular, less connected to others, less able to appreciate what other people produce and think and envision than they ever were'* (Flugge, 1994: 210). **You were referring to books in translation. Now, 20 years later, is this still the case?**

Klaus: No I think it's probably improved a little, I think the blame is with the fact that there are still relatively few foreign books being published. In this country it is something to do with insularity. There is still a certain segment that is insular; for example, we have an author/illustrator called Max Velthuijs and people can't pronounce his name. The Random House sales director who used to sell our books frequently said that if we changed his name to Max Fieldhouse we would get 50 per cent more sales. That was some years ago but even now people still hesitate about buying foreign books. There is not enough interest or inquisitiveness in what is published in countries such as France, Germany or Russia, let alone in countries such as China, Japan or India. I think some countries are being neglected.

Janet: In 2012 I asked if you would consider publishing some lesser known and very challenging picturebooks by the award-winning, Danish man and wife team, Oscar K and Dorte Karrebaek. Despite speaking to their publishers at the Bologna book fair you felt that these books would not sell on the British market. **Why did you make this decision? Is the translation of such books not financially worthwhile and could this be why they are not published in countries such as the UK and USA?**

Klaus: If I am convinced a book is good then it must be published but in this case I felt the books were just too extreme. I looked at them and they were too radical in my opinion. The Danes are famous for having avant-garde books, they are not frightened of tackling difficult and morbid subjects like *The Undertaker* . . . .

Janet: *The Children's Undertaker.*

Klaus: . . . *The Children's Undertaker?* Even worse! I think in some places in Scandinavia the government supports publishers with grants so that they can publish certain, difficult books. These certainly are very difficult, controversial picturebooks.

Janet: In Scandinavian countries children are expected to become independent thinkers. At times it seems that British children are living and growing up in a nanny state where we wrap them up in cotton wool and overprotect them by doing their thinking for them.

Klaus: I can see your point.

Janet: Many controversial picturebooks from other countries, particularly Scandinavia, are not translated and published in the UK and yet these countries publish picturebooks from British publishers. **Why do you think this is the case and what do you think about books in translation for the English market?**

Klaus: Well first of all there is an economic consideration. To publish a difficult book in Denmark if you're very lucky, as a publisher, you sell 2,000 copies. Whereas here you know there are more opportunities to sell co-productions than the Danes or the Finns or the Norwegians who are coming up with much more difficult subjects so they need to buy in certain books and I think the British are great at producing certain books that are internationally acceptable. So it's been getting tougher to sell co-productions and the reason for that is that other countries too have had their library budgets cut. They can't buy 3,000 copies any more; you know in Denmark they now buy 1,300 copies instead of 2,500–3,000 copies. In most countries outstanding picturebooks are bought by librarians, so if the libraries have less money as happens to be the case in Germany, France and other countries, they have to cut down on what they can buy. So, it's not just Britain but Britain is worse off. I think that for a highly developed country like Britain, to close down libraries is, in my opinion, a total disaster.

Janet: I totally agree but it is happening everywhere.

Klaus: Yes but not as much as it is happening here. The Americans have not cut their budgets as much as here.

Janet: In one of our previous conversations you said that 'Controversial books are getting ever more difficult to sell as they need committed librarians to get them to parents and teachers. Alas with ever more cuts in library spending the market is shrinking and the print runs for full colour picture books are becoming uneconomical' (Personal correspondence, May 2013).

What role do libraries have to play in relation to publishing of challenging picturebooks?

Klaus: As I have previously said, librarians (with money!) were the most important customers. With good picturebooks, in fact with good fiction and good everything but especially picturebooks because they are not that easy to produce, you need to have a certain print run to make sense. The fact that there are fewer libraries around is going to affect a publisher's print run and it will also affect the number of picturebooks being published in the future. I'm quite sure of that. I already know some publishers who have cut down picturebooks.

Janet: We are in a sad situation really aren't we?

Klaus: Well, touch wood we will go on. We have picturebook creators like David McKee and Tony Ross and Quentin Blake and Michael Foreman and new ones. Really new ones are however difficult to come by because art colleges are not teaching illustration as much any more, they are concentrating on computer graphics. There used to be a dozen colleges that taught illustration, now there are just three or four so it is more difficult to find people.

Janet: What about Martin Salisbury at Anglia Ruskin University?

Klaus: Yes, he stands out as a leading light in the world of illustration, especially children's book illustration. His course is the most important in the country.

Janet: Klaus, you are the incredibly well respected, award-winning managing director and owner of Andersen Press. It has been a real pleasure to talk to you about the thing that you, in fact both of us, love so very much, children's books, in particular, picturebooks.

Just before we finish I would like to briefly mention one of your rather different publications, Letters to Klaus *(2013), the proceeds of which all go to the Save the Children*

FIGURE 13.10 *Letters to Klaus.*

Fund [Figure 13.10]. This book is a delightful collection of 100 stunning, idiosyncratic and avant garde, illustrated envelopes sent to you over the years from your friends and picturebook artists. People such as David McKee, Satoshi Kitamura, Susan Varley, Philippe Dupasquier, Tony Ross, the late Max Velthuijs, and many others.

You have over 300 illustrated envelopes and your collection started when David McKee sent the first one and you put it on your office wall. Many of these artists create strange and challenging illustrations in their professional work and this is clearly evident from the envelopes, many of which make reference to you and your own quirky, often maverick way of looking at life. The envelopes celebrate you as a person. They also show that you are a tremendously valued and dear friend to the people who sent them [Figures 13.11A (Plate 32), 13.11B and 13.11C].

Closing words

It is a true honour to converse with Klaus about his great love, picturebooks, and their place in our contemporary society. He talks about them with fervour, enthusiasm and with an intensity bordering on love. He really cares for books, their creators and their future and he is obviously devoted to Andersen Press – his personal creation! Klaus has such generosity of spirit and it is this, along with his appetite to search out and promote new talent in the field of children's publishing, whilst keeping a firm grip on what and who has already been successful, that makes him such a knowledgeable and exciting person to talk to about children's publishing. Andersen Press is one of the most innovative and of course successful independent publishing houses and this is due primarily to Klaus. His passion is infectious, he is an inspiring person to be with and his personal company is top quality, just like Andersen, his professional company. He once said, 'Fiction has the unique ability to make contact with the imagination at its deepest level.'

This is so true. Thank you Klaus.

FIGURE 13.11A (Plate 32) Klaus on beach by David McKee.

FIGURE 13.11B Aztec Klaus by Satoshi Kitamura.

FIGURE 13.11C Smoking Klaus by Satoshi Kitamura.

Academic references

Evans, J. (ed.) (2009) *Talking Beyond the Page: Reading and Responding to Picturebooks*. London: Routledge.

Flugge, K. (1994) Crossing the Divide: Publishing Children's Books in the European Context. *Signal: Approaches to Children's Books,* No. 75(September). Stroud: The Thimble Press.

Flugge, K. (ed.) (2013) *Letters to Klaus*. London: Andersen Press.

Iser, W. (1978) *The Act of Reading*. London: Johns Hopkins University Press.

Triggs, P. (1984) The Man Behind the Books – Klaus Flugge, *Books for Keeps*, No. 24(January).

Children's literature

Jarman, J., illus. Varley, S. (2014) *Lovely Old Lion*. London: Andersen Press.

McKee, D. (1964) *Two Can Toucan*. London: Abelard Schumann.

McKee, D. (1978) *Tusk Tusk*. London: Andersen Press.

McKee, D. (1980) *Not Now, Bernard*. London: Andersen Press.

McKee, D. (1982) *I Hate My Teddy Bear*. London: Andersen Press.

McKee, D. (1984) *Elmer*. London: Andersen Press.

McKee, D. (1985) *Two Monsters*. London: Andersen Press.

McKee, D. (1987) *The Sad Story of Veronica Who Played the Violin*. London: Andersen Press.

McKee, D. (1996) *Charlotte's Piggy Bank*. London: Andersen Press.

McKee, D. (2005) *Three Monsters*. London: Andersen Press.

McKee, D. (2010) *Denver*. London: Andersen Press.

McKee, D. (2012) *Melrick the Magician*. London: Andersen Press.

Oram, H. & Kitamura, S. (1982) *Angry Arthur*. London: Andersen Press.

Varley, S. (1984) *Badger's Parting Gifts*. London: Andersen Press.

Velthuijs, M. (1991) *Frog and the Birdsong*. London: Andersen Press.

Willis, J., illus. Ross, T. (2003) *Tadpole's Promise*. London: Andersen Press.

Willis, J., illus. Ross, T. (2014) *Chicken Clicking*. London: Andersen Press.

INDEX